PHOTOGRAPHY DEGREE ZERO

PHOTOGRAPHY DEGREE ZERO

REFLECTIONS ON ROLAND BARTHES'S *CAMERA LUCIDA*

EDITED BY GEOFFREY BATCHEN

THE MIT PRESS
CAMBRIDGE, MASSACHUSETTS
LONDON, ENGLAND

MIT Press books may be purchased at special quantity discounts for business or sales promotional use. For information, please e-mail special_sales@mitpress.mit.edu or write to Special Sales Department, The MIT Press, 55 Hayward Street, Cambridge, MA 02142.

This book was set in Adobe Garamond Pro and Engravers Gothic by The MIT Press. Printed and bound in the United States of America.

Library of Congress Cataloging-in-Publication Data

Photography degree zero : reflections on Roland Barthes's *Camera lucida* /
edited by Geoffrey Batchen.
   p. cm
   Includes bibliographical references and index.
   ISBN 978-0-262-01325-3 (hardcover : alk. paper)
   1. Barthes, Roland, Chambre claire. 2. Photography—Philosophy. 3.
Photography, Artistic. 4. Photographic criticism. I. Batchen, Geoffrey.
   TR642.B3736 2009
   770.1—dc22

10 9 8 7 6 5 4 3 2 1

Cover image: Idris Khan, Every Page . . . from Roland Barthes's *Camera Lucida, 2004, digital C-print. Courtesy of Yvon Lambert Gallery, New York.*

This book is gratefully dedicated to Richard Howard. His translations have allowed a generation of English-speaking readers to share in the pleasures of French literature.

CONTENTS

All intellectual work is based on collective labor, and nowhere is this more evident than in an edited volume of essays. I gratefully thank all the authors who have contributed to *Photography Degree Zero* for their willingness to participate and share their thoughts on *Camera Lucida*. Without their generosity and support, this volume would not have been possible.

Douglas Nickel helped initiate the project and worked on an earlier version of the proposal, preparing a foundation for its eventual publication. A number of people made helpful comments on drafts of my introduction, including Anne Ferran, Nancy K. Miller, Carol Mavor, and Gordon Hughes. It is much the better for their insights. Sarah Caylor is to be thanked for skillfully gathering together a folio of reviews of *Camera Lucida*, again adding extra substance to my introduction. Mitra Abbaspour, Nikolas Drosos, Tomas Dvorak, Media Farzan, Teresa Mendes Flores, Philip Glahn, Aud Sissel Hoel, Yoshiaki Kai, Jeehey Kim, Peeter Linnap, Antonella Pelizzari, Anna Tellgren, Yuko Teshima, Yulia Tikhonova, and Chu-chiun Wei all generously provided me with information about or even actual copies of translated editions of *La chambre claire*. Several students kindly helped give this project some necessary order; they include Jenny Bantz, Amanda Brown, and Pete Marinucci. I especially want to thank Elizabeth DeRose for organizing all the reprint permissions, an essential contribution.

Idris Kahn kindly allowed us to use one of his artworks as the cover image for the book, greatly enhancing its impact. I thank Yvon Lambert Gallery, New York, for making this possible.

Richard Howard graciously agreed to be interviewed, sharing his memories of working with Roland Barthes and patiently answering all my subsequent queries.

This book owes its existence to the support of Roger Conover at The MIT Press. I hope it meets with his approval. I also want to thank Marc Lowenthal for his assistance with the preparation of the manuscript, Sandra Minkkinen for her editorial guidance, and Yasuyo Iguchi for the book's elegant design.

Permission to reproduce previously published essays was given by the following copyright holders and authors and is gratefully acknowledged:

CHAPTER 2: Victor Burgin. "Re-reading *Camera Lucida*." *Creative Camera* 215 (November 1982): 730–4. Reprinted by permission of *Creative Camera* (London).

CHAPTER 3: Jane Gallop. "The Pleasure of the Phototext." *Afterimage* 12, no. 9 (April 1985): 16–8. Reprinted by permission of *Afterimage* (Rochester, New York).

CHAPTER 4: Margaret Iversen. "What Is a Photograph?" *Art History* 17: 3 (September 1994): 450–64. Reprinted by permission of Blackwell Publishing (Oxford, UK).

CHAPTER 5: Margaret Olin. "Touching Photographs: Roland Barthes's 'Mistaken' Identification." *Representations* 80 (Fall 2002): 99–118. Reprinted by permission of the Regents of The University of California.

CHAPTER 6: Jay Prosser. "Buddha Barthes: What Barthes Saw in Photography (That He Didn't in Literature)." *Literature and Theology* 18, no. 2 (June 2004): 211–22. Reprinted by permission of Oxford University Press.

CHAPTER 7: Eduardo Cadava and Paola Cortés-Rocca. "Notes on Love and Photography." *October* 116 (Spring 2006): 3–34. Reprinted by permission of The MIT Press Journals (Cambridge, MA).

CHAPTER 8: Michael Fried. "Barthes's *Punctum*." *Critical Inquiry* 31, no. 3 (Spring 2005): 539–75. Reprinted by permission of The University of Chicago Press.

CHAPTER 9: James Elkins. "What Do We Want Photography to Be? A Response to Michael Fried." *Critical Inquiry* 31, no. 4 (Summer 2005): 938–57. Reprinted by permission of The University of Chicago Press.

CHAPTER 13: Shawn Michelle Smith. "Race and Reproduction in *Camera Lucida*." In J.J. Long, Andrea Noble, and Edward Welch, eds., *Photography: Theoretical Snapshots* (Milton Park, Abingdon: Routledge, 2009). Reprinted by permission of Taylor & Francis Books (UK).

PHOTOGRAPHY DEGREE ZERO

PALINODE

AN INTRODUCTION TO *PHOTOGRAPHY DEGREE ZERO*

GEOFFREY BATCHEN

"One day, quite some time ago, I happened on a photograph of Napoleon's youngest brother, Jerome, taken in 1852. And I realized then, with an amazement I have not been able to lessen since: 'I am looking at eyes that looked at the Emperor.'"[1] A first-person anecdote about the wonder induced by an otherwise ordinary photograph: thus begins Roland Barthes's *Camera Lucida: Reflections on Photography*, perhaps the most influential book yet written about the photographic experience. *Photography Degree Zero: Reflections on Roland Barthes's* Camera Lucida pays tribute to that book and to that influence in the best possible way—by subjecting both to analysis and critique.

This volume came into being when a number of its contributors discovered that we had a common interest in *Camera Lucida*, an interest in part driven by our frustration with being unable to get beyond it. All of us frequently quoted from the book. Indeed, we found we could rarely write an essay on photography without having first to pay our respects to ideas and vocabulary established by Roland Barthes. And so it has been for many other scholars too; this is surely the most quoted book in the photographic canon.[2] At a recent conference in Spain, its organizer announced that anyone heard quoting from *Camera Lucida* would be levied with a fine. The joke is further evidence of the book's ubiquity but also of a certain fatigue. Terms established by Barthes, such as *studium* and *punctum*, have become part of the standard lexicon of photographic debate, along with a particular understanding of photographic time and of photography's relationship to death and a certain narcissistic way of speaking. All these aspects of *Camera Lucida*, and more, have come to be so frequently repeated in the works of others that they have congealed into what Barthes himself would call a *doxa*: "Public Opinion, the mind of the majority, petit bourgeois consensus, the Voice of Nature, the Violence of Prejudice."[3] Perhaps, some of us said to each other, we all should write essays about this conundrum and by this means bring *Camera Lucida* back to life or, better yet, get it out of our systems altogether. *Photography Degree Zero* is the end result of this impulse.

It is, of course, not the first book to be published about Barthes's discussion of photographic images. Nancy Shawcross's commentary, *Roland Barthes and Photography: The Critical Tradition in Perspective*, appeared in 1997 and still offers a provocative overview of the topic.[4] In focusing her attention on *Camera Lucida*, Shawcross locates it in relation to themes found in Barthes's other works and to the writings of predecessors like Charles Baudelaire and contemporaries such as Marguerite Duras. Later in this same year, an anthology of essays edited by Jean-Michel Rabaté was also published. Based on a 1994 conference held at the University of Pennsylvania, *Writing the Image after Roland Barthes* comprised nineteen papers on a variety of aspects of Barthes's work, including his writing on photography.[5] Another impressive anthology, *Critical Essays on Roland Barthes*, edited by Diana Knight, appeared in 2000; its chapters include both an early French review of *La chambre claire: note sur la photographie* (of which *Camera Lucida* is an English translation) and a number of challenging essays, mostly by French authors, in which that book is a central concern.[6]

Coming almost ten years later, *Photography Degree Zero* supplements and extends these important predecessors. But it also differs from them in a number of respects. *Photography Degree Zero* presents an exclusively Anglo-American perspective, investigating the significance of *Camera Lucida* for a select group of scholars who are based in the United States and Great Britain. The focus of these scholars is on this particular book and its contribution to an understanding of photography rather than on, say, Barthes's broader contributions to literature or criticism.[7] The hope is that the act of gathering these essays together here will allow for a productive conversation between a diversity of points of view and give new readers an opportunity to compare and contrast these views. It is assumed that a reader of *Photography Degree Zero* will also have a copy of *Camera Lucida* nearby and will be able to consult its pages and examine its illustrations when necessary. The two books should, in other words, be read together.

Something needs to be said about this anthology's choice of title. *Photography Degree Zero: Reflections on Roland Barthes's* Camera Lucida implies a continuity of purpose that links Barthes's last book, *Camera Lucida*, with his first, *Writing Degree Zero*.[8] Published in 1953 (although based on essays written between 1947 and 1950), *Writing Degree Zero* was written as a response to Jean-Paul Sartre's 1947 book *What Is Literature?*[9] Sartre's existential polemic suggested that all texts involve a mutually productive exchange of responsibilities between reader and writer. Barthes's book agrees with this basic premise but argues that how a text is written, its form, is as important to the politics of this exchange as what the text says. Among the subversive textual strategies that Barthes discusses is "colorless writing," a kind of writing then fashionable that attempts to achieve a neutral or "zero degree" of form—a form of writing that, like most photographs, denies it even has a form. But even this writing, Barthes concludes, has a noticeable style "loaded with the most spectacular signs of fabrication" (*WDZ* 64).

Thirty years later, on the first page of *Camera Lucida*, Barthes acknowledged his debt to the work of Sartre by dedicating his new book to the older man's 1940 study *L'imaginaire*.[10] The two books share a common theme (photography and memory), a "tragic dimension,"[11] and a phenomenological heritage (Barthes describes his approach to photography in *Camera Lucida* as "a vague, casual, even cynical phenomenology," *CL* 20). But Barthes is also writing his book the year after teaching a class at the Collège de France on a state of being he called *le neutre* (usually translated as "the neutral"[12]), a theme that was inspired, he claims, by his disappointment that a bottle of pigment of that name turned out to be "a color like the others."[13] As a form of words, then, *Photography Degree Zero* succinctly recalls both this long, complex history and these multiple, enduring interests.

Barthes on Photography

Camera Lucida was by no means Barthes's first effort at writing about photography. In fact, photographs had been a frequent talking point in his earlier work. Between 1954 and 1956, for example, Barthes wrote a series of short essays that were about the imagery he encountered in everyday life and were primarily for publication in the monthly French journal *Les lettres nouvelles*. Fifty-three of these were eventually to appear as a single collection under the title *Mythologies* (the 1972 English translation of the same name includes only twenty-eight of them).[14] As he tells us in his preface, "The starting point of these reflections was usually a feeling of impatience at the sight of the 'naturalness' with which newspapers, art and common sense constantly dress up a reality which, even though it is the one we live in, is undoubtedly determined by history. . . . I resented seeing Nature and History confused at every turn" (*M* 11). His aim is to unmask this naturalization and to account in some detail for precisely *how* it occurs. Photographic images of various kinds turn out to be central to this process.

Among the essays in *Mythologies* is one titled "Photography and Electoral Appeal," an urbanely sarcastic commentary on the mythical personas conveyed by the portraits that politicians attach to their election materials: "what is transmitted through the photograph of the candidate are not his plans, but his deep motives, all his family, mental, even erotic circumstances, all this style of life of which he is at once the product, the example and the bait" (*M* 91). In a few short words, Barthes manages to skewer a genre of photography that we tend to take for granted; his acidic observations restore its strangeness to it. His review of *The Family of Man*, Edward Steichen's famous 1955 exhibition devoted to the "essential oneness of mankind throughout the world," is less jocular, more urgent:[15] "Everything here, the content and appeal of the pictures, the discourse which justifies them, aims to suppress the determining weight of History: we are held back at the surface of an identity, prevented precisely by sentimentality from penetrating into this ulterior zone of human behavior where historical alienation introduces some 'differences' which we shall here quite simply call 'injustices'" (*M* 101). Barthes mentions the apparently "universal" experiences of birth and death, experiences that, he points out, are in fact always mediated by historical and thus political circumstances. Echoing a famous remark by Bertolt Brecht, he contends that "the failure of photography seems to me to be flagrant in this connection: to reproduce death or birth tells us, literally, nothing."[16]

Another exhibition, at the d'Orsay Gallery, induces a meditation on what Barthes calls "shock photos."[17] In a remark that seems prescient of those that will follow in *Camera Lucida*, he suggests that "the photographer must do more than signify the horrible, if we are to feel horror. . . . straight photography leads you to the scandal of horror, not to horror itself" (*CC* 33–34). Complaining of the degree to which his reactions to such photographs have been preordained by the photographer ("by the use of contrasting and complementary elements"), he compares them unfavorably to certain heroic "literary" paintings (he seems to be thinking of Jacques-Louis David's *Napoleon Bonaparte Crossing the Alps at Saint-Bernard Pass* of 1801) that exhibit "a sort of disturbing recklessness, leading the reader of the picture into a kind of astonishment more visual than intellectual" (*CC* 34). For him, the only photographic pictures at the exhibition that induce this same response—that induce "the *critical* catharsis demanded by Brecht"—are those that are unstudied and obstinately literal: "these images astonish because they seem at first sight strange and unfamiliar, almost calm" (*CC* 34).

Barthes's commentaries in *Mythologies* are informed by his recent encounter with the work of the Swiss linguist Ferdinand de Saussure as well as by a Brecht-inspired Marxism that, as he says in a 1970 preface, sees the "essential enemy" as "the bourgeois norm" (*M* 9).[18] In a long afterword titled "Myth Today," Barthes offers a semiotic analysis of the kinds of myths that he has been talking about, equating them with an identifiable *system* of representation—that is, with language (*M* 110). Accordingly, he wants to consider everyday images as operating like sign systems. He turns for an example to a seemingly innocent photographic image on the cover of *Paris Match* magazine of a "young Negro in a French uniform . . . saluting, with his eyes uplifted" (*M* 116) and sees there not just a mystification of French imperialism but a greater semiological system at work whose ultimate goal is to depoliticize speech of any kind (*M* 143). By providing a brief account of the rhetorical figures and structured internal relationships that facilitate this depoliticization, Barthes hopes to also provide a means for their interpretation and contestation (a means that came to be called *structuralism*). But what he doesn't yet provide is a discussion of the importance of the *photographicness* of this example to its functioning within his schema. This is the issue he will address in a group of essays published in the early 1960s.

In the first of these, "The Photographic Message," written in 1961, he considers the press photograph as a type of ideological message orchestrated by its makers and distributers.[19] He quickly concludes that, due to "the unique structure that a photograph constitutes," the photographic image has a special status: "*it is a message without a code*" (*IMT* 16–17). A photograph appears to have no form of its own; we automatically look through the surface of a photograph to see what it is of.[20] Other types of image, such as drawings, combine a *denoted* message (its analogical content, the thing the drawing depicts) and a *connoted* message (its style of representation but also "the manner in which the society to a certain extent communicates what it thinks of it," *IMT* 17). In a photograph, Barthes observes, these two qualities—denotation and connotation—are inseparable. Indeed, Barthes contends that "of all the structures of information, the photograph appears as the only one that is exclusively constituted and occupied by a 'denoted' message, a message which totally exhausts its mode of existence" (*IMT* 18). This special status makes a photograph (or at least a press photograph that is seemingly transparent to its subject) a paradoxical sort of sign because it is simultaneously "objective" and "invested," natural and cultural. But it also makes it a powerful ideological weapon because photography works to naturalize a view of the world that is in fact always political and interested.

In 1964, in an essay titled "Rhetoric of the Image," Barthes returned to these same issues but this time with an advertising image as his object of analysis.[21] In the process of considering whether photography should be considered to operate like a language, he examines an advertisement for pasta sauce to skim off the different messages that it contains. He begins with the linguistic messages contained in its caption and labels and even in the "Italianicity" (one of Barthes's many apt neologisms) implied by the product's own name ("Panzani"). He then moves on to discuss the play between the denoted or literal elements of the image (what it's of, the arrangement of these elements, the colors deployed in the image) and their symbolic meanings (freshness, plenty, Italianicity again), which he collectively calls *connotation*. Barthes's interest is in how these various elements systematically relate to each other to impart these messages to us transparently. He is once more anxious to separate photography from both drawing and cinema, describing the former as an "anthropological revolution . . . in man's history" and even as a "truly unprecedented" type of consciousness (*IMT* 44). He does so on the basis of photography's introduction of a "new space-time category: spatial immediacy and temporal anteriority"—an experience that he sums up as the "having-been-there" that is the basis of every photograph's sense of witness. Many of these concepts, even if not the vocabulary or semiotic analysis that accompanies them here, will reappear in *Camera Lucida*.

As important to *Camera Lucida* as these early efforts at photographic critique is Barthes's developing character as a writer. In one of his most famous essays, "The Death of the Author" (from 1967),[22] he advocates a kind of self-conscious writing that he describes as "performative" (*IMT* 145)—an open-ended textual practice that, he argues, is "truly revolutionary since to refuse to fix meaning is, in the end, to refuse God and his hypostases— reason, science, law" (*IMT* 147). Shifting critical emphasis from the traditional notion of a singular originating author to multiple, newly empowered readers, he finishes with a call that continues to reverberate even now: "the birth of the reader must be at the cost of the death of the Author" (*IMT* 148). Subsequent books such as *The Pleasure of the Text* (1973), *Roland Barthes by Roland Barthes* (1975), and *A Lover's Discourse: Fragments* (1977) offer versions of this performative style of writing, in each case inviting the reader to induce something from Barthes's text that exceeds the intentions of its author.[23] This interaction, a kind of consummation of text and reader, conjures themes that have now become central to Barthes's work—pleasure, desire, and the body (the body of the writer, the body of the reader, and even the body of writing itself).[24] These various bodies are also broached in his book on photography, as are a number of his earlier concerns. As we have seen with his use of denotation and connotation, Barthes often liked to structure his arguments around two opposing terms of his own invention (his deployment of *plaisir* and *jouissance* in *The Pleasure of the Text* is another example) and this tactic recurs in *Camera Lucida*.[25] In *Roland Barthes by Roland Barthes*, he also rehearses the play of image and text that one finds in the later book by opening with a series of personal photographs accompanied by erudite, meditative captions. The particular tone of these captions—at once philosophical and autobiographic, poetic and analytical, questioning and assured—makes them a kind of foreword to his last major writing project.

WRITING *CAMERA LUCIDA*

Camera Lucida emerged as a consequence of a commission by *Les cahiers du cinema* for a contribution to its series of short books on cinema. Barthes had been elected a member of the Collège de France in March 1976, and the following year's publication of *A Lover's Discourse*, which sold very well, brought him an added measure of celebrity. He opened 1977 with a short commentary on the work of photographer Richard Avedon and then published others on French photographers Daniel Boudinet and Bernard Foucon (to be followed in 1978 with a brief text on the photography of Wilhelm von Gloeden).[26] However, 1977 was also the year in which his mother, Henriette Barthes, died, on October 25, thus depriving him of a beloved companion with whom he had lived most of his life. His introspective mood is indicated in an interview with Angelo Schwarz late in that year, where he describes every encounter with a photograph as "a contact with death . . . at least, this is how I experience photography: as a fascinating and funereal enigma."[27] It was perhaps the traumatic event of his mother's passing, as much as his admiration for the writer, that also led to Barthes's lecture at the Collège de France in October 1978 on Proust's novel *In Search of Lost Time*.[28] The opportunity presented by the invitation from *Cahiers du cinema* therefore allowed him to bring together a number of themes preoccupying him during this period—photography, remembrance, and death.

On December 23, 1978, Barthes was interviewed on French radio, and he again discussed his long interest in photography and suggested the possibility of writing a book to explain that interest: "In the final analysis, what I really find fascinating about photographs, and they do fascinate me, is something that probably has to do with death. Perhaps it's an interest that is tinged with necrophilia, to be honest, a fascination with what has died but is represented as wanting to be alive."[29] With his mother's death very much on his mind, this fascination, then, was what he decided to write his next book about.

Barthes began writing his manuscript on April 15, 1979, and completed it, as he tells us in a concluding note in *La chambre claire*, just forty-nine days later, on June 3. The inference of such a note is that he wrote a section a day, or close to it, as the finished book comprises exactly forty-eight distinct sections. It also suggests that the book was written at high speed, implying in turn an unrehearsed, almost conversational flow of thought. The idea is further reiterated in his choice of subtitle, the self-consciously modest *Note sur la photographie*. However, it is likely that Barthes had for some time been preparing index cards or paper slips covered in notes to himself with this project in mind, as he had for previous books.[30] Using these slips as prompts, Barthes's habit was to write his manuscripts in blue ink, using a fountain pen, and then to type them up on his electric typewriter, revising the text as he went. The index card had provided an organizing logic for previous books, such as *A Lover's Discourse* and *Roland Barthes*, where each of their subsections is headed by a key word or phrase. *La chambre claire's* forty-eight discrete sections are, in contrast, designated by a number in the body of the text, with added titles appearing only on the contents page (which in the French edition comes at the back of the book). Although the sections vary in length, the book is divided into two equal parts, twenty-four sections in each, giving it the added gravitas of an internal symmetry. It is yet another sign that every aspect of this book has been carefully thought out and calibrated.[31]

The manuscript incorporated the diverse range of Barthes's own reading, such that one finds, for example, marginal references to the work of psychoanalyst Jacques Lacan and a book on Zen Buddhism on the same page.[32] Other pages acknowledge the influence of Italo Calvino, Proust, Paul Valéry, and of course Sartre. His bibliography also includes philosophical works by Julia Kristeva, Jean-François Lyotard, Philippe Lacoue-Labarthe, and Edmund Husserl as well as books on photography by Raul Beceyro, Pierre Bourdieu, Susan Sontag, and Gisèle Freund.[33] Barthes also consulted the 1964 edition of Beaumont Newhall's *The History of Photography* and several photographic issues of more recent French magazines.[34] The most notable of these was the November 1977 issue of *Nouvel observateur*, which contained, among other things, a French translation of Walter Benjamin's 1931 essay "Little History of Photography" (which Barthes does not single out for acknowledgment in his bibliography).[35]

These various sources and influences are transposed into a voice that is very much Barthes's own. The language that this voice uses is at once accessible and difficult, including obscure and learned vocabulary, popular expressions and witticisms, and terms whose meanings he invents on the spot. As one of Barthes's French reviewers put it, *La chambre claire* launches "a series of new, uncommon, disparaged, neological or outdated words, which bring new life to language before congealing in their turn."[36] Having begun in the first person, *La chambre claire* has the intimate tone of an autobiography, and it does indeed contain a number of references to Barthes's own life, including the recent death of his mother and his own grief at her passing.

However, its narrative structure also resembles a kind of philosophical detective novel, a quest where the protagonist, Barthes himself, pursues an elusive quarry (the answer to the question "what is photography, in itself?") through recourse to various clues and red herrings. Barthes had opened *Roland Barthes by Roland Barthes*, his book about autobiography, with the hand-written warning: "It must all be considered as if spoken by a character in a novel." And in his classes around this time, Barthes certainly expressed interest in writing a novel or at least in "the novelistic" as a mode of discourse.[37] Barthes makes a number of references to Proust in *La chambre claire*, and the meditative style of his manuscript could also well be described as Proustian. In short, posing neither as fiction nor nonfiction but containing elements of both, *La chambre claire* refuses to adhere to any one literary genre.

His choice of title is similarly abstruse. The words *la chambre claire* mean literally "the light room" or "the clear room," as if to provide an antidote to the camera obscura, or "dark room," an apparatus that had historically formed the basis of the photographic camera. But *chambre claire* is also a technical term used by the French to refer to an optical instrument known (in Latin, the language of science) by English speakers as a camera lucida. This instrument had been patented by Englishman William Wollaston in 1806, well before photography's invention was announced in 1839, and was in principle quite different from the camera obscura. Barthes may well have read the description of a camera lucida given by Newhall in *The History of Photography*. This, at any rate, is where he found the illustration of it in use that came to grace the cover of *La chambre claire*.[38] The instrument consists of a three-sided glass prism suspended before the eye of the draftsman, such that a subject and the piece of paper beneath the prism meld together onto the back of the draftsman's retina. Thus, the image produced by a camera lucida is seen only by the draftsman and by no one else, except in the form of a tracing.[39] Here, then, was an apt metaphor for Barthes's own text.

Barthes makes frequent references to particular photographs in his book, but only twenty-four of these are illustrated. Reproduced in black and white, they were drawn mostly from sources close at hand and particularly from that special issue of *Nouvel observateur* devoted to photography and published in November 1977. There seems to be no particular rationale behind their choice beyond personal taste and rhetorical convenience. As he says in one interview: "The photographs I chose have an argumentative value. They are the ones I use in my text to make certain points."[40] Ten come from the nineteenth century and fourteen from the twentieth, but they are reproduced in no particular chronological order. Most of them fall within the realm of portraiture or journalism. There is only one landscape (more accurately an architectural study, by Charles Clifford), and even it has a figure in it. There is also one still life picture. A number of famous photographers are represented—Stieglitz, Nadar, Avedon, Kertész, Sander—but their work is joined by some ordinary, even generic images, as well as by two photographs by unknown photographers. These images are presented with short italicized captions, usually (but not always) versions of Barthes's own words in the main text.[41]

Barthes first saw the Polaroid photograph by French photographer Daniel Boudinet that he chose as the frontispiece to his book when he attended an opening reception for a Boudinet exhibition on April 25 while in the middle of writing *La chambre claire*.[42] Dated 1979 and titled only *Polaroid*, it is the most recent and only color (printed a monochrome blue-green) image to appear in the book. Barthes gives it further emphasis by having it printed on a special glossy paper stock and surrounding it with a line; it thus comes to us already framed, like an artwork. However, he never directly refers to it in his text.

Reading *Camera Lucida*

As masterful works of literature, Roland Barthes's texts are never simply transparent to meaning (they are, in Barthes's own terms, *writerly*) and produce their full effects only in the process of being read.[43] *Camera Lucida*, in particular, is marked by frequent double meanings, asides, learned allusions, self-assured aphorisms, and a sheer beauty of expression that all need to be appreciated at firsthand. Nevertheless, it is useful to have a general sense of how the book proceeds.

Barthes opens his manuscript, as we have already heard, with an expression of amazement at photography's capacity to touch him across time and space. As he goes on to suggest, "a sort of umbilical cord links the body of the photographed thing to my gaze" (*CL* 81). This indexicality, this direct physical link between a photograph and the thing it represents, led him to what he calls an "'ontological' desire: "I wanted to learn at all costs what Photography was 'in itself,' by what essential feature it was to be distinguished from the community of images" (*CL* 3). Perversely, given his prior association with at least two of these same discourses, he decides that analytical methods derived from sociology, semiology, and psychoanalysis are inadequate to this task and that he will instead take himself and especially his own bodily responses to certain images as the measure of photographic knowledge (*CL* 9). He thus confines his study to the realm of the spectator, ignoring the question of how photographs are produced in favor of an extended exploration of their reception.

Following some wry passages about the experience of being photographed (*CL* 11–15), he posits his notorious opposition of two Latin terms, *studium* and *punctum*, as a way of accounting for his different reactions to photographic pictures (*CL* 26–27).[44] Some photographs, he says, elicit in him nothing but polite interest: "they please or displease me without pricking me. . . . The *studium* is that very wide field of unconcerned desire, of various interest, of inconsequential taste. . . . To recognize the *studium* is inevitably to encounter the photographer's intentions" (*CL* 27). He contrasts this response with a more complicated one he calls *punctum*, which is induced, he says, by an "element which rises from the scene, shoots out of it like an arrow, and pierces me" (*CL* 26). Barthes continues to offer suggestive and physically palpable similes, as if any simple definition cannot do the experience justice: "this wound, this prick, this mark made by a pointed instrument" (*CL* 26), a "sting, speck, cut, little hole—and also a cast of the dice" (*CL* 27). In short, he says, "a photograph's *punctum* is that accident which pricks me (but also bruises me, is poignant to me)" (*CL* 27).

The remainder of Part One continues to meditate on this distinction, digressing from time to time to ponder the nature of photography's effects on him: "ultimately, photography is subversive not when it frightens, repels, or even stigmatizes, but when it is *pensive*, when it thinks" (*CL* 38). The *punctum*, he proposes, is an element of a picture that evades analysis ("what I can name cannot really prick me" *CL* 51)—very often an incidental detail (he mentions several examples), an uncoded aspect of the photograph that is sometimes recalled in memory or even transformed *by* memory (*CL* 53). This suggests that a photograph's *punctum* is not necessarily something to be found within the image itself: "Last thing about the *punctum*: whether or not it is triggered, it is an addition: it is what I add to the photograph and *what is nonetheless already there*" (*CL* 55). As he has said a little earlier, "it animates me, and I animate it" (*CL* 20), and this makes any *punctum*-like experience a necessarily personal, subjective one.

Despite having constructed this complex analytical armature, Part One of *La chambre claire* concludes with a confession: "I had perhaps learned how my desire worked, but I had not discovered the nature (the *eidos*) of Photography" (*CL* 60). To do so, he says, he will have to both "descend deeper into myself" and "make my recantation, my palinode" (*CL* 60).

A palinode is an ode or song in which the author retracts something said in a previous poem.[45] And indeed, in Part Two of his book, Barthes shifts his search for the essence of photography from an investigation of many photographs to an intense analysis of just one. This is the famous Winter Garden Photograph of his mother, which he found in November 1977 after her death. It shows her in 1898 standing at the age of five next to her seven-year-old brother. Although he refuses to reproduce it ("for you, it would be nothing but an indifferent picture" *CL* 73), Barthes describes the photograph in detail, both its physical attributes ("old . . . the corners blunted from having been pasted into an album, the sepia print had faded" *CL* 67) and its image (apparently the two children are standing near a wooden bridge railing in a glassed-in conservatory at their childhood home, she a little back and holding one finger in her other hand). But what he finds in this picture is not exactly visible to others. It is "something inexpressible" (*CL* 107), the "air" of his deceased mother (*CL* 107), "the truth of the face I had loved" (*CL* 67), what he henceforth wants to call "utopically, *the impossible science of the unique being*" (*CL* 71).

Having discovered "something like an essence of the Photograph . . . in this particular picture" (*CL* 73), Barthes traces its source to photography's peculiar articulation of time—the way photography simultaneously conjures past, present, and future in a single image form. "I now know that there exists another *punctum* (another 'stigmatum') than the 'detail,'" Barthes writes, in a continuation of his palinode. "This new *punctum*, which is no longer of form but of intensity, is Time, the lacerating emphasis of the *noeme* (*'that has been'*), its pure representation." He looks at an 1865 photograph of Lewis Payne, who is about to be hanged for an attempted assassination, and sees there "at the same time: *This will be* and *this has been*" (*CL* 96). At the moment in 1979 when Barthes gazes on his photograph, Payne is already long dead, but at the moment this photograph was taken, he is still yet to die. In the future anterior tense of the photograph, Payne is both dead ("this has been") and is going to die ("this will be"). Although a "still," every photograph always represents this passing of time from past to future and therefore always also signals the eventual passing of the person looking at it (always contains, as Barthes says, "this imperious sign of my own death," *CL*

97). Hence Barthes's insistence that photography is inescapably haunted by the morbid promise of death: as he puts it, "whether or not the subject is already dead, every photograph is this catastrophe" (*CL* 96).

Barthes has already told us that "every photograph is a certificate of presence" (*CL* 87). Photographs, he suggests, offer us a truth-to-presence (they certify that something was indeed there before the lens in some past moment in space and time) even if not a truth-to-appearance (they do not necessarily look like their referent). As a consequence, he tells us, the photograph of his mother as a child has an effect on him that "becomes at once evidential and exclamative; it bears the effigy to that crazy point where affect (love, compassion, grief, enthusiasm, desire) is a guarantee of Being. . . . It then approaches, to all intents, madness" (*CL* 113). Photography, it seems, is both mad and tame, and Barthes's language takes on an extra poetic resonance to convey its familiar strangeness to us—"a bizarre *medium*, a new form of hallucination: false on the level of perception, true on the level of time . . . a mad image, chafed by reality" (*CL* 115). Mad or tame? The choice, Barthes says, is ours, depending on our willingness to either confront photography's "intractable reality" or politely suppress it as a mere illusion (*CL* 119).

In that spirit, *La chambre claire* finishes with an enigmatic quotation on its back cover that is taken from a 1976 book titled *Practice of the Tibetan Way*: "Marpa was very moved when his son was killed, and one of his disciples said: 'You have always told us that all is illusion. Is it not so with the death of your son, is not that an illusion?' And Marpa replied: 'Indeed, but the death of my son is a super-illusion.'"[46]

This, then, was the manuscript that was submitted to *Cahiers du cinema* in June of 1979 and that was subsequently published in France by a collaboration of Cahiers, Gallimard, and Editions du Seuil. By January 25, 1980, *La chambre claire: note sur la photographie* was back from the printers, and Barthes was soon sending copies to friends, inscribed with suitable dedications. By late February, reviews were about to appear in the French press; Barthes had also conducted some interviews in which he discusses his new book.[47] Despite the intimations of his own mortality contained within *La chambre claire*, no one could have guessed what was about to occur. On the afternoon of February 25, after a lunch with politician François Mitterand in the company of a small group of other French intellectuals, Barthes was hit by a van while crossing the street on his way home. Although he survived the initial accident, his health gradually deteriorated while in hospital, and he died a month later on March 26, 1980, at the age of sixty-four.[48] Virtually all subsequent discussions of *Camera Lucida* are mediated by this fact. It has become a book marked by Barthes's indissoluble association of photography with death and by two actual deaths—the death of the author's mother (the event that inspired its writing) and the death of the author himself.

By this point, Barthes's work was eagerly read in the United States and Britain, and a number of his previous books were available in English editions. An English translation of *La chambre claire* was in fact already in the works by the time Barthes died. The American edition was translated by New York poet Richard Howard, a friend of the author's who had performed the same service for a number of Barthes's earlier books. Howard remembers receiving the proof sheets for *La chambre claire* before it appeared in bookstores in France (perhaps in January 1980) and began working on it almost immediately.[49] He had found in the past that Barthes took relatively little interest in the creative decisions entailed in translation and was content to trust Howard's judgment. This was the case with *La chambre claire*, and Howard does not recall Barthes making any corrections to his English version (Barthes had only a basic reading ability in English). When necessary, Howard was able to consult Susan Sontag about any particular translation problems, although this manuscript contained no memorable ones.

Howard decided on the English title—*Camera Lucida: Reflections on Photography*—with the change in subtitle driven by the translator's desire to avoid the diminution of substance implied by the word *note* and by his thinking that the word *reflections* incorporated a suitably photographic metaphor.[50] It was the publisher's decision to delete the marginal notes, bibliography, illustration list, and Tibetan quotation found in the French original and to change the cover design (the engraving of a camera lucida in use was replaced by a sketch of a small camera on a tripod). The American edition, published by Hill and Wang, appeared in 1981 and by August 23 had been reviewed in the *New York Times*.[51] However, reviews of *La chambre claire* had already appeared in the British and American press, such as Stephen Bann's in the *Times Literary Supplement* in November 1980 and Pepe Karmel's commentary in *Art in America* in March 1981.[52]

Before considering the book's reception in more detail, it is worth pausing for a moment to discuss the differences between the French and American editions. The deletion of the Tibetan quotation implies that it is of no great importance, certainly that it is not a part of Barthes's original text. Many scholars would disagree.[53] But this relatively small intervention also points to greater liberties taken by the publishers of other editions. Versions of *La chambre claire* are available in most languages, including in Spanish, German, Italian, Portuguese (one from Brazil and another from Portugal), Turkish, Greek, Czech, Russian, Chinese (one published in Taiwan and another in China), Korean, Japanese, Danish, Swedish, and Norwegian, as well as English.[54] There have even been two unauthorized editions published in Farsi.[55] These all vary considerably in their degrees of faithfulness to the layout of the French original. Like the American edition, a 1981 Portuguese translation deletes the Tibetan quotation, as do a 1980 Italian translation, a 1984 version published in Brazil, a 1985 German translation, a 1986 edition in Swedish, a 1994 Czech translation, a 1996 Korean edition, a 1996 Danish edition, an English edition published in London in 2000, both Farsi editions, and a Norwegian version issued in 2001. More surprising still is the elimination of the color image by Boudinet from a 1989 Spanish edition, as well as from the German, Czech, British, and one of the Farsi versions (several others save money by reproducing it in black and white).[56] Is this image so unimportant to the purpose of Barthes's book that it need not even be included?

A number of scholars have argued that Boudinet's *Polaroid* is a central, perhaps even *the* central, image in Barthes's argument, despite never being mentioned by him. As Diana Knight has explained, the Boudinet image was lifted from a larger sequence titled *Fragments of a Labyrinth* that the artist shot at night in his own apartment between dusk and dawn and using only available light.[57] There is not much to see. We can make out the edge of a bed or couch with a pillow resting on it, but most of the picture is taken up with a diaphanous drawn curtain that overlaps in the center, obscuring our vision of what lies beyond. It parts a little as it touches the bed, allowing a flash of illumination. This, it seems, is a place for contemplation, rest, and sleep and perhaps also for sex (the curtains are drawn, after all). As the first image you see in *Camera Lucida*, its monochrome blue-green color creates a melancholy mood, setting a tone for the text that is to follow. But its significance goes further than that.

According to Knight, "Boudinet's dawn polaroid is certainly an integral part of Barthes's symbolic narrative of refinding his mother in the literal *chambre claire* of the glass conservatory."[58] Barthes even refers to the "blue-green of her pupils" (*CL* 66) when speaking of his mother's eyes. Moreover, he tells us (in a reference that surreptitiously links his Winter Garden Photograph to Boudinet's) that "all the world's photographs formed a Labyrinth. I knew that at the center of this Labyrinth I would find nothing but this sole picture" (*CL* 73). In keeping with this reference, Beryl Schlossman sees the Boudinet image and its "voluptuous textured curtain scene" as a symbolic stand-in for Barthes's absent mother and "the maternal body" and points to its "allegorical quality of absence-presence."[59] Mary Lydon is more circumspect about the meaning of the picture but again underlines its importance to Barthes's book given that, in *La chambre claire*, it is "so eloquently placed between Barthes's homage to Sartre's *L'imaginaire* and his own text."[60]

Polaroid (reproduced in color but never discussed by Barthes) is, it seems, the other to the Winter Garden Photograph, that much discussed but never reproduced *imaginaire* in which Barthes finds the essence of both his mother and photography. These two photographs are presented by him as inseparable manifestations of the same labyrinth—one (barely) visible, the other not at all (except in our mind's eye). Borrowing an analogy pursued by Barthes in *Empire of Signs*, his 1970 book about his impressions of Japan, one might say that the Boudinet picture represents "the visible form of invisibility [hiding] the sacred 'nothing.'"[61] Its presence is necessary to maintain the binary dynamic that animates every aspect of this book. Accordingly, any translated edition of *La chambre claire* that does not include the Boudinet image should be regarded as fatally flawed.

A Liminal Moment

Camera Lucida arrived on the scene at a liminal moment in the history of photographic discourse. As Barthes himself mentioned in an interview published three days before his accident: "there does seem to be a kind of 'theoretical boom' in photography. . . . People who are not technicians, historians, or aestheticians are becoming interested in it."[62] In France, Susan Sontag and Michel Tournier had just published their own books on photography (Sontag's is in Barthes's bibliography), and he also points out that the University of Aix-Marseilles had recently accepted a proposal from Lucien Clergue for a doctoral program in photography—"but in the Chemistry Department!"[63] To these events, we might add the establishment of a photography collection at the Musée d'Orsay in Paris in 1978, the special issue of *Cahiers de la photographie* published in 1981 under the title "Quelle histoire la photographie!," and the creation of the Centre de la Photographie in Paris in 1982.

The situation in the United States was a little different. It became possible to study for a master of fine arts degree in art photography in the United States in the mid-1960s, and by the late 1970s, photography, whether as historical object or professional practice, had become fully institutionalized, having at last found a secure niche in universities, art schools, art museums, and the marketplace, as well as in the culture at large.[64] For various reasons, this proliferation in turn generated an anxiety about the status of photography among its intelligentsia, evidenced equally in self-conscious art practices and a newly invigorated critical writing. Some examples of this turn might include the special issue of *Artforum* devoted to photography in September 1976 (incorporating Nancy Foote's essay "The Anti-Photographers" and A. D. Coleman's "The Directorial Mode: Notes toward a Definition"), the publication of Susan Sontag's *On Photography* in 1977, the special issue of *October* magazine devoted to photography in 1978 (in which its editors called for "a radical sociology of photography to force upon us, to disclose to view, the structural and historical nature and implications of our present photographic revisionism"), and the lecture series organized in 1979 by the Art Institute of Chicago titled "Towards the New Histories of Photography."[65]

To this list could be added the practices of artists like Cindy Sherman (who produced her now canonical *Untitled Film Stills* in New York between 1977 and 1980) and the essays that promoted them, in particular Craig Owens's "The Allegorical Impulse: Toward a Theory of Postmodernism, Part 2" (which appeared in *October* 13, Summer 1980) and Douglas Crimp's "The Photographic Activity of Postmodernism" (*October* 15, Winter 1980).[66] Both of these essays refer to and draw on the 1977 publication of Barthes's essays in *Image Music Text*. Using concepts proposed by Barthes himself, they also both posit a critique of modernism in general and of photography in particular that they call "postmodernism."[67]

This, then, was the general cultural context in which *Camera Lucida* appeared in the United States. The situation in Britain was a little different, given that country's strong left-wing intellectual tradition and closer proximity to France, along with the existence of a number of little magazines dedicated to critical discussions of photography and related media (in the 1980s, these included *Screen, Screen Education, Camerawork, Creative Camera* and *Ten.8*).[68] The character of the debate in the United Kingdom might be summed up in the title of a 1979 anthology, *Photography/Politics: One*, and in essays in this period by Victor Burgin and John Tagg that sought to reconcile a Marxist tradition with semiotics (including the earlier work of Barthes), psychoanalysis, and the work of Michel Foucault. This was an effort embodied in the influential 1982 volume *Thinking Photography*.[69] What postmodern critics from both countries shared was an opposition to a kind of modernist formalism most often identified with John Szarkowski and the art photography favored by the Museum of Modern Art in New York. As Szarkowski proposed in 1962, "it should be possible to consider the history of the medium in terms of photographers' progressive awareness of characteristics and problems that have seemed inherent in the medium."[70] In other words, Szarkowski too claimed to be seeking the essence of photography, in his case by privileging the specific qualities of the photographic medium.[71]

Given this context, some readers were not sure what to make of *Camera Lucida*, a book that seemed to combine the ontological quest of a conservative modernism with the sophisticated vocabulary and pedigree of a postmodern semiotics. Many reviewers struggled to explain the relation of *Camera Lucida* to Barthes's earlier, more overtly political structuralist work. On the one hand, they tried to fathom how a subjective division of pictures between *studium* and *punctum* could possibly further a critical analysis of photography, and on the other, they worried about Barthes's reliance on what Michael Starenko called "the heresy of sentiment."[72] Every reviewer concedes the seductive quality of Barthes's writing, especially in its role as a moving eulogy to his deceased mother, but some were distinctly hostile to its more general discussion of photography: as Sam Vernedoe put it, "*La Chambre Claire* is the kind of book photography does not need now."[73]

Despite this ambivalence, the book was extensively reviewed at the time of its publication (in one case, by three critics in the same journal).[74] More important, it quickly found a responsive English-speaking audience (it went through eighteen printings by 1996), and its distinctive vocabulary and elliptical style soon came to influence photographic writing of all kinds.[75] That influence continues, although today it is evidenced less powerfully by the ubiquity of the word *punctum* or an obsession with indexicality than by the attention now being paid to ordinary and vernacular photographs and by the popularity of subjective, novelistic, and affective modes of writing about them.[76] In that guise, the *Camera Lucida* effect promises to resonate within photodiscourse for some time to come.

CAMERA LUCIDA NOW

Indeed, as many of the essays in *Photography Degree Zero* attest, *Camera Lucida*'s intellectual density and evocative prose remain more than capable of stimulating significant debate. The earliest essay in the present book is Victor Burgin's 1982 review of *Camera Lucida*, first published in *Creative Camera* as "Re-reading *Camera Lucida*." Burgin provides a sympathetic overview of Barthes's book as a literary text, relating it to his earlier work and arguing that, despite Barthes's adoption of a phenomenological approach that "rejects the concept of the unconscious," "Barthes's approach to the photograph in *Camera Lucida* is compatible with the sort of psychoanalytic/intertextual approach" that Burgin himself advocated. Jane Gallop's 1985 essay, "The Pleasure of the Phototext," was first published in *Afterimage* as part of a group of texts concerned with the representation of sexuality.[77] In it she draws a comparison between *Camera Lucida* and *The Pleasure of the Text* as a way of "pursuing the idea of a relation between sexuality and the medium of photography, which is not sexuality *in* photography, but is something like the sexuality *of* photography."

From these relatively early discussions, we move to Margaret Iversen's 1994 essay "What Is a Photograph?," another effort to argue that Barthes's brand of phenomenology, steeped as it is in the author's own desire, is "psychoanalytical through and through." The work of Jacques Lacan serves as a touchstone for Iversen's analysis of Barthes's text, allowing her to emphasize its relation to the gaze, trauma, and the death drive. Margaret Olin's 2002 essay, "Touching Photographs: Roland Barthes's 'Mistaken' Identification," examines the privileged relation of the photograph to its referent posited by *Camera Lucida*, pointing out Barthes's own mistaken identification of a detail in a James Van Der Zee photograph that he reproduces. She even speculates that the famous Winter Garden Photograph involves a similar displacement, "mistakenly" conjuring an image of Kafka as a child and thereby casting doubt on the role of truth in Barthes's narrative.

Jay Prosser's contribution, "Buddha Barthes: What Barthes Saw in Photography (That He Didn't in Literature)," suggests a correspondence between what Barthes found in photographs and what he sought in Buddhism. First published in 2004, Prosser's essay argues that the photographic flash that illuminates the darkness is the equivalent, for Barthes, of the mystic's light of revelation. Eduardo Cadava and Paola Cortés-Rocca combine voices in a 2006 meditation on love and loss inspired by *Camera Lucida*. Their "Notes on Love and Photography" examines "the general relay between photography and the mother" in terms that acknowledge the photograph's "magical and uncanny power to procreate," associating this power with music and even with "the entire logic of our relation to the world."

Michael Fried's 2005 essay, "Barthes's *Punctum*," is one of a series he has written on photography in which he seeks to locate his discussion of the medium in relation to his own interest in what he calls "*antitheatrical* critical thought and pictorial practice."[78] He seeks to underline what he regards as common claims in *Camera Lucida* and his own 1967 essay "Art and Objecthood."[79] Fried's discussion of *Camera Lucida* has in turn generated several responses, including one by James Elkins, also from 2005, that ponders the centrality of Barthes's book as a text about photography given what Elkins regards as "its limited value in the history or criticism of photography."[80] Rosalind Krauss also offers a short commentary on Fried's text for this book, pointing to a number of important questions of translation and emphasizing Barthes's interest in escaping the "fascism of language."

In another previously unpublished essay, "*Camera Lucida*, circa 1980," Gordon Hughes reads *Camera Lucida* as a lament for a kind of photographic experience and practice that Barthes sees as increasingly under threat, most seriously by the photographic avant-garde. Carol Mavor, in her essay "Black and Blue: The Shadows of *Camera Lucida*," regards Barthes's "obvious, erroneous readings of race" and explores, in a deeply personal text, the figuring of blackness throughout *Camera Lucida*. Race is also the major concern of Shawn Michelle Smith's 2007 commentary, "Race and Reproduction in *Camera Lucida*," a theme through which she reveals the book's "most evocative power and its most frustrating limitations." My own contribution, "*Camera Lucida*: Another Little History of Photography," builds on an earlier essay of the same name that pursues the possibility that Barthes's book might productively be read as a history rather than a theory of photography.

Thirteen essays, then, plus this introduction: Barthes's modest text is still capable of provocation, still able to make us think about photography. And this despite the frequent predictions in recent years of photography's own demise, a death induced—it has been variously suggested—by a combination of its own success (whereby it has managed to eclipse "the very notion of a medium"), by the introduction of digital technologies that have displaced its most fundamental properties and undermined its truth values, or more generally by an "evolution taking place in the whole framework that provided photography with a cultural, instrumental and historical context."[81] In other words, for some, *Camera Lucida* appeared on the scene just as the photography it sought to describe was about to disappear from view. Has the photography pursued by Barthes perhaps already gone, transformed into a mere ghost of its former self? Can we any longer feel the affect that so transported Barthes as he looked at certain photographs?

"It has already disappeared," says Barthes in 1979. "I am, I don't know why, one of its last witnesses . . . and this book is its archaic trace" (*CL* 94). Exactly what photography, then, are we today trying to be the witnesses of? What are the contemporary identities, the political economies, the physical and conceptual forms of this phenomenon that continues unabated, even after all the obituaries have been written? Any account of photography written after *Camera Lucida* is haunted by such questions, just as surely as by the specter of the photographic image. What we don't know yet is quite how these questions should be answered. It is fair to say that we are now at a moment that sees itself as being after postmodernism but that has yet to attract the burden of a proper name or the motivation of an enabling politics. The invention of such a politics and with it a mode of critical writing that is appropriate for the times in which we live therefore remains the most pressing task to face the present generation of photography's interlocutors. What *Photography Degree Zero* proposes is that, even twenty-five years and more after its initial publication, *Camera Lucida* remains a good place from which to begin.

Notes

1. Roland Barthes, *Camera Lucida: Reflections on Photography* (1980), trans. Richard Howard (New York: Hill and Wang, 1981), 3 (henceforth *CL* in the main text). This is the English translation of Roland Barthes, *La chambre claire: note sur la photographie* (Paris: Cahiers du Cinéma, Gallimard, Seuil, 1980).

2. Note, for example, the central role assumed by *Camera Lucida* in the various discussions gathered in James Elkins, ed., *Photography Theory* (New York: Routledge, 2007). The canonical status of *Camera Lucida* is evidenced also by the frequency with which extracts from the book itself are included in anthologies devoted to photographic history and theory. See, for example, Julia Thomas, ed., *Reading Images* (New York: Palgrave, 2001), 54–61, and Liz Wells, ed., *The Photography Reader* (London: Routledge, 2003), 19–30. The British photographic artist Idris Khan pays further homage to the book's influence in a multiple-exposure image titled *Every page . . . from Roland Barthes'* Camera Lucida (2004). In this work (as the title suggests), one gets to see every page of the book at the same time. See Geoff Dyer, "Between the Lines," *The Guardian* (London), September 2, 2006: http://www.guardian.co.uk/artanddesign/2006/sep/02/art (accessed 16 January 2009).

3. Roland Barthes, *Roland Barthes by Roland Barthes* (1975), trans. Richard Howard (New York: Hill and Wang, 1977), 47.

4. Nancy Shawcross, *Roland Barthes and Photography: The Critical Tradition in Perspective* (Gainesville: University Press of Florida, 1997).

5. Jean-Michel Rabaté, ed., *Writing the Image after Roland Barthes* (Philadelphia: University of Pennsylvania Press, 1997).

6. Diana Knight, ed., *Critical Essays on Roland Barthes* (New York: Hall, 2000). For French commentaries, see also Jean Delord, *Roland Barthes et la photographie* (Paris: Créatis, 1981), and Gilles Mora, ed., *Roland Barthes et la photo: le pire des signes* (Paris: Contrejour, 1990).

7. Numerous surveys of Barthes's career have been published. A useful introduction, including summaries of previous surveys, can be found in Graham Allen, *Roland Barthes* (London: Routledge, 2003).

8. Roland Barthes, *Writing Degree Zero* (1953), trans. Annette Lavers and Colin Smith (London: Jonathan Cape, 1967) (henceforth *WDZ* in the main text). The continuity of *Writing Degree Zero* and *Camera Lucida* is discussed by, among others, Jacques Derrida, in "The Deaths of Roland Barthes" (1981), in Hugh Silverman, ed., *Philosophy and Non-Philosophy since Merleau-Ponty* (London: Routledge, 1988), 259–296.

9. Jean-Paul Sartre, *Qu'est-ce que la littérature?* (1947), published in English as Jean-Paul Sartre, *What Is Literature?*, trans. Bernard Frechtman (New York: Philosophical Society, 1949).

10. Jean-Paul Sartre, *L'imaginaire* (1940), published in English as Jean-Paul Sartre, *The Imaginary: A Phenomenological Psychology of the Imagination* (1940), trans. Jonathan Webber (London: Routledge, 2004).

11. See Jean-Michel Rabaté, "Introduction," *Writing the Image after Roland Barthes*, 6–8.

12. See Rosalind Krauss, "Translator's Introduction," *October* 112 (Spring 2005): 3–6. She also comments that "The fantasy on which Barthes's penultimate course 'Le Neutre' is based . . . held steady . . . over the trajectory that took him from *Writing Degree Zero*, with the zero degree an early version of 'le neutre,' through all the rest of his books" (4). Indeed, in *Camera Lucida*, Barthes laments: "if only Photography could give me a neutral, anatomic body, a body which signifies nothing!" (12).

13. Roland Barthes, "From *The Neutral*: Session of March 11, 1978," *October* 112 (Spring 2005): 9. In his "Session of May 6, 1978," Barthes ruminates (under the heading "Oscillation") on some possible meanings of *neutral*, including "degree zero." He concludes with "in short: Neutral = to cancel and/or to scramble." Roland Barthes, *The Neutral: Lecture Course at the Collège de France (1977–1978)*, trans. Rosalind E. Krauss and Denis Hollier (New York: Columbia University Press, 2005), 130.

14. Roland Barthes, *Mythologies* (Paris: Édition du Seuil, 1957); Roland Barthes, *Mythologies*, trans. Annette Lavers (New York: Hill and Wang, 1972) (henceforth *M* in the main text).

15. The phrase comes from Edward Steichen, "Introduction," *Family of Man* (New York: Museum of Modern Art, 1955), 4.

16. In his "A Short History of Photography" (1931), Walter Benjamin refers to Brecht's thinking as follows: "For the situation, Brecht says, is complicated by the fact that less than ever does a simple *reproduction of reality* express something about reality. A photograph of the Krupp works or of the A.E.G. reveals almost nothing about these institutions." See Walter Benjamin, "A Short History of Photography" (1931), in Alan Trachtenberg, ed., *Classic Essays on Photography* (New Haven: Leete's Island Books, 1980), 213.

17. "Photos-Chocs," in Barthes, *Mythologies*, 119–121. An English translation (originally published in *Creative Camera* in the United Kingdom in July 1969) can be found reproduced as "The Scandal of Horror Photography," in David Brittain, ed., *Creative Camera: Thirty Years of Writing* (Manchester: Manchester University Press, 1999), 32–34 (henceforth *CC* in the main text). The essay is translated as "Shock-Photos" in Roland Barthes, *The Eiffel Tower and Other Mythologies*, trans. Richard Howard (New York: Hill and Wang, 1979), 71–73.

18. Algirdas Julien Greimas remembers introducing Barthes to the work of Saussure in 1949 or 1950 while they were both working in Alexandria. Barthes claims that he first read Saussure in 1951. See Louis-Jean Calvet, *Roland Barthes: A Biography*, trans. Sarah Wykes (Bloomington: Indiana University Press, 1995), 94–95. Barthes knew the work of Brecht from his role as a theater critic in the 1950s, positively reviewing the Berliner Ensemble's production of *Mother Courage* in Paris in May 1954. However, he also wrote several more general essays on Brecht's method. See Roland Barthes, "Diderot, Brecht, Eisenstein" (1973), *Image, Music, Text*, trans. Stephen Heath (London: Fontana, 1977), 69–78; and Roland Barthes, "Brecht and Discourse: A Contribution to the Study of Discursivity" (1975), *The Rustle of Language*, trans. Richard Howard (New York: Hill and Wang, 1986), 212–222. See also Philippe Roger, "Barthes with Marx," in Rabaté, *Writing the Image after Roland Barthes*, 174–186. Barthes sums up his view of Brecht's theatrical work in *Camera Lucida*: "this impasse is something like Brecht's: he was hostile to Photography because (he said) of the weakness of its critical power; but his own theatre has never been able to be politically effective on account of its subtlety and its aesthetic quality" (36).

19. Roland Barthes, "The Photographic Message" (1961), *Image Music Text*, 15–31 (henceforth *IMT* in the main text).

20. Barthes, of course, does the same; in each of his examples, he looks at a photomechanical reproduction and sees through it to the photograph at its origin.

21. Roland Barthes, "Rhetoric of the Image," *Image Music Text*, 32–51.

22. This essay was first published in English (having been translated by Richard Howard) in the United States, appearing in 1967 as part of *Aspen*, numbers 5 + 6, an art project posing as a magazine. This issue consisted of twenty-eight numbered items gathered in a box, including essays by Barthes, Susan Sontag, and George Kubler. It was edited and designed by Brian O'Doherty and published in 1967 by Roaring Fork Press, New York. As its editor, artist Brian O'Doherty, recalls: "To my distress several people, including Barthes, didn't get paid. Barthes was in Philadelphia at that time and he came to New York to talk about the project. He got it immediately. My notion that art, writing etc., was produced by a kind of anti-self that had nothing to do with whoever 'me' was, an excellent preparation for our conversation. He said, 'I think I may have something for you.' When 'The Death of the Author' arrived, I knew it was revolutionary." See "In Conversation: Brian O'Doherty with Phong Bui," *The Brooklyn Rail* (June 2007): http://www.brooklynrail.org/2007/06/art/doughtery (accessed 16 January 2009) and Alex Alberro, "Inside the White Box: Brian O'Doherty's 'Aspen 5+6,'" *Artforum* 40, no. 1 (September 2001): 170–174. Barthes's essay was published in French in *Mantéia* 5 (1968): 12–17, and was also included, in a translation by Stephen Heath, in the 1977 anthology *Image Music Text*, 142–148.

23. See Roland Barthes, *A Lover's Discourse: Fragments* (1977), trans. Richard Howard (New York: Hill and Wang, 1978); Roland Barthes, *The Pleasure of the Text* (1973), trans. Richard Miller (New

York: Noonday Press, 1975); Barthes, *Roland Barthes*. For an appreciation of Barthes as a writer, see Susan Sontag, "Writing Itself: On Roland Barthes," in Susan Sontag, ed., *A Barthes Reader* (New York: Hill and Wang, 1982), vii–xxxvi.

24. Graham Allen sees this shift as a tactical one that is designed to avoid the absorption of Barthes's work into the *doxa*. "The body of the writing subject is that, according to Barthes, which seems most scandalous to both bourgeois and petit-bourgeois culture (with its ideas of perversity and sexual deviance) and Marxist-inspired left-wing discourses (with their ban on the personal, the sentimental, that which is pleasurable). Conservative and left-wing discourses seem to conspire together to ban the writing subject from indulging in the pleasures and perversities of the body. . . . Against such orthodoxies, on the right and left sides of the political spectrum, Barthes defiantly takes post-structuralist theory and directs it at his own body and his own pleasures." Allen, *Roland Barthes*, 101. Barthes ensured that his writing about such pleasures encompassed all possible sexualities. In *A Lover's Discourse*, for example, he refers to the "beloved object" rather than to a specific sexed subject. When asked about this, he replied: "I think that exactly the same *tonality* can be found in a man who loves a woman or a man, and a woman who loves a man or a woman. And so I was careful to de-emphasize the sexual difference." Roland Barthes, "The Greatest Cryptographer of Contemporary Myths Talks about Love" (*Playboy*, September 1977), *The Grain of the Voice: Interviews 1962–80*, trans. Linda Coverdale (New York: Hill and Wang, 1985), 293. Since Barthes's death, his own homosexuality has become a topic of discussion. See, for example, D. A. Miller, *Bringing Out Roland Barthes* (Berkeley: University of California Press, 1992).

25. In *The Pleasure of the Text*, Barthes distinguishes two kinds of experience that can be had from texts—*plaisir* (pleasure) and *jouissance* (bliss, ecstasy). The first "comes from culture and does not break from it, is linked to a *comfortable* practice of reading," whereas the second "imposes a state of loss, the text that discomforts." Barthes, *The Pleasure of the Text*, 14.

26. In his 1980 review of *La chambre claire*, Hervé Guibert lists recent essays by Barthes on the work of Avedon (for *Photo*), Faucon (for *Zoom*), Boudinet (for *Créatis*), and von Gloeden (for "a German publication"—actually, for *Wilhelm von Gloeden* [Naples: Amelio editiore, 1978]). See Hervé Guibert, "Roland Barthes and Photography: The Sincerity of the Subject" (*Le monde*, 28 February 1980), trans. Diana Knight, in Knight, *Critical Essays on Roland Barthes*, 115. Barthes's essay on Wilhelm von Gloeden is translated into English in Roland Barthes, *The Responsibility of Forms: Critical Essays on Music, Art, and Representation*, trans. Richard Howard (Berkeley: University of California Press, 1985), 195–197. For a commentary by Renaud Camus on Barthes's essay on Boudinet, see Renaud Camus, "Barthes and the Discourse of Photography" (1979), in Knight, *Critical Essays on Roland Barthes*, 112–114.

27. See Roland Barthes, "On Photography" (an interview with Angelo Schwarz from late 1977 published in *Le photographe*, February 1980), *The Grain of the Voice*, 356.

28. The text of this lecture, delivered in November 1978 in New York as "Proust and I," has been published in English under the title "*Longtemps, je me suis couché de bonne heure . . .*," in Barthes, *The Rustle of Language*, 277–290.

29. Barthes was interviewed by Bernard-Henri Lévy and Jean-Marie Benoist, as quoted in Calvet, *Roland Barthes*, 220.

30. About 12,250 such slips are now stored as part of the Barthes bequest at Institute Mémoires de l'édition contemporaine in Paris. See Denis Hollier, "Notes (on the Index Card)," *October* 112 (Spring 2005): 35, 40. For reproductions of some of these slips, see also Marianne Alphant and Nathalie Léger, eds., *R/B: Roland Barthes* (exhibition catalogue, Paris: Centre Pompidou, 2002).

31. It has been pointed out that, if you're inclined toward such calculations, there is even a numerological aspect to *La chambre claire's* organization: if you add together forty-eight chapters, twenty-four illustrations, and twelve bibliographic items it comes to a total of eighty-four, the age of Barthes's mother when she died. See Jay Prosser, "Roland Barthes's Loss," *Light in the Dark Room: Photography and Loss* (Minneapolis: University of Minnesota Press, 2005), 24.

32. See *La chambre claire*, 15, and *Camera Lucida*, 4–5.

33. The books on photography in Barthes's bibliography include Raul Beceyro, *Ensayos sobre fotografia* (Mexico: Arte y libros, 1978); Pierre Bourdieu et al., *Un art moyen* (Paris: Minuit, 1965); Gisèle Freund, *Photographie et societé* (Paris: Seuil, 1974); Susan Sontag, *Le photographie* (Paris: Seuil, 1979).

34. Beaumont Newhall, *The History of Photography* (New York: Museum of Modern Art, 1964). For a commentary by William Klein on Barthes's use of his particular images in *Camera Lucida*, see William Klein, "Sur deux photos de William Klein," in Mora, *Roland Barthes et la photo*, 30–31.

35. Walter Benjamin's "A Little History of Photography" was first published in *Literarische Welt* in the September and October issues of 1931. It was first published in English in a translation by Stanley Mitchell that renders it as "A Short History of Photography," in *Screen* 13, no. 1 (Spring 1972): 5–26. Although Barthes doesn't list the French translation of the essay in his bibliography in *La chambre claire*, he does say, in an interview from late 1977: "There are few great texts of intellectual quality on photography. I don't know of very many. There is Walter Benjamin's essay, which is good because it is premonitory." See Barthes, *The Grain of the Voice*, 354. However, he may well have been referring to "The Work of Art in the Age of Mechanical Reproduction," a 1936 essay by Benjamin that was translated into French that same year by a friend of Barthes's, Pierre Klossowski. Speaking of influences, Colin MacCabe has commented on the similarities of Barthes's "ontological quest" to that of André Bazin, whose 1945 essay, "Ontology of the Photographic Image," is also absent from Barthes's bibliography (although Barthes does refer to Bazin in his text; see *CL* 55). See Colin MacCabe, "Barthes and Bazin: The Ontology of the Image," in Rabaté, *Writing the Image after Roland Barthes*, 71–76.

36. Hervé Guibert, "Roland Barthes and Photography," in Knight, *Critical Essays on Roland Barthes*, 117.

37. In a 1975 interview with Jean-Jacques Brochier, Barthes described the style of discourse found in *Roland Barthes by Roland Barthes* as "novelistic rather than intellectual." Barthes, "Twenty Key Words for Roland Barthes" (*Le magazine littéraire*, February 1975), in Barthes, *The Grain of the Voice*, 223. Nancy Shawcross has argued that *Camera Lucida* represents a "third form" of writing that partakes of both the essay and the novel. See her chapter "Contextualizing *Camera Lucida*: 'The Third Form,'" in Shawcross, *Roland Barthes on Photography*, 67–85.

38. Newhall, *The History of Photography*, 14.

39. See Geoffrey Batchen, "Detours: Photography and the Camera Lucida," *Afterimage* 18, no. 2 (September 1990): 14–15.

40. Roland Barthes, from an interview with Guy Mandery, December 1979, in Barthes, *The Grain of the Voice*, 358.

41. Barthes reproduces an 1863 portrait of Queen Victoria on horseback (*CL* 56) along with a caption that appears nowhere in his text: "'*Queen Victoria, entirely unaesthetic . . .* ' (Virginia Woolf)." The same caption appears, in English, in *La chambre claire* (92). In 1961, Barthes described the interplay between photograph and caption in "The Photographic Message": "The caption, by its very disposition, by its average measure of reading, appears to duplicate the image, that is, to be included in its denotation." Barthes, *Image Music Text*, 26.

42. Barthes describes going to the opening (by bus in the rain) in his journal entry for April 25, 1979, under the heading "Futile evening": "At the (crumbling) Galerie de l'Impasse, I was disappointed: not by D.B.'s photographs (of windows and blue curtains, taken with a Polaroid camera), but by the chilly atmosphere of the opening. . . . D.S., beautiful and disturbing, said to me: 'Lovely, aren't they?' 'Yes, very lovely' (but it's thin, there's not enough here, I added under my breath)." Roland Barthes, "Deliberation," *The Rustle of Language*, 368. Mary Lydon has suggested that the passage from which this description comes features "three characters from *La Chambre Claire*: Barthes, his mother, and Daniel Boudinet, whose initials, as they are sounded in French, so markedly punctuate the enigmatic title: '*Délibé*ration.'" Mary Lydon, "Amplification: Barthes, Freud, and Paranoia," in Steven Unger and Betty R. McGraw, eds., *Signs in Culture: Roland Barthes Today* (Iowa City: University of Iowa Press, 1989), 134.

43. In *S/Z* (1970), Barthes compares "readerly" texts with "writerly" ones. As Terence Hawkes summarizes, "*writerly* texts require us to look at the nature of language itself, not *through* it at a preordained 'real world.'" See Terence Hawkes, *Structuralism and Semiotics* (Berkeley: University of California Press, 1977), 114–115. See also Shawcross, *Roland Barthes and Photography*, 79.

44. For a discussion of the history and implications of the palinode, see Prosser, *Light in the Dark Room*, 12–14, 163–164.

45. A number of scholars have pointed out that the distinctions conjured by these terms are prefigured in a 1970 essay titled "The Third Meaning" in which Barthes discusses a series of stills from Eisenstein's film *Ivan the Terrible*. He is particularly taken with an opposition between "*the obvious meaning*" and "*the obtuse meaning*" of these stills, with the second of these emerging from various details: "the supplement that my intellection cannot succeed in absorbing, at once persistent and fleeting, smooth and elusive." See Roland Barthes, "The Third Meaning: Research Notes on Some Eisenstein Stills," *Image Music Text*, 52–68, and also Steven Unger, "Persistence of the Image: Barthes, Photography, and the Resistance to Film," Unger and McGraw, *Signs in Culture*, 153–155, and Allen, *Roland Barthes*, 126.

46. This translation is from the essay by Victor Burgin in this volume, chapter 2, Re-reading *Camera Lucida*.

47. See the interviews with Laurent Dispot (published in *Le matin*, February 22, 1980) and Guy Manderey (published in *Le photographe*, February 1980) in Barthes, *The Grain of the Voice*, 351–352, 356–360. See also Hervé Guibert's review (published in *Le Monde* on February 28, 1980, and translated by Diane Knight) in Knight, *Critical Essays on Roland Barthes*, 115–117.

48. Jean-Paul Sartre died shortly thereafter on April 15, 1980, and his funeral, which drew a crowd of 50,000 people, somewhat eclipsed that of Barthes. See Calvet, *Roland Barthes*, 254.

49. From an interview by the author with Richard Howard, New York, August 7, 2008.

50. For a commentary on the implications of this decision, see Shawcross, *Roland Barthes and Photography*, 69–70. See also Mary Lydon's comments on the losses and gains in the transference of title from *La chambre claire* to *Camera Lucida* in Unger and McGraw, *Signs in Culture*, 119–138.

51. Andy Grundberg, "Death in the Photograph," *New York Times,* August 23, 1981, 11.

52. Stephen Bann, "Emanations of the Real," *Times Literary Supplement,* November 14, 1980, 1301; Pepe Karmel, "Photography," *Art in America* (March 1981): 19.

53. See, for example, Jay Prosser's essay in this volume, chapter 6, Buddha Barthes: What Barthes Saw in Photography (That He Didn't See in Literature), and his "Roland Barthes's Loss," *Light in the Dark Room*, 51–52.

54. See, for example, *La camera chiara: nota sulla fotografia*, trans. Renzo Guidieri (Turin: Einaudi, 1980); *A câmara clara,* trans. Manuela Torres (Lisbon: Edicoes 70, 1981); *A cámara clara: nota sobre a fotografia*, trans. Júlio Castañon Guimarães (Rio de Janeiro: Editora Nova Fronteira, 1984); *O foteinos thalamos: seimioseis gia ti fotografia*, trans. Giannis Kritikos (Athens: Rappa Editions, 1984); *Akarui heya: shashin ni tsuite no oboegaki,* trans. Hikaru Hanawa (Tokyo: Misuzu Shobo, 1985, 1997); *Camera lucida: sajin e gwanhan note*, trans. Gwang Hee Cho (Seoul: Youlhwadang, 1986, 1997); *Det ljusa rummet: tankar om fotografiet*, trans. Mats Löfgren (Stockholm: Alfabeta Bokförlag, 1986); *La cámara lúcida: nota sobre la fotografía*, trans. Joaquim Sala-Sanahuja (Barcelona: Paidós Ibérica, 1989); *Světlá komora: vysvětlivka k fotografii,* trans. Miroslav Petříček (Bratislava: Archa 1994); *Det lyse kammer: bemaerkninger om fotografiet,* trans. Karen Nicolajsen (Copenhagen: Raevens Sorte Bibliotek, 1996); *Camera lucida: fotograf uzerine dusunceler*, trans. by Reha Akcakaya (Istanbul: Alti Kirkbes, 1996); *Ming shi: she ying zha ji*, trans. Chi-Lin Hsu (Taipei: Taiwan she ying gong zuo shi, 1997); *Camera Lucida: komentariy k fotografiiam*, trans. M. Ryklin (Moscow: Ad Marginem 1997); *Camera Lucida: Reflections on Photography,* trans. Richard Howard (London: Vintage, 2000); *Det lyse rommet: tanker om fotografiet*, trans. Knut Stene-Johansen (Oslo: Pax Forlag, 2001); *Ming shi: she ying zong heng tan*, trans. Kefei Zhao (Beijing: Wen hua yi shu chu ban she, 2003); *La camera lucida*, trans. Pianta M. Cristina (Rome: Nicolodi, 2003); *Světlá komora: vysvětlivka k fotografii*, trans. Miroslav Petříček (Prague: Fra 2005); *A câmara clara: nota sobre a fotografia*, trans. Manuela Torres (Lisbon: Edicoes 70, 2008).

55. *Otagh-e roshan: taamolati dar bab-e akkasi*, trans. Farshid Azarang (Tehran: Mahriz, 2001); *Otagh-e roshan: andishehayi darbare-ye akkasi,* trans. Niloufar Motaref (Tehran: Cheshmeh, 2001).

56. In contrast, the latest Japanese edition (2007) has the Boudinet image in color on its cover as well as inside. A 2001 Norwegian edition reproduces the Boudinet *Polaroid* in black and white inside the book but has a color detail of the diaphanous curtain as its cover image and a full, color reproduction of *Polaroid* on its back cover. The Korean edition has deleted the Boudinet image from the inside of the book but reproduces it in color on the cover.

57. Diana Knight, "The Woman without a Shadow," in Rabaté, *Writing the Image after Roland Barthes*, 138.

58. Ibid.

59. Beryl Schlossman, "The Descent of Orpheus: On Reading Barthes and Proust," in Rabaté, *Writing the Image after Roland Barthes*, 149.

60. Lydon, in Unger and McGraw, *Signs in Culture*, 132.

61. Barthes's *Empire of Signs* is quoted in Allen, *Roland Barthes*, 72.

62. Barthes, interviewed by Laurent Dispot (*Le Matin*, February 22, 1980), in Barthes, *The Grain of the Voice*, 351.

63. Ibid. He refers to the publication of Susan Sontag, *La photographie* (Paris: Seuil, 1979), and Michel Tournier, *Des clefs et des serrures* (Paris: Chêne/Hachette, 1979).

64. See, for example, David Travis and Elizabeth Siegel, eds., *Taken by Design: Photographs from the Institute of Design, 1937–1971* (Chicago: University of Chicago Press, 2002).

65. Nancy Foote, "The Anti-Photographers," and A. D. Coleman, "The Directorial Mode: Notes toward a Definition," *Artforum* 15, no. 1 (September 1976): 46–61. This particular issue of *Artforum* was edited by John Coplans (with Max Kozloff as managing editor). Susan Sontag, *On Photography* (New York: Farrar, Straus and Giroux, 1977). Rosalind Krauss and Annette Michelson, eds., "Photography: A Special Issue," *October* 5 (Summer 1978): 4. For one overview of this moment, see Douglas Fogle, ed., *The Last Picture Show: Artists Using Photography 1960–1982* (Minneapolis: Walker Art Center, 2003).

66. Cindy Sherman, *The Complete* Untitled Film Stills (New York: Museum of Modern Art, 2003); Craig Owens, "The Allegorical Impulse: Toward a Theory of Postmodernism, Part 2," *October* 13 (Summer 1980): 58–60; Douglas Crimp, "The Photographic Activity of Postmodernism," *October* 15 (Winter 1980): 91–101.

67. As John Rajchman unkindly puts it: "Postmodernism is what the French learned Americans were calling what they were thinking." John Rajchman, "Postmodernism in a Nominalist Frame: The Emergence and Diffusion of a Cultural Category," *Flash Art International Edition* 137 (November–December 1987): 49. For another history of the advent of the discourse of postmodernism in the United States, see Andreas Huyssen, "Mapping the Postmodern," *New German Critique* 33 (Fall 1984): 5–52.

68. Barthes's essay "Rhetoric of the Image" (1964), for example, was translated in Britain by Brian Trench as early as spring 1971 in *Working Papers in Cultural Studies*, No. 1 (Birmingham: University of Birmingham, 1971).

69. Terry Dennett and Jo Spence, eds., *Photography/Politics: One* (London: Photography Workshop, 1979). See also John Tagg's essay "Power and Photography," in *Screen Education* 36 (Autumn 1980): 17–55, and Victor Burgin's three essays in Victor Burgin, ed., *Thinking Photography* (London: Macmillan Education, 1982). This important anthology, put together by Burgin in 1980, includes essays by himself, Walter Benjamin, Umberto Eco, John Tagg, Alan Sekula (the lone American contributor), and Simon Watney. Burgin mentions *La chambre claire* in passing in his introduction (13), while explaining that "Rhetoric of the Image" is absent from the book only because it was already widely known in English translation. The fractious tone of the period is captured in Richard West's account of a conference about photography in Britain in the 1980s held at the University of Derby in 2005. See Richard West, "Photography in Britain since 1968: The '80s," *Source* 42 (Spring 2005): 3–4. For a direct comparison of *Thinking Photography* and *Camera Lucida*, see Edward Welch and J. J. Long, "Introduction: A Small History of Photography Studies," in J. J. Long, Andrea Noble, and Edward Welch, eds., *Photography: Theoretical Snapshots* (Milton Park, Abingdon: Routledge, 2009), 1–15.

70. John Szarkowski, *The Photographer's Eye* (New York: Museum of Modern Art), unpaginated.

71. See Geoffrey Batchen, *Burning with Desire: The Conception of Photography* (Cambridge, MA: MIT Press, 1997), for an extended discussion of the relationship of formalism and postmodernism.

72. Michel Starenko, "Roland Barthes: The Heresy of Sentiment," *Afterimage* (November 1981): 6–7.

73. Sam Varnedoe, "Roland Barthes, *La Chambre Claire*," *Art Journal* (Spring 1981): 75.

74. In addition to the reviews already listed, see also Douglas Davis, "The Magic Box," *Newsweek,* September 21, 1981, 105; Clive James, "That Old Black and White Magic," *New York Review of Books,* December 17, 1981, 37; Steven Marks, "*Camera Lucida: Reflections on Photography,*" *New Art Examiner* 9, no. 1 (1981): 27; Vivien Raynor, "How We See Pictures," *The New Leader* 64, no. 17 (1981): 15–16; Phillip Monk, "The Violent Lens," *The Canadian Forum* 61, no. 714 (1981–82): 36–37; Victor Burgin, "Re-reading *Camera Lucida*," *Creative Camera* 215 (1982): 730–734, 744; Sarah Charlesworth, "*Camera Lucida: Reflections on Photography,*" *Artforum* 20, no. 8 (1982): 72–74; Michael Halley, "Argo Sum," *Diacritics* 12, no. 4 (1982): 69–79; John Roberts, "*Camera Lucida,*" *Artscribe* 35 (1982): 68–70; Susan Butler, "Barthes: The Real Thing," *Creative Camera* 219 (1983): 862–64; Steve Baker, "Against *Camera Lucida,*" *Creative Camera* 219 (1983): 864–865; Christopher Norris, "*Camera Lucida,*" *Critical Quarterly* 25 (1983): 88–91.

75. The book has also continued to attract a diverse array of commentaries. See, for example, Minette Lehmann, "How Lucid Is *Camera Lucida*?," *San Francisco Camerawork* 16, nos. 2–3 (Summer–Fall 1989): 32–36; Anselm Haverkamp, "The Memory of Pictures: Roland Barthes and Augustine on Photography," *Comparative Literature* 45, no. 3 (Summer 1993): 258–279; Kris Cohen, "Locating the Photograph's 'Prick': A Queer Tropology of Roland Barthes's *Camera Lucida*," *Chicago Art Journal* 6 (Spring 1996): 5–14; Johnnie Gratton, "The Subject of Enunciation in Roland Barthes's *La Chambre Claire*," *French Studies* 50 (April 1996): 170–181; Johnnie Gratton, "Text, Image, Reference in Roland Barthes's *La Chambre Claire*," *Modern Language Review* 91, no. 2 (1996): 355–364; Kas Saghafi, "Phantasmphotography," *Philosophy Today* (2000): 98–111; Meir Wigoder, "History Begins at Home: Photography and Memory in the Writings of Siegfried Kracauer and Roland Barthes," *History and Memory* 13, no. 1 (Spring 2001): 19–59; Carol Mavor, "Roland Barthes's Umbilical Referent," in Richard Meyer, ed., *Representing the Passions: Histories, Bodies, Visions* (Santa Monica, CA: Getty Research Institute, 2003), 175–205; Andrew Fisher, "Beyond Barthes: Rethinking the Phenomenology of Photography," *Radical Philosophy,* 148 (March/April 2008), 19–29.

76. See (to name just a few recent books that acknowledge the influence of *Camera Lucida*), Christopher Pinney, *Camera Indica: The Social Life of Indian Photographs* (London: Reaktion Books, 1997); Marianne Hirsch, *Family Frames: Photography, Narrative and Postmemory* (Cambridge, MA: Harvard University Press, 1997); Carol Armstrong, *Scenes in a Library: Reading the Photograph in the Book 1843–1875* (Cambridge, MA: MIT Press, 1998); Martha Langford, *Suspended Conversations: The Afterlife of Memory in Photographic Albums* (Montreal: McGill-Queen's University Press, 2001); Ulrich Baer, *Spectral Evidence: The Photography of Trauma* (Cambridge, MA: MIT Press, 2002); Alex Hughes and Andrea Noble, eds., *Phototextualities: Intersections of Photography and Narrative* (Albuquerque: University of New Mexico Press, 2003); Geoffrey Batchen, *Forget Me Not: Photography and Remembrance* (New York: Princeton Architectural Press, 2004); Elizabeth Edwards and Janice Hart, eds., *Photographs Objects Histories: On the Materiality of Images* (London: Routledge, 2004); Carol Mavor, *Reading Boyishly: Roland Barthes, J. M. Barrie, Jacques Henri Lartigue, Marcel Proust, and D. W. Winnicott* (Durham: Duke University Press, 2007).

77. For a later discussion of *Camera Lucida* by Gallop, see Jane Gallop and Dick Blau, *Living with His Camera* (Durham: Duke University Press, 2003).

78. See Michael Fried, *Why Photography Matters as Art as Never Before* (New Haven: Yale University Press, 2009).

79. Michael Fried, "Art and Objecthood," *Artforum* 5 (June 1967): 12–23.

80. See also James Elkins, "Camera Dolorosa," *History of Photography* 31, no. 1 (Spring 2007): 22–30. Elkins introduces this essay as follows: "This is a fragment of a book I am working on, written in the first instance against Roland Barthes's *Camera Lucida.*"

81. Rosalind Krauss has proposed that photography's various successes heralded what she calls a "postmedium condition": "Photography's apotheosis as a medium—which is to say its commercial, academic, and museological success—comes just at the moment of its capacity to eclipse the very notion of a medium and to emerge as a theoretical because heterogeneous object. But in a second moment, not too historically distant from the first, this object will lose its deconstructive force by passing out of the field of social use and into the twilight zone of obsolescence." Rosalind Krauss, "Reinventing the Medium," *Critical Inquiry* 25, no. 2 (Winter 1999): 295. The "postmedium condition" that she describes joins "the death of photography," "postphotography," and "photography after photography" as phrases coined by scholars to describe an identity crisis for photography that is said to have emerged in the 1960s but became fully apparent only with the introduction of digital technology in the 1980s. See, for example, Anne-Marie Willis, "Digitisation and the Living Death of Photography," in Philip Howard, ed., *Culture, Technology and Creativity in the Late Twentieth Century* (London: John Libbey, 1990), 197–208; Geoffrey Batchen, "Burning with Desire: The Birth and Death of Photography," *Afterimage* 17, no. 6 (January 1990): 8–11; William J. Mitchell, *The Reconfigured Eye: Visual Truth in the Post-Photographic Era* (Cambridge, MA: MIT Press, 1992); Geoffrey Batchen, "On Post-Photography," *Afterimage* 20, no. 3 (October 1992): 17; and the various essays in Hubertus V. Amelunxen et al., eds., *Photography after Photography: Memory and Representation in the Digital Age* (Munich: Siemens Kulturprogramm & G+B Arts, 1996). Juan Fontcuberta has argued that technological changes were but one aspect of a larger process of epistemological and social change that has meant photography can no longer simply be itself. See Joan Fontcuberta, "Revisiting the Histories of Photography," in Joan Fontcuberta, ed., *Photography: Crisis of History* (Barcelona: Actar, 2003), 10–11.

VICTOR BURGIN

(those who fail to re-read are obliged to read the same story everywhere)
—(*S/Z* 15–16)

La Chambre Claire—Note sur la photographie was the last book by Roland Barthes to be published during his lifetime; the translation, *Camera Lucida—Reflections on Photography,* is the latest of about a dozen works by Barthes to become available in English. There has been a tendency amongst those who have so far written about *Camera Lucida* to regard it as Barthes's last word on photography. In the strictly literal sense this is of course true; in any other sense it makes a nonsense of what Barthes stood for. In a preface of 1963 he characteristically remarks that to write is, "to become someone to whom *the last word* is denied; to write is to offer others, from the start, the last word" (*CE* xi). Of course that "last word" offered to his commentator is itself no more than a thread in a web of texts which will grow for as long as Barthes's work is discussed—as long as the *written* Barthes survives.

Barthes was first of all a literary theorist; one of the many aspects of literature he wrote about was the way in which a reader constructs the image of a whole character from the fragmentary indications offered by the text. Barthes reminded us of such truths, contrary to common intuition, as that the narrator of a story is a character amongst the others: "the *I* which writes the text, it too, is never more than a paper-*I*" (*IMT* 161). Thus, on the otherwise blank page which opens his "autobiography," *Roland Barthes by Roland Barthes,* he inscribes (in his own handwriting, to get the most out of the paradox): "All this must be considered as if spoken by a character in a novel." I never knew Barthes in person, "in the flesh"; the Barthes I know is a person "in the text"—as contradictory, and otherwise complicated, as any corporeal being; in the brief space available to me here I want to follow some of the traces of Barthes's written-*I/eye* as they emerge within a discourse on photography.

If Barthes had never written specifically about photography he would still be a figure of primary importance for the theory of photography because of his pioneering work in "semiology." Although it had long been common for people to speak loosely of "the language of" this or that activity—including, of course, "the language of photography"—it was only in the late-1950s to mid-1960s that Barthes, and others, undertook to interrogate the supposed analogy between "natural language" (speech and writing) and signifying systems other than language *from the standpoint of linguistic science.* These early investigations demonstrated that there is no single signifying system upon which all photographs depend (in the sense in which all texts in English ultimately depend upon the English language); there is, rather, a heterogeneous complex of codes upon which photography may draw. Each photograph signifies on the basis of a plurality of these codes (for example: codes of gesture, of lighting, and so on), the number and type of which varies from one image to another, and very few of which are unique to photography. (I would emphasise, "signifies *on the basis of,*" as it was never claimed that the consideration of such codes would *exhaust* the signification.)

By the early-1970s semiology had undergone a radical transformation from within, in the course of which the linguistic model became displaced within a broader complex of methodologies—most notably those of Freudian and Lacanian psychoanalysis. Within the area of theory today the term "semiology" is most commonly used to refer to the early approach, with its almost exclusive emphasis on (Saussurian) linguistics; the word "semiotics" is now most usual to designate the ever-changing field of cross-disciplinary studies whose common focus is on the general phenomenon of *meaning* in society. (Other, more or less equivalent, expressions for its current forms include: "textual semiotics," "deconstructive analysis," and "post-structuralist criticism.") In this second revolution in theory, all the more surprising in that it followed so closely on the massive upheaval of structuralism itself, emphasis was shifted, as the title of one of Barthes's essays from this period puts it, "From Work to Text" (*IMT* 155). In structuralist semiology the particular object of analysis (novel, photograph, or whatever) was conceived of as a self-contained entity, a "work," whose capacity to *mean* was nevertheless dependent upon underlying formal "structures" common to all such works—the task of theory was to uncover and describe these structures. This approach provided what we might call an "anatomy" of meaning production; however, as an "anatomical" science, it was unable to say anything about the constantly changing "flesh" of meaning. *Text,* as conceived of by Barthes (with the prompting of, mostly notably, Jacques Derrida and Julia Kristeva), is seen not as an "object" but rather as a "space" between the object and the reader/viewer—a space made up of endlessly proliferating meanings which have no stable point of origin, nor of closure. In the concept of "text" the boundaries which enclosed the "work" are dissolved; the text opens continuously into other texts, the space of *intertextuality.* Perhaps the most simple example I can offer here, to give a rough idea of the notion of "intertextuality," is of the drink advertisement which shows a glass slipper containing ice-cubes and a measure of vermouth; consciously or not, I am referred instantaneously to: "Cinderella" (rags to riches; romantic love); "drinking from a slipper" (*fin-de-siècle* playboys and chorus-girls; physical sexuality); "American-ness" ("on the rocks"—for example, scenes in B-movies of drinking in piano-bars); "failure" (for example, an unsuccessful marriage is conventionally referred to as "on the rocks"); and so on. All of this, and more, belongs to the fields of what Barthes calls the "*déjà-lu*": the "already read," "already seen," everything we already know and which the text may therefore call upon, or "accidentally" evoke. These intertextual fields are themselves, of course, in constant process of change (another reason why there can be no final closure of meaning). This brief example is perhaps already enough to show the impossibility of assigning a "sum" of signification: the parts will not add up to a non-contradictory whole. I am of course aware that, in the case of advertising certainly, but also in most other cases of the use of photographs, the proliferation of connotations is "controlled" by means of an "anchoring" caption—if there were more space available to me I would argue that such apparent "closure" is ultimately spurious; even without the argument, however, it may be appreciated—from the work of graffiti artists, for example—that though the caption may come dressed as a policeman it may be made to play the clown. It might also be objected that my associations in respect of the advertisement cited take the trajectory of a phantasy— romantic attraction; sexual possession; post-coital disillusion—which is the pattern of a vast number of actual narratives (films, books, TV plays, and so on), and as such is itself subject to narrative *closure;* but it is not the *only* phantasy projection possible here, and if it were to be *told* then the telling would itself open out onto other, mutually contradictory, texts, which in turn, . . . and so on.

One of the most far-reaching consequences of textual analysis has been what Barthes called, in the title of another essay, "The Death of the Author." The Author, says Barthes, is a conception which:

suits criticisms very well, the latter then allotting itself the important task of discovering the Author (or its hypostases: society, history, psyche, liberty) beneath the work: when the Author has been found, the text is "explained"—victory to the critic. Hence there is no surprise in the fact that, historically, the reign of the Author has also been that of the Critic. (IMT *147*)

To Barthes's (infinitely extensible) list of "hypostases," the "ghosts" in the textual machinery, there can of course be added "structure"; the semiological writings which have survived (in the sense they are still used) are those in which "structure" functions in the analysis as a heuristic device rather than a real goal. It would be wrong however to view "post-structuralism" as the negation of "structuralism"; Barthes himself remarks:

the frayed nature of the codes does not contradict structure (as, it is thought, life, imagination, intuition, disorder, contradict system and rationality), but on the contrary (this is the fundamental affirmation of textual analysis) is an integral part of structuration. It is this "fraying" of the text which distinguishes structure—the object of structural analysis, strictly speaking—from structuration—the object of . . . textual analysis (V 157).

My task here is to provide a (re-)reading of Barthes's work on photography which pays attention both to the "fraying" of his texts (where "his" meanings "edge out" into the seas of intertextuality), and to their structure (consistency of analytic "motifs," and their patterning, repetitions, transformations, across the totality of his work). It should be clear that this is no hunt for that Chimera of dominant criticism, what Barthes "really said"; even less (even greater conceit), what Barthes "really meant." My purpose is simply to negotiate the shifting currents of his texts in the hope they will carry me in a direction in which I wish to go.

If, in the spirit of early structuralism, we were to reduce the corpus of Barthes's writings on photography to its "bare bones" we would find that his analysis is invariably *binary*, the nature of the opposition between the two terms being subject to some transformation. Proceeding less formally, but in accordance with this insight, the following chronology emerges:

Barthes's semiology begins with the final section of *Mythologies*, "Myth Today," written in 1956. In the course of this essay he discusses a photograph. On the cover of *Paris Match* he sees a picture of a black soldier giving the French salute: "a rich, fully experienced, spontaneous, innocent, *indisputable* image"; but Barthes discerns an additional message at work here, which is: "there is no better answer to the detractors of an alleged colonialism that the zeal shown by this Negro in serving his so-called oppressors" (*M* 116). Thus, the very "naturalness" of the photograph, Barthes observes, here lends the ideology ("myth") of imperialism the status of an indisputable truth. This distinction between the image and the concept which appropriates it is retained by Barthes in his 1961 essay "The Photographic Message," where he introduces linguistic concepts to refine the distinction and give it the status of a general law: the "brute fact" (for example, "there is a black soldier saluting") is the *denotation*, the parasitic message (for example, "the indigenous population is not exploited") is the *connotation*. In these terms he now identifies what he calls, "the photographic paradox": "the co-existence of two messages," where a, "connoted (or coded) message develops on the basis of a *message without a code*" (*IMT* 19); (the distinction is carried over, in virtually the same words, into his 1964 paper, "Rhetoric of the Image," *IMT* 32).

In a short preface to the 1970 edition of *Mythologies* Barthes repudiates the form of his project in that book (albeit not the project itself—the "capital enemy" remains "the bourgeois norm"). Semiological analysis, he remarks, "has become more developed, precise, complicated, differentiated; it has become the theoretical site where there can play . . . a certain liberation of the signifier." Precisely what this "play of the signifier" entails I have already tried to indicate—it can be seen most fully in his *S/Z* (1970) the classic demonstration of "textual analysis" (just as Barthes's *Système de la Mode,* soon to appear in translation, is the classic work of structuralist semiological method). In the opening pages of *S/Z,* a lengthy analysis of a short story by Balzac, Barthes remarks: "denotation is not the first meaning, . . . it is ultimately no more than the last of the connotations" (*S/Z* 9). Put more briefly: *all* meaning is *in* culture (to return to the man on the cover of *Paris Match*—what is there which is truly "innocent" in the attribution, "black," and, "soldier"?). The idea of the "pure" fact, literally *insignificant,* nevertheless persists. Barthes's other book published in 1970 is *L'Empire des Signes,* his book about Japan (or, more strictly, as he himself remarks, about his *fantasy* of Japan), and his own favourite amongst his works (because, he once said, of its associations with a happy period in his love-life). *L'Empire des Signes* is, in effect, a book of sustained praise of the attitude of the *haiku.* Amongst the *haiku* he quotes is one by Bashô, which is itself, contradictorily (a 'meta-*haiku*'?), about the attitude of the *haiku:*

How admirable
He who does not think: 'Life is ephemeral'
On seeing a flash of lightning.   (*E* 96)

The *haiku,* Barthes says (in a passage he will repeat almost word for word ten years later), "does not make meaning of the subject," it merely, "reproduces the designating gesture of a small child who points a finger . . . while saying only: that!" The *haiku* may instruct us in that mental discipline which can appear to silence meaning, but the appearance is illusory—to be outside of language, in real terms, means infancy; to be outside of all meaning whatsoever means death. Psychoanalysis has shown us that the mental processes of which we are conscious are not the only meaning-producing processes which are taking place: the coveted "absence" of meaning may mean merely that meaning has left the room, and is holding a party in the basement. I shall return to this point. For the moment, in respect of Barthes's "photographic paradox" of the "message without a code," we should remember that there is no paradox in the real, only in the way the real is *described;* the paradox is a purely linguistic (more specifically, *logical*) entity. Barthes's particular paradox is born of the uneasy union of two inherently contradictory discourses: semiotics and phenomenology.

The terms "denotation"/"connotation" do not appear in Barthes's 1970 essay on photography, "The Third Meaning," but the trace of the opposition so important to classic semiology may nevertheless be discerned, in this essay, in the distinction between "informational" and "symbolic" levels of meaning. Far from being seen as radically distinct, however, these two are now classed together as that which, "presents itself quite naturally to the mind"—which Barthes now calls the *obvious* meaning. The "obvious" meaning covers all of the semantic area which was previously divided between denotation and connotation, but a small portion of territory has now been ceded to support a "third meaning": "the supplement that my intellection cannot succeed in absorbing," which Barthes terms the *obtuse* meaning. This meaning is supported by, "what, in the image, is purely image (which is in fact very little)" (*IMT* 61). It is this "very little" which Barthes is now concerned to isolate. Semiotics had already accounted in some detail for the manner of production and circulation of those meanings which are fully in the *public* domain. Barthes now turned his attention to that *slight,* but nevertheless important, meaning-effect/affect of photographs which had previously slipped into the interstices of an analysis which had privileged social meaning at the expense of the private. This level of meaning, says Barthes: "is that of *signifiance,* a word which has the advantage of referring to the field of the signifier . . . and of linking up, via the path opened up by Julia Kristeva who proposed the term, a semiotics of the text" (*IMT* 54). Barthes opens up several paths in "The Third Meaning" without travelling very far down any of them. I shall return to the directions in which these paths lead, for the moment I must observe only that Barthes's final essay on photography—a decade later—will only assert the futility of such journeys.

Barthes has been quoted as saying: "it is necessary to choose between being a terrorist and being an egoist"; it is the exercise of this choice which distinguishes Barthes's work from 1975 onwards from all his work before that year. *Roland Barthes by Roland Barthes* institutes the "privatisation" of Barthes's discourse, his abandoning of the voice of the *tutor,* which continues with *A Lover's Discourse* and *Camera Lucida.* In *Camera Lucida* Barthes is concerned with photographs only in so far as they contribute to "those little touches of solitude" of which, he says, life consists. Contemplating a photograph of his recently deceased mother he has, "no other resource than this *irony:* to speak of the 'nothing to say.'" This photograph, and others, "touch" him in a certain way. That aspect of a photograph which may *move* an individual, in a way which is strictly incommunicable, Barthes calls the *punctum.* It is the *private* nature of the experience which defines the *punctum.* Certainly there are photographs which many people, in common, will find moving, but here, "emotion requires the rational intermediary of an ethical and political culture"; it, "derives from an *average* effect, almost from a certain training"; it is a matter of general "human interest." This *common ground* of

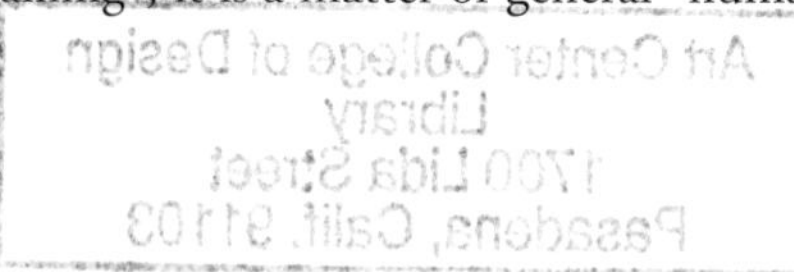

meaning—whether it concerns the emotional, the practical, the historical, or whatever other aspect of shared experience—Barthes terms the *studium.* Clearly, we are here back to the "two levels of meaning," which is the basis of all Barthes's writing on photography; specifically, we are returned to the distinction in "The Third Meaning," between the "obvious" and "obtuse" meanings of a photograph. Now, however, the tentativeness of the earlier essays is absent, the boundaries are now fixed, the paths are closed. The "obvious meaning" becomes the *studium,* the "obtuse meaning" becomes the *punctum*—the translation into an inert language, a *dead* language, signals that we have arrived at a terminus. The process of change is now *arrested* (Latin is also a juridical language) in the name of an experienced certitude. It is to the nature, and status, of this certitude that I now wish to turn.

Barthes describes his project in *Camera Lucida* as a search for the "essence" of photography. In terms of everyday language, to speak of a "search for essence," sounds rather mystical, ineffable. To people who have been raised in the English-speaking world it can conjure up those images of consumptive and spiritually anguished poets which are the bequest of our domestic Romantic tradition. We would be wrong however to situate Barthes's use of the term within such a context. Barthes quite explicitly relates his project to that of *phenomenology.* Barthes dedicates *Camera Lucida* to Sartre's book *L'Imaginaire,* which is an extended discussion of mental imagery from the point of view of phenomenology. In the technical language of phenomenology, "essence" (*eidos*), is simply the common factor, or factors, which unites all of our otherwise very different encounters with, in this case, photographs. I say "unites our encounters," rather than "unites photographs," because phenomenology sets out to describe subjective experiences rather than material objects. The reason for this is that the phenomenologist would say that the only thing I can be *certain* of about the material world is that I have mental representations of (it). I place "it" (the world) in brackets here because that is what the phenomenologist would have me do: my consciousness is too laden with the baggage of everyday commonsense assumptions that I see only what I *know,* I must therefore store this baggage out of the way, put my knowledge "on the shelf" (even if it is "scientific" knowledge) in order to "reduce" my experience of the world to the terms of "raw" apprehension. It is in this sense that we should take Barthes's assertion in *Camera Lucida* that, looking at certain photographs, he, "wanted to be a primitive" (*CL* 7).

A further concept crucial to phenomenology, is that of "intention": things exist for me only in that I *actively* "intend" them in consciousness (I do not simply, *passively,* "perceive" things). The mind is not simply a *screen* upon which the world projects its appearances; in "making something" of appearances the mind, in a sense, is also a *projector,* projecting a world of things *onto* those appearances. To give only a most basic and familiar example,

I never see a "cube" *as such*, I can see no more than three sides at any one time; or again, I "intend" circular coins where I almost invariably *see* only a variety of ellipses. The notion of "intentionality" is crucial to a reading of the account of photography in *Camera Lucida*, which is in fact practically identical to Sartre's descriptions in *L'Imaginaire*. Here is Sartre, early in the book, talking about a photograph:

My intention is here now; I say: "This is a portrait of Peter," or, more briefly: "This is Peter." Then the picture is no longer an object but operates as material for an image . . . Everything I perceive enters into a projective synthesis which aims at the true Peter, a living being who is not present.

The real object therefore, present to perception (here, the photograph) is, "an 'analogue' of another object," and no more or less an analogue than is a purely *mental* "representative" of the absent object of "intention." An immediate problem, therefore, for a theory of photography based exclusively on phenomenology would be that it would not distinguish between a photograph and, for instance, an image "seen" in a crystal ball (another of Sartre's examples). In fact Barthes in *Camera Lucida* is, like Sartre, concerned not so much with the general phenomenon of the photograph as such, but rather with the yearning "intentionality" of the imagination. At the beginning of the final section of *The Psychology of the Imagination* (the English translation of *L'Imaginaire*), Sartre writes: "the act of the imagination is a magical one. It is an incantation destined to produce the object of one's thought, the thing one desires, in such a way that one can take possession of it. In that act there is always something of the imperious and the infantile." These words might have come straight out of *Camera Lucida* (where Barthes does in fact speak of photography as "a magic"). Of course, to become *infantile* is another way in which we may understand the phrase "be a primitive." I shall come back to this point by way of a comment on the translation of Barthes's book.

On the very first turn of the page of Barthes's text in *Camera Lucida* I read, "what Lacan calls the *Tuché*," whereas the French gives me simply, "the *Tuché*," together with a margin note referring me to pages 53–66 of Lacan's *Le Séminaire, Livre XI*. Only four lines later I read, "*tathata*, as Alan Watts has it, the fact of being this"; again, the French has it, "*tathata*, the fact of being this," together with a reference to page 85 of Watts's *Le Bouddhisme Zen*. It cannot be objected that there would be little point in referring English readers to French publications, the Lacan text cited here has been translated (as, *The Four Fundamental Concepts of Psychoanalysis*, Hogarth, 1973—the relevant pages are 53–69), and Alan Watts's writings are originally in English. Just as the translation is, in the matter of margin notes, under-researched, so there are points at which the sense of it seems to me to be inadequate. Immediately after the mention of Watts, the translation reads, "*tat* means *that* in Sanskrit and suggests the gesture of the child pointing his finger at something and saying: *that, there it is, lo!*" Other readers may have shared my own incredulity at this child who speaks like a character in a Hollywood Biblical epic. In fact Barthes's child says not, "*that, there it is, lo!*," but, "*Ta, Da, Ca!*." The original, "*Ta, Da, Ca!*," is first of all a subversive joke, a mimicry of *Tathata* which reduces a dramatic and mysterious incantation to childish prattle; but it is *doubly* subversive in that, in the same movement, it points to what is *serious* in the prattle. What is "overheard" here is an utterance produced during the child's transition from the infantile world of brute experience "without mediation, satiety, or void" ("infant" is from *infans*—"without speech"), to a world of *things* ordered by words. The child here *plays* with "its" language (as it might play with its food), jubilating in the demonstration of its grasp of the representative function of the sounds, yet no less aware of their material substance and its structuring (an awareness it will later lose, language coming to appear increasingly "transparent"). There is an instance of such play which is famous in the literature of psychoanalysis: in *Beyond the Pleasure Principle,* Freud describes watching a child alternately expel from its cot, and then recover, a cotton reel on a string, to the accompaniment of its utterance of "ooh!" and "da," which Freud interprets as approximations of the German words *fort* and *da*—"gone" and "there." Freud interprets the child's "game" as its attempt to master the painful experiences of its mother's absences: the disappearance and reappearance of the mother being symbolised by the absence and presence of the reel. Lacan's own discussion of Freud's interpretation focuses on the fact that the opposition "absence/presence" is in turn symbolised by a phonemic opposition: O/A (*ooh/da*). Lacan argues that what Freud allows us to observe here is a moment in the infant's entry into language, the language that will later permit it to *communicate* its experience to others, but only at the cost of stripping the experience of its irreducible and unrepeatable *particularity.* No verbal statement will ever succeed in expressing *that* child's experience of the absence of *this* mother under *those* circumstances (nor, ideologies of the "purely visual" notwithstanding, will any other form of representation). According to Lacan it is in such gaps between the plenitude of experience and the paucity of symbolism that *desire* is born. The "fort/da" game is invoked by Lacan in the specific passage cited by Barthes: the *Tuché* is the specific "encounter with the real" which nevertheless will always elude the subject's grasp: in trying to signify it, we lose it. In a Lacanian terminology I can say that what we encounter in the *Real* (as a plenitude which is effaced in the very moment it is experienced), which slips our grasp in the *Symbolic* (language, and all other socially conventional forms of signification), we will strive to "conjure up" in the *Imaginary* (for my purposes here, the realm of imagination and *phantasy*).

It is a commonplace to observe that desire and phantasy are closely connected (together, they result in the "day-dream"), and that photographs are commonly involved in our "phantasising." In adopting the spelling "*ph*antasy" I locate the term within the context of psychoanalysis, (which we might call the *science* of phantasy). In a classic, Freudian, setting the word "phantasy" refers to imaginary scenarios which can be *conscious* (as in the day-dream), *preconscious* (not conscious, but which may emerge into consciousness under favourable conditions), and *unconscious* (radically inaccessible to consciousness, except in the disguised form of dreams, slips of the tongue and other lapses—and, of course, *conscious* phantasies). I have written elsewhere on the topic of photographic imagery as a vehicle of phantasy investments, and I shall not try to summarise what I have already said, as the account is already condensed. Without going into detail, I wish simply to note that, *in its point of departure,* Barthes's approach to the photograph in *Camera Lucida* is compatible with the sort of psychoanalytic/intertextual approach I have suggested. I say "in its point of departure" as Barthes's method in *Camera Lucida,* although it is founded on the idea of subjective *investment* (here, "intention") in the photograph, may not draw upon psychoanalytic concepts for the simple reason that phenomenology does not recognise the *unconscious.* (Although Barthes uses Freudian and Lacanian psychoanalytic theory very extensively throughout his work, he nevertheless writes of himself: "His relation to psychoanalysis is not scrupulous (though without his being able to pride himself on any contestation, any rejection). It is an *undecided* relation" (*RB* 150).)

Camera Lucida, then, for all its reference to Lacan, is based on a method of analysis— phenomenology—which rejects the concept of the unconscious. Such a rejection has severe consequences in that it denies photography theory a body of research which, I believe, is crucial to its development. Freud made it clear enough, in various parts of his work (see his discussions of voyeurism, fetishism, and psychogenic disturbances of vision), and Lacan has since made it perfectly explicit in his introduction of the notion of the *scopic drive,* that unconscious desire operates in our looking and being looked at. (We are all, of course, well aware of the occasions when the link between desire and looking is apparent to consciousness. I would stress that it is not the character of our *experience,* as such, which is in dispute—Lacan's discussions of looking owe much to Sartre's own in chapter 4 of *Being and Nothingness*—it is the operation of *unconscious* processes within the experience which is at issue.) Although *Camera Lucida,* we might say, represses the notion of the unconscious, Barthes's paper, "The Third Meaning" invokes the concept of the unconscious through its reference to *signifiance.*

Julia Kristeva distinguishes between *signification* and *signifiance* (a term she adopts from Benveniste): *signification* is meaning which is produced on the side of what she calls (after Lacan) the *symbolic*—that is the area within which the Barthes of *Camera Lucida* would locate the *studium,* the public arena of socially determined meaning production; *signifiance,* on the other hand, is radically distinct in that it belongs to what Kristeva calls the *semiotic.* Kristeva's use of this word is very particular and should not be confused with the more general use of the term: The *semiotic* is that area of meaning which must be repressed in the process of socialisation of the "speaking subject"; it is anterior to language and intimately linked to rhythms and pulsions of the *body;* it is (dis)covered in terms of the "primary processes" of the unconscious (metaphor and metonymy) which are in turn known only through the disturbances they create in the orders of rational discourse. Kristeva's work is situated within a Lacanian problematic, even while critical of it, and is not to be assimilated to the biologistic reductionism which has tended to be the fate of psychoanalytic theory in the English-speaking world. Freud himself was quite explicit in situating the "drives" "at the boundary of the somatic and the psychic." Anglo-Saxon empiricism would turn a blind eye to the "boundary area" and shift the entire question of the origins of subjectivity onto the body alone—thus supporting the conservative myth of the "timelessness" of "human nature," supposedly determined by the (undoubtedly) perpetual facts of birth, ageing, death, and so on. (To appreciate that this is a conservative position we need only consider its consequences for feminism.) Barthes himself succinctly replied to this ubiquitous mythologising of "the human condition" (central to all liberal-humanist ideology—in the area of art/photography criticism see, for example, the writings of John Berger and Peter Fuller) in his short essay on Steichen's "Family of Man" exhibition (*M* 100–102).

The concept of *signifiance* in the work of Kristeva is bound up with considerations of the infantile period of life, that period before speech when the nurseling is most intimately identified with the body of the *mother.* Psychoanalytic theory has described how, in the primitive stages of emergence of language, sound imagery joins with other forms of imagery (visual, tactile, and so on) around certain early encounters with the real to establish "elementary signifiers" of the unconscious: certain "image fragments" become associated with certain early experiences which thereby make a "lasting impression" on the infant/child; these images, and the emotional charge they carry, remain in the unconscious mind of the adult; from time to time, some conscious event (for example, looking at a photograph) will have some aspect to it which will "allow" an associative connection with the unconscious fragment; the emotional charge carried by the unconscious fragment will then "spark" across the gap to the configuration in conscious perception, investing it with a "feeling" for which there is no rational explanation. It is in this way (albeit the account I have given is highly simplified) that I would account for Barthes's "*punctum.*" Barthes himself provides support for this account. In *Camera Lucida* he writes about a photograph of an American family by James Van der Zee; the detail which "touches" him in this image, he says, is the strapped shoes of one of the women: "This particular *punctum* arouses great sympathy in me, almost a kind of tenderness" (*CL* 43). Barthes makes no further comment until, some ten pages later, he "remembers" the photograph ("I may know better a photograph I remember than a photograph I am looking at," p. 53); he now realises that it was not the shoes which moved him, it was the *necklace* the woman wore: "for (no doubt) it was this same necklace (a slender ribbon of braided gold) which I had seen worn by someone in my own family." The relative he has now been reminded of is a deceased maiden aunt: "I had always been saddened when I thought of her dreary life"; after the aunt died her necklace remained, "shut up in a family box of old jewelry." We can here see the process of *signifiance* at work: the investment of emotional "affect" (*cathexis*) in the ankle-strap; the metaphorical displacement from the circle round the ankle to the circle round the throat; the metonymical displacement from the woman in the photograph to the maiden aunt, "whose necklace was shut up in a box"; we quickly arrive at the sources of the emotion in the themes of death and sexuality, played out within a family scenario, which are the very substance of psychoanalysis. (The identification of such "sources" is *not* however, the aim of textual semiotics—this, strictly, here, would be a matter between Barthes and his analyst. Semiotics is interested in the potential field of such displacements and their "mechanisms," in so far as this bears on the general phenomenon of the production of meaning).

Barthes is well aware of all this. In introducing the Van der Zee picture he remarks: "Very often the *punctum* is a 'detail,' that is, a partial object. Hence, to give examples of *punctum* is, in a certain fashion, to *give myself up.*" The French at the end of this last sentence reads, "*me livrer,*" which certainly means, "give myself up" (in the sense of a surrender to justice), but the verb *livrer* also carries the meaning, "to betray a secret." Further, "partial object" certainly translates the original "*objet partiel,*" and communicates the idea of *bias,* but *objet partiel* is also the standard translation of the English psychoanalytic term *part-object,* introduced by Melanie Klein in her account of the phantasy world of the child to designate a real or phantasied part of the body (for example, the breast), and its symbolic substitutes, towards which a "component instinct" is directed.

The "encounter with the real" which we may expect to be represented most strongly in the unconscious is the *trauma* (for example, in the "fort/da" case, the mother's absence). "Trauma" is from the Greek word for "wound," its Latin equivalent is *punctum.* In 1963 Barthes spoke of the difficulties of writing a letter of sympathy to a friend who has just lost someone he loves; the "phrases" he invents do not satisfy him; he realises that the message he wishes to communicate, "could after all be reduced to a simple word: *condolences*"; but this, the most "sincere" message, is the least possible, it would appear cold. Barthes observes that the warmth and sincerity of his sympathy can only be communicated by *artifice,* by invention. He recognises in this the very condition of literature itself: "Like my condolence note, everything written becomes a work only when it can vary, under certain conditions, an initial message (I love, I suffer, I sympathise)." *Camera Lucida,* written in the brief interim between the death of Barthes's mother and Barthes's own death, says, "I suffer," and says it with surpassing artifice. Its originality is in its deployment of a number of radically heterogeneous discourses (for example, psychoanalysis and phenomenology), whose synthesis is achieved not at the level of theory (which would be impossible), but at the level of *literature. Camera Lucida,* as a totality, may be read as the autobiographical novel that Barthes often said he wished to write. A novel which in its originality does not announce itself *as* a novel (such "obvious" novels Barthes despised as complicit with an exhausted "sociolect"; as belonging to the "readerly" (*lisible*), rather than the "writerly" (*scriptible*).

The review of *Camera Lucida* as a work of fiction is yet to be written. My task here has been to take the book at face value (so often a mistake with Barthes) as a contribution to photography theory. *Camera Lucida,* in this perspective, is primarily an evocation of *intentionality* as it strives to conjure the image of a loved person through the intermediary ("*medium*") of a snapshot. Its significance for theory is the emphasis thus placed on the *active* participation of the viewer in producing the meaning/affect of the photograph. The theoretical perspectives this entails, in terms of Barthes's own work as a whole, are those centred on the notions of intertextuality and *signifiance.* These perspectives are alluded to, in respect of photography, in "The Third Meaning"—they are only "spelled out" in detail in connection with Barthes's first love, literature; however, he observes:

Our aim is to manage to conceive . . . the plurality of the text, the opening of its "signifiance." It is clear then that what is at stake in our work is not limited to the university treatment of the text . . . nor even to literature in general; rather it touches on a theory, a practice, a choice, which are caught up in the struggle of men [sic] and signs.

An indication of what a consideration of "the plurality of the text" might mean in terms of a photographic *practice* is to be found in a lengthy footnote to "The Third Meaning." Barthes has posited a hypothetical "filmic of the future" which will lie not in movement, "but in an inarticulable third meaning that neither the simple photograph nor figurative painting can assume since they lack the diagetic horizon, the possibility of configuration" (*IMT* 66). In the footnote with which he interrupts himself at this point, he cites those existing practices which *do* combine still and story—the photo-novel and the comic strip—and he remarks:

I am convinced that these "arts," born in the lower depths of high culture, possess theoretical qualifications and present a new signifier (related to the obtuse meaning) . . . There may thus be a future—or a very ancient past—truth in these derisory, vulgar, foolish, dialogical forms of consumer subculture.

Roland Barthes was a teacher, several of his books are the products of seminars conducted with his students. He complained of a particular difficulty of teaching—to be required to impose a generally applicable body of knowledge and techniques (to be systematic, scientific), while yet wishing to relate to one's audience at an individual level (to be spontaneous, "natural"): "The choice is gloomy: conscientious functionary or free artist, the teacher escapes neither the theatre of speech nor the Law played out on its stage" (*IMT* 192). Given the situation, neither attitude of the teacher can ever appear to be entirely convincing. The problem is not confined to teaching: *all* discourse issues not only from some *position* (no possibility of "neutrality"—moral, political, economic, aesthetic, or whatever), but also from some *one*. It would be "bad faith" for me to pretend I have no *stake* in what I am saying; but equally, I am not doing my job as a *critic* if I simply assert my views without explaining how and why I think they have a general validity, a validity which is independent of the personal history of he or she who utters them. It is partly because this existential situation of the critic has led to two quite different types of project that it has become necessary today to distinguish between "criticism" and "theory"—the former being the most widely encountered; the latter, culturally marginalised, encountered mainly in specialist journals and seminar rooms.

"Theory" is generally indicted by criticism as *obscure,* and no one was put in the dock more often on this charge than Barthes himself. In *Mythologies* he asks:

Why do critics thus periodically proclaim their helplessness or their lack of understanding? It is certainly not out of modesty: no-one is more at ease than one critic confessing that he understands nothing about existentialism; . . . and no-one more soldier-like than (another) pleading for poetic ineffability.

Barthes concludes: "All this means in fact that one believes oneself to have such sureness of intelligence that acknowledging an inability to understand calls in question the clarity of the author and not that of one's own mind." It is, finally, a way of soliciting the complicity of the public by saying, in effect: "I whose profession it is to be intelligent, understand nothing about it; now you wouldn't understand anything about it either; therefore, it can only be that you are as intelligent as I am" (*M* 34).

Such conflicts aside (it has always been the fate of theory which announces itself as such to be called before the bar of conservatism), the existential dilemma remains—*Camera*

Lucida is one response to it. Early in the book, Barthes speaks (again) of a "discomfort" he had "always suffered from": "the uneasiness of being a subject torn between two languages, one expressive, the other critical." The critical language (theory), moreover, divides him, "between several discourses, those of sociology, of semiology, and of psychoanalysis." Dissatisfied with any one discourse, alert always to its reductive capacity, he would, "gently leave it and seek elsewhere." In *Camera Lucida* (appearances notwithstanding) he abandons the discourse of theory (abstract, general) as inappropriate to the object of his text—which is his *mother* (all the photographs illustrated in the book are substitutes for the one he does not show—the "Winter Garden" picture of his mother—which is in turn nothing but a means of access to his mother). The "leave-taking" in *Camera Lucida* is not all gentle; Barthes expresses impatience with those of, "Photography's commentators (sociologists and semiologists)," who turn a theoretically blind eye to the (phenomenological) *experience* of the photograph, its "magic." Barthes here attacks what the methodologies he himself did so much to advance have become in the hands of certain practitioners. In his essay on teaching he remarks that he has no desire to see the "notes" taken during his courses—partly out of discretion (such notes are very personal things), but, more likely, from fear of contemplating himself in a reduced state, "like a Jivaro treated by his fellows." Where the "shrinking" of Barthes has taken place, however, it has more often been the work of the critics than of his students: there is another side to the critical coinage which announces its lack of understanding—it is the side which claims to understand very well the "Jivaro head" it substitutes for the original, and which can then serve it as an Aunt Sally, or a talisman, as the need arises.

Although Barthes was for most of his career reviled by "popular opinion" (which is to say, by those critics who pretend to speak on behalf of it), the situation changed when in the last few years of his life he began to speak "not as a terrorist but as an egoist"—here at last was a Barthes with whom the critics could identify. The passage in *Camera Lucida* where Barthes lambasts the scientist of the sign (his own other self) has become widely quoted amongst precisely the sorts of critics Barthes opposed. Barthes was once asked at the end of a lecture, by someone obviously irritated by what they took to be Barthes's wilful "difficulty," if the Freudian "super-ego" wasn't *really* just what we all know as "conscience." Barthes replied: "Yes, if you leave out all the rest." It was rather like being asked if "lightning" isn't the same thing as "Zeus's thunderbolt"—yes it is, if you're happy to ignore the difference between the "world-view" of modern meteorology and that of classical mythology. On page 88 of *Camera Lucida* does Barthes reject systematic approaches to photography, or does he not? Yes, he does, if you leave out all the rest. *Camera Lucida* itself leaves something out; in a strictly literal sense, in respect of *this* book at least, it is Barthes's last word: I close my copy of *Camera Lucida*. The back cover is, entirely, a photograph of Barthes. I close my copy of *La*

Chambre Claire. There is no photograph. The back cover carries an emblematically enlarged quotation from a work called, *Practice of the Tibetan Way.* It seems peculiarly apt to me that the English-language version of this work should conclude with a portrait of the author; whereas the author chose to end it all with a paradoxical text which again sets in play that hopelessly irresolvable choice he faced as writer and teacher: the oscillation between the "two languages," between egoism and terrorism, actor and policeman—now set in the testing context of personal grief. The quotation reads:

Marpa was very moved when his son was killed, and one of his disciples said: "You have always told us that all is illusion. Is it not so with the death of your son, is not that an illusion?" And Marpa replied: "Indeed, but the death of my son is a super-illusion."

Abbreviations

CC	*La Chambre Claire,* Editions du Seuil, 1980
CE	*Critical Essays,* Northwestern, 1972
CL	*Camera Lucida,* Jonathan Cape, 1982
E	*L'Empire des Signes,* Skira, 1970
IMT	*Image-Music-Text,* Fontana, 1977
M	*Mythologies,* Paladin, 1973
RB	*Roland Barthes by Roland Barthes,* Hill & Wang, 1977
S/Z	*S/Z,* Jonathan Cape, 1975
V	Textual Analysis of Poe's 'Valdemar,' in R. Young (ed.), *Untying the Text,* Routledge & Kegan Paul, 1981

The Pleasure of the Phototext

Jane Gallop

I'd like to talk about the word "in" in the phrase "sexuality in art and the media." That word "in" implies a relationship of container and contained, a relationship in which sexuality is something interior to—contained within—art or the media, something that is represented. It implies that sexuality is something that is within the work of art rather than in some relation the viewer or the artist has to the work of art. Is that how we want to think about the relation between sexuality and art? Do we want to think about it as something that is represented in art, as something whose image we see in a work of art, or do we want to think about it as somewhere else?

I entitled my talk "The Pleasure of the Phototext," which is close to the title of a book by Roland Barthes, *The Pleasure of the Text.*[1] I inserted the *photo* because I am not going to talk too much about the literary text, the text as a piece of writing, but I am going to make reference to some of Barthes's ideas about the sexuality of reading, about the eroticism of a certain relation with the text, as those ideas show up in his book on photography, *Camera Lucida: Reflections on Photography,*[2] written seven years after *The Pleasure of the Text.* That word "of" in Barthes's title is actually ambiguous: it can refer to the pleasure in the text, which the text contains, but it can also refer to the pleasure the text affords us, the pleasure the text offers. The play of that which is within and yet offered is what I would like to propose as an alternate preposition, an alternate spatial model, to the "in." So, rather than sexuality *in* art, the pleasure *of* the phototext.

In order to think about the relation between inside and outside, I want to quote a passage from *The Pleasure of the Text,* from a chapter entitled "Representation." "Certainly, it happens very often that representation takes as its object of imitation desire itself." Barthes has just asserted that the erotic relation to the text, the pleasure of the text, is different from representation, but he, of course, recognizes that one of the things that often gets represented is pleasure—erotics, sexuality, desire. He is not trying to deny that the whole history of representative art, of representative literature, is a history whose themes have often been those of desire and sexuality.

Certainly, it happens very often that representation takes as its object of imitation desire itself; but then, this desire never leaves the frame, the picture [his word is tableau, *which could also mean* scene*]; it circulates among the characters; if there is an addressee, his addressee remains interior to the fiction. (. . . Representation is just that: when nothing comes out when nothing leaps out of the frame: of the picture [*tableau, scene*], the book, the screen.)*

It is noteworthy that this is also one of the few places in *The Pleasure of the Text* where Barthes mentions other media besides writing. His formulation implies that the relation of representation works the same for the book, the screen, and the picture. Barthes defines representation as a case in which something remains totally inside.

Barthes is writing *against* representation, which for him is a means of containing and co-opting desire, pleasure, sexuality. He defines it as a situation in which nothing comes out, where everything remains inside, where nothing leaps out of the frame. Of course there may be desire, there may be sex (sex is, after all, the commonest theme of art and literature), but it is all contained within. The desire circulates, but it circulates among the characters; it does not come out. It is addressed from one character to another; it is not some relation that might include the artist, that might include the viewer.

In *Camera Lucida,* Barthes is no longer specifically talking about pleasure, but he is specifically talking about photography, and in that book he defines two elements of the photograph. One is the *studium.* It is what we might call the theme or the subject of the picture, what the photographer is trying to say, but it also has to do with ideas and general culture. According to Barthes, the *studium* can be interesting, significant, and important, but a picture that has only a *studium* is like representation: everything is enclosed within the field of the picture, and nothing comes out. Then there is a "second element" that Barthes says, "comes and breaks up the *studium.*" If you think of the *studium* as a kind of enclosure, breaking it up suggests breaking something open, allowing seepage. "This time," he continues, "it's not me who goes after it (like I invest with my sovereign consciousness the field of the *studium*), it's it that goes off from the scene, like an arrow, and comes and pierces me." When Barthes tries to define the other element of the photograph, he refers to something that goes off from the scene, precisely something which is not within representation, not within the frame, within the scene. Barthes refers to this element in striking terms: "it goes off from the scene, like an arrow, and comes and *pierces me* (emphasis mine)."

There is a lot of work in film theory on voyeurism—numerous analyses that describe how the gaze is an aggression upon that which is seen. Barthes's consideration of photography does not concur with the notion that the photograph as object of the gaze is passive while the viewer is in an active, even aggressive, relationship to it. In this relationship there is a passive and an aggressive term which are often lined up as female and male, as so often we line up aggressive with male, passive with female. In Barthes something quite different *sometimes* happens, but not all the time. He says, in fact, that a picture which is all *studium* is just a passive object: inert, immobile, lying there. But when there is that second element, the element that breaks up the *studium,* something happens which is quite the opposite of the relationship which occasions complaints about the male gaze and the female object of the gaze. Something happens: the second element goes off from the scene like an arrow and comes and pierces the viewer. There is a reversal: something in the photograph is aggressive and penetrates the viewer.

Barthes has not yet named the second element. He continues: "A word exists in Latin to designate that wound, that prick, that mark made by a pointed instrument . . . I will thus call it *punctum* . . . The *punctum* of a photo, it's that accident which, in it, stings me." He is talking about something that hurts him: wounds, stings, pierces. He mostly uses the Latin word to name it, but when he wants to define the Latin word, the French equivalent he gives it is *piqûre,* which I am amused to find can be translated as "prick." Not, of course, our vulgar word for the male genital, but the word for something that pierces, something that wounds.

My point is not that it is original to see the viewer as passive. Susan Sontag in her book *On Photography* writes: "One is vulnerable to disturbing events in the form of photographic images in a way that one is not to the real thing. That vulnerability is part of the distinctive passivity of someone who is a spectator twice over, a spectator of events already shaped, first by the participants and second by the image maker."[3] What interests me is the particular kind of passivity that Barthes is talking about. The piercing arrow brings us close to a tradition of a certain mystic discourse in which otherness enters you in some way that is ecstatic. Ecstasy etymologically derives from the Greek *ekstasis,* from *ex-,* "out" + *histanai,* "to place." Thus, it means something like "placed out." Ecstasy is when you are no longer within your own frame: some sort of going outside takes place. In Barthes's *The Pleasure of the Text,* he talks about the most intense form of pleasure, which he calls *jouissance,* which can be translated as "ecstasy." (Richard Miller translates it as "bliss.") The *punctum* which is not in all photography but is in his favorite photographs, the ones that move him, produces something like a *jouissance,* an ecstasy.

In *Camera Lucida,* the imagery used to describe this ecstasy carries connotations of pain. The arrow reminds us of Cupid's arrow, of a tradition in which love comes from the outside and not according to your intention, attacks you, pierces you, changes you, takes you outside yourself, puts you in a state of passivity that (at least in the Western tradition) is seen as a violation of the body, a penetration of the self, something dangerous and threatening and yet at the same time terribly pleasurable, something wonderful.

Later in the book, Barthes once again explains how the *punctum* works, this time by means of a contrast between cinema and photography: "The cinema has a power which at first glance photography has not: the screen (Bazin noted) is not a frame, but a mask; the character who leaves it continues to live." Once again we encounter the notion of something that goes outside the frame, something that is not still, immobile within the frame but that leaves it and continues to live. Barthes continues: 'A blind field' [Bazin's term] incessantly doubles the partial vision." The idea here is that in photography everything is contained within the photograph, whereas in cinema things continue to live outside the field of vision, and that continuity which we cannot see, Bazin calls the "blind field." Barthes continues: "Now, before thousands of photos, including those that possess a good *studium*, I don't sense any blind field: everything that happens within the frame dies absolutely, once outside that frame." This is Barthes's definition of the bad photograph: the photograph with a good *studium*, with good intentions, good ideas, the well-made photograph, but the photograph where everything is within the frame and does not continue to live outside the frame. He is talking about a kind of violence; he uses the word "dies." He is not talking about death within the frame, or about the representation of violence; he is using violent imagery for something representation does. He is talking about what happens when a photograph has a good *studium* but no *punctum.* As soon as there is a *punctum,* however, a "blind field" is created or divined. A *punctum* thus does the same thing that cinema does. I will not go into whether or not this is how cinema works. What interests me is this image of the photograph where everything is contained within the frame and the photograph where things continue to happen outside the frame.

Barthes cites a photograph by James Van der Zee of a black family of three, in which the *punctum* is a necklace one of the women is wearing. "Because of her round necklace, the Negress in her Sunday best has, for me, an entire life outside her portrait." The *punctum,* by breaking open the *studium,* breaks open a sterile enclosure which does not allow anything to pass through, and allows what Barthes calls "life" to pass through, to permeate the frame.

What Barthes calls "life" has something to do with a kind of eroticism that he valorizes in this book. He has a strong sense of good and bad in eroticism. At various points in *Camera Lucida,* as well as in *The Pleasure of the Text,* he contrasts erotica and pornography to the detriment of the latter. What Barthes valorizes has something to do with the "life" that passes outside the frame. Continuing to talk about this "blind field," he comes to talk specifically about eroticism: "The presence of this blind field is, I believe, what distinguishes the erotic photo from the pornographic photo." For Barthes, pornography is pure *studium* whereas the erotic occurs when there is a *punctum.* "Pornography ordinarily represents the sex-organ, it makes it into an immobile object (a fetish), to which we burn incense, like a god that doesn't leave its niche." This kind of erotic relationship in which the sex-organ is represented within the frame is sexuality *in* art, and it is described negatively by being likened to religion, by being represented as a god that does not leave its niche, to which we burn incense (in this context, a quite provocative image). For Barthes, pornography is a self-enclosed image: it is sexuality contained, sexuality that does not leave its frame. The viewer can worship it in a kind of masturbatory way but can neither touch it nor be touched by it.

He continues: "For me, no *punctum* in the pornographic image; at most it amuses me (and still, boredom comes fast). The erotic photo, on the contrary (it's its very condition) does not make the sex-organ a central object; it can very well not show it; it draws the spectator out of its frame." That last phrase is ambiguous in French. It could also read: it draws the spectator out of *his* frame. The word would be the same in French. There is a double meaning here: the sense of *two* things coming out of their enclosures. (I do not agree that pornography always makes the sex-organ a central object nor that in erotic photography the sex-organ is never a central object. I think that is a false distinction as it is based upon what goes on within the frame. I am much more interested in the distinction between pornography as "a god that doesn't leave its niche" and erotica as "drawing the spectator out of the frame").

Barthes continues: "and it's in this way that this photo, I animate it and it animates me." It is in this way, because of the *punctum,* because the erotic photo draws the spectator out of its frame, out of his frame, out of her frame (all of which are perfectly legitimate translations of Barthes's French). With the erotic photo, "I animate it and it animates me." Earlier Barthes seemed to define the spectator as passive, as, indeed, a victim of aggression, and yet now his definition seems a lot more complicated, a complex of activity and passivity. There is some sort of reciprocal activity occurring where one is both the subject and the object of the verb "animate," a verb that echoes this notion of life that Barthes talks about. Behind all of this is the contrast between that which dies outside the frame and that which continues to live outside the frame, animation as opposed to the inanimate. The erotic photograph is different finally not because of what occurs inside the photograph, not what is represented, but precisely because something occurs between the photograph and the viewer: a relation of reciprocity, if one can imagine a reciprocal relation with a photograph, a relation of mutual animation.

A few pages earlier Barthes writes that the *punctum* is "what I add to the photo and which nonetheless is there already." On the other hand, it is "what I add to the photo," implying a highly active viewer who puts something there, who is in some way creating the photograph. However, what he is creating is something that is already there, something that is *in* the photograph. In the late '60s, Barthes's great move in literary criticism was his promotion of the notion of active reading as opposed to passive consumption. He called for a kind of reading in which the reader actively contributes to the text, in a sense, writes the text. Yet this is, finally, a subtle activity. He is not talking literally about writing; we know what writing is and that is not the kind of reading he means.

In relation to photography this means adding to the photograph something which is already there. This suggests a contact we might call "active passivity," an active viewing in which one contributes to seeing something that is really out there. This "active passivity," this complex, is what he is trying to gesture toward, or at least what I am trying to gesture toward, because, after all, this is my reading of his book, and I may be all too actively adding things which I only hope are already there. I would have it that he gestures toward some sort of contact with alterity, some sort of contact with something that is out there in the world already, that is not simply a projection, but that we nevertheless do not just take in as purely passive consumers. That is how I understand this notion: "I animate it and it animates me."

I am trying to read *Camera Lucida* by means of an analogy between viewing a photograph and some sort of erotic relation to an "other." I am (or he is) trying to think around a way to touch, to contact, to encounter the real of the other. As I have said, when Barthes talks about the sting and the wound and the arrow that pierces me, he is pointing to a tradition of mysticism. In Western thought, mysticism is the great tradition of openness to alterity, of total receptivity to being overwhelmed by otherness. But there is something else here that I find interesting because I am not really interested in a purely passive relation. There is also the relation of the "I animate it and it animates me," the relation of what I add to the photograph which is nonetheless *already* there. In sex the subject must desire, must fantasize, must imagine. Things must come from the mind and cause one to view the other as the object of desire. Yet, at the same time, there is also a wish to encounter the other as something real, out there, beyond one's fantasies, not the god in the niche to whom we burn incense, not the pornographic image, but a relation to some real other. This wish is at play in the notion of the *punctum:* something that leads us outside of the frame.

The analogy interests me not simply because I am interested in sex, not simply because sex is the topic of this journal [a special issue of *Afterimage*], but because it seems a suggestive way to talk about photography. It is often said that photography is a strange hybrid of nature and art, of art and the real. Photography is art like sex is fantasy, desire, imagination. It is one's own ideas projected onto the world, shaping and distorting the world, framing the world and making it into an object of art or an object of desire. Photography is also something else. Besides being art, it seems to have some quite special relation to the real.

Photography interests Barthes because of this special relation to the real. He says that the photograph necessarily always takes its referent with it, takes the thing in the world that it refers to with it. Photography is at once representation, and yet also, some sort of direct registration of the real. According to Barthes: "The photo is literally an emanation of the referent. From a real body, that was there, rays went out that came to touch me, me who is here . . . the light, although impalpable, is certainly here a carnal medium, a skin that I share with he or she who was photographed." For Barthes the photograph is magical because what gets registered on the film actually comes from the real object. I am not sure that this is exactly how photography works, that we are actually looking at a record, or that the object really comes and touches us. Barthes's sense of photograph is both very mystical and very naive.

In the passage just quoted, Barthes uses a number of metaphors related to the body: the skin, touch, the carnal. It seems to me that this body imagery bespeaks his attempt to think some relation to the real, to the body that is really out there, the referent if you like, to some thing that touches him. He is trying to think some relation to the referent through a notion of erotic contact, hence the difference between the body that touches me and that god in his niche to whom I burn incense without any real contact. There is a real body, the rays, the light which is a skin that touches me. Yet, this still implies the passivity of the spectator and the activity of either the photograph or the photographic object, its referent. But then there is the last part of the sentence, "the light, a skin that I share with he or she who was photographed." The image of sharing a skin is extraordinary. If you say something touches you, there is a subject and an object of that verb, which has an active and a passive meaning. But if you are sharing a skin, there is another relation.

At the end of the sentence Barthes writes that he shares the skin "with he or she who was photographed." That locution might not sound too unusual to us because nowadays we are all pretty careful to say "he or she," or that sort of thing. But Roland Barthes is an author who never talks about sexual difference, who never sexually differentiates his erotic objects when he describes them. To my knowledge, this is the only place in his work where he sexually differentiates: he actually uses two pronouns, a masculine and a feminine pronoun. The inelegance of "he or she," of the double pronoun, is not only a recognition of sexual difference, but, I think, it also signals an attempt to talk about the real.

I am pursuing the idea of a relation between sexuality and the medium of photography, which is not sexuality *in* photography, but is something like the sexuality *of* photography. In August 1984 I heard Leslie Bellavance, a Milwaukee artist and teacher, make a similar point: "Erotica and photography have what seems to be parallel paradoxes. The erotic paradox is the meeting point of dependence and independence. The photographic paradox is the meeting point of nature and art." Bellavance's paradoxes resemble Barthes's statement that the *punctum* is what I add that is already there. The erotic paradox is this strange combination of dependence and independence. In order to be erotic, the object must depend on the viewer, on the aroused one, on our fantasies, our imagination, our constructs, our framing, and yet, the object must also remain independent, still real, still other. Eroticism itself is a relation to something that is very much part of our imagination, our projection, our desires. Our eroticism is what is most narcissistic or most imperialistic in our relation to the world, and yet, there is also some relation between our desires and something that is really out there, that is independent of our fantasies.

Bellavance defines the photographic paradox as the meeting point of nature and art. Nature is a word we have used for a long time to talk about what is out there, outside of culture, outside of our constructions, our frames, outside of our art. In *On Photography,* Sontag writes that photographs "trade simultaneously on the prestige of art and the magic of the real. They are clouds of fantasy and pellets of information." My goal here is to provoke you to think toward a relation between sexuality or eroticism and photography, a relation between two "paradoxes," two contradictory projects, two perhaps impossible projects, in which neither one is contained within the other, a relation of the "of" or the "and," rather than of the "in." I do not want to talk about the representation of sexuality *in* photography. Nor do I want to reproduce photography to a manifestation of sexuality. I would rather attempt to think about what it is in the photographic project which uncannily resembles the paradox of sexuality.

In his explanation of the *punctum,* Barthes says:

Certain details could "sting" me. If they don't, it's undoubtedly because they were put there intentionally by the photographer. . . . the detail that interests me is not, or at least not rigorously, intentional, and probably it must not be; it finds itself in the field of the thing photographed like a supplement at once inevitable and obliging; it does not necessarily attest to the photographer's art.

A lot of photographers would resent that statement and they would not be wrong. Barthes is interested in that element in the photograph which he does not think the photographer intended. He actually waffles about it; the issue seems pretty complicated for him. He says, "the detail that interests me is not," which sounds like a decisive, negative assertion, but then he adds, "at least not rigorously, intentional, and probably it must not be." There is something about the question of the intentionality of the interesting detail that seems to trouble him. Early in *Camera Lucida,* Barthes states that there are three ways to talk about photography: from the point of view of the photographer, from the point of view of the person photographed, and from the point of view of the viewer. He then says that he will not talk about it from the point of view of the photographer because he is not a photographer. This is consistent with Barthes's larger project, at this stage of his career, that is, the project of a subjective science, a science in which he speaks from his own subjective experience. It stands in marked contrast with Sontag's book *On Photography* in which, although not a photographer either, she writes about photography from her notion of the photographer's point of view.

Sontag may be hard on photographers, constantly talking about their appropriative desire, but Barthes's relation to the photographer is ultimately, if more subtly, aggressive. He is saying: I am interested in *my* relation to the photograph; I am not interested in your relation to the photograph. That is not all: he is most interested in the things that he thinks *he* adds to the photograph. It may be "already there," but if the photographer did not intend to put it there, it *therefore* constitutes some relation to the real. The erotic relation to the photograph, like so many other erotic relations, may produce a certain kind of rivalry. Thus, Barthes lays claim to the most erotic place in the photograph, the *punctum.* He proclaims: it is mine, it is not the photographer's. I put it there. It is there already, but that is the erotic paradox: what I put there is already there. This could be the less seemly side of Barthes's erotic relation to the photograph, or even the less seemly side of every viewer's relation to the photograph. This is the moment in eroticism when we say: Yes, yes, I am open to otherness; I want to encounter you, but I do not want you to encounter anyone else! This is my relation to you!

As unseemly as it may be, when viewed from this jealous angle, I want to examine further the notion of the questionable intentionality of the *punctum.* The poster for this series, "Sexuality in Art and the Media," is a photograph by Harry Bowers, *Black and White #6.* To discuss its *studium,* it is a photograph of a naked man and a clothed woman, which clearly quotes from the history of representational art. But for me, finally, the object of greatest fascination, the point which takes me outside the frame and whose intentionality remains uncertain, is neither the man's naked body nor the woman's clothed body. Both these bodies, however attractive, are within the frame of representation. The object that most draws out my imagination is the wedding ring on the man's finger. I find myself wondering whether the photographer wanted it there, or did not realize it was there, or was indifferent. What it does to me bears out Barthes's notion of something that seems to have a "blind field" and lives outside the frame. Because of it, this naked man—coded there as an object for my desire, as an object of my gaze—seems to have a (sexual) life and history outside the frame. Because of it, he is not just an object to whom I burn my incense, but he is also a "real person."

In the passage that I quoted before in which Barthes defines what happens in the erotic photo, he continues: "The *punctum* is thus a sort of subtle outside-the-field, as if the image flung desire beyond what it offered to view: not only toward "the rest" of the nudity, not only toward the fantasy of a practice, but toward the absolute excellence of a being, body and soul mingled." I am embarrassed by the phrase "absolute excellence of a being, body and soul mingled." These sorts of words are not in fashion in the post- and anti-humanist circles where Barthes is read. "Soul" is not a word intellectuals and critics use much anymore. The embarrassment caused by the phrase "body and soul mingled" is like the embarrassment I feel when I say that the man's wedding ring makes him a "real person." The phrase "real person" is an attempt to indicate that he exists, that he has a life that goes outside the frame. The question is, what is beyond the frame? I think we run into trouble when we start talking about what is beyond the frame. We get into a kind of troubling essentialism and start talking about "souls" and the "absolute excellence of being." I am wary of positing what is outside the frame, because when we posit that, we are once again within a long tradition of ontological and metaphysical projection—projection of what God is, what the real is, what the noumenal world is beyond phenomena. Photography and eroticism both occupy a space that is neither quite outside nor inside the frame, but are rather in some very conflicted and powerfully dynamic relation to inside and outside. In this space we confront the paradoxes of dependence and independence, nature and art, nature and the real, what I add and what is there already, what animates me and what I animate. For me, finally, that is the sexuality *of* art and the medium of photography.

Notes

1. Roland Barthes, *Le Plaisir du texte* (Paris: Seuil, 1973). Translations mine. Richard Miller has translated this book as *The Pleasure of the Text* (New York: Hill and Wang, 1975).
2. Roland Barthes, *La Chambre claire: Note sur la photographie* (Paris: Gallimard Seuil, 1980). Translations mine. Richard Howard has translated it as *Camera Lucida: Reflections on Photography* (New York: Hill and Wang, 1981).
3. Susan Sontag, *On Photography* (New York: Dell, 1977), 169.

What Is a Photograph?

Margaret Iversen

Barthes's last book, *Camera Lucida* (1980), begins with the words, "One day, quite some time ago . . . ," clearly announcing its status as a fiction, as art.[1] The central character is a scholar who, throwing off his academic robes—his whole culture even—retires to his study rather like Descartes and meditates in the first person on photography. More precisely, he meditates on his desire in relation to those photographs that somehow move him. These few instances then furnish a bedrock of personal but irrefutable evidence from which he hopes to extrapolate the essence of photography in general. It's a lovely, alluring story in which we want to believe but by which we ought not to be completely taken in. Rather, we should inquire why the book is written in this form. There are, no doubt, many answers to this question, chief among them being Barthes's avowed desire to write fiction. My proposal is that the book is a kind of fable about photography that, despite its apparent antitheoretical stance, was deeply influenced by the difficult, frequently impenetrable, seminar given by Jacques Lacan in 1964 and published in English as *The Four Fundamental Concepts of Psycho-analysis*.[2] Lacan gave Barthes an inscribed copy of the book when it was published, and it survives, lightly annotated, in an archive in Paris.[3] Barthes's accessible little book, in effect, mediated Lacan's thinking about the real and the function of the gaze as *objet petit a* (object little *a*), without too many overt references to Lacan. In this essay, I set the two texts side by side, elucidating Lacan through Barthes's reading of him and, conversely, interpreting *Camera Lucida* in the light of *The Four Fundamental Concepts*.

The dramatic opening gesture of eschewing all technical, semiological, sociological, and historical approaches to photography has the consequence of drawing Barthes closer to the tradition of phenomenological description of lived experience. In fact, the book is dedicated to Sartre and his *L'imaginaire*.[4] But Barthes adds something often lacking in that tradition—

affect. His kind of phenomenology would be "steeped in desire, repulsion, nostalgia, euphoria" (21) and, I will argue, through and through psychoanalytical. *Camera Lucida* is in many ways a somber book, haunted as it is by the recent death of the author's mother and, for us, in retrospect, his own. It circles around the thought that the essence or specific character of photography is a "that-has-been"—a certificate of the presence of something that is past. A photograph weaves together presence and absence, present and past.[5] The nature of the medium as an indexical imprint of the object means that any photographed object or person has a ghostly, uncanny presence that might be likened to the return of the dead. Yet the title of the book is anything but somber. *La chambre claire* literally means "the light or bright room." It also refers, we are told, to a draughtsman's technical aid, quite unlike the dark chamber of the camera obscura, which projects an image onto paper by means of a prism (106). For those who have read the book, it might also evoke its key though unreproduced photograph of Barthes's mother as a child in a conservatory or winter garden.

The Real

The occasion for writing the book, according to the fiction, was the death of the mother and the son's melancholy search for her in a pile of old photographs. But its underlying theme is taken from Lacan's account of the encounter with the real, which is ultimately an encounter with the persistently denied fact of one's own mortality. Barthes declares that every photograph contains "an imperious sign of my future death" (97). Looking at an old photograph, one thinks simultaneously of a future ("he is going to die") and of an absolute past ("he has died") (96)—a recognition that collapses time and seals one's own fate. But Barthes develops this painful recognition from a negative into a positive, from dark to light, through Freud's conception of the death drive as mediated by Lacan.

The death drive is not something that had previously much concerned Barthes, although it might well be argued that his earlier aesthetics of *jouissance* or bliss (also a Lacanian conception but owing much to Bataille's theories of eroticism) in *The Pleasure of the Text* already carried something of what is beyond the pleasure principle: "he enjoys the consistency of his selfhood (that is his pleasure) and seeks its loss (that is his bliss)."[6] The topography of instinctual drives developed by Freud in *Beyond the Pleasure Principle* set the pleasure principle in opposition to the death drive.[7] As we have already noted, the first principle relates to the theory of constancy whereby the psychical apparatus tries to keep levels of excitation low or constant through the discharge of unpleasurable tension. It has to do, therefore, with the maintenance of a homeostatic system, the preservation of life, libidinal satisfaction, and the stability of the ego—in short, everything that Freud groups under the rubric of life instincts, or Eros.[8] Barthes's constant association of pleasure with what is coded, cultural, and collective fits in with Freud's conception of the pleasure principle as integrative. And Barthes follows Lacan's rather low estimation of pleasure evident in statements such as, "Pleasure limits the scope of human possibility—the pleasure principle is a principle of homeostasis" (31). "Bliss" must then participate in the disintegrative energies of the death drive, which would include pain, loss, and the shudder of annihilation. However, the sexual frisson inherent in the French term *la jouissance* (which also means orgasm) is muted in *Camera Lucida*. The book is not about the transgressive and dangerous dimension of desire but the trauma of separation, loss, and death.

The Lacan text that I'm suggesting was Barthes's touchstone is itself a meditation on Freud's *Beyond the Pleasure Principle*. It concerns the third, rather elusive term in Lacan's tripartite topography in which the relation between the imaginary and symbolic orders is complicated by the real. *The Four Fundamental Concepts* contains several chapters exploring the real as it is manifested in the visual field (that is, as the gaze), so the book bears on matters directly relevant to the visual arts. There is admittedly little overt evidence in *Camera Lucida* to support my case for the central importance of Lacan's *Seminar XI*, except that in the French version there is a brief bibliography that cites it. However, Lacan gave Barthes a copy of his book when it was published, and his marginal notations indicate the interest that Barthes took in the sections on the missed encounter with the real. For instance, he paid oblique tribute to some of the most vivid passages in *The Four Fundamental Concepts* about the dream of the burning child. Finding the photograph of his dead mother as a child, he repeats the searing words uttered by the dead child in the father's dream: "*je brûle*" (I'm burning) (100). The finding of the Winter Garden Photograph, like the father's dream, is a missed encounter with the real. At the beginning of the book, Barthes observes that the defining characteristic of photography is its attachment to "the absolute particular, the sovereign Contingency, matte and somehow stupid, the This . . . , in short, what Lacan calls *Tuché*, the Occasion, the Encounter, the Real, in its indefatigable expression" (4). The fifth chapter of *The Four Fundamental Concepts* is called "Tuché and Automaton." (*Tuché* might have been more readily recognizable as the name of the Greek principle of fate in its usual English transliteration as "Tyche"). The terms are borrowed from the second book of Aristotle's *Physics* in a discussion of causality, but Lacan redefines them as "the encounter with the real" and "the network of signifiers," respectively. While the automaton or network of signifiers involves the subject in his or her relation to the machinery of the symbolic register, the *tuché* or real is a relation outside that system. The significance of this is that the subject is not exhausted by or subsumed into the symbolic, linguistic, conceptual apparatus of culture. Lacan explicitly connects the automaton to "the insistence of the signs by which we see ourselves governed by the pleasure principle" (53–54). *Tuché,* on the contrary, is experienced by the subject as a painful intrusion, as a trauma.[9]

Lacan is adamant that this painful encounter with a real beyond the pleasure principle was the constant object of Freud's research. In "The Subversion of the Subject," for example, he writes, "for to ignore the death instinct in his doctrine is to misunderstand that doctrine entirely."[10] Lacan's reading of Freud no doubt privileges the post-1920 topography, but it does at least have the virtue of directing our attention to those moments in Freud's thought where the unconscious is given a fateful, accidental character as, for example, in his paper on the uncanny.[11] In *The Four Fundamental Concepts,* Lacan delves into the early *Interpretation of Dreams* (1900) and comes up with a dream that is riven by trauma and does not at all conform to the general thesis of the book that dreams are disguised, hallucinated wish-fulfillments — the dream of the burning child.[12] Like the nightmares of Freud's shell-shocked soldiers, this dream is a (missed) encounter with the real—that is, with the irredeemable loss of the child. "How can the dream," inquires Lacan, "the bearer of the subject's desire produce that which makes the trauma emerge repeatedly—if not its very face, at least the screen that shows that it is still there behind" (55).

The real would seem, then, to be a hitch in the circuit of life-preserving, pleasure-seeking drives that cannot be smoothed over and that insistently repeats. The "compulsion to repeat" is, for Freud, the hallmark of what cannot be assimilated or subdued. An example of such repetition discussed by Freud in *Beyond the Pleasure Principle* is the "fort-da" game invented by his one-and-a-half-year-old grandson.[13] The little boy repeatedly threw a cotton-reel attached to a piece of thread into his cot where it disappeared from view and then reeled it back, accompanying these alternating actions with sounds meaning "gone" and "there." For Freud, the game is a reenactment and a working through of the original trauma of the boy's separation from his mother. For Lacan, the cotton-reel is a small piece of the subject with which he attempts to span the "ditch," the "ever-open gap" around his cot created by the mother's absence (62).

The most obvious connection between this "repetition compulsion" and photography is the fact of mechanical reproduction and Barthes picks up on this link: "the photograph mechanically repeats what could never be repeated existentially" (4). It has, therefore, some of the uncanny, fateful character of the compulsive repetition discussed by Freud. But Barthes tends to locate the photograph's uncanniness more in its insistence on the absent referent. The object isn't just represented as in a drawing or a painting—rather, it clings to the photograph in a disconcerting way. One way of reading *Camera Lucida* is as a reassessment of realism by an ardent modernist. But realism, in this context, must be detached from the collection of threadbare academic conventions and aligned with the Lacanian real.[14] Not all photographs, however, are susceptible to this realignment. In Lacan's terms, the photograph can either be fully integrated in the network of signifiers or it can be tychic. Or as Barthes observes, it can either be experienced as tame (that is, "tempered by aesthetic and empirical habits") or as mad (119). Barthes's "mad" realism is clearly related to surrealism in which a disruptive reality unsettles the "civilized codes" (119).

Shock

Although my aim is to read *Camera Lucida* through *The Four Fundamental Concepts*, I want to pause here to consider what I take to be another important, though unacknowledged inspiration for the book—"Little History of Photography" (1931), a text by a writer deeply marked by surrealism, Walter Benjamin.[15] Part of that essay concerns photographic studies of anonymous subjects made by the Scottish painter, David Octavius Hill.[16] With paintings of such subjects, Benjamin notes, interest in the identity of the sitters soon fades. "With photography, however, we encounter something new and strange." Confronted, for example, by Hill's Newhaven fishwife "there remains something that cannot be silenced, that fills you with an unruly desire to know what her name was, the woman who was alive there, who even now is still real and will never consent to be wholly absorbed in art."[17]

Barthes's sense of the photograph as an insistent presence of the real emanating from the past is clear enough here, but with his next example Benjamin adds another dimension important for Barthes—trauma. He writes of a photograph by Karl Dauthendey of himself and a woman that Benjamin says is Dauthendey's fiancée, whom he was to find, shortly after the birth of their sixth child, lying in the bedroom with her arteries severed. Benjamin reflects:

No matter how artful the photograph, no matter how carefully posed his subject, the beholder feels an irresistible urge to search such a picture for the tiny spark of contingency, of the Here and Now, with which reality has (so to speak) seared the subject, to find the inconspicuous spot where in the immediacy of that long-forgotten moment the future nests so eloquently that we, looking back, may rediscover it.[18]

This clearly refers to Freud's theory of the trauma. But why should the camera be able to spot the trace left by the original trauma, making it possible for us to predict retrospectively the future disaster? Benjamin seems to indicate that it may be the camera's inability to censor the "inconspicuous spot": "For it is another nature which speaks to the camera rather than to the eye: other above all in the sense that a space informed by human consciousness gives way to a space informed by the unconscious."[19] The camera's blind mechanism, Benjamin seems to suggest, is similar to the surrealist's use of psychic automatism. Unfortunately, this promising suggestion then quickly deteriorates into Benjamin's familiar and disappointing parallel between the technical devices of photography (the fraction of a second, enlargement, and so on) that "reveal secrets" opening up an "optical unconscious," just as the techniques of psychoanalysis reveal the instinctual unconscious. But do the stop-motion photographs of Muybridge and Marey or the enlarged plants of Karl Blossfelt give us insight into an unconscious dimension in anything like a Freudian sense? I doubt it. In her book *The Optical Unconscious*, Rosalind Krauss points out the difficulty of thinking of the visual field as having an unconscious in these terms but develops the idea in other ways.[20] When we understand, with Lacan, how the real appears in the visual field as the gaze, the difficulty unravels. In my view, this is what Barthes proposes in *Camera Lucida*.

Before moving on to consider the Lacanian conception of the gaze, we need to return to the psychoanalytic understanding of trauma and Barthes's appropriation of it. There is little point in pausing too long here, however, because the job has already been thoroughly done by Andrew Brown in his monograph called *Roland Barthes: The Figures of Writing*, which closes with a chapter called simply "The Trauma."[21] For Freud, the trauma is linked to what he termed the primal scene: the child witnesses or experiences something at an age too young to comprehend its meaning. This unassimilable memory is preserved until, at a later date, another perhaps innocuous event occurs that recalls the first and floods it with sexual meaning. By a process of "deferred action," then, the childhood experience becomes traumatic. A good example of this process is given in Freud's case study known as "The Wolf Man."[22] The adult patient reported to Freud a frightening dream that he had at five years old: wolves were sitting motionless in the branches of a tree outside his bedroom window and staring at him. Freud suggests that the effect of the dream derives from a much earlier impression, although key aspects of that event are reversed and filtered through fairy-tale scenarios. As an infant, he had woken and stared transfixed at a scene of violent motion—his parents copulating "in the manner of animals." The unconscious recollection of such a scene would have confirmed the reality of castration once that eventuality had become, with the onset of the Oedipus complex, a burning issue for the boy. The traumatic primal scene can hardly be said to have taken place since the trauma lags so far behind the event. Lacan adds to this that the trauma is real insofar as it remains unsymbolizable—a kernel of nonsense at the heart of the subject. *Camera Lucida* is structured around the idea of the trauma. The recent death of the mother, we may suppose, had reactivated in Barthes the original wound of separation. In one of the fragments of *A Lover's Discourse*, he recalls his suffering as a child: "interminable days, abandoned days, when the mother was working away."[23] His search for her authentic photographic image, then, is tinged with this original bereavement.

As Brown rightly points out, there is a close connection between the theory of the trauma and the aesthetics of shock.[24] For Benjamin, traditional art was for the most part ego-sustaining; it kept its distance, and this constituted its aura. But now that we are bombarded from all sides by the unassimilable shocks of modern life, our psyches require something beyond the pleasure principle. We subject ourselves to the shock effects of violent cinema images, for example, as a way of "binding" threatening stimuli and of building up a protective "crust" (Freud's terms). For instance, the short strip of amateur film that records John F. Kennedy's assassination or the TV images of the attack on the World Trade Center are endlessly replayed to a nation unable to overcome its trauma. Yet it would be misleading to assimilate the shock effects of Benjamin's antiauratic art to Barthes's traumatic photographs. The sections of "Little History of Photography" that clearly interested Barthes were those that dealt with auratic, early photography with its atmospheric effect of "light struggling out of darkness."[25] Barthes seems interested in restoring the shock of precisely those portrait photographs. Photography is particularly susceptible to this treatment because, as Barthes points out, it has an inherently "traumatic" structure: I witness something in the past by "deferred action" (10). Brown draws attention to an interesting passage from Freud's *Moses and Monotheism* where an analogy is drawn between photographic and psychic deferred action: the latter may be made "more comprehensible by comparing it with a photographic exposure which can be developed after any interval of time and transformed into a picture."[26] To assess what is distinctive about Barthes's notion of the traumatic photograph, we have to understand his theory of the *punctum*.

The first half of *Camera Lucida* is taken up with a discussion of the distinction that Barthes makes between two fundamentally different types of interest we take in photography. The *studium* of a photo generates a generalized interest, pleasure, or concern in the viewer. Photographs with a *studium* we judge "good." But in some photographs, a detail or *punctum* takes the viewer by surprise—"pricks" him or her and completely alters the sense of the image. The detail does not prompt a reinterpretation that would subsume it dialectically and integrate it into the whole. It shares with the trauma and Lacan's anamorphic stain an uncoded, unassimilable quality. It is unnamable, and, writes Barthes, "what I can name cannot really prick me. The incapacity to name is a good symptom of disturbance" (51). In discussing one photograph that has this lacerating detail for him, Barthes first lights on a woman's strapped shoes (43) and then, like an analysand working through screen memories toward the original trauma, shifts to her necklace, which reminds him of one that was worn by his unmarried aunt but since her death has been kept in a jewelry box (53). Jane Gallop's interesting discussion of Barthes's distinction, in her *Thinking through the Body*, emphasizes the way that a photograph with only a *studium* stays put within the confines of the picture. Its coherence is entirely internal. In contrast, the *punctum* breaks up that coherence and bursts through the frame and plane. The photograph endowed with a *punctum* has a "blind field," something equivalent to what is masked on the edges of the cinema image.[27] There is, then, a kind of symmetry between the photograph's and the subject's openness to alterity.[28]

Barthes's *studium/punctum* distinction recalls aspects of his earlier essay on still photographs from Eisenstein's films. In "The Third Meaning" (1970), he points to the presence in these stills of an "obtuse" meaning that exceeds the "obvious" signification of symbolism and narrative. Certain details "hold" or touch him but without his being able to say why.[29] They remain mute signifiers and open on to the field of *signifiance* as understood by Kristeva.[30] Although there may be some overlap between the *studium* and the *punctum*, the concepts have exactly opposite connotations of blunt and sharp. The saving bluntness of the third meaning, its ungraspable resistance to conceptual consumption, preserves the image-text from any fixity of interpretation. The sharpness of the *punctum*, on the other hand, cuts through the deliberate decorum of the pose and the prop and reactivates a trauma.

The Gaze

Barthes's opposition between the *studium* and the *punctum* of photographs can be further elucidated by reference to Lacan's critique, in *The Four Fundamental Concepts*, of classical optics and perspective construction. The point of carrying out the critique is to explode the idealist illusion of "seeing oneself seeing oneself" (83)—that is, the optical equivalent of the illusion of self-reflective consciousness ("I think, therefore I am"). More than once, Lacan here acknowledges his indebtedness to Merleau-Ponty and particularly to a posthumous work that had just appeared, *The Visible and the Invisible* (1964). He refers to a chapter of that book called "The Intertwining / the Chiasm," where the philosopher is trying to show that our own corporeality, making us objects of sight in the world, is the necessary condition of our being subjects of sight.[31] While I look at things, I am looked at. My activity, then, is equally a passivity. Visual perception, tied to the body, is necessarily partial. As Lacan observes, "I see only from one point, but in my existence I am looked at from all sides" (72). Merleau-Ponty's reflections on vision helped Lacan to formulate his sense of the necessary preexistence of the gaze, which, in the visual register, shows the subject not as an autonomous, rational subject but as constituted by the desire of the Other. The subject is thus decentered in relation to any point of sight. In this context, the traffic between the two thinkers was two-way: Merleau-Ponty used Lacan's 1949 essay "The Mirror Stage" in formulating his conception of the "visible seer."

A key characteristic of our relation to the *studium* of a photograph is our confident self-possession: "I invest the field of the *studium* with my sovereign consciousness" (26). This sort of perception has similarities with geometral perspective in which a single point of sight inaugurates and organizes the field. For Lacan, this system is the optical equivalent of the classical concept of consciousness as formulated by Descartes: the Cartesian subject, he notes, "is itself a sort of geometral point" (86). And, he urges, this conception of self-reflective consciousness is founded on a misrecognition, which in the visual register would be called a *scotoma*—that is, a blanking out of something that is traumatic. What is blanked out is, in either case, the fact that the subject is not just a subject of consciousness but also a subject of unconscious desire. This latter subject, who can be heard only in the lacunae of discourse, can be glimpsed only in the gaze. My suggestion is that Barthes's *punctum* is equivalent to Lacan's gaze or, in other words, to what is elided in classical optics. Because, as Lacan argues, desire is constituted by a lack (separation from the mother, symbolic castration), that lack as gaze inevitably looms up in the visual field and disorganizes it (89). The *punctum*, as we've seen, also reverses the direction of the lines of sight and disorganizes the visual field, erupting into the network of signifiers that constitute reality: "This time it is not I who seek it out, it is this element which rises from the scene, shoots out of it like an arrow, and pierces me" (26).[32] The terms that Barthes uses to describe this experience (*prick, wound, hole*) clearly suggest their relation to lack.

Lacan's discussion of anamorphosis illustrates the disparity between one's position as sovereign subject of sight (*studium*) and as object of the gaze (or the *punctum*). From an orthodox position, the viewer of Holbein's *Ambassadors* (1533) shares their confidence and vanity; he is master of all he surveys. But something incomprehensible, a shadowy phallic shape, floats in the foreground. Only when one starts to leave the room and casts an oblique glance back does the shape resolve itself into a human skull: "It reflects our own nothingness, in the figure of the death's head" (92). In other words, only when the position of illusory mastery is vacated does the gaze come into full view. The two positions are mutually exclusive: the world of representation is given only if the immediacy of the real is sacrificed, and conversely, the real is glimpsed only when the vanity of the world conceived as my representation is renounced. There is, then, a blind spot in the orthodox perceptual field that Lacan calls the stain (*la tache*), defined, like the gaze, as "that which always escapes from the grasp of that form of vision that is satisfied with itself in imagining itself as consciousness" (75). Barthes takes up this term in one of his definitions of the *punctum*: "For *punctum* is also, sting, speck (*petite tache*), cut, little hole—and also a cast of the die. A photograph's *punctum* is the accident which pricks me" (27, French 49) This same spot also makes an appearance in a passage from the book *Working Space* (1986) by the American artist Frank

Stella, helpfully cited by Malcolm Bowie. The painter "worries that there is something that he cannot see, something that is eliding him . . . a dark spot."[33] It would seem that this stain or spot must be approached indirectly, viewed awry, glancingly, without conscious deliberation. One requires visual equivalents of the strategies of indirection invented by Freud to approach the unconscious—dreams, free association, transference. As Lacan notes, "It is not, after all, for nothing that analysis is not carried out face to face" (78).

The gaze as spot or stain stresses the opacity and negativity of what is both object and cause of the scopic drive. This contrasts with the transparency and fullness of vision normally associated with the imaginary register's specular mirroring of the ego.[34] The difference is attributable to the fact that the gaze does not represent the ego but rather gestures toward the unrepresentable subject. It reflects not the body image as idealized, coherent, and coordinated but the subject as castrated and in the grip of desire.[35] This subject, called punningly by Lacan *le sujet troué* (the subject full of holes), uses an *objet trouvé* (a found object) to figure both the hole and the missing bit.[36]

To understand the way in which this subject can be shown, it is necessary to return to a consideration of Lacan's formulation of the *objet petit a*. His account of the constitution of the subject involves a series of painful self-alienations that are described almost as bodily automutilations. One's very birth involves the casting off of a vital part of the organism, the placenta. Then one is weaned from the breast, understood by the infant as coextensive with its own body. One "gives up" urine and feces. Finally, symbolic castration seals one's fate as a desiring subject who is haunted by lack and who retrospectively turns all other infantile experiences of loss into forms of castration. In each case, a cut is made that initiates both an erotogenic zone (lips, rim of anus, tip of penis, slit of eyelids) and an object (nipple, feces, urinary flow, phallus as imaginary object, "the phoneme, the gaze, the voice—the nothing").[37] The "part objects" formed by the cut are the *objets petit a*: "The *objet a* is something from which the subject, in order to constitute itself, has separated itself off as organ. This serves as a symbol of lack, that is to say, of the phallus, not as such, but in so far as it is lacking" (103). The gaze as *objet petit a* must refer to the lost parental gaze from which the infant ardently sought recognition, or since entry into the symbolic order (the acquisition of language) involves a sacrifice of being for meaning, a residue of one's "pre-Oedipal" vision may emerge between the cracks in the symbolic as though from outside. These lost morsels of flesh, the hollowed out bits of one's being, play a critical role in Lacan's understanding of the subject's relation to the world. If it weren't for them, we would be caught between the specular idealizations of the imaginary and the impersonal law of the symbolic.

Lacan's references to visual art in *The Four Fundamental Concepts* are taken mostly from the history of painting. However, he does mention photography once, admittedly in a context that indicates that we are not supposed to take it literally. He is insisting on the externality of the gaze that has the effect of turning me into a picture:

What determines me, at the most profound level, in the visible, is the gaze that is outside. It is through the gaze that I enter light and it is from the gaze that I receive its effects. Hence it comes about that the gaze is the instrument through which light is embodied and through which—if you will allow me to use the word, as I often do, in a fragmented form—I am photo-graphed. (106)

If traditional optics can be represented by a triangular diagram showing an eye at the geometral point from which it views an image correlated to an object, then the geometral point is where the ego's eye is installed. It is essentially an Albertian model of representation, transposed into a Kantian model of experience in which phenomena are correlated with (unknowable) noumena. This is the story that consciousness tells itself about vision. But the unconscious also sees, throwing onto a screen its projected desires, fantasies, and fears. The diagram of geometral perspective must accordingly be intersected by an inverted triangle showing a point of light projecting a picture onto a screen. The subject of representation is figured as a single point, and from the perceptive of the gaze (point of light) the subject is represented as the base of a triangle—anamorphically distorted and blurred. If the subject is to appear in the picture, it must be as a screen casting a shadow, creating a blind spot, a hole, in the passing spectacle.

Lacan insists that the point of light is outside: "In the scopic field, the gaze is outside, I am looked at, that is to say, I am a picture" (106). This insistence is consistent with Lacan's conception of the unconscious as an intersubjective relation (desire is the desire of the Other) and with his view of the subject as radically split by the castrating intervention of the register of the symbolic. Lacan suggests that we can observe this fracturing even in the animal kingdom in the phenomenon of display when an animal swells or grimaces, turning itself into a semblance to ward off its predator (107). But this split can be observed not just in the mimicry of intimidation but also in camouflage. An insect, for example, can accommodate itself so well to its environment that it becomes invisible. Roger Caillois's 1935 essay on mimicry in the surrealist magazine *Minotaure* and in *Méduse et cie* (much admired by Lacan) proposed that this activity amounts to a kind of death drive in which the organism loses its integrity and is swallowed up by space. Lacan's double dihedral diagram is a modified version of one described by Caillois in "Mimicry and Legendary Psychasthenia," where he is discussing the dangerous "temptation by space" evidenced in mimicry. Caillois describes a diagram formed by the intersection of two dihedrals—a "dihedral of action" (the vertical base of which is formed by a standing person) and a "dihedral of representation" (whose base is set at the distance where the object appears). It becomes clear that the latter dimension of space carries the same force as Lacan's point of light or gaze. In this space, writes Caillois, "the living creature, the organism, is no longer the origin of the coordinates, but one point among others." And further, "the feeling of personality, considered as the organism's feeling of distinction from its surroundings, of the connection between consciousness and a particular point in space, cannot fail in these conditions to be seriously undermined."[38]

The composite diagram of visuality, first proposed by Caillois, also makes clear the reversibility of the positions of object and subject produced by this intersubjectivity and splitting. Lacan illustrates this point with an amusing anecdote about his student days when he joined working fishermen for the summer. One of the fishermen had pointed to a floating sardine can glinting in the sun and joked, "See that sardine can? Well, it doesn't see you!" But it did. Lacan has been photo-graphed and suddenly feels very ill at ease in the picture (95). This reversal of subject and object is facilitated by the phenomenological fact that "I see outside" or, to put it another way, that "perception is on the objects that it apprehends" (88).

Barthes often acknowledges this externality and passivity in relation to the *punctum*. We have already seen how for him "it fills the sight by force" (91). There is also a discussion, useful in this context, about posing in front of the camera. Posing involves putting on a look drawn from the image repertoire: "I transform myself in advance into an image" (10). But then, suddenly, something intervenes that shatters this ego-protecting shield. The shutter clicks, and "I then experience a micro-version of death," the sound "breaking through the mortiferous layer of the pose" (14–15). Here is perhaps an example of an aural *punctum* finding a chink in the armor of the imaginary. If assuming the 'mortiferous' pose involves the negation of myself as unique subject, then this "micro-version of death" is paradoxically revivifying.[39]

Another discussion that bears on Lacan's sense of being photographed comes when Barthes is stressing the greater importance of chemistry for photography over that of its relation to the camera obscura, which after all it shares with painting. The optical device does not fix the image, and it is the magic of light-sensitive paper that gives the photograph its essential nature as a "that-has-been":

The photograph is literally an emanation of the referent. From a real body which was there, proceed radiations which ultimately touch me, who am here. . . . A sort of umbilical cord links the body of the photographed thing to my gaze: light, though impalpable, is here a carnal medium, a skin I share with anyone who has been photographed. (81)

This passage also connects with the chapter in Lacan's book called "The Line and Light." Here again geometral optics is the target of criticism, but now its inadequacy as a theory of vision is attributed to the fact that what it calls rays of light can easily be figured as threads or sticks. It is really a spatial mapping that even a blind man could comprehend and so would seem to miss entirely what is essential about vision. As Rosalind Krauss points out, the contrast that Lacan is making is between a tactile visuality that is palpably obvious and easily mastered and an optical visuality or "atmospheric surround" in which the viewer, no longer a surveyor, is "caught within the onrush of light."[40] As Lacan observes: "Light may travel in a straight line, but it is refracted, diffused, it floods, it fills—the eye is a sort of bowl—it flows over, too" (94). What both Lacan and Barthes wish to express is the chiasm of vision: I may see objects, but I am also enveloped by a light or gaze that unsettles the position I want to occupy as source of the coordinates of sight.

TAME OR MAD?

In the chapters called "The Line and Light" and "What Is a Picture?," Lacan broaches the question of the function of art from the point of view of psychoanalysis. The artist, he says, wants to present himself as subject, as gaze, and the gaze is there (even in paintings with no pair of eyes) in what we call *style*. There is "something so specific to each of the painters that you will feel the presence of the gaze" (101). If, as I've suggested, the *objet petit a* is that (missing) morsel of one's being outside of symbolic matrixes and public images, then it follows that the *objet petit a* as gaze would inhere in that individuality of style. Lacan also considers the function of art from the spectator's side. Painting, he says, is an opportunity "to lay down one's gaze," and he calls this effect the *dompte-regard* (the tamed-gaze) and adds, "This is the pacifying, Apollonian, effect of painting" (101). Art offers something for the eye and gives the spectator a sense of mastery in relation to the visual field and a sublimated pleasure that compensates for instinctual renunciation (111). Yet, he continues, there is a whole field of painting, expressionism, for example, that answers the scopic drive: it offers something for the gaze. The difference between these two functions is illustrated by the retelling of the classical tale of the competition between Zeuxis and Parrhasios. Zeuxis deceived the eye of a bird that flew down to peck on his painted grapes, but Parrhasios, in reply, painted a veil that incited Zeuxis to ask, "What have you painted behind it?" For Lacan, the latter is the true case of *trompe l'oeil*—a triumph of the gaze over the eye (103, 111–112). The veil animates the desire of the viewer, and its full effect is felt only when one realizes that nothing lies behind it.[41]

Do *dompte-regard* and *trompe l'oeil* correspond to what Barthes calls tame and mad receptions of photography? I think so, but with the difference that Lacan seems to accept the legitimacy or psychic value of both functions, whereas Barthes challenges us to choose between two incompatible possibilities, tame or mad: "Such are the two ways of the Photograph. The choice is mine: to subject its spectacle to the civilized code of perfect illusions, or to confront in it the wakening of intractable reality" (119).

These are the last lines of the book. A retrospective glance through the plates reminds one that the frontispiece reproduces a strange color photograph of an interior showing only thin curtains drawn against a brilliant light.[42]

NOTES

1. Roland Barthes, *Camera Lucida: Reflections on Photography* (1980), trans. Richard Howard (New York: Hill and Wang, 1981), trans. of *La chambre claire: note sur la photographie* (Paris: Cahiers du Cinéma, Gallimard, Seuil, 1980) (all subsequent page references to the English edition will appear in the text between parentheses).

2. Jacques Lacan, *The Four Fundamental Concepts of Psycho-analysis*, ed. Jacques-Alain Miller, trans. Alan Sheridan (London: Penguin Books, 1977), trans. of *Le Séminaire de Jacques Lacan,* Livre 11, *Les quatre concepts fondamentaux de la psychanalyse* (Paris: Éditions du Seuil, 1973).

3. The text is in the Institute mémoires de l'édition contemporaine, Paris. It is inscribed by Lacan as follows: "Plaisir du texte: vous connaissez,—moi j'aime. À l'occasion de qui j'envoi mon 'truc' à Roland Barthes. Le 20 II 73. Jacques Lacan" (The Pleasure of the Text: you know—I love it. On the occasion when I send my 'thing' to Roland Barthes.) The clusters of marks that Barthes made in the margin in this copy fall on pages 64–68, 81–86, 118–119, 133–134.

4. Jean-Paul Sartre, *L'imaginaire: psychologie phénoménologique de l'imagination* (Paris: Gallimard, 1940), trans. as *The Psychology of the Imagination* (London: Methuen, 1972). A long passage from this book is quoted in *Camera Lucida* (19–20), the burden of which is that it is quite possible to regard things represented as unreal. For Barthes, photographs with a *punctum* escape this fate. Jean-Michel Rabaté regards this text as the "philosophical foundation" of *Camera Lucida*. See Jean-Michel Rabaté, ed., *Writing the Image after Roland Barthes* (Philadelphia: University of Pennsylvania Press, 1997).

5. This point is stressed in Derrida's homage to Barthes, which was written shortly after his death. Jacques Derrida, "The Deaths of Roland Barthes," in Hugh J. Silverman, ed., *Philosophy and Non-Philosophy* (New York: Routledge, 1988), 259–296, esp. 281. See also Johnnie Gratton, who stresses the illogical conjunction or paradox of "here" and "past" that is characteristic of Barthes's understanding of the photograph. Reference in *Camera Lucida*, he says, "can never be separated from a certain loss or absence." See John Gratton, "Text, Images, Reference in Roland Barthes's *La Chambre Claire*," *Modern Language Review* 91 (1996): 356. Michael Fried's interesting essay, "Barthes's *Punctum*," stresses the photographer's lack of intentionality with respect to the *punctum* and connects this with his own concept of absorptive painting. The essay appeared in *Critical Inquiry* 31 (Spring 2005): 539–574.

6. Roland Barthes, *The Pleasure of the Text* (1973) trans. Richard Miller (New York: Hill and Wang, 1975). See also Georges Bataille, *Eroticism*, trans. Mary Dalwood (London: Boyars, 1987), and J. Mitchell and J. Rose, eds., *Feminine Sexuality: Jacques Lacan and the École Freudienne,* trans. J. Rose (London: Macmillan, 1982).

7. Sigmund Freud, *Beyond the Pleasure Principle* (1920), trans. James Strachey, *The Standard Edition of the Complete Psychological Works of Sigmund Freud* , ed. James Strachey (London: The Hogarth Press , 1955), 18: 3–64. See also helpful discussions of the pleasure principle, the death drive, and related concepts in J. Laplanche and J.-B. Pontalis, *The Language of Psycho-analysis*, trans. Donald Nicholson-Smith (London: Hogarth Press, 1980). See also my book *Beyond Pleasure: Freud, Lacan Barthes* (University Park, Pennsylvania: Penn State University Press, 2007), for an extended discussion of the legacy of Freud's conception of the death drive in art and theory from surrealism to contemporary art.

8. Freud, *Beyond the Pleasure Principle*, 42–43.

9. "Le réel est *au-delà* de l'automaton," he writes, echoing the French term for "beyond" in the French translation of *Beyond the Pleasure Principle*. Several writers make the connection between the *punctum* and the Lacanian real but do not develop the idea: Victor Burgin, "Re-reading *Camera Lucida*," in *The End of Art Theory: Criticism and Postmodernity* (London: Macmillan, 1986), 71–95; Michael Moriarty, *Roland Barthes* (London: Polity, 1991), 204 ff. Some commentators don't make any reference to Lacan: Nancy M. Shawcross, *Roland Barthes on Photography: The Critical Tradition in Perspective* (Gainesville: University Press of Florida, 1997); Gilles Mora, ed., *Roland Barthes et la photo: le pire des signes* (Paris: Contrejour, 1990). See also Ulrich Baer, *Spectral Evidence: The Photography of Trauma* (Cambridge, MA: MIT Press, 2002); Carol Armstrong, *Scenes in a Library: Reading the Photograph in the Book* (Cambridge, MA: MIT Press, 1998); and Eduardo Cadava, *Words of Light: Theses on the Photography of History* (Princeton, NJ: Princeton University Press, 1997), all of which are influenced by Barthes's book.

10. Jacques Lacan, "Subversion of the Subject," *Ecrits: A Selection*, trans. Alan Shridan (London: Tavistock, 1977), 301.

11. Sigmund Freud, "The Uncanny" (1919), *Standard Edition*, 17: 217–252.

12. Sigmund Freud, *The Interpretation of Dreams*, *Standard Edition*, 4: 509–511, 533–534; and Lacan, *The Four Fundamental Concepts*, 34, 56–60.

13. Freud, *Beyond the Pleasure Principle*, 14–17. The child was his daughter Sophie's son, who tragically died around the time of his writing this book. On the effects of this, see Elisabeth Bronfen, *Over Her Dead Body: Death, Femininity and the Aesthetic* (Manchester: Manchester University Press, 1992), 15 ff.

14. Hal Foster has dubbed this "traumatic realism." See Hal Foster, "Death in America," *October* 75 (Winter 1996): 37–60, and his "The Return of the Real," *The Return of the Real* (Cambridge, MA: MIT Press, 1996), 127–170.

15 15. Walter Benjamin, "Little History of Photography" (1931), *Selected Writings*, ed. Marcus Bullock, Michael Jennings, et al., Vol. 2, *1927–1934* (Cambridge, MA: Harvard/Belknap, 1999), 506–530; Walter Benjamin, "A Small History of Photography," *One-Way Street and Other Writings,* trans. Edmund Jephcott and Kingsley Shorter (London: Verso, 1979), 240–257. Barthes does mention Benjamin's "premonitory" "Work of Art" essay on photography in an interview from the late 1970s. See Roland Barthes, "On Photography," *The Grain of the Voice: Interviews 1962–80*, trans. Linda Coverdale (Berkeley: University of California Press, 1981), 354. **"Little History"** was first translated into French in 1971. Another text important for Barthes, but not discussed here, was Susan Sontag, *On Photography* (London: Penguin Books, 1978).

16. The pictures were the product of collaboration between Hill and Robert Adamson. See Mary Price, *The Photograph: A Strange Confined Space* (Stanford: Stanford University Press, 1994), 37.

17. Benjamin, "Little History of Photography," 510.

18. Ibid., 510. "Little History of Photography" is translated as "Petite histoire de la photographie" in *Études photographiques* 1 (November 1996) (available online). The scholarly footnotes (15 and 16) point out that the woman in the picture is in fact Karl Dauthendey's second wife, so it would seem that Benjamin has projected something quite "fantasmatic" onto the young woman's expression.

19. Ibid.

20. Rosalind Krauss, *The Optical Unconscious* (Cambridge, MA: MIT Press, 1993), 178–179. See her chapter 2 for a critical use of Lacan's theory of visuality. Her sense of the phrase, like mine, has to do with the way that artists find in the visual field an unconscious reality that is repressed or foreclosed in conscious thought.

21. Andrew Brown, *Roland Barthes: The Figures of Writing* (Oxford: Clarendon Press, 1992), 236–284. Many monographs are devoted to Barthes. I'll mention only Annette Lavers, *Roland Barthes: Structuralism and After* (London: Methuen, 1982); Michael Moriarty, *Roland Barthes* (Oxford: Polity, 1991); Steven Ungar, *Roland Barthes: The Professor of Desire* (Lincoln: University of Nebraska Press, 1983). See also Martin Jay, *Downcast Eyes: The Denigration of Vision in Twentieth-Century French Thought* (Berkeley: University of California Press, 1993), which has chapters devoted to Lacan and Barthes. For an excellent collection of critical essays, see Diana Knight, ed., *Critical Essays on Roland Barthes* (New York: Hall, 2000).

22. Sigmund Freud, "From the History of an Infantile Neurosis (The 'Wolf Man')" (1918 [1914]), *Standard Edition*, 17: 1–122, also in Pelican Freud Library, Vol. 9, *Case Histories II*, 227–366 (Harmondsworth: Penguin Books, 1979).

23. Roland Barthes, *A Lover's Discourse: Fragments,* trans. Richard Howard (New York: Hill and Wang, 1978).

24. Brown, *Roland Barthes*, 275–277.

25. Benjamin, "Little History of Photography," 517; Benjamin, "A Small History of Photography," 248.

26. Brown, *Roland Barthes*, 270; Sigmund Freud, *Moses and Monotheism: Three Essays* (1939), *Standard Edition*, 23: 3–132, Pelican Freud Library, Vol. 13, *The Origins of Religion*, 237–386.

27. Barthes uses the term "blind field" on page 57 of *Camera Lucida*. For an extended discussion of the concept, see Pascal Bonitzer, *Le champ aveugle: essais sur le cinéma* (Paris: Gallimard, 1982). See chapter 2 of Iversen, *Beyond Pleasure,* on Hopper and the blind field of painting. I originally wrote on the blind field in Edward Hopper's work: "In the Blind Field: Hopper and the Uncanny," *Art History* 21, no. 3 (September 1998): 409–429.

28. Jane Gallop, *Thinking through the Body* (New York: Columbia University Press, 1980), 151–155. See Norman Bryson's distinction in the chapter called "The Gaze and the Glance" of his *Vision and Painting: The Logic of the Gaze* (London: Macmillan, 1983), which has affinities with Barthes's *studium* and *punctum*.

29. Roland Barthes, "The Third Meaning: Research Notes on Some Eisenstein Stills," *Image/Music/Text,* trans. Stephen Heath (London: Fontana Press, 1977), 52–68. The theory of the *punctum* is more nearly approximated in a still earlier essay on photography, "The Photographic Message" (1961),

where Barthes considers the possibility of a photograph without connotation: "If such a [pure] denotation exists, it is perhaps not at the level of what ordinary language calls the insignificant, the neutral, the objective, but, on the contrary, at the level of absolutely traumatic images." in *Image/ Music/ Text,* 30.

30. Julia Kristeva, *Revolution in Poetic Language* (1974), trans. Margaret Waller (New York: Columbia University Prress, 1984), 17. See Victor Burgin, "Re-reading *Camera Lucida*" and his discussion of photography and *significance* in *The End of Art Theory: Criticism and Postmodernity* (London: Macmillan, 1986), 71–95.

31. Maurice Merleau-Ponty, *The Visible and the Invisible,* ed. Claude Lefort, trans. Alphonso Lingis (Evanston, IL: Northwestern University Press, 1968), 130–155.

32. This is why the *punctum* is volatile and subject to displacements. See Margaret Olin, "Touching Photographs: Roland Barthes's 'Mistaken' Identification," *Representations* 80 (Fall 2002): 99–118.

33. Malcolm Bowie, *Lacan* (London: Fontana, 1991), 169; Frank Stella, *Working Space* (Cambridge, MA: Harvard University Press, 1986), 6–9. Bataille's notion of *la tache aveugle* is also relevant here. See Denis Hollier's illuminating discussion of it in *Against Architecture: The Writings of Georges Bataille,* trans. Betsy Wing (Cambridge, MA: MIT Press, 1989), 94–98. See also Hollier's article on surrealist indexicality in "Surrealist Precipitates: Shadows Don't Cast Shadows," *October* 69 (Summer 1994): 111–132.

34. See my critique of this one-sided reception of the mirror stage in chapter 3 of Iversen, *Beyond Pleasure,* on Dalí and paranoia.

35. Joan Copjec reads the analysis of vision (and particularly the "sardine can" anecdote) in *The Four Fundamental Concepts* as a revised version of the mirror stage, which in some ways it clearly is. I am concerned, however, to preserve as distinct moments the mirror stage and the subject's relation to the real in the visible even if there are overlaps. Joan Copjec, "The Orthopsychic Subject: Film Theory and the Reception of Lacan," *October* 49 (Summer 1989): 53–71, reprinted in *Read My Desire: Lacan against the Historicists* (Cambridge, MA: MIT Press, 1994), 15–38. The anecdote is an interesting variation on the famous one told by Sartre in *Being and Nothingness,* to which Lacan refers, where a voyeur bent over a keyhole thinks he hears footsteps and is covered in shame. Jean-Paul Sartre, *Being and Nothingness: An Essay on Phenomenological Ontology,* trans. Hazel Barnes (London: Methuen, 1957), pt. 3, chap. 1, sec. 4, "The Look," 252–302. On this, see Stephen Melville, "Division of the Gaze, or, Remarks on the Color and Tenor of Contemporary 'Theory,'" *Seams: Art as a Philosophical Context* (Amsterdam: G&B Arts International, 1996), 111–129.

36. Lacan, *The Four Fundamental Concepts,* 184.

37. Lacan, *Écrits,* 315.

38. Roger Caillois, "Mimicry and Legendary Psychasthenia" (1935), trans. John Shepley, *October* 31 (Winter 1984): 17–32, reprinted in *October: The First Decade, 1976–1986* (Cambridge, MA: MIT Press, 1987), 58–75 (the citation is on p. 70), originally published as "Mimétisme et psychasthénie légendaire," *Minotaure* 7 (June 1935). See also Roger Caillois, *Méduse et cie* (Paris: Gallimard, 1960). For an interesting commentary, see Denis Hollier, "Mimesis and Castration, 1937," *October* 31 (1984): 3–15. Rosalind Krauss also makes this connection in her essay "Corpus Delicti," in Rosalind Krauss and James Livingstone, eds., *L'Amour Fou: Photography and Surrealism* (Washington, D.C.: Corcoran Art Gallery and New York: Abbeville Press, 1986), 57–144.

39. This strand of thought is part of Barthes's Lacanian inheritance, which in turn is informed by Heidegger's conception of authentic being as being toward death. See Jonathan Dollimore's excellent *Death, Desire and Loss in Western Culture* (London: Penguin Books, 1998).

40. Krauss, *The Optical Unconscious*, 33.

41. For a quite different interpretation of Lacan on painting, which confines it to the Apollonian function, see Jonathan Scott Lee, *Jacques Lacan* (Boston: Twayne, 1990), 159–161.

42. I am sorry to see that recent English editions of the book do not include the photograph by Daniel Boudinet called *Polaroid*, 1979.

Touching Photographs

Roland Barthes's "Mistaken" Identification

Margaret Olin

A photograph enjoys an unusually close relationship to its referent, according to a widespread theory about the nature of photography. As this theory would have it, the key moment in photography occurs when the shutter opens, allows light into the dark chamber within, and gives lasting representation to whatever is in front of its lens.[1] This view of photography, however, characteristically ignores another, equally important moment: the moment of identification. Someone must identify photographic images, group them according to various criteria, and place them together in photographic albums or art books.

The moment of identification, unlike that of illumination, does not distinguish photography from other visual images, or even from encounters in the world at large. At work in any personal exchange, identification plays an integral role in the formation of groups. Moreover, it is not just identification *of* a subject that is at stake but, often, identification *with* it.[2] The personal and social position through which the beholder is looking can bring what she or he sees into focus, or distort it beyond recognition. The encounter with an image might seem more one-sided than a meeting with a person, but it, too, is susceptible to the slippage between one kind of identification and the other. Whether scholars seek to avoid such slippages in their work, or to confront or exploit them, they disturb the simple relation between representations and subjects, between images and people, between photographs and their referents. Something had to be in front of the camera. Does it matter what?

Roland Barthes's last book, *Camera Lucida: A Note on Photography,* published in 1979, is grounded, ostensibly, in a statement of faith in a photograph's relation to its referent. The inseparability of referent and image that it seems to assume explains the extraordinary series of slippages between people and images; and between modes of identification that punctuate its exposition.[3] The Roland Barthes character in this book, as I will call his first-person exposition, lays out in two parts a theory of photographic reception on the basis of the adherence of the photograph to its referent.[4] Barthes (the author as opposed to the narrator of *Camera Lucida*) had developed a theory of photography based on its indexical nature in his 1964 essay "Rhetoric of the Image." That theory built on earlier writings about the nature of the modern "myth," in which Barthes examined everyday myths that support community identity: the Tour de France, the Eiffel Tower, the French menu.[5] "Rhetoric of the Image" examined photography's remarkable suitability for mythmaking through an ad for packaged pastas and sauces.[6] Italianicity, he wrote, was evoked by the name of the company, Panzani, and the color—red pepper, green tomatoes—of the Italian flag. A string bag with these vegetables tumbling out of it, along with packages of pasta and cans of sauce, evoked the idea of shopping in an open-air market and the cultural associations of still lifes and cornucopiae. But the fact that the ad was photographed, rather than drawn or painted, meant that these cultural and national associations seemed to come directly, naturally.

The naturalness of the associations came from the way photography represents its object: "although the Panzani poster is full of 'symbols,' there nonetheless remains in the photograph a kind of natural *being-there* of objects, insofar as the literal message is sufficient: nature seems to produce the represented scene quite spontaneously."[7] This "natural *being-there*" is Barthes's replacement for the usual term in such arguments, index, or indexical, borrowed loosely from Charles Peirce.[8] In Peirce, as in most discussions of photography, the *index* is opposed to the *icon,* which represents its object through resemblance. In relation to photography, similarity generally means visual resemblance: a photographed portrait, like a painted one, is an icon. An index, however, represents its object through contact: it points at its object, or it is itself a trace of, or mark made by, that object. A thumbprint is an index. Because the item had to be there for an indexical representation of it to exist, it is often thought that an index is inherently more persuasive than an icon. A photograph is both an icon and an index; it is like an icon with a seal of approval, or, as Barthes calls it, a "certificate of presence."[9] Because the pasta had to be there to be photographed, we feel as though we are looking at it directly, not through a representational medium. The connotation of Italianicity gets a free ride on indexicality; it seems to be in the photograph along with the green peppers. All this seeming natural gives the myth—that one can get Italianicity and freshness out of a can—its persuasive force.

Camera Lucida uses a different strategy to move in a more agonized direction, but it, too, starts with the idea of the photographic index. The person—and here it is most often people, and never pasta, who are the subject (I shall return to pasta later)—must have been there for a photograph to have been taken: "I call the 'photographic referent' not the *optionally* real thing to which an image or a sign refers but the *necessarily* real thing which has been placed before the lens, without which there would be no photograph."[10] The photograph, then, is a trace, a remnant, of the person who was there. The trace is tactile, like a footprint, or perhaps more accurately like a navel, given that in one passage Barthes describes photography as an umbilical cord.[11] In a description that draws on the imagery of a medieval theory, rays move from the subject of the photograph, to the sensitive plate, to the finished photograph and finally to the viewer of the photograph, who is literally touched (nourished?) by the photograph.[12] While the first part of *Camera Lucida* develops the theory through "random" looking at mostly famous photographs, the second part raises the personal stakes: it engages Barthes's grief for his recently deceased mother on the basis of a photograph of her when she was five years old. Because of this communication between the past and the present, a photograph has a memorial element, and relates directly to death, even if the person in question is alive still. Instead of the index that seemed to guarantee the myth, *Camera Lucida* dwells on the "That-has-been" of the photograph.[13]

The division into two parts may suggest a separation between mind and emotion, the scholarly versus the personal. But both parts are personal. In part one, Barthes bases his theory of photography on his search for photographs that "exist" for him. To explain the ways that photographs can "exist," he uses two Latin terms: *studium* and *punctum*. The *studium* denotes the field of its cultural or educational possibilities: emotion requires the "rational intermediary of an ethical and political culture."[14] This unitary "field" is pierced by the second element, the *punctum,* which breaks out of the cultural field and into the personal. It "shoots out of it like an arrow, and pierces me."[15] The *studium* is the "field" and the *punctum* is that which pierces the field.

The *punctum* is always personal to the viewer, and is often a detail, "Barthes" tells us. As an example, he illustrates a photographic portrait by the Harlem photographer James Van Der Zee. Thematically, Van Der Zee is close to the heart of *Camera Lucida.* He is known for *The Harlem Book of the Dead,* containing funerary photographs taken in the 1920s, published in 1978.[16] Roland Barthes may have seen it in New York on his visit there in November of that year.[17] If he did, the recently bereaved Barthes may have been struck, and perhaps horrified, especially by Van Der Zee's photographs of his own mother, both alive and after her death.

Barthes did not, however, use a photograph from the book of the dead to illustrate his notion of the *punctum* but a portrait of a family that was alive when Van Der Zee photographed them in his studio in 1926. Barthes describes the portrait's *studium* in the following language: its enunciation of "respectability, family life, conformism, Sunday best, an effort of social advancement in order to assume the White Man's attributes (an effort touching by reason of its naïveté)."[18] Given that the subject was the *studium,* its cultural field could have been literature of or about the exponents of the "New Negro," or he could have acquired his ideas about the context of the photograph in the course of reading the work of W. E. B. Dubois and others, who exhorted Negroes to emulate whites in order to be accepted by them.[19] Van Der Zee himself was engaged as an official photographer of Marcus Garvey's Universal Negro Improvement Association.[20] The "Sunday best" might actually have been "borrowed best," since Van Der Zee kept fashionable clothes on hand for clients with aspirations or imaginations beyond their means.[21] Such observations indicate directions for further investigations of this *studium.*

But actually, Barthes's *studium* was not very studious; he adapted his remarks from the commentary on the photograph in *Le nouvel observateur,* a special issue on photography that was the source for many of the photographs in *Camera Lucida.*[22] The commentary tries to do justice to the family's identity: "visibly American, and clearly something else."[23] The family is "desirous of giving itself an image conforming to the marks of prosperity of the American Way of Life."[24] At that time, according to the writer in *Le nouvel observateur,* "black is beautiful" was not a cry of defiance and despair.[25]

"Barthes's" judgment of the family's "naïveté" is no less problematic for the fact that both he and the editor of the French literary journal were viewing Van Der Zee's subjects from the Harlem of the 1920s through the lens of the American 1960s as seen from Paris in the 1970s. Why are the sitters naïve? To think that the acquisition of "Sunday best" and jewelry (or to have themselves photographed in such costumes), will make them like whites? Or are they naïve to think that whites will treat them better if they see them in such garb? Which attributes does Barthes mean? Why does Barthes take the "American Way of Life" to mean "attributs du Blanc," rather than attributes of the middle class, surely an aspiration of many of Van Der Zee's sitters, and entry into which a portrait by Van Der Zee may already have certified? Are there attributes that are more properly theirs, and that they could display if they were less touchingly naïve? What "*Imaginaire*" (image-system or repertoire, to use Barthes's expression) would they have created for themselves, had they chosen to construct their visual identities without the resources of Van Der Zee's studio?[26] Van Der Zee photographed more imaginatively costumed clients, but were they more authentic? To what image of blacks in Harlem should Van Der Zee's sitters have conformed? Why does Barthes call their identity into question? Do they misidentify themselves? What are they "by nature"?

I dwell on these questions because among Roland Barthes's early "mythologies of the month," were those in which he pointed out and deconstructed the myths that white people held of black people.[27] There he did not indulge in commonplaces about the "attributes of Whites" or "touching naïveté." To the Barthes of *Mythologies,* whites are just as naïve when they brandish their own attributes. The clue to "Barthes's" use of the term *naïveté* may be his use of the modifier "touching." That he finds the identification with whites not only interesting but "touching," suggests that the *studium* conveys feeling just as does the *punctum* and, therefore, that the difference between *studium* and *punctum* may just be a difference of degree. The *studium,* while it may touch Barthes, however, does not prick him. The *punctum* that punctures the field of the *studium* is "the belt worn low by the sister (or daughter)—the 'solacing Mammy'—whose arms are crossed behind her back like a schoolgirl, and above all her *strapped pumps* (Mary Janes—why does this dated fashion touch me? I mean: to what date does it refer me?). This particular *punctum* arouses great sympathy in me, almost a kind of tenderness."[28]

The detail that stabs him is actually two details; rather, one detail, around the waist, strikes Barthes first, but another detail becomes more convincing as his eye moves down toward the feet. But later, without the photograph to distract him, a third detail, above the others, comes to him, making this work by Van Der Zee the prime example of another quality of the *punctum:* it illustrates the way in which (like the experience of a Romantic poet, although Barthes does not make this connection) the true significance can often only be specified later, when the image, no longer there, has "*worked* within me."[29] Having moved from the spreading waist to the feet, he settled around the neck, and realized that the *punctum* in Van Der Zee's portrait was not a pair of shoes, not a belt, but a necklace. "I realized that the real *punctum* was the necklace she was wearing; for (no doubt) it was this same necklace (a slender ribbon of braided gold) which I had seen worn by someone in my own family, and which, once she died, remained shut up in a family box of old jewelry. . . . I had just realized that however immediate and incisive it was, the *punctum* could accommodate a certain latency (but never any scrutiny)."[30]

Never any scrutiny indeed. The reason that Barthes could only have recognized this *punctum* when he wasn't looking at it, is that the detail he picks out, the slender ribbon of braided gold, is not there. The lady wears a string of pearls, as does her seated relative. Most readers probably do not notice "Barthes's" mistake, since the Van Der Zee photograph is several pages into the past by the time Barthes recognizes the *punctum*. Possibly for this reason, few writers have commented on it, and those that do merely puzzle over it, remarking that it is, after all, personal, or chalking it up to the reproduction, where "it looks white and rather thick."[31]

In fact, the *punctum* does exist, but it is in a different photograph, which Barthes reproduced, along with several other photographs of his family, in *Roland Barthes / par Roland Barthes*. This mistaken detail, then, not the necklace actually pictured, led Barthes to the center of pain in the photograph, and to the time of the "strapped pumps." Indeed, the wearer of the necklace, Barthes's Aunt Alice, occupies the same place as Van Der Zee's "solacing Mammy" in the family picture, or at least in the picture of the family, and the composition of a photograph, not the pumps or the necklace on a real person, enabled him to make the identification. Presumably, Barthes recognized the family constellation, even though to do it he had to move the detail, the *punctum,* from one photograph to another.

Barthes's mistake may seem like a simple case of missing the forest for the trees. But the detail he thought he needed to search for was indeed important, if absent. His effort, then, illustrates other highly significant aspects of the *punctum:* the *punctum* may be the composition; the *punctum* may be forgotten; the *punctum* may be in a different photograph. The example illuminates an important aspect of memory: the deception at its heart, its ability to embroider and change, to be displaced, when it is "working on" one, like the details in a Freudian dream interpretation.[32] Not just the memory of whatever incident or person the *punctum* reminds one of, but memory of the photograph, the spur to memory, can itself enact this displacement. But the mistaken memory opens up the possibility of comprehension. When Barthes's memory replaced the pearls with the necklace that should have been there, the aunt who occupied the "solacing Mammy's" place magically appeared. This braided gold necklace was, perhaps, the *punctum* of Barthes's family photograph. He recognized, poignantly, the necklace he had seen his aunt wear and that lay, after her death, shut up inside a "family box," inside a dark chamber, rather than the light chamber, or camera lucida, of Barthes's title, a contrast to the better known camera obscura.[33] But perhaps Van Der Zee's portrait only reminded him of having seen the photograph of his aunt's family, and even the jewelry shut up in the family box had itself lived, for Barthes, only in a photograph. As Art Spiegelman wrote, concerning his attempt to use family photographs in his own work: "Snapshots illuminate my past like flares in the darkness. . . . Although often they only help me remember having seen the photos before!"[34]

Could Barthes's mistaken identification of the *punctum* illuminate his "mistake" (surely it was one) about the naïveté of the sitters in the *studium?* The naïveté he sees in the portrait can only be "touching" if the respectable family picture covers up a grimmer reality. It turns out that the touching naïveté he sees in the portrait, the respectable family life, indeed covers up the dreary life of a woman who, in her utter respectability, is utterly pitiable. But it is not the black family in Harlem whose naïveté is exposed. It is that of a white family in France, Barthes's family. "This sister of my father never married, lived as an old maid near her mother and it always distressed me to think of the sadness of her provincial life."[35] And whether or not the black family identified with white attributes, certainly Barthes identified his own family with the black family's attributes. He identified with their touchingly naïve, and mistaken, self-identification. But what is touching in someone else's family is wounding in one's own. Did Barthes understand these reversals, did he know that the necklace was not there? Surely Barthes, the author, understood. Otherwise, "Barthes" the narrator, would never have remarked parenthetically that the *punctum* will not bear any scrutiny, thus, perhaps slyly, warning readers not to turn back several pages to look at the picture.[36]

The concept of the *punctum* is further complicated with the introduction of a second source of *punctum* described as "the lacerating emphasis of the *noeme* ('*that-has-been*')," the pure representation of the passage of time that connotes death.[37] Any photograph has this about to die/already dead, quality, even if the subject is not dead—yet—and even though not all photographs will have this effect in the immediate sense that Barthes describes upon seeing a portrait by Alexander Gardner of a soon-to-be-executed would-be assassin.[38] The extreme example that causes the narrator the most pain is not that of a convict, however, but a photograph of his mother taken when she was a small child. He found it shortly after her death, while sorting photographs in search of one in which he could do more than recognize her, in which he would find "the truth of the face I had loved."[39] He found several pictures, some more characteristic than others, but one finally gave him what he was looking for. He christened it the "Winter Garden Photograph," because it was taken in a greenhouse.

My mother was five at the time (1898), her brother seven. He was leaning against the bridge railing, along which he had extended one arm; she, shorter than he, was standing a little back, facing the camera; you could tell that the photographer had said, "Step forward a little so we can see you"; she was holding one finger in the other hand, as children often do, in an awkward gesture.[40]

It is a pale, yellowed photograph; his mother's face, unclear, is in danger of disappearing altogether. Yet it was revealing. It showed "a figure of a sovereign *innocence*, . . . In this little girl's image I saw the kindness which had formed her being immediately and forever." Unlike the other photographs he discusses, he chooses not to reproduce this picture in his book, ostensibly because it would mean nothing to his readers.

But most likely there was no Winter Garden Photograph to reproduce, or perhaps only the one of Franz Kafka at the age of six, described, with its palm trees and Kafka's soulful eyes, as well as an oversized hat, by Walter Benjamin in his essay "A Short History of Photography."[41] Benjamin placed the setting tentatively in a "kind of winter garden landscape," but the French translation that appeared in *Le nouvel observateur*'s special issue on photography places Kafka definitively in a winter garden.[42] Like that of Barthes, Kafka's Winter Garden Photograph also remained unreproduced in this translation, but the editor illustrated the essay with several other photographs, among them Van Der Zee's portrait of a family.[43] If there was indeed no Winter Garden Photograph of Barthes's mother and uncle, then Benjamin's description inspired Barthes to reposition the photograph of the two children away from the frosty old grandfather of *La souche,* a family photograph Barthes provides later in *Camera Lucida,* and into a nurturing Winter Garden, where he could preserve his mother. The grandfather's large hat, like one Benjamin describes in Kafka's photograph, may have helped Barthes bridge the gap between the picture of Kafka and that of Barthes's mother. The resemblance between Barthes's described, but not reproduced, Winter Garden Photograph and *La souche* has until recently barely been remarked. Like the pearls that were exchanged for a slender ribbon, the distance between the description and the reproduction of the photograph may have disguised the resemblance for some, although here it is the photograph, rather than the description, that is delayed. The reader who reaches *La souche* with the faded Winter Garden Photograph firmly in mind may have been meant to smile knowingly, like a reader of a meandering novel who comes upon a sudden turn of events that forces a reconsideration of all that has gone before. If so, the author would have been disappointed had he lived to realize how few readers had done so. Not that the resemblance has completely escaped notice, even from the beginning. It has puzzled some readers, one of whom wonders why the Winter Garden Photograph was so much more powerful than this one, while another mistakes *La souche* for a portrait of Barthes's father.[44] Yet, when Diana Knight finally raised in print the likelihood that *La souche* is the Winter Garden Photograph, few readers were willing to follow this twist of the plot.[45]

Perhaps justifiably. Certainly there could have been a Winter Garden Photograph. Maybe whenever his mother and her brother posed, they automatically took the same positions, she nestling one finger in her other hand, standing back a bit, he, coming forward, leaning on and extending his hand on whatever was handy, railing or knee. They posed the same way wherever they were: at the end of a wooden bridge or at the end of a life; among the branches and palms of a flourishing winter garden, or around and between their grandfather, on the bare dirt of a garden in winter, with no trees except themselves, two offshoots of the *souche* (stock of tree, founder of a family), as Barthes calls the old man. But even if the Winter Garden Photograph was always in that chamber of light, where an unclouded vision could have seen it at any moment, what needed to be hidden, unlike Edgar Allen Poe's purloined letter, was not the photograph but its meaning.[46] The reader must be discouraged from wondering how this banal photograph could have inflicted such a wound, and the children must be placed in a winter garden, by themselves, not in the distracting company of this old man. "What relation can there be between my mother and her grandfather," he wrote, concerning this photograph, "so formidable, so monumental, so Hugolian, so much the incarnation of the inhuman distance of the Stock [*souche*]?"[47] Indeed, if *La souche* is the Winter Garden Photograph, then not only did the fabrication of the winter garden translate his mother's photograph to suit Barthes's metaphor of a bright room, it removed the inconvenient grandfather at the same time. The braided gold necklace should have been there; the old man should not. Man and necklace are present but absent. The *punctum* is the detail that is not there, or that one wishes were not there. Absence, in this book about loss, is presence. Like Jean-Paul Sartre's mental image in *L'imaginaire,* to which *Camera Lucida* is dedicated, the *punctum* is "a certain way an object has of being absent within its very presence," or perhaps present within its absence.[48] The *punctum*'s Lacanian counterpoint is the gaze that traps the eye.[49]

But the displacement of the detail is just as Freudian as it is Lacanian. And the detail is displaced here, just as in the photograph by James Van Der Zee. Barthes emphasizes his mother's look of sovereign innocence as the picture's distinguishing mark. He mentions, however, other details in the picture as well, for example, that "awkward gesture" of his mother's, "holding one finger in the other hand, as children often do." How often do children make that gesture after all? Perhaps they do every day, although a search through several generations of my own family photographs failed to turn up any examples of it. Assuming there really was a Winter Garden Photograph, then Barthes's mother presumably made that gesture more than once. That would make a minimum of three such gestures in Roland Barthes's family album, two by Barthes's mother and one by Barthes himself as a small child, published by Barthes in *Roland Barthes.* Perhaps here, as supposedly in the portrait by James Van Der Zee, the *punctum* is a detail. In the Winter Garden Photograph, Roland Barthes discovered not his mother, or not only his mother, but also himself, himself as a child, specifically as a child known from photographs. A chain of photographs leads Barthes, searching from image to image, to the unexpected discovery of himself as his own mother, just as he had been his mother's mother while he cared for her during her last illness.[50]

But he was Aunt Alice as well. How different was this woman, who never married but lived alone near her mother all her life, from Barthes himself, who, as he does not fail to tell us later in the book, lived alone with his mother until her death, two years before his own? In *Camera Lucida* he wrote that, in certain photographs, he had his "father's sister's look."[51] They have been compared by Diana Knight, the perceptive observer of several of the anomalies of Barthes's favorite photographs, because "between them [they] incarnate the termination of the paternal line."[52] Indeed, although they were both unfertile limbs of the family tree, what struck Barthes about her was her loneliness, not her lack of progeny. "The father's sister: she was alone all her life," reads the caption of a portrait of Alice in *Roland Barthes.*[53] Did the graceful portrait of Alice with her parents on the preceding page cover up the sadness exposed in her childhood portrait? The portrait of Barthes as a young man also sparks an insight into "*l'irréductible*" in himself: "in the child, I read quite openly the dark underside of myself," an original darkness that inhabits the man as well.[54]

The displacement of the *punctum* leads to another, less personal, meaning of the Winter Garden Photograph that its absence disguises. If the *punctum* is displaced, like an alibi, then the detail that is not there, the "that-has-been," never was. And neither was the indexical power of the photograph. The fact that something was before the camera when the photograph was taken is no longer unproblematically the source of the photograph's power. I do not imply that *Camera Lucida* would suffer if the Winter Garden Photograph turned out to be an invention. To the reader of *Camera Lucida* it should matter little whether it existed or not.[55] The fictional truth of the unseen Winter Garden Photograph is powerful enough to survive its possible nonexistence, just as the missing necklace of Van Der Zee's sitter only gains in power through its misplacement in a similarly novelistic turn. But the fact that it does not matter has consequences for any theory of photographic indexicality. To raise the possibility that these images do not exist, and to realize how little their existence matters is to cast this founding concept into question. The fact that something is in front of the camera matters; what that something was does not. What matters is displaced.

Barthes's identification of the irreducible does matter. Barthes's sadness and that of his aunt Alice, like his mother's transparent simplicity, shone through their childhood photographs. Just as the Italianicity and euphoria of Panzani appear to be directly represented in the ad through the indexicality of the photograph, so Barthes's irreducible darkness, his sister's loneliness, and the kindness that had formed his mother's being, were visible in their youthful photographs. The photograph is traced to an originary being in front of the camera, and the person is traced to an originary childhood. One sees right through the pasta to its Italian ethnicity. A child, no more able than a vegetable to disguise its essence, reveals the "irreducible" just as indexically as the Panzani vegetables reveal their Italianicity. With one difference: the telling details, whose presence before the camera guarantees the authenticity of the ad, are absent. Essence is not guaranteed.

Yet the pain is there, even when the necklace is not. If the immense power of the photograph does not come from that which was in front of the camera, it lies elsewhere. To find it, we can look in the network of identifications that these photographs establish. They begin with Barthes's family, but they go beyond it as well. If Barthes identifies with Aunt Alice, then in a cross-gender, cross-Atlantic, interracial identification, through his tender care of his mother become daughter, he is also the "solacing Mammy" in Van Der Zee's photograph, the woman who "on account of her necklace," had, for Barthes, "a whole life external to her portrait."[56] Barthes's aunt gave him piano lessons on his boyhood visits to the provinces, and he went to stay with her after the death of her own mother, Barthes's grandmother.[57] But when Barthes's mother died, his aunt was not there to solace him, her necklace already encased in a "family box."

Barthes's "identification" of these people links multiple photographs in a chain of identificatory relationships. His community of photographs that "exist" for him links his family to a series of strangers. But as an encounter with either a portrait or a family, Barthes's encounter with Van Der Zee's sitters, like most encounters in this tragic narrative, is at best missed. In order to make the sitters part of his family, he emptied their identity of everything but their status as representatives of a marginalized class open to assimilation by the narrator. Indeed, marginalized figures take up a large share of the illustrations in *Camera Lucida,* including among its twenty-five photographs, a gypsy, retarded people, a condemned man, slum children from Little Italy, three African-Americans including Van Der Zee's sitters, and an African. These subjects were perhaps important objects of identification for Barthes, who enumerated most of his own claims to marginal status in *Roland Barthes*.[58] There may have been a wishful element as well. Barthes could well have interpreted the black woman's stance, and her fashionable clothes of the 1920s, as displaying a self possession that he could well have wished for his aunt.[59] Barthes's relation to the lady in her Sunday best is one-sided, misleading, and unknowable, but poignant and meaningful all the same. The rhetorical analyst Barthes, of an earlier moment, would have unmasked his comments about this picture as an example of mythological thinking; the earlier Barthes, however, wrote essays. *Camera Lucida,* as I have tried to show, is not an essay. Rather than expose the naïveté that makes pasta ads effective, he places himself "in the situation of a naïve man, outside culture, someone untutored who would be constantly astonished at photography."[60]

This naïve viewer is perhaps everyone when photography enters the delicate sphere of human relations. Relations to people can be as one-sided as relations to photographs. Even people do not determine our response to them through preexisting essences. We endow them with attributes we need them to have, hang gold ribbons around their necks when they would prefer pearls. One might say that not only do we misidentify them, we misidentify *with* them. A reading of *Camera Lucida* suggests that the most significant indexical power of the photograph may consequently lie not in the relation between the photograph and its subject but in the relation between the photograph and its beholder, or user, in what I would like to call a "performative index," or an "index of identification." *Camera Lucida* allows us to see its narrator use photography to satisfy his desire to possess or commune with his mother, to absorb her into himself and preserve her there through his identification with her. Photography is a winter garden, like a *chambre claire* that lets in light in the winter and keeps alive artificially that which should otherwise have died.

The narrator of *Camera Lucida* performs, rather than argues, the meeting in the winter garden because he, like many an art historian or critic, is caught up in the rhetoric of proof and existence, the truth of his mother's face. He looks for what a photograph is "in itself."[61] But an "in itself," a "truth," could only have been an external guarantee of the relation that was his goal, a relation established, like most relations, with no guarantees at all.

NOTES

I am grateful to members of audiences in Amsterdam, Houston, and Los Angeles, whose perceptive questioning of my presentations enabled me to develop my ideas; to the students in my seminars at the School of the Art Institute over the last nine years for reading and rereading Barthes with me; and to Katherine Bergeron for her insightful reading for this journal.

1. I refer to a widespread position. It has been critiqued many times, however, for example long ago by Joel Snyder and Neil Walsh Allen, in "Photography, Vision, and Representation," *Critical Inquiry* 2 (1975): 143–169, and as recently as William J. Mitchell, *The Reconfigured Eye: Visual Truth in the Post-Photographic Era* (Cambridge, Mass., 1992).

2. An important example of the growing literature on identification is Diana Fuss, *Identification Papers* (New York, 1975).

3. Roland Barthes, *La chambre Claire: Note sur la photographie* (Paris, 1980); translated as *Camera Lucida: Notes on Photography,* trans. Richard Howard (New York, 1981). I will cite the English translation, sometimes amended (henceforth abbreviated *CL,* page references to the French edition immediately following those of the U.S. edition). A good deal has been written about Barthes's interest in photography. Besides the sources mentioned below, see especially, Jean Delord, *Roland Barthes et la photographie* (Paris, 1981); Nancy M. Shawcross, *Roland Barthes on Photography: The Critical Tradition in Perspective* (Gainesville, Fla., 1997); and the essays in Jean-Michel Rabaté, ed., *Writing the Image After Roland Barthes* (Philadelphia, Pa., 1997).

4. In two excellent essays, Johnnie Gratton has explored the staging of Barthes's individuality in *Camera Lucida.* Johnnie Gratton, "The Subject of Enunciation in Roland Barthes's *Camera Lucida,*" in Diana Knight, ed., *Critical Essays on Roland Barthes* (New York, 2000), 266–278; and Johnnie Gratton, "Text, Image, Reference in Roland Barthes's *La Chambre Claire,*" *Modern Language Review* 91 (1996): 355–364. I will place Barthes's name in quotation marks when I believe the reader is in danger of taking the narrator of *Camera Lucida*—unproblematically—for the writer Roland Barthes.

5. Most of them were originally published primarily in the journal *Les lettres nouvelles,* beginning in 1953. They were collected in Roland Barthes, *Mythologies* (Paris, 1957). A smaller number were translated in Roland Barthes, *Mythologies,* trans. Annette Lavers (New York, 1972).

6. Roland Barthes, "Rhetoric of the Image" (1964), in Roland Barthes, *The Responsibility of Forms: Critical Essays on Music, Art, and Representation,* trans. Richard Howard (New York, 1985), 21–40.

7. Barthes, "Rhetoric of the Image," 34, original emphasis.

8. I use C. S. Peirce's terms because they are used more consistently in art historical analysis, even though Peirce's argument is actually thereby distorted. See C. S. Peirce, "Logic as Semiotic: The Theory of Signs," in *Philosophical Writings of Peirce,* ed. Justus Buchler (New York, 1955), 98–119; Michael Leja, "Peirce, Visuality, and Art," *Representations* 72 (2000): 97–122. Barthes also uses the terms *metaphor* and *metonymy* to mean roughly what is designated by the terms *icon* and *index.* For an example of the use of Peirce, see Rosalind Krauss, "Notes on the Index," in *The Originality of the Avant-Garde and other Modernist Myths* (Cambridge, Mass., 1985), 196–219. More recently, Carol Armstrong described the photograph as "first and foremost an indexical sign—that is, an image that is chemically and optically caused by the things in the world to which it refers"; Carol Armstrong, *Scenes in a Library: Reading the Photograph in the Book, 1843–1975* (Cambridge, Mass., 1998), 2.

9. *CL,* 87/135.

10. *CL,* 76/120, original emphasis.

11. *CL,* 81/126–127.

12. *CL,* 80–81/126. On the medieval theory of visual rays, which involved the controversy between intromission (Barthes's assumption) and extramission, see David C. Lindberg, *Theories of Vision from Al-Kindi to Kepler* (Chicago, 1976), 61–85. Kenneth Scott Calhoon also effectively reveals the haptic rhetoric in *Camera Lucida;* Kenneth Scott Calhoon, "Personal Effects: Rilke, Barthes, and the Matter of Photography," *Modern Language Notes* 113, no. 3 (1998): 612–634, esp. 612–618.

13. *CL,* 77/120–121. In the French edition, this essence is referred to, in Latin, as the "*interfuit,*" and in French, as the "*Ça-a-été.*" I plan to develop the memorial character in the beholding of images further, in an expansion of the present essay.

14. *CL,* 26/48.

15. *CL,* 26/49.

16. James Van Der Zee, Owen Dodson, Camille Billops, *The Harlem Book of the Dead* (Dobbs Ferry, N.Y., 1978).

17. Louis-Jean Calvet, *Roland Barthes: A Biography,* trans. Sarah Wykes (Bloomington, Ind., 1994), 233.

18. *CL,* 43/73.

19. See Henry Louis Gates Jr., "The Face and Voice of Blackness," in *Facing History: The Black Image in American Art, 1710–1940* (San Francisco, 1990), xxix–xlvi; and Henry Louis Gates Jr., "The Trope of a New Negro and the Reconstruction of the Image of the Black," *Representations* 24 (1988): 129–155. See also Melville J. Herskovits, "The Negro's Americanism," in Alain Locke, ed., *The New Negro* (1925; reprint, New York, 1969), 353–360; and other essays in this important collection of the movement.

20. Roger C. Birt, "A Life in American Photography," in *Van Der Zee: Photographer, 1886–1983,* ed. Deborah Willis-Braithwaite (New York, 1998), 46–48.

21. Ibid., 44–45.

22. Barthes lists his photographic sources in the French edition only. Barthes, *La chambre claire,* 187.

23. [Robert Delpire?], in *Le nouvel observateur,* Special Photo 2, ed. Robert Delpire (1977), 19.

24. Ibid.

25. Ibid.

26. Barthes uses the concept of an "*Imaginaire*" (translated "image repertoire" in *CL*, 11/25) and Roland Barthes, *Roland Barthes/par Roland Barthes* (1975), 2d ed. (Paris, 1995), 98–99. In the English translation "imaginaire" is rendered "image system"; Roland Barthes, *Roland Barthes by Roland Barthes,* trans. Richard Howard (New York, 1977), 105. Hereafter the U.S. edition of this work will be cited, with references to the French edition immediately following. The concept echoes ideas in Jean-Paul Sartre, *L'imaginaire: psychologie-phénoménologique de l'imagination* (Paris, 1940); translated as *The Psychology of Imagination* (New York, 1948). Barthes dedicates *La chambre claire* "In Homage To *L'Imaginaire* by Jean-Paul Sartre."

27. For example, Roland Barthes, "Bichon and the Blacks," in *The Eiffel Tower and Other Mythologies,* trans. Richard Howard (New York, 1979), 35–38. The essay appeared in the original French edition of *Mythologies.*

28. *CL,* 43/73–74, original emphasis.

29. *CL,* 53/87, italics in the English translation only.

30. *CL,* 53/87–88.

31. Derek Attridge writes, in a footnote, "It is Barthes who identifies the necklace as a 'slender ribbon of braided gold': one cannot see this in the reproduction, where it looks white and rather thick—and identical to the other necklace in the picture, from which no *punctum* shoots. This discrepancy is of no account, however; even if we did see what Barthes describes, we would remain impervious to the *punctum's* laceration"; Attridge, "Roland Barthes's Obtuse, Sharp Meaning and the Responsibilities of Commentary," in Rabaté, *Writing the Image After Roland Barthes,* 88 n. 4. Diane Knight refers to "the supposed retrospective punctum of her necklace"; Knight, *Barthes and Utopia: Space, Travel, Writing* (Oxford, 1997), 263.

32. Sigmund Freud, *The Standard Edition of the Complete Works of Sigmund Freud,* vol. 4, *The Interpretation of Dreams* (1899), trans. James Strachey (London, 1953), 277–309.

33. The "camera lucida" is contrasted to the "camera obscura" in chapter 44 of *CL,* 106/164.

34. Art Spiegelman, "Mein Kampf (My Struggle)," in *The Familial Gaze,* ed. Marianne Hirsch (Hanover, N.H., 1999), 100.

35. *CL,* 53/88, translation slightly revised.

36. The French author Georges Perec records a subjective mistake concerning a family photograph in a novel originally published in 1975. His narrator records his own mistake, however. Barthes, perhaps intentionally, allows the reader to find his narrator's mistake; Georges Perec, *W, or the Memory of Childhood,* trans. David Bellow (Boston, 1988), 27 and 33 n. 1. I am grateful to my student Timothy Straveler for the reference to Perec.

37. *CL,* 96/148.

38. Ibid., 96/148–150.

39. Ibid., 67/106.

40. Ibid., 67–69/106.

41. Walter Benjamin, "Kleine Geschichte der Photographie" (1931), in *Gesammelte Schriften,* ed. Rolf Tiedemann and Hermann Schweppenhäuser, vol. 2, bk. 1 (Frankfurt, 1977), 375; translated as "A Short History of Photography," trans. P. Patton, in *Classic Essays on Photography,* ed. Alan Trachtenberg (New Haven, Conn., 1980), 206.

42. Walter Benjamin, "Les analphabetes de l'avenir," *Le nouvel observateur,* Special Photo 2 (1977), 16.

43. *Le nouvel observateur,* Special Photo 2 (1977), 19.

44. Carol Armstrong, "From Clementina to Käsebier: The Photographic Attainment of the 'Lady Amateur,'" *October* 91 (2000): 106; and Ralph Sarkonak, "Roland Barthes and the Spectre of Photography," *L'esprit créateur* 22 (1982): 56–57. Liliane Weissberg assumes that "The Stock" is "open to speculation: it may represent the author's family and it may not"; Weissberg, "Circulating Images: Notes on the Photographic Exchange," in Rabaté, *Writing the Image After Roland Barthes,* 113.

45. Knight raises the issue in *Barthes and Utopia,* 265–66. See, for an example of a response, the rather hesitant reference to Knight's "suggestion" in Attridge, "Roland Barthes's Obtuse, Sharp Meaning," 86 and 89 n. 9. It never seriously occurred to me that there really was a Winter Garden Photograph, but, like Knight, I have had mixed success convincing others.

46. Diana Knight refers to Edgar Allen Poe in relation to the Winter Garden Photograph, *Barthes and Utopia,* 266. Barthes used the Poe story as a parable relating to the concealment of meaning; Daniel Ferrer, "Genetic Criticism in the Wake of Barthes," in Rabaté, *Writing the Image After Roland Barthes,* 225.

47. *CL,* 105/163–64, translation slightly amended.

48. Sartre, *Psychology of Imagination,* 104.

49. Margaret Iversen brings out Lacanian elements in Barthes, including that of the important relation to Lacan's discussion of the gaze; Margaret Iversen, "What is a photograph?" *Art History* 17 (1994): 450–63. See also Jacques Lacan, *The Four Fundamental Concepts of Psycho-Analysis,* ed. Jacques-Alain Miller, trans. Alan Sheridan (New York, 1977), 65–119.

50. *CL,* 72/112.

51. Ibid., 103/161.

52. Knight, *Barthes and Utopia,* 264.

53. Barthes, *Roland Barthes by Roland Barthes,* 14/20.

54. Ibid., 22/28. In the U.S. edition, a slight change in spacing made the caption for this photograph look as though it went with a different photograph, of Barthes as a toddler.

55. Although to some in the audiences to which I have spoken it has mattered a lot.

56. *CL,* 57/90–91.

57. Calvet, *Roland Barthes,* 43.

58. Barthes, *Roland Barthes by Roland Barthes,* 131/118.

59. This speculation is my response to a series of astute observations on the photographs by Sally Stein.

60. Roland Barthes, *The Grain of the Voice: Interviews 1962–1980,* trans. Linda Coverdale (New York, 1985), 357.62. *CL,* 3/13.

61. *CL,* 3/13.

Buddha Barthes

What Barthes Saw in Photography (That He Didn't in Literature)

Jay Prosser

Roland Barthes's last book is on photography and it is about the limits of words. The last word in it goes to Chögyam Trungpa, in which the Tibetan Buddhist writer discusses the response of a lama to the loss of his son. "Marpa was very upset when his son was killed, and one of his disciples said, 'You used to tell us that everything is illusion. How about the death of your son? Isn't it illusion?' And Marpa replied, 'True, but my son's death is a super-illusion.'"[1] Like a *koan,* the question and answer between master and student in Zen Buddhism, the anecdote is designed less to explain the truth than provoke an awakening to truth words conventionally cover over. The truth of a *koan* "cannot be understood by logic; it cannot be transmitted in words; it cannot be explained in writing; it cannot be measured by reason."[2] In response to the *koan* Barthes had written earlier that we should try "not to solve it, as if it had a meaning, nor even to perceive its absurdity (which is still a meaning), but to ruminate it 'until the tooth falls out.'"[3] Marpa's response has itself dropped out for readers of the English translation of *La chambre claire.* It doesn't appear in *Camera Lucida,* inside the text or as it does in the French version on the rear cover. Beginning with the dropped out words of one Buddhist lama recalled by another Buddhist lama allows us to ruminate on the importance of Buddhism for Barthes. At the end of his life Buddhism leads him to a reality in photography that had eluded him in his life in literature. Almost at the point of death, Barthes finds in photography a reality beyond words: a revelation of death.

Buddhism infuses particularly "late" Barthes, the personal yet elliptical turn his work took in his last five years. In the book prior to *Camera Lucida* it is used to name the turnings of the mind and their cessation or blowing out, in the words Barthes borrows from the Sanskrit for the sufferings of love in *A Lover's Discourse,* "vritti" and "nirvana."[4] Before this it appears in *Roland Barthes by Roland Barthes,* where the Zen fragment or "torin," the "method of abrupt, separated, broken openings," is claimed as the model for Barthes's own fragmented form.[5] The thematically explicit Buddhist text is *Empire of Signs,* which was inspired by a visit to Japan in 1966 and repeated visits over the next year. It depicts Japan as a "system," in its art, rituals, and cultural expressions archetypically Zen in exemption from meaning (*ES* 3). In Japan the "centre is empty (*ES* 30)." Representation is "a suspension of language . . . which erases in us the reign of codes" (*ES* 75), "an escheat of signification (78)." The haiku is emblematic of the emptying of discourse: "*it's that, it's thus,* says the haiku, *it's so.* Or better still: *so! (ES* 83)." Barthes finds in Japan an opposition to the Western metaphysical tradition of representation in which the centre holds meaning, often uncovered through rational discourse—what he hopes will be "The Destruction of the West."[6] Yet Barthes turns Japan into discourse, a system made up of signification in its food, city organization, theatre. It becomes another sign in Barthes's growing empire of signs as a semiotician. *Empire of Signs* is above all an eloquent book, more in keeping with the semiotic virtuosity of *The Fashion System* and *Elements of Semiology* with which it is contemporary than the later word-faltering phase.[7] Like other Western writers travelling to the East to escape Western discourse, Barthes leaves out the emptiness at the heart of form in Buddhism that would stop explanation. Luce Irigaray's attempt to reverse the West's "cleverness of technique" with the yogic breath is another recent theoretical example.[8] Such "Buddhist modernism" as it has been called has been a danger since Western colonial officials began translating the Pali canon that introduced the Buddha's words to the West.[9]

In *Empire of Signs* Buddhism is most present in the photographs, which the prefatory note tells us do not "illustrate" the text but create "the onset of a kind of visual uncertainty" or the "loss of meaning Zen calls a *satori (ES* xi)." In them or rather in the "interlacing" of text and image we are supposed to "read the retreat of signs (*ES* xi)." It's telling that the text needs to tell us this, as if to be certain that we'll see the uncertainty. The note undoes itself by elevating the verbal sign precisely to the level of "gloss" or meaning the note denies. Nevertheless Barthes compares the satori, the sudden awakening or enlightenment in Zen Buddhism, to a photograph, to "a flash, a slash of light: *When* [Barthes quotes Shakespeare] *the light of sense goes out, but with a flash that has revealed the invisible world; . . . it is the* flash of a photograph one takes very carefully . . . but having neglected to load the camera with film (*ES* 84)." In *Camera Lucida* Barthes loads the film into the camera and works the analogy the other way round. Now the photograph is like the haiku in an "immense immobility."[10] In this *Note sur la photographie,* his sustained meditation on photography, Barthes pays attention to the emptiness at the heart of form.

The emptiness revealed by the form of photography has been recognised by two recent books linking Taoism and photography.[11] Photography's focus concentrates the mind, like the one-pointedness of meditation, or *samadhi*. As the most instantaneous medium it draws attention to the present moment. It literalises observation while putting in the background the mediating powers of the artist-ego. Above all photography is not language and as such lends itself to the ineffable that has been the object of mystics in every world religion. For in the opening lines of the *Tao Te Ching,* "The tao that can be told is not the eternal Tao."[12] Or as Wittgenstein puts it in a similar definition of mysticism at the end of his *Tractatus Logico-Philosophicus,* "There are, indeed, things that cannot be put into words. They *make themselves manifest.* They are what is mystical."[13] What is notable about Wittgenstein's extraordinary turn away from logical positivism is the faith that the mystical will nevertheless manifest in the visual (Wittgenstein himself has been thought to have albeit inadvertent connections to Buddhism).[14] Taoism prepared the way for the reception of Buddhism in China where it would form Ch'an Buddhism, which as it migrated to Japan mutated to Zen. *Ch'an* means "meditation" and like the *Tao* or "way" in Taoism offers a similarly direct access to reality, not by means of reason, narration, explanation—language. As Zen evolved, the skilful arts of direct access to reality flourished: along with the haiku and *koan* in Japan, brush-stroke painting, calligraphy, archery, and gardening were perfected.[15] With such arts produced simply and with one-pointed mind, the superfluity of the sign was reduced, form emptied. It is natural that Barthes should be attracted to the Zen tradition in making the connection between photography and Buddhism.

Camera Lucida is Barthes's most felt Buddhist text, more than *Empire of Signs, Roland Barthes by Roland Barthes,* and *A Lover's Discourse.* Barthes's texts become more Buddhist perhaps corresponding to his discursive explanations dropping out. The essence Barthes finds in photography which he calls *punctum,* the poignant detail that wounds us about photography, is referenced with the pointing in Zen Buddhism. "In order to designate reality, Buddhism says *sunya,* the void; but better still: *tathata,* as Alan Watts has it, the fact of being thus, of being so; *tat* means *that* in Sanskrit and suggests the gesture of the child pointing (*CL* 5)." Barthes had read Alan Watts's *The Way of Zen* by this main conduit of Zen in the West in the 1960s and 1970s and cites it in his bibliography (also not translated in *Camera Lucida*). In Watts "*nama-rupa* or 'name-and-form,' the signs we use to classify our world, are said to be ultimately void."[16] At the heart of *nama-rupa* is *sunyata,* the emptiness of form. In the gesture of the child pointing at that nothing Barthes reverses his previous writings on photography. These serve as an index to his career but had always been about form. In the fifties at the beginning of his career Barthes was the mythologist analysing the mythology or ideology of the photograph in contexts such as Edward Steichen's anthropological exhibition, "The Family of Man."[17] In the sixties as a semiologist and structuralist he read the "rhetoric of the image"—the title he gave to an essay which is exemplary in treating photography as a linguistic-like structure made up of Saussurean "signifieds" and "signifiers."[18] Then the poststructuralist Barthes in the seventies placed photographs at the beginning of his autobiography, *Roland Barthes by Roland Barthes,* now revealingly in excess of the signifier, in the margins of the unravelling linguistic structures, marker that Barthes's empire was becoming undone. Yet Barthes's attraction to photography was not in spite of but because of its diremption of meaning from the sign. Though he had made analysis of signs his career he had sought since his first book a cessation of signification, what he called then the zero degree and which he here so blatantly doesn't recover in literature.[19]

He first recognises what is distinct about photography in an essay published in 1961 from the same structuralist era as "The Rhetoric of the Image." Yet while "The Photographic Message" is a self-declared "structuralist analysis," it is important for showing how photography is a "structural paradox," a paradox for structuralism.[20] Like any other text analysed by structuralists, photography works according to various "connotation procedures," the text/ captions, photographic composition and layout in publication that seek to "connote" the photographic message (*IMT* 20). On the other hand photography "transmit[s] . . . literal reality," is a "perfect *analogon*" of the thing represented and hence "*it is a message without a code* (*IMT* 17)." The code is "not strictly part of the photographic structure (*IMT* 20)." And yet—and here's the paradox—Barthes writes that we cannot isolate denotation that is the essential state of photography. The message can only be accessed through linguistic signifiers. Toward the end of the essay, however, Barthes foretells in an eerie prophecy what might enable him to point to an empty form that is photography:

These few remarks sketch a kind of differential table of photographic connotations, showing, if nothing else, that connotation extends a long way. Is this to say that a pure denotation, a this-side-of language, is impossible? If such a denotation exists, it is perhaps not at the level of what ordinary language calls the insignificant, the neutral, the objective, but on the contrary at the level of absolutely traumatic images. The trauma is a suspension of language, a blocking of meaning. (IMT *30)*

Camera Lucida is famously preceded by the trauma of Barthes's own life. It is the trauma of losing his mother that propels his return to photography to seize on the "this-side-of-language" that it is. Henriette Binger Barthes died in October 1977. Barthes had already promised to write a short piece for *Les cahiers du cinema* on photography, his biographer notes. *Camera Lucida,* the book-length essay written almost at one sitting in early 1979, is the result.[21] The single book that Barthes had left in him turns out to be about his mother's loss through photography. In *Camera Lucida* he says he wanted "to write a little compilation about her, just for myself (*CL* 63)." The second part of *Camera Lucida*'s two-part structure begins with the scene of Barthes's loss, enacted through photographs. "Now, one November evening shortly after my mother's death, I was going through some photographs. I had no hope of 'finding' her . . . I had acknowledged that fatality, one of the most agonising features of mourning, which decreed that however often I might consult such images, I could never recall her features (summon them up as a totality) (*CL* 63)." He catches her in fragments, "which is to say that I missed her *being,* and that therefore I missed her altogether (*CL* 66)." In photographs he searches for her, "gradually moving back in time with her, looking for the truth of the face I had loved. And I found it" (*CL* 67)—momentarily in the famous Winter Garden Photograph that shows his mother as a child in front of a winter garden, or conservatory. But looking at the Winter Garden Photograph Barthes does not get over his loss. He has "nothing to say," exactly like Zen according to Watts and corresponding to melancholia in Freud's famous distinction between mourning and melancholia.[22] "The horror is this: nothing to say about the death of one whom I love most, nothing to say about her photograph . . . I have no other recourse than this *irony:* to speak of the 'nothing to say' (*CL* 93)." The Winter Garden Photograph is therefore not reproduced in the book, the empty sign. Instead Barthes writes the reason he can't reproduce it, itself in parenthesis as if outside whatever is essayistic about these "Reflections on Photography": it would be part of our "*studium,*" or codes or connotation to be studied; "(. . . but in it, for you, no wound) (*CL* 73)." Etymologically *punctum* is "pricking" or "puncturing," as *trauma* is "wounding."

What photography's flash, its slash of light, illuminates is time. The *punctum* is wounding because it points at lost time, not that can be recovered in Proustian writerly memory—there is "nothing Proustian in a photograph (*CL* 82)," Barthes writes—but because it points to what is intractably, irremediably gone. Barthes revises *punctum* from direct pointing to direct pointing at what is over. The tense of photography is in *La chambre claire* preterite: "*Ça-a-été*" (*CL* 120), "*interfuit*" (*CL* 121). Light and time are photography's elements, as indeed enlightenment and attention to the present moment might be thought of as Buddhism's. *Punctum* corresponds in Barthes's apprehension with the definition of satori he gives, "at once the past and the real (*CL* 82)." Photography's emptiness is hooked into death. Death is literally in many of the photographs of *Camera Lucida,* such as in "sheet carried by the weeping mother" around the corpse of a child in Nicaragua (*CL* 24). But *every* photograph presents death, every photograph reveals "He is dead and he is going to die (*CL* 95)," for "the Photograph always carries its referent with itself . . . like the condemned man and the corpse" (*CL* 5–6); like Barthes carrying his dead mother. "In Photography, the presence of the thing (at a certain past moment) is never metaphoric . . . if the photograph then becomes horrible, it is because it certifies, so to speak, that the corpse is alive, as *corpse:* it is the living image of the dead (*CL* 78–79)." The *tathata,* thus-goneness, is what Buddhism illuminates about time, for it is the non-solidity of objects and their constant transience that make the centre empty, and name and form, *nama-rupa,* which Barthes concentrated on before, a retroactive attempt to give solidity to fluidity and emptiness—delusively. Consciousness is a five-step process of *skandhas,* "heaps" or "groups," in which emptiness is transformed into form, giving the illusion of solidity of self and separateness of other. The failure to perceive the reality of emptiness is the cause in Buddhism of our suffering—our desire for what we think we do not have, our loss for what we thought we had; our not wanting what we have. Barthes in his suffering, his trauma, has a tantric-like transformation. On tantra, transforming energy, Trungpa writes one must be an "open wound."[23] This is not a system, the mastery of form of *Empire,* but beyond perfect control. Buddhism is not a theory (modernism) but a practice and the end of systems. Barthes in *Camera Lucida* pleads "resistance to any reductive system" and questions prior discourses, expressing "the uneasiness of being a subject torn between two languages, one expressive, the other critical (*CL* 8)." His return to the imaginary this side of language comes to rest in the image, photography.

From the time of his mother's death to the time when he began writing his book on photography, Barthes spoke of having been involved in "dismembering language" and called for a return to the imaginary: "I think we may see a return to what I would call a writing of the imaginary."[24] The return takes place not just in language but in reality; the death of his mother and death in photography collided with his own. A month after *La chambre claire* was published, Barthes was knocked down by a laundry van and after languishing in hospital— there was nothing physically wrong with him, doctors said; he didn't die of the accident—he died a month later. When he writes in *Camera Lucida* that after his mother's death "From now on I could do no more than await my total, undialectical death (*CL* 72)," language could not be more real. The English translation, *Camera Lucida,* was posthumous.

His return to the imaginary in photography is a wish to return to—to return—his mother. What Barthes loses in his mother is "one whom I love most (*CL* 93)." Barthes lived with his mother, chose to live with her his whole life, which some have tried to see in terms of theory's discourses of gender and sexuality—homosexuality or an Oedipal plot; critics invariably link these. But Barthes's mother is outside discourse. He has lost not "the mother," he insists, but his mother (*CL* 75). "As if our experts cannot conceive there are families 'whose members love one another (*CL* 74).'" And it is a love that has no need for language. Not only is his grief unspeakable, but "in a sense I never 'spoke' to her, never 'discoursed' in her presence, for her; we supposed, without saying anything of the kind to each other, that the frivolous insignificance of language, the suspension of images, must be the very space of love (*CL* 72)." The photographs, especially in Barthes's response to the child of the Winter Garden

Photograph, capture the space of love. Photographs always pointed to that love, poignantly suspending what the text says. In the autobiography the photographs of Barthes as a child with his mother get underneath what the captions say. They evidence not the coded version of love told in "The Demand for Love" and "The Mirror Stage: that's you" as the inexpressibility of that love in language.[25] Theirs is a love, and thus Barthes's a grief, that exceeds conventional explanation. "It is always maintained that I should suffer more because I have spent my whole life with her; but my suffering proceeds from *who she was;* and it is because she was who she was that I lived with her (*CL* 75)." His mother's kindness "belonged to no system" and "she never made a single 'observation (*CL* 69).'" The last piece of writing for a talk he never gave found on Barthes's desk at his death was entitled: "One always fails in speaking of what one loves."[26] In it music (the medium which most empties the sign of meaning) is a space "*outside of language*" (*RL* 302) expressing love, generating a "kind of aphasia (*RL* 303)." In *Camera Lucida* the Winter Garden Photograph is compared to Schumann's *Gesang der Frühe* (Song of Dawn), which he wrote right before his death and which, Barthes writes, "accords with both my mother's being and my grief at her death; I could not express this accord except by an infinite series of adjectives, which I omit, convinced however that this photograph collected all the possible predicates from which my mother's being was constituted (*CL* 70)." To love Schumann, he wrote in an essay the same year as *Camera Lucida,* is to return to an indissoluble connection with the mother. Schumann "is truly the musician of solitary intimacy, of the amorous and imprisoned soul that *speaks to itself . . .* in short of the child who has no other link than to the other . . . This is a music at once dispersed and unary, continually taking refuge in the luminous shadow of the Mother (the *lied,* copious in Schumann's work, is, I believe, the expression of this maternal unity)."[27]

In *Camera Lucida* Barthes points to the Winter Garden Photograph of his mother with the gesture before language, the that-ness or *tathata* of the child. The photograph shows his "mother-as-child (*CL* 71)," which corresponds to reality at the end of her life: "she had become my little girl, uniting for me that essential child she was in her first photograph [. . .] I who had not procreated, I had, in her very illness, engendered my mother (*CL* 72)." But in other photographs Barthes realises loss is generic as well as personal, that a generational and progressive loss is not the point. Slippage of generations characterises several of the photographs in *Camera Lucida,* most notably in the photograph that *could be* Barthes's mother in the absence of the Winter Garden Photograph: "Nadar: The Artist's Mother (or Wife) (*CL* 68)." Really it is the artist's ill wife, but what does it matter, for Barthes has, as he says, gone mad for the sake of pity, "taking into my arms what is dead, what is going to die (*CL* 117)." Or in another example, "The Stock" which appears in a chapter entitled "Lineage," another generational uncertainty occurs: "Sometimes I am mistaken, or at least I hesitate: a medallion represents a young woman and her child: surely that is my mother and myself? But no, it is her mother and her son (my uncle) (*CL* 103).” Another interchangeability appears in Barthes's comments on a photograph, again parenthetical: “the sister (or daughter) (*CL* 43).” In Buddhism every being is a possible mother. According to the Dalai Lama a Tibetan term for human beings, “dear old mother sentient beings,” is based on the fact that, in the doctrine of rebirth, you really *could* be my mother.[28] Seeing into death or *sunyata* for all is the source of *karuna,* compassion—pity-with. Compassion entails egolessness, the dissolution of false dualities, becoming the other in interchangeability and absolute identification. From this comes the mind of limitless love. Barthes writes that if anything can give him the zero degree it is “perhaps only my mother,” “that it is not indifference which erases the weight of the image . . . but love, extreme love (*CL* 12).”

In writings on death by mystics from different creeds the return to the mother or beloved is often an image for death but also for union with the ineffable that we name provisionally: *Sunyata/Nirvana;* Tao; God. Such union without need of intermediary is the kernel of many mystical traditions. Barthes engages a mysticism all the more remarkable for emptying his work of its critique of mythologisation, a turnabout that has exasperated critics: “he affirms the powerful myth he taught us to resist.”[29] It is as if Barthes drops work for life, for the life and death of his mother. Barthes was raised in the Protestant religion of his mother, notable in Catholic France (he had just given her a Protestant funeral). According to his biographer Barthes thought both that Protestantism was more Christian than Catholicism because of its reduction of the sign and that it could be summed up by the one principle of life: the rejection of pride, which was an obstacle to love. In the elliptical final works Barthes's eclectic mysticism combines love and death leading to union with the beloved dead mother. In *A Lover's Discourse* from the *Tao Te Ching,* for the man who lives the Way: “I alone am different from other men,/ For I seek to suckle at my mother's breast.”[30] And alongside St Augustine and Kierkegaard, St John of the Cross who in his *Dark Night of the Soul* shows how a soul must conduct itself to gain union with God, the only way it can be one with its Beloved. Two phases of bereavement are undergone: the dark night of the senses in which the body dies, departs form as if from a house; and the dark night of the soul, in which the spirit falls into despair, a deeper darkness. From this Barthes quotes “And the night illuminated the night (*ALD* 171).”

In *Camera Lucida* mysticism travels from Zen to Tibetan Buddhism. The direct pointing of Zen leads Barthes to look at the void beneath form. Of all the schools visualisation and iconography are most central in Tibetan Buddhism, the most secretive, ritualistic and mystical. As in St John of the Cross death is a gateway to awakening. The night that illuminates the night St John describes as a “ray of darkness”; his dark night of the soul is equivalent to Buddhism's *sunyata,* St. John's most recent translator thinks, suggesting how Barthes was able to make this journey to Tibetan Buddhist mysticism.[31] In the Vajrayana tradition of Tibetan Buddhism death is the best chance of enlightenment. *Vajra-yana* means the "diamond or lightning way" and its works are filled with imagery of mystical light, and therefore darkness. This is particularly so of the *Bardo Thötröl, The Tibetan Book of the Dead,* which Chögyam Trungpa had just translated a few years before Barthes began *Camera Lucida.*[32] (From the Vajrayana tradition himself, it was his encounter with Zen that enabled Trungpa to translate Vajrayana to the West.[33]) Here darkness is characterised by luminosity. The *Bardo Thötröl* consists of instructions for the dying person (or to be read by the living to the dying) for how to attain *nirvana* in *sunyata,* enlightenment in the void. The *bardo* is a gap, between death and life, but there is also a *bardo* of meditation, and a *bardo* of existence. *Bardo* is our living situation, constant change, any transitional experience which is confusing that provides an opportunity to see in confusion. *Bar* means "in between"; *do,* "island." Commentators in Tibetan Buddhism have an extraordinary notion of death as "a sensitive period," a bit like travelling, for "how do we transit from this life to the bardo and from the bardo to our next reincarnation"? "It is like a transfer, or a station where you catch the next train."[34] And if you keep your eyes open, awareness attains union with luminous emptiness. In the *Bardo Thötröl* the union is compared to that of mother and child, the child of awareness returning to the arms of the mother of luminous emptiness: "When they come together, it is as though the child runs and leaps into its mother's arms after a long separation." The mother in Vajrayana Buddhism is "the creative power that gives birth. She is the space (*dhatu*), the zero dimension of emptiness (*shunyata*) from which all phenomena arise."[35] The vision is of healed dualism, not only between self and other, life and death, but representation and the real. *Samadhi,* that one-pointedness of meditation, means "union," from *Samdah,* the "tomb" of a yogi who has become one with the ultimate at death. Writing *Camera Lucida* in that island between his mother's death and his own—and thinking about the gap of her loss, the generational gap, and the gap separating life and death—Barthes finds in that gap the zero degree he had been searching for.

Death awareness is a major part of Buddhism but has not been embraced with much enthusiasm by Western interpreters, who have gone for enlightenment, transcendence, light—above all the direct reality of Zen without contemplating the void being pointed to. In the West, Trungpa writes in his introduction to *The Tibetan Book of the Dead,* death is denied, which is "a fundamental rejection of love, that nobody is really willing to help a dying person's state of mind (*TBD* 68)." In the *Bardo Thötröl* the reader is there with the dead, fully relating and in instructing a dying person and confronting death "you are really talking to yourself (*TBD* 73)." In the Tibetan tradition death awareness is the ultimate meditative practice. Monks went into charnel grounds not to overcome fear of death but to touch it. Surrounded by bones and skulls, they would have been faced with the aliveness of death, as in Barthes's photograph, the live corpse. The *Bardo Thötröl* is about how to see the thus-goneness and hence to become a buddha or "tathāgata," which, Trungpa writes, "literally means 'thus-gone' which can be paraphrased as 'he who has become one with the essence of what is.' It is synonymous with *Buddha* ('awakened') (*TBD* xxiii)." This *Book of the Dead,* which could just as easily be called the book of birth, "can show us how to live (*TBD* xxvii)." Or as Larry Rosenberg suggests how to live a Buddhist life in the light of death, "We must die every day. We must die every moment. We must die now."[36] In the foundation of mindfulness the third reality the Buddha saw—after ageing and sickness—was a corpse, and *then* the contemplative life. "This body is of the same nature, will become like that, is not exempt from that fate," the Buddha suggests as meditation.[37]

As death has not been seen in Buddhism, the reference of photography has been transformed into signs. In both the attention has been to form and not emptiness. The closing of *Camera Lucida* tells us that the real for Westerners is now hidden. Death is not in modern secular society, is nowhere except in photography. Since the second half of the nineteenth century, death or our contact with it passed from religion to photography. The invention of photography coincided with a crisis in religious belief and this is why it comes to hold the vestiges of the dead's being, for Barthes and almost as much for Walter Benjamin, who writes that, in "the cult of remembrance of loved ones, absent or dead," "the aura emanates from early photography in the fleeting expression of a human face."[38] But for both Barthes and Benjamin loss of faith in the aura or essence has meant the renunciation of the mystical in photography. *Camera Lucida* ends astoundingly given Barthes's career in signs, with criticism of the contemporary hegemony of signs, "where everything is transformed into images" which "completely de-realises the human world of conflicts and desires (*CL* 118)." Barthes longs for a naïve—a childish—relation to images, the abolition of the sign and contact with the real. Because photography is not an aide-mémoire but a *memento mori,* not a memorialisation of the dead but a reminder of all death, it "has something to do with resurrection" and our "astonishment" at it if nothing else is "religious (*CL* 82)." The flash of photography illuminates darkness. *La chambre claire/Camera Lucida* ("light room"), though written in the dark room of Barthes's loss, brings him to the mystic's light.

With its journey for the truth of the dead *Camera Lucida* is close to *The Tibetan Book of the Dead,* the *Bardo Thötröl.* As such *Camera Lucida* too, like that prayer (in Tibetan the word is "wish-path"), maps the path to come through the path of the dead. Photographs are like the footprints the dead person leaves behind when she is gone that must be attended to by the living in the Tibetan tradition. In the darkness Barthes attains something like his enlightenment or awakening: Buddha Barthes. Returning to Trungpa's *koan* I find it hard to explain and it occupies me like a decaying tooth. But I see a coincidence with Barthes's closing lines about two approaches to photography, one that reads it as "the civilized code of perfect illusions," the other that madly "confront[s] in it the wakening of intractable reality (*CL* 119)." It is clear that *Camera Lucida* chooses madness over civilization, awakening to reality rather than the illusion of code. It is less clear, but perhaps possible, that death is an illusion because it is like everything in life, only a gap; and yet also that the death of the one whom one loves most is a super-illusion because it is nevertheless irreversible and insufferable, beyond words. The passing moment in Buddhism is both cause of our suffering, in our failure to see it, and key to our enlightenment if we waken to its reality. The past moment is gone, yet when we realise this and relax into it, we enter a kind of space: emptiness. In another *koan* that Barthes read before he died, two monks see some wild geese flying overhead. "Where are they going?" asks Ma-tsu. Po-chang replies: "They've already flown away." "How," shouts Ma-tsu, "could they ever have flown away?"[39]

ABBREVIATIONS

ALD	*A Lover's Discourse*
CL	*Camera Lucida*
ES	*Empire of Signs*
IMT	*Image Music Text*
TBD	*Tibetan Book of the Dead*

NOTES

This chapter is a slightly revised version of the paper that appeared in *Literature and Theology* 18, no. 2 (June 2004).

1. C. Trungpa, *Cutting Through Spiritual Materialism*, J. Baker and M. Casper (eds) (Boston: Shambhala, 1987), p. 49. Cited in French on the rear cover of Roland Barthes, *La chambre claire: Note sur la photographie* (Paris: Gallimard, 1980).
2. I. Miura and R. F. Sasaki, *The Zen Koan* (New York: Harcourt Brace 1965), p. 5.
3. Barthes, *Empire of Signs,* trans. R. Howard (London: Cape, 1982), p. 74.
4. Barthes, *A Lover's Discourse: Fragments,* trans. R. Howard (New York: Farrar, 1978), p. 224.
5. Barthes, *Roland Barthes by Roland Barthes,* trans. R. Howard (New York: Farrar, 1977), p. 94.
6. Barthes, *The Grain of the Voice: Interviews 1962–1980,* trans. L. Coverdale (Berkeley: California UP, 1985), p. 85.

7. Barthes, *The Fashion System,* trans. M. Ward and R. Howard (Berkeley: California UP, 1990). Barthes, *Elements of Semiology,* trans. A. Lavers and C. Smith (London: Cape, 1967).

8. L. Irigaray, *Between East and West: From Singularity to Community,* trans. S. Pluháček (New York: Columbia UP, 2002), p. 10.

9. D. Keown, *Buddhism: A Very Short Introduction* (Oxford: Oxford UP, 1996), p. 122.

10. Barthes, *Camera Lucida: Reflections on Photography,* trans. R. Howard (London: Vintage, 1993), p. 49.

11. T. Ang, *Tao of Photography* (London: Mitchell Beazley, 2000). P. L. Gross and S. I. Shapiro, *The Tao of Photography: Seeing Beyond Seeing* (Berkeley: Ten Speed Press, 2001).

12. L. Tzu, *Tao Te Ching,* trans. S. Mitchell (London: Kyle Cahie, 2000), p. 1.

13. L. Wittgenstein, *Tractatus Logico-Philosophicus,* trans. D. F. Pears and B.F. McGuinness (London: Routledge, 2001), p. 89.

14. C. Gudmunsen, *Wittgenstein and Buddhism* (London: Macmillan, 1977).

15. A. Bancroft, *Zen: Direct Pointing to Reality* (London: Thames and Hudson, 1995), p. 5.

16. A. W. Watts, *The Way of Zen* (London: Penguin, 1990), p. 62.

17. Barthes, *Mythologies* (1957), trans. A. Lavers (New York: Farrar, 1972), pp. 100–102.

18. Barthes, *Image Music Text,* trans. S. Heath (London: Fontana, 1977), p. 35.

19. Barthes, *Writing Degree Zero,* trans. A. Lavers and C. Smith (London: Cape, 1967).

20. Barthes, *Image Music Text,* p. 19.

21. L.-J. Calvet, *Roland Barthes: A Biography,* trans. S. Wykes (Oxford: Polity Press, 1994).

22. A. W. Watts, *The Way of Zen,* p. 97. S. Freud, "Mourning and Melancholia," trans. J. Strachey, *On Metapsychology,* Vol. II, *Penguin Freud Library,* A. Richards (ed.) (London: Penguin, 1991), pp. 245–268.

23. C. Trungpa, *The Essential Chögyam Trungpa,* C.R. Gimian (ed.) (Boston: Shambhala, 1999), p. 119.

24. Cited in Calvet, p. 219.

25. Barthes, *Roland Barthes by Roland Barthes,* pp. 4, 9.

26. Barthes, *The Rustle of Language,* trans. R. Howard (Oxford: Blackwell, 1986), pp. 296–305.

27. Barthes, *The Responsibility of Forms: Critical Essays on Music, Art, and Representation,* trans. R. Howard (New York: Farrar, 1985), pp. 293–294.

28. His Holiness the XIV Dalai Lama, *Transforming the Mind: Teachings on Generating Compassion* (London: HarperCollins, 2000), p. 68.

29. J. Culler, *Barthes* (Glasgow: Fontana, 1983), p. 122.

30. Barthes, *A Lover's Discourse,* p. 213.

31. St John of the Cross, *Dark Night of the Soul,* trans. M. Starr (London: Random House, 2002), p. 100.

32. Guru Rinpoche according to KarmaLingpa, *The Tibetan Book of the Dead: The Great Liberation through Hearing in the Bardo,* trans. F. Fremantle and C. Trungpa (Boston: Shambhala, 1992).

33. D. Mukpo, "Here Comes Chögyam," *Shambhala Sun* 12 (2003) pp. 56–61.

34. G. Rimpoche, with G. Alhadeff and M. Magill, *Good Life, Good Death* (New York: Riverhead Books, 2001), pp. 30, 32.

35. F. Fremantle, *Luminous Emptiness: Understanding the Tibetan Book of the Dead* (Boston: Shambhala, 2001), pp. 243, 258.

36. L. Rosenberg, *Living in the Light of Death: On the Art of Being Truly Alive* (Boston: Shambhala, 2001), p. 17.

37. *The Long Discourses of the Buddha: A Translation of the Dīgha Nikāya,* trans. M. Walsh (Boston: Wisdom, 1995), p. 338.

38. W. Benjamin, *Illuminations* (London: Fontana, 1992), p. 219.

39. Watts, *The Way of Zen,* p. 142.

Notes on Love and Photography

Eduardo Cadava and Paola Cortés-Rocca

When my gaze meets yours, I see both your gaze and your eyes, love in fascination—and your eyes are not only seeing but also visible. And since they are visible (things or objects in the world) as much as seeing (at the origin of the world), I could precisely touch them, with my finger, lips, or even eyes, lashes and lids, by approaching you—if I dared come near to you in this way, if I one day dared.
—Jacques Derrida, *On Touching*

I desire you. I desire only you. . . . Where are you? I am playing hide and seek with ghosts. But I know I will end up finding you, and the whole world will be newly lit because we love each other, because a chain of illuminations passes through us.
—André Breton, *Mad Love*

To be on an island inhabited by artificial phantasms was the most insupportable of nightmares; to be in love with one of these images was worse than being in love with a phantasm (perhaps we always have wanted the person we love to have a phantasmatic existence).
—Adolfo Bioy Casares, *The Invention of Morel*

Is Roland Barthes dreaming when he writes Camera Lucida? *Does he think of his mother every day, or of the mother of whom he dreams every day (he tells us at one point that he only dreams of his mother), or of the mother that he both knew and did not know, saw and did not see, or of the mother that was never herself? Is he haunted by the ruin of all the memories of her that he wished to capture, in the writing of this book, for every day and always? Or by what happens, one day, between photographic technology and the light that helps bring to life a photograph of his mother when she was five years old—a photograph in which he claims to find the truth of the face he loved, and from which he seeks to "derive" all photography? Or else by what happens, all at once—within the movement of his thoughts and writing, and in relation to his body— among photography, the work of his unconscious, the ghostly experience of music, the traumatic experiences of death and mourning, and the pangs of love? Barthes dreams (and writes) his vision (offering us something like photography itself: what he calls "a new form of hallucination"), the fire of a declaration of love that, as he says, burns and consumes him, a "floating flash" that, blinding him, disorienting him, enables him to experience and touch his finitude; and if we listen to the muteness of his mournful song, to the cry of his writing, we can perhaps hear him say:*

> *I approach myself as I wait for you, today, my love, and for all time, but I know that, with your death, but also in your life, the self I approach is lost and cannot be found. In the midst of this loss, I experience the madness of a single desire: to affect time with time, secretly, in the night, and with the hope that, like the click of a camera, I may yet live to archive the music of my love for you. I love you, I desire you, I want to see and touch your body, I cannot live without you, and, with your death, I am no longer myself, even though I know that, even before your death, and because of my love for you, I already was not myself. If I have been wounded by your death—if it has pierced me and struck me—it is because this wound already was "mine," already was the signature of my love. Like the punctum about which I soon will tell you, your death has been added to my life, even if, from the very beginning, it already was there. No longer simply alive, but not yet dead, at the threshold of life and death, I offer you this book in the hope that it can suspend and derange time, and that, confessing my enduring love, my enduring wound, it can transform "the corpus I need" into "the body I see," the body I touch.*

I

Photography is mad, and, in the world of Roland Barthes's *Camera Lucida*, its delirium and danger are related to the experience of love, and, more particularly, to what he calls the "pangs of love," "extreme love."[1] But what is love, and in what way does it pain us, pierce us, strike us, and offer us a glimpse of our mortality? What is its relation to death, mourning, music, and photography? What does love have to do with the ruin, loss, and dissolution of the self? What does it mean to love a photograph, and in what way does love mean nothing else than loving a photograph (is it even possible to love something other than a photograph)? What is the relation, within the space of photography, between the "observed subject" and the "subject observing" and how does this relation, at least according to Barthes, require a reconceptualization of both photography and love? These are the questions raised by Barthes's strange but moving meditation on photography and the death of his beloved mother. Barthes's text carries the signature of a vigil that is more than simply an experience of mourning, more than simply a surviving testimony or a meditation on photography, since, as is legible in nearly every one of its sentences, it remains amorously related to a mother who has died (perhaps even more than once), but is still living, and not only in his memory. Indeed, we could even say that, within the logic of the book, it is his mother's survival, her living on, even after her death, that indicates that things pass, that they change and transform, and, minimally, because this survival asks us to think not of the impossibility of a return to life but of the impossibility of dying, not life or death, but life and death, or perhaps, even more precisely, "life death." It is this ghostly survival—as a metonym for all such survivals—that defines the madness of the photograph, since it is there, within the medium of photography, that we simultaneously experience the absence of the "observed subject" and the fact of its "having-been-there," the relation between life and death, between testimony and its impossibility, between the self and an other, and among the past, the present, and the future. Within the delirious space of photography, all these apparent oppositions are suspended and ruined in order to be rethought in relation to the madness of love "itself," since the experience of love also breaks down and shatters these same oppositions, along with many others (including the relation between interiority and exteriority, presence and absence, singularity and repetition, lucidity and blindness, and necessity and chance). This means, among other things, that this little book on photography is also, and perhaps most essentially and significantly, a text on love and eroticism. It is Barthes's true "lover's discourse," and this because, as he suggests, to speak of photography is always to speak of love.

Barthes reinforces this point when, in the first few pages of his book, he confesses that when he looks at a photograph he sees "only the referent, the desired object, the beloved body" (*CL* 7/*CC* 19). It is precisely "love," he explains, "extreme love," that enables him to "erase the weight of the image" (*CL* 12/*CC* 27), to make the photograph "invisible" (*CL* 6/*CC* 18), and thereby to clear a path for him to see not the photograph, but the object of his desire, his beloved's body. If, at first glance, it would seem that the force of love, and particularly of "extreme love," enables him to pass through the photographic surface to reach the referent, to exceed the limits of the photographic medium in order to see his beloved, Barthes soon makes it clear that there can be no love without photography and no photography without love. But to state this chiasmic axiom is merely to articulate the beginning of a mystery, since what is really at stake in this context is the possibility of understanding what "love" and "photography" mean here, especially since, like all the other terms he mobilizes within his text—including "*studium,*" "*punctum,*" "music," "death," "mourning," "identity," and even "mother" (we would like to call these terms "Barthemes" to signal his effort to singularize his use of them, to make them "his")—these two words or concepts can never be understood outside of their relation to other words and concepts.

Like the lover who wishes to address the singularity of his beloved without recourse to the lover's discourse he inherits, Barthes seeks to invent a language that would be more faithful to what he "perceives" to be the singular, paradoxical, and contradictory character of photography.[2] He suggests that, in order to submit to the photographic adventure, to surrender to the unprecedented experience of photography, we must invent a language with which we can approach it, even if we know we may never seize or capture it. Like all lovers, the Barthesian lover therefore seeks to name a world that has never yet existed before his eyes, as if his language might, in calling it forth, touch it for the first time. Indeed, as we know from his earlier analysis of the lover's discourse, language desires nothing more and nothing else than to touch the beloved's body—and the world in which it exists.

In the same way that the lover's language wishes to approach and touch his beloved, Barthes desires to approach and touch photography: to touch its essence, to touch on what differentiates it from other modes of representation. In the opening paragraph of his text, he confesses, in a wonderfully ambiguous formulation that signals both photography's singularity and its intimate relation with cinema: "I decided I liked Photography *in opposition* to the Cinema, from which I nonetheless failed to separate it. This question grew insistent. I was overcome by an 'ontological' desire: I wanted to learn at all costs what Photography was 'in itself,' by what essential feature it was to be distinguished from the community of images" (*CL* 3/*CC* 13–14). Overwhelmed by desire, the writer seeks to discover the "ontology" of photography, but, rather than looking for concepts that might distinguish and define the fundamental elements with which we might determine photography's singularity, he suggests that there can be no reflection on photography that does not begin with the revision of the words or concepts with which we speak and think about images, and through which we look at them. Barthes signals and reinforces the fact that his "Barthemes," "his" words or concepts, designate something other than what we usually would expect them to mean through a series of typographical strategies, including the capitalization of terms, italicization, and the strategic use of quotation marks.[3] Given the way in which each Bartheme condenses and encrypts a series of associations that prevent it from remaining self-identical to itself, we could even say that its condition of possibility can only be the impossibility of its ever having a fixed semantic content. This is why Barthes frequently uses quotation marks (in this passage, around the word "ontological" and the phrase "in itself"); they signal that the word, name, or concept enclosed within them is never simply monosemic, but rather—

like the subject whose entry into photographic space announces the "advent" of himself as an other—is always in the process of becoming something else. As is so often the case with Barthes, each element of his writing—its typographical eccentricities, its rhythm and movement, its echolalia and repetitions, its diction and distribution—works to enact what he wishes to convey.

If Barthes creates a text whose movement and circulation, whose words and names, embody and enact its semantic drift, in this instance it is because he wants to suggests that what makes love and photography love and photography is that neither they nor their amorous or photographic subjects ever remain the same. This means, among other things, that, before anything else, Barthes's text is an assault on the constitution of a "safety zone" for any theory of photography in which it would be possible to delineate strict borders that would separate, define, and establish the elements that would be indispensable for thinking photography "in itself." Among the words that have become the most essential to any reflection on photography there is perhaps no more important set of terms than "subject," "image," and "reference." Barthes invents a heretical language that questions and redefines this "Holy Trinity" in order to destabilize the unity and integrity of each of its terms—to work in favor of processes and not positions, of multiple forms of becoming and not unities that would be identical to themselves—and therefore to reconceptualize photography altogether. Dissolving the distinction between one term and another, *Camera Lucida* proceeds in a way that could be said to belong to the experience of love; it proposes a theory of photographic becoming in which the photograph is a force of transformation: in which models become images, images become subjects, and subjects become photographs.

Within this logic of transformation and metamorphosis, it is impossible to sustain the abstraction we call "reference." The relation between the represented object and its representation, between reference and image, does not presuppose an object whose being and existence precede, or remain outside, the process through which it becomes an image. On the contrary, Barthes suggests that photographic representation stages—makes absolutely "literal"—what is at the heart of modern representation, and this is precisely the putting into crisis of a temporal order in which first there is an object and then later its representation. What stands in front of the photographic apparatus—an object or subject that gives way to a portrait—does not "exist" before the camera's click. As Barthes explains, "once I feel myself observed by the lens, everything changes: I constitute myself in the process of 'posing,' I instantaneously make another body for myself, I transform myself in advance into an image" (*CL* 10/*CC* 25). This "active" transformation is not that of someone who offers himself to the camera, like some sacrificial victim, in order to be reproduced, but rather that of someone who knows that what makes him what he "is"—and therefore prevents him from ever being simply "himself"—is the multiplicity that *inhabits* "him." In the same way that the being of an object does not exist before its representation, there also is never a single, homogeneous object that—even before it is placed in front of the camera—coincides with itself. What Barthes engages here, in an extremely systematic and rigorous manner, is nothing less than what produces the difficulty of all contemporary reflections on photography: the absence of the subject. But, as he suggests—and here lies his strength and courage—this absence does not result from disappearance or effacement, but, on the contrary, from multiplication and proliferation. As he puts it,

> *in front of the lens, I am at the same time: the one I think I am, the one I want others to think I am, the one the photographer thinks I am, and the one he makes use of to exhibit his art. In other words, a strange action: I do not stop imitating myself, and because of this, each time I am (or let myself be) photographed, I invariably suffer from a sensation of inauthenticity, sometimes of imposture (comparable to certain nightmares). (CL 13/CC 29–30)*

Photography—and the portrait as its genre *par excellence*—constitutes a radical and absolute destabilization of the Cartesian subject, "comparable to certain nightmares," and not unlike the one advanced by psychoanalysis, in which "I think where I am not, therefore I am where I do not think."[4] Like psychoanalysis, photography shatters the subject of reason—a subject that would be complete and coincidental with itself—by introducing a plurality that is not produced by the metonymic force of unconscious desire, but by affects and the gaze: "I see, I feel, hence I notice, I observe, and I think" (*CL* 21/*CC* 42). It tells me that I do not exist before my image—that I exist only as an image, or, more precisely, only as a series of images, none of which are ever one. It redeems me from the immobility of a "self" and tells me that the I that is reproduced in each new image, and in every copy of each of these images, is never even one at the moment in which it poses before the camera. "I only resemble," Barthes notes, "other photographs of myself, and this to infinity: no one is ever anything but the copy of a copy, real or mental" (*CL* 102/*CC* 159). Undoing every contemplative act that would presume a distance between "itself" and the image on which it focuses, *Camera Lucida* puts the category of an observer—as the neutral subject of a process that presumably occurs outside him—into crisis.

The provocative statement that "a photograph is always invisible" (*CL* 6/*CC* 18)—because it is possible to pass through it in order to move directly to the referent—should be read not as a means of devalorizing or overcoming the materiality of the image, but as a way of contesting historical and sociological readings and understandings of the image. If Barthes claims, from the very beginning, that he is "'scientifically' alone and disarmed" (*CL*, 7/*CC*,

20), it is because he refuses to imagine himself as someone who, sheltered and protected by a critical, sociological, historical, and even, in the end, an affective distance, rigorously and completely analyzes a photographic corpus. The I who speaks in *Camera Lucida* contemplates a series of photographs that he holds in his hands without imagining that he is a neutral witness of a relation or bond that has excluded him: on the contrary, the singular adherence that binds the image to its referent also includes him. This is why, far from reinforcing the assumption of an ontological difference between the subjectivity—the "humanity"—of the observer and the materiality of the chemical paper or metal plate that forms a photograph, *Camera Lucida* works to destabilize this frontier: the image becomes a subject and the subject becomes an image. They are bound together in a relation that, acquiring a certain privacy or intimacy, reveals itself to be an amorous one: the encounter between the subject and the photograph he holds in his hands produces the spark that subjectivizes the image (that "animates" it) and that simultaneously illuminates his own photographic being.[5]

Closer to pleasure than to science, the act of looking at a photograph therefore does not differentiate between a subject and an image, but rather brings together "two experiences: that of the observed subject and that of the subject observing" (*CL* 10/*CC* 24). To look at a photograph also is to recognize the photographic dimension of my "self," to identify a particularity that seizes my gaze, to register or acknowledge that I already am, and in advance, a kind of photograph.[6] This is why, as Barthes suggests in the early pages of his text, he can take "himself" as a "mediator for all Photography," and why he can become "the measure of photographic 'knowledge'" (*CL* 8–9/*CC* 22). This also is why representation or testimony are never innocent: the camera is never here or there in order to register "reality," and the image does not exist to confirm how different it is from us. Instead, Barthes suggests that the essence of photography lies in its affirmation of becoming. Photography names (without naming) the process whereby something stops being what it "is" in order to transform itself into "something else." It "represents that very subtle moment when, to tell the truth, I am neither subject nor object but a subject who feels he is becoming an object: I then experience a micro-version of death (of parenthesis): I am truly becoming a specter" (*CL* 14/*CC* 30). Between life and death, subject and object, subject and image, in a kind of parenthesis, the specter I am becoming declares that the only image or subject that could really be an image or subject would be the one that shows its impossibility, its disappearance and destruction, its ruin.

To look at a photograph therefore means to contemplate the singular adherence that transforms me into an image and what the image demonstrates to me (without demonstrating anything at all) about what it means to be a photographic subject. The relation between the object and its image, among the image-object, the object-image, and my gaze, links me to the adventure of experiencing the photographic fragment as a mirror that returns me to my own image. As Barthes explains, "I am the reference of every photograph, and this is what generates my astonishment in addressing myself to the fundamental question: why is it that I am alive *here and now?*" (*CL* 84/*CC* 131). In other words, why am I not *there*—in the fragment of paper that I hold in my hand or in the place in which the photograph was taken? Why am I not there *then,* in the moment in which the click of the shutter was heard, in the precise instant in which what the image shows me was transformed into this image? If photography is "the cunning dissociation of consciousness from identity" (*CL* 12/*CC* 28), it is not only because photography signals a crisis in the identity of the subject but also because it introduces a mediation and break into the very interior of the concept of identity. Within the photographic space, I "discover" that I am never self-identical to myself, and that there is no object, no act, no instant that ever coincides with "itself." Each time we hold an image in our hands, the magic of photography returns to repeat itself and the photographed and the photographic apparatus encounter themselves again as if for the very first time, in part because the observer, haunted and constituted by this earlier encounter, is himself a photographic apparatus. Photography prevents us from ever recognizing this or that identity—ours, but also that of someone or something else—because "photography" is the name of the destruction of any consciousness of identity.

This law of both love and photography—a law that interrupts identity by marking it with the sign of difference and transformation—belongs to what makes Barthes's meditation on love and photography so radically provocative: against a sense that photography's signature lies in its capacity to fix and preserve—to arrest—what is before the camera, he mobilizes a network of associations that, practically and textually, seek to disorganize and destabilize the opposition or difference between opposing terms, such as stasis and movement, preservation and destruction, survival and death, and memory and mourning. That this work of disorganization and destabilization is shown to be at the heart of the experience of love—as Barthes would have it, love is nothing else than a process of disorganization and destabilization—is what we are meant to trace, as if we were tracing and listening to a kind of secret, and as we follow the Ariadne's thread which, like the Winter Garden Photograph of his mother as a child, brings together photography, love, and death.

||

What would it mean to formulate an ontology for photography—for this medium that, according to Barthes, is characterized only by "contingency, singularity, adventure" (*CL* 20/*CC* 40)? *Camera Lucida* opens with this ontological desire and, as the text advances, ontology gives way to a space entirely devoted to desire: "I was interested in Photography only for 'sentimental' reasons," Barthes writes, "I wanted to explore it not as a question (a theme) but as a wound" (*CL* 21/*CC* 42). If photography is not to be thought as a theme (or as a question to which we might provide an answer), it is because it cannot be reduced to a theme; it is because, "unclassifiable" (*CL* 4/*CC* 15), it wounds the very possibility of theme and, in particular, of the theme or concept of photography. This is why the language and concepts mobilized throughout this text require a reading attentive to what he calls, at the end of the first part of the book, his "palinode," his retraction of his desire to name or conceptualize photography in a determinate manner. We might even say that this palinode—as a mode of assertion that countersigns a kind of withdrawal from what is being asserted—is one of the text's signatures. It belongs to an effort of conceptualization that moves the text in one direction in order later to follow the reverse path in search of a language willing to risk a relation to "affect," a language that, as he puts it, can only "speak of desire or of mourning" (*CL* 21/*CC* 41). The entirety of *Camera Lucida,* in other words, proceeds by seeking a language commensurate with the paradoxical character of the photograph—a language that is guided and interrupted by the desire for the very thing that, always lost, and never comprehended, remains to be mourned: photography itself.

The notorious distinction that Barthes makes between the photograph's *punctum* and *studium*—a distinction that, as we will see, is only the simulacrum of a distinction (even if, at the same time, these two terms always remain different from each other)—appears to be the exemplary instance of this paradoxical compromise with desire or mourning. As he would have it—at least initially—the *studium* is a field of predictability and repetition: "it always refers to a classical body of information"; it is what "I perceive quite familiarly as a consequence of my knowledge, my culture" (*CL* 25/*CC* 47). It constitutes (or "figures") a totality that always refers to something that precedes the image: the intention that might govern the photograph's production, whether it is generated by the photographer, the technology, or the object captured in the image. This field is scanned by the detail that Barthes calls the *punctum,* which he claims is excluded from the field of intentions, in the strongest sense of the term "intentionality"—that is, in terms of a subject's will of expression—but also in the sense of what this or that photographic technology or photographed subject can or wishes to say. "Certain details may 'prick me,'" he writes, "If they do not, it is doubtless because the photographer has put them there intentionally" (*CL* 27/*CC* 49). The *punctum* therefore escapes from what counts as the art of the photographer, but also from what we could call the art of the photographic technique or of the object—the capturing of the present moment, the precision of technical processes, the exhibition of rarities—precisely because *punctum* is the name with which Barthes seeks to designate what cannot be seen in advance, "that accident which pricks me (but also bruises me, is poignant to me)" (*CL, 47/CC, 79*).

Defined as a detail that fascinates, but also as a wound that interrupts the *studium,* that cuts or pricks the image and the corporeal gaze that would view it, the *punctum* points directly toward that affective field opened by images—a field that always evokes enjoyment as both pleasurable and wounding.

If the *studium* would seem to be on the side of legibility, the effect of a "certain training" (*CL,* 26/*CC,* 48) or "education" (*CL,* 28/*CC,* 51), if it evokes the range of cultural and historical contexts from which we may draw information that enables us to engage a photograph (even if only in a general way), the *punctum* is what disturbs this legibility, what punctures or strikes through the surface of reproduction: "it arises from the scene, shoots out of it like an arrow, and pierces me"; it "disturbs" the *studium* (*CL,* 26–27/*CC,* 49). Emerging with the ghostly force of the supplement, the *punctum* appears as a kind of transit or relay between the photograph and the viewer that, despite its violence, despite its singularity, nevertheless can be drawn into a network of associations. Like the language that moves in relation to affect, in relation to desire and mourning, the *punctum* works in relation to the *studium.* As Derrida explains in the elegy he wrote shortly after Barthes's death,

> *as soon as the punctum ceases to oppose the studium, all the while remaining heterogeneous to it, as soon as we can no longer distinguish here between two places, contents, or things, it is not entirely subjugated to a concept, if by "concept" we mean a predicative determination that is distinct and opposable. This concept of a ghost is scarcely graspable in its self as the ghost of a concept. Neither life nor death, but the haunting of the one by the other.*

"The 'versus' of the conceptual opposition," he adds, "is as unsubstantial as a camera's click."[7]

If at first glance it would seem that the *punctum/studium* couple names the opposition between a cultural or historical canon and its interruption or between what is predictable and what is irreducibly singular—a claim that seems to be supported by Barthes's assertion that "the *studium* is ultimately always coded, the *punctum* is not" (*CL* 51/*CC* 84)—the parenthesis that follows this assertion "(I trust I am not using these words abusively)" dissolves this pure antagonism in order to complicate and reformulate not only the opposition between singularity and predictability, contingency and repetition, detail and totality, but also between intentionality and nonintentionality. In *Camera Lucida,* the *punctum/studium* couple does not speak to us of antagonistic elements, of two forces opposed to one other, and identical to themselves; rather, it names the "co-presence" (*CL* 42/*CC* 72)—in the here and now of the space of every image—of two forces in transformation, two streams that tend toward each other, without ever coinciding with one another. This is why, if the *studium* names a kind of education, knowledge, and civility that produces a general interest, an *average* effect, it does so in the form of a simulacrum. "Photography cannot signify (aim at a generality) except by assuming a mask" (*CL* 34/*CC* 60–61), Barthes notes in relation to a portrait taken by Richard Avedon. The *studium* designates an imposture, a fiction of generality that can only take the form of a myth. "This is why the great portrait photographers are great mythologists" (*CL* 34/*CC* 60–61), he adds, explaining that they are capable of capturing a face (the absolute mark of peculiarity) or a gesture (an act of pure contingency) and presenting it *as if it were* the face of a race, a nation, or a class. Indeed, in the same way that generality is nothing but a masquerade of generality, it is impossible to posit, within any image, a space of absolute transgression. Barthes's amorous language seeks a radical difference, an object capable of interrupting the terrain of the always-the-same, and it finds it in the detail that captures its gaze and that he calls the *punctum.* But just as chance belongs to the amorous repetition, the *punctum* is far from being pure contingency or pure singularity: its regular appearance in each image adopts the form of a rule "plausible enough" (*CL* 25/*CC* 47) that it can be systematized as one of the two "themes in Photography" (*CL* 27/*CC* 49).

That Barthes both preserves and dissolves this opposition between difference and repetition, that he seeks to have it enact the paradoxical character of the photograph, is perhaps even more legible if we trace the way in which it is mobilized within his text a little more carefully. For example, it is legible when, in the moment in which he confronts the Winter Garden Photograph, he admits: "I gave myself up to the Image, to the Image-Repertoire. Thus I could understand my generality; but having understood it, invincibly I escaped from it. In the Mother, there was a radiant, irreducible core: my mother" (*CL* 75/*CC* 117). Registering that his engagement with this photograph of his mother (before she was his mother) is informed and shaped by the Image-Repertoire (perhaps another name for the *studium*), he nonetheless suggests that what distinguishes his suffering from the suffering of another person in similar circumstances, what even increases it, is the fact that he has spent his whole life with her and that his suffering "proceeds from *who she was*" (*CL* 75/*CC* 117). Precisely in order to articulate and maintain the particularity of his mourning, Barthes confesses that, "like the Proustian Narrator at his grandmother's death: 'I did not insist only upon suffering, but upon respecting the originality of my suffering'; for this originality was the reflection of what was absolutely irreducible in her, and thereby lost forever" (*CL* 75/*CC* 117–118). But how is it possible to believe in the originality of Barthes's suffering if he himself tells us that it is "like" the suffering of Proust after the death of his grandmother? How can we believe in the originality of someone who is not an unprecedented figure in his life but a person who is repeated in the life of others, a figure almost as archetypal as the mother? In signaling originality through the words of another, Barthes stages the paradoxical character of mourning. Effectively, he suggests, the pain or grief that we experience before a loss is always contradictory: each time that we lose someone, we go through, at least structurally (even if not in every detail), exactly the same series of experiences as someone who has suffered a similar loss: we surrender to the same rituals, we reproduce the same set of sentences and formulas. At the same time, and like everyone else, we think that our suffering is entirely unique. And we are not wrong here, because, paradoxically, what is repeated each time that we fall in love or that we lose someone is precisely the radical originality of love or loss. Photography, like love or death, is the experience of the singularity that is repeated or of the repetition that appears as something singular.[8]

This structural relation between singularity and repetition reappears in another form within Barthes's discussion of the *punctum/studium* couple. The *punctum* and *studium* do not belong entirely to the image or to the mode of perceiving it—they are neither only attributes of the image nor only a projection of the gaze—but rather are points of connection between the history of the image and the history of the gaze. This is why Barthes can say that the *punctum* is "what I add to the photograph and *what is nonetheless already there*" (*CL* 55/*CC* 89). Between what "I add" and what "is already there," or, more precisely, between what "I add" and what "*was* already there," there is always a temporal dissymmetry: every image is like a clock that is always a little behind or a little ahead. This is why the true *punctum* sometimes comes a little later. There is "[n]othing surprising," Barthes admits, "if sometimes, despite its clarity, the *punctum* should be revealed only after the fact, when the photograph is no longer in front of me and I think back on it. It happens that I may know better a photograph I remembered than a photograph I am looking at, as if direct vision oriented its language wrongly, engaging it in an effort of description which will always miss its point of effect, the *punctum*" (*CL* 53/*CC* 87). As he suggests, every photographic experience is always an experience of the past, of what is converted into an experience, not in the present of the living, not in the now of the camera's click or of the gaze, but later, when—as happens in Barthes's response to the family portrait taken by Van der Zee, which he analyzes in his discussion of the *punctum*—this or that photograph continues to haunt him, when it has, as he puts it, "worked within me" (*CL* 53/*CC* 87). Reading this portrait of a black family in 1926, and after first identifying its *punctum* as the belt and then as the "*strapped pumps*" of the standing black woman, he later claims that the "real *punctum* was the necklace she was wearing; for (no doubt) it was this same necklace (a slender ribbon of braided gold) which I had seen worn by someone in my own family, and which, once she died, remained shut up in a family box of old jewelry (this sister of my father never married, lived with her mother as an old maid, and I had always been saddened whenever I thought of her dreary life)" (*CL* 53/*CC* 87–88). That he identifies this *punctum* through a series of associations and displacements that evoke his history, his affections, and his inscription within a language, a culture, and a familial network that precede him, means that the *punctum* emerges in relation to elements of the *studium.* If this particular detail moves him, if he registers this particular wound, it is because this wound already is *in* him, somewhere in *his* history, even if in a displaced, encrypted, and illegible manner. It is because this wound appears, after a period of latency, like an "unexpected flash" (*CL* 94/*CC* 148), within his psychic and bodily memory. Moreover, this sequence of associations and displacements—from the belt to the pumps to the necklace, from the necklace of the black woman to the necklace of his aunt, from the photograph in front of him to an earlier photograph from his family's history, and from the sadness or death sealed within one image to that inscribed within another—enacts the "power of expansion" that he already had associated with the *punctum* (*CL* 45/*CC,* 74). In other words, the *punctum,* in all its singularity, in its absolute irreducibility, encrypts an entire network of substitutions that, composing and decomposing it at the same time, prevent it from ever being what it is, from ever being self-identical to itself. What makes this series of substitutions possible, however—and Barthes is entirely rigorous here—is time "itself," and it is no accident that the term he associates most closely with accident and contingency—the *punctum*—is another word for time. Indeed, as he tells us, "there exists another *punctum* (another 'stigmatum') than the 'detail.' This new *punctum,* which is no longer of form but of intensity, is Time, the lacerating emphasis of the *noeme* ('*that-has-been*'), its pure representation" (*CL* 96/*CC* 148). If time lacerates the surface of the photograph, this wounded photograph also interrupts the movement of time, in a manner that has, not the form of time, but rather the form of time's interruption, the form of an "*intense immobility*" (*CL* 49/*CC* 81), of an explosion. It wounds the form of time, intensely and irrecuperably. This disorder is introduced by the photograph from the very beginning, however, since every photograph is marked by the singular moment in which it was taken, a moment that, because it cannot be reproduced or repeated, because it is not redeemable in the present, inhabits the present like a kind of ghost. This is why every photograph signals "the return of the dead" (*CL* 9/*CC* 23), a return in which the photographed becomes a "Total-Image, which is to say, Death in person" (*CL* 14/*CC* 31).

The photograph therefore does not only look backward—it does not only evoke lost time and melancholy—but it also opens onto a future: it is in fact displaced toward the future. As Barthes notes, the metonymic force of the detail opens the photograph to "a kind of subtle beyond" (*CL* 59/*CC* 93). This beyond is not a spatial beyond or a crossing of the limits of codified knowledge or cultural sentiments; it is a "blind field" (*CL* 57/*CC* 91), a beyond that, composed of time, is like the future, something to which we always remain blind. It is the field of the possible, of what, within the photograph, cannot be said to be simply here and now, but rather evoked, like a promise, in relation to the past and to an unknown future which is still to come, but has, as its horizon, our future death. This is why, bound together like the copy and its negative, the *punctum* and the *studium* are the two fictional poles of photography: each image pretends to reach them but never entirely succeeds. *Punctum* and *studium* are the two threads that, together, constitute the materiality of photographic language: contingency, chance, gratuitousness, singularity, and difference, on the one hand, and necessity, predictability, composition, regularity, and repetition, on the other. In this way, every photograph not only shows what it exhibits—not only shows a relation between an observed subject and a subject observing captured on a piece of photographic paper—but also says, exhibits, or performs what photography *is*. Photography is an amorous experience, magical and paradoxical: an objective chance, a necessary gratuitousness, "the tireless repetition of contingency" (*CL* 5/*CC* 17).

III

There is something uncanny in every photograph—a force of destabilization, something that leaves us in suspense even as it fascinates us. This perhaps is because, when we look at an image, we encounter, directly in front of us, and no matter how elusive it may remain, the first sign of chance and contingency—again, what Barthes calls the *punctum*—and, like all encounters with contingency, this one also produces a certain terror and bedazzlement. But perhaps it is something else altogether: perhaps photography distances itself from all civilized and sympathetic contemplation and directly interrogates enjoyment because what we notice when we look at an image is the peculiar relation that a photograph maintains with what was (but is no longer) before the camera. Within the photographic world of *Camera Lucida,* the photograph enables an experience of pleasure because it promises the possibility of our being able to conjure, and perhaps even to touch, the material remainder of the referent's lost body. Even if the referent is no longer present or living—and this absence or death is what wounds us, even if, as Barthes reminds us, this wounding is never experienced without a certain degree of pleasure—the trace of its "having-been-there" belongs to what makes a photograph a photograph. This is why the photograph always appears as a form of haunting which, evoking a material trace of the past, condenses, among so many other things, the relation between the past and the present, the dead and the living, and destruction and survival.

Unlike other modes of representation, photography effectively establishes an existential relation with the object because, within the photograph, "the presence of the thing (at a certain past moment) is never metaphoric" (*CL* 78/*CC* 123), even if we can only encounter its ghostly remains. This nonmetaphorical, real presence does not imply that the image bears "testimony" to anything or offers an "objective" or "faithful" representation of the object. The relation between indexicality and truth or testimony is not a characteristic of the index but a particular mode of reading or perceiving the photographic image that simultaneously brings together a conception of the subject, language, and representation. *Camera Lucida* distances itself from this relation between photography and truth precisely when it signals that the body that poses for the camera is a photographic body, a subjectivity that does not exist before its representation but that instead constitutes itself in the act of sitting in front of the camera. If, within classical semiotics, the process of representation begins and ends in the stability of the "referent," Barthes undoes this certainty at the very moment he identifies this point of departure and arrival with a plural subjectivity, when he renames it a "little simulacrum," the "Spectrum of the Photograph" (*CL* 9/*CC* 22–23). Far from demonstrating the truth of reference, the indexical character of the photograph stages its phantasmatic being, its presence in the past and its absence in the present. The photograph is an index of the photographed, in the same way that his smell, his fingerprints, or the footprints he leaves in the sand are indices of him. They are traces or fragments left behind by a body that work as "a certificate of presence" (*CL* 87/*CC* 135), as a sign of something that was present then but now is not. The index is a sign linked to mourning and melancholy, and never to truth or testimony. Indeed, recalling the way in which photography was perceived in its beginnings in the nineteenth century, we may confirm that the idea that technology has the power to bring an occult "truth" to visibility is precisely the result of a historical perception. To put it differently: the confidence that what we call the referent or subject of an image is an entity that is stable and identical to itself, a full presence that exists before representation, that stands in front of the photographic apparatus and of which the camera (or language) gives us a "faithful" or "true" representation, corresponds not to a characteristic proper to photography, but to a policing use of photographic technology. To naturalize a policial use of photographic technology and to convert this reading of the photograph into "the" reading of it is, like any ideological operation, the result of a dehistoricization of the multiple modes in which the photographic image is circulated and read. Nevertheless, it is precisely because there is no single way to read indexicality that an index—for example, a photographic portrait or a lock of hair—says something different to a detective in a police story than to the protagonist of a romance novel. This is why Alphonse Bertillon and Francis Galton sought a mode of ordering what to their eyes seemed evident: the correspondence between a subject and his image. In response, and to the contrary, Barthes confesses that "'myself' never coincides with my image" (*CL* 12/*CC* 26–27).[9]

Indexicality is not linked to truth or testimony, but to the body. As an index, the photograph bears, according to Barthes, a material relation to the body of the photographed, which is why he can suggest that in photography the presence of that body within a unique moment in the past can never be metaphorical. As he notes, "I am delighted (or depressed) to know that the thing of the past, by its immediate radiations (its luminances), has really touched the surface, which in its turn my gaze will touch" (*CL* 81/*CC* 126). The photographic index is a corporeal trace, a luminous "emanation," captured by a chemical process. From the perspective of its most absolute materiality—that is, as a chemical effect produced by light—photography acquires magical traits. The photographic index displays its magic, its alchemy, by joining—as if it were "a sort of umbilical cord" (*CL* 81/*CC* 126)—the body that earlier marked that photographic plate or film with its presence and the body that holds the image in its hands and looks it over with its eyes. What delights and, at the same time, depresses is the double character of the photographic trace. On the one hand, the image is a real (nonmetaphorical) fragment of a body that belonged to the past. This means that from the very beginning the indexical character of photography offers the promise of immortality. This utopic hope of interrupting or stopping time, of immobilizing the present and freezing it on a two-dimensional surface, is legible in the first uses of photography—particularly in the nineteenth-century custom of taking portraits of the dead—and it remains inscribed within the desire of all photographic technology and, indeed, touches every image the camera takes. This is why a photograph can be considered an index, in the same way that a fossil or a ruin are indices: a fragment that comes to us from the past and permits us to dream that the totality that produced it is still here and, moreover, still belongs to us. On the other hand, as a trace, as an emanation of a body, an index—for example, a photograph or a footprint on the beach—never gives us precise information about the body that posed for the camera or that sank its feet in the sand. Nevertheless, what cannot be neglected here is that we are left only with an absence—before the camera and on the sand. An index maintains an existential relation with the photographed body only because it signals, with an unforeseen "prick," the wake of its disappearance.

If the index's double character simultaneously delights and depresses, then, it is because it says that the body that was there was there in such a convincing manner that it was able to leave a small fragment of itself, a fragment that we touch with our gaze as if we were touching this body. But every index is also the sign of a fatality (*CL* 6/*CC* 18), because it simultaneously signals an irrecoverable time and a lost object. This perhaps is why photography evokes a greater sense of melancholy than other indexical objects: "in photography, something *has posed*" (*CL* 78/*CC* 123) in front of the camera, and this something has not slipped away but rather appears to have stayed there, arrested, if only for an instant. This promise of surrender that produces the immobile object before the tiny hole of the camera is perhaps what returns this absence most mournfully. It is also the sense of stability produced by photography when, embalming time, it moves us to imagine, as we contemplate a photographic portrait, that we are before an embalmed body.

This is why *there is something uncanny in every photograph—a force of destabilization, something that leaves us in suspense even as it fascinates us.* Like a "floating flash," its "effect is certain but unlocatable, it does not find its sign, its name; it is sharp and yet lands in a vague zone of myself; it is acute yet muffled, it cries out in silence" (*CL* 51, 53/*CC* 87). It is the force of a mark: the force of the index or of that past existence that has only an image as its trace, the force of the *punctum* or chance that wounds every image. The force of the photograph resides in its capacity to fascinate us and to leave us defenseless because photography—which often has been associated with the field of the Imaginary—does nothing else than point toward the very center of the Real, toward that place where we remain without words or without a gaze. This is why we so often remain mute in front of an image: it is as if, for a fleeting second, we are viewing what cannot be named. This also is why Kafka's phrase—that we "photograph things in order to drive them out of our minds"—connects the compulsion to photograph not to the necessity of registering or possessing the world, but to the possibility of not seeing it, and this is because, ultimately—or at the limit—photography points toward the Real itself, toward what we do not wish to name, toward what we do not wish to see: the *punctum,* the index, contingency, death. Nevertheless, whether we seal our lips, close our eyes, or take photographs of everything, the "floating flash" will not fade away or disappear. Perhaps to see a photograph we do not need to open our eyes to its literal brutality, but neither do we need to close them. Ultimately—or at the limit—perhaps we can view a photograph best when we look at it with our eyes half-closed, as when we look at the sun.

IV

As an index, every image is an emanation of a body from the past that, disappearing and no longer here, nonetheless has left behind a fragment of itself. When we contemplate this remnant, that is, this photograph, we look at it quickly in order to arrest the gaze in a new fragment, in a detail that Barthes calls the *punctum.* In this way, index and *punctum* are two names for designating the experience of the fragment or the fragmentation of experience that we call "photography." As a fragment, a photograph offers itself to be read as a kind of remnant or corpse; it is what remains of a totality that now is absent. But, as a new totality, it signals the violence enacted in every photographic act, and in photographic language itself. After all, a photograph is a cut that the eye or the camera realizes in the world, even if only in this fragmentary way. As Barthes suggests, while looking at a series of photographs of his mother and trying to discover her essence in them: "According to these photographs, sometimes I recognized a region of her face, a certain relation of nose and forehead, the moment of her arms, her hands. I never recognized her except in fragments, which is to say that I missed her being, and that therefore I missed her altogether" (*CL* 66/ *CC* 103). These photographic fragments enable him to "dream about her," but not to "dream her" (*CL* 66/ *CC* 104). Or rather, if they "dream her," they can only dream her as fragmented, as shattered, as only present in the absence that Barthes insistently and passionately wishes to overcome. The result of this fragmented dream is the object that, ungrateful and without memory, we call an image, a fragment that appears before our eyes only as a "counter-memory" (*CL* 91/ *CC* 142), and as if it were a matter of an autonomous whole.

Camera Lucida perfectly identifies the ontological violence that characterizes photographic technology and translates it into a kind of grammar that names the effects of the image on the body of the observed subject and of the subject observing: it pierces, pricks, scans, and tears a hole. Nevertheless, Barthes reads this photographic violence—perhaps another name for the force of decontextualization that takes place in any photograph—in relation not only to melancholy or tragedy but also to enjoyment. The image is comparable, then, to the haiku. It shares with this poetic form the "essence (of a wound)," this feature of the fragment in which nothing is missing because "everything is given," which neither asks for development nor provokes "even the possibility of a rhetorical expansion" (*CL* 49/ *CC* 81). This identification between the photographic image and the haiku is pervasive within Barthes's writings and can be traced in his essay "The Third Meaning," in his book on Japan, *Empire of Signs,* and in his other quasi-autobiographical text, *Roland Barthes by Roland Barthes.*[10] In each instance, the haiku, like the image, is a kind of "anaphoric gesture," where "meaning is only a flash, a slash of light," in which what is developed is, as he puts it, "undevelopable" (*CL* 49/*CC* 81), and in which "the wake of the sign which seems to have been traced" within the photographic image "is erased."[11] Somewhat different from melancholy and tragedy, and as a fragment that becomes a new totality and does not ask to be expanded, the image therefore acquires the brilliance and splendor of the haiku and, in this context, of the fetish.[12]

Indeed, the fetish is that fragment that initially receives special attention because it refers to an absent object in order to hide it and to occupy its place. The image becomes a fetish when the thin cord tying it to the object is cut and the gaze sinks into it in search of an increasingly minuscule detail whose "mere presence changes my reading" (*CL* 42/*CC* 71). Before the images of Mapplethorpe, Barthes is unmoved by the spectacle that photography offers, and instead focuses on the image of the underwear taken at very close range in order to register "the texture of the material" (*CL* 42/*CC* 71). Like the detective who concerns himself only with those details most pertinent to the resolution of the crime, the analyst who investigates the minute slip that will conduct him to the truth, and the lover who isolates a particular trait or feature in relation to which he surrenders himself to the beloved object, the close-up fragments the world and gathers details that make us forget the whole to which they at one time belonged.

The photographic gaze is fetishistic; it functions like an infinite blowup, and enlarges the image in order to search for "a 'detail,' *i.e.,* a partial object" (*CL* 43/ *CC* 73). As Michelangelo Antonioni's film or Julio Cortázar's story confirms, however, to enlarge an image, to approach its details, is perhaps always to go in search of the mystery of our own image. "To give examples of *punctum,*" Barthes confesses, "is, in a certain fashion, to *give myself up*" (*CL* 43/ *CC* 73). In *Camera Lucida* there is one detail that insists and captures Barthes' gaze with great regularity, as if each portrait were a kind of magnet that attracts him to it. At first, it emerges as a "cultural or historical" question: "many of the men photographed by Nadar have long fingernails: an ethnographical question: how long were nails worn in a certain period?" (*CL* 30/ *CC* 52, 54). But later, this detail appears again, and with another tone, when Barthes contemplates a portrait of the young Tristan Tzara. What holds his attention is not the face of the photographed Tzara, nor even the fact that he is wearing a monocle; rather, Barthes suggests, "the grace of the *punctum* is Tzara's hand resting on the door frame." He then proceeds to a close-up that focuses on something even smaller, the true *punctum* of the photograph: here, "a large hand whose nails are anything but clean" (*CL* 45/ *CC* 74) would seem to be the most adequate analog to whatever it is that seduces us within an image. What dazzles us, what wounds us, when we look at a photograph is a marginal and unexpected detail—a kind of emanation of the unconscious within the body or in the image—which is excluded from the intentionality of the photographer or the photographed subject or object, and thereby opens the door for chance to enter. The *punctum* is a fetish, a fulgurating detail that, irradiating its light, does not occult, but nevertheless makes the rest of the image opaque. This is what seems to happen in Duane Michals's portrait of Andy Warhol, in which Warhol covers his face with his hands but nevertheless manages to hide nothing. Warhol "offers his hands to read, quite openly; and the *punctum* is not the gesture," but, as happens in the earlier image, "the slightly repellent substance of those spatulate nails, at once soft and hard-edged" (*CL* 45/ *CC* 77). The *punctum* is this soft and spatulate detail that captures us; it is, at the same time, this "slightly repellent substance," the remains left behind by a body, an object, or instant that we love as a fetish, as an index, or photograph. If this attention to nails is a kind of permanent interest for Barthes (it already appears in "The Third Meaning"), it is perhaps because fingernails seem to embody the fetish: the fact that they continue to grow even after the body to which they belong has died—we could even say that they represent that part of the living body that most closely resembles dead matter—means that, like the photograph, and like the fetish, they shatter the border between life and death, and presence and absence. Fragments of the body, they magnetize Barthes's attention and desire because, among so many other things, they belong to his meditation on the contradictory character of photography. If a photograph is a fragment that steals the show from the totality that at one time had housed it, it is because what dazzles us within a photograph is, like Barthes's nails, a marginal fragment, a detail that, fulgurating within the image, leaves everything else in shadows. This mobile and elusive detail is charged with a metonymic force. It condenses the image and displaces it like a ghost, it can be seen here and then there, it appears now and reappears later. The fragment we call a photograph and the fragment that illuminates it have the power to tear both time and our gaze: "it is phantasmatic, deriving from a kind of second sight which seems to bear me forward to a utopian time, or to carry me back to somewhere in myself" (*CL* 40/*CC* 68). Photography is the amorous fetish *par excellence,* a fragment of the present that, like the relation between two lovers, links and realizes both the past and the future and, in doing so, deranges time altogether.

V

In his discussion of the question of resemblance, Barthes claims that when he gets close to a photograph, when he feels he almost can touch his "desired object, his beloved's body," he finds himself "burning" (*CL* 100/*CC* 157), as if consumed by a kind of fire. This experience of burning registers not only the extremity of his desire and love but also, at the very edge of this extremity, the conflagration of his identity. Indeed, the entire discussion of resemblance belongs to Barthes's polemic against identity in general. If a photograph implies a resemblance to an identity, he suggests, this identity is always "imprecise" and "even imaginary"; it is only an "absurd, purely legal, even penal affair" (*CL* 100–101/*CC* 157, 160). This is why a photographic portrait always "looks like anyone except the person it represents," and why he can find the "splendor" of his mother's truth in the Winter Garden Photograph (*CL* 102–103/*CC* 160). In this "lost, remote photograph"—in which the little girl he never knew, the little girl who neither resembles nor looks "like" his mother, nevertheless evokes the "lineaments" of his mother's truth—Barthes encounters a photographic principle: "In front of the photograph of my mother as a child," he writes, "I tell myself: she is going to die: I shudder, like Winnicott's psychotic patient, *over a catastrophe which has already occurred. Whether or not the subject is already dead, every photograph is this catastrophe*" (*CL* 96/*CC* 150). If the photograph of his mother as a child already bears the trace of her future death, it is certainly because, at the moment in which Barthes finds it and views it, she *is* dead (the catastrophe "*has already occurred,*" and he only can view the photograph through the lens of this death), but it is also because the photograph, at the very moment it was taken, already had mortified and immobilized its subject (the catastrophe *"had already occurred,"* and not only before he views the photograph but also before his birth or his mother's death). Whether or not the mother "is already dead," then, *literally* dead, she already will have experienced (a kind of) death.

The photograph always brings death to the photographed, because death is the photograph's *"eidos"* (*CL* 15/*CC* 32).[13] What survives in a photograph, what returns in it, is therefore always also the survival of the dead, the appearance of a ghost or phantom. This is why, within the space of the photograph, the dead always are alive, and the alive always are dead without being dead. This axiom enables Barthes to generalize his experience of the Winter Garden Photograph into a claim about the photograph in general, but it also leads him to read his own death not only in relation to that of his mother, but in relation to the death that is announced by every photograph: as he puts it, every photograph "always contains this imperious sign of my future death" (*CL* 97/*CC* 151). Observing a photograph, the viewer spectralizes himself in relation to a death that, through an uncertain and phantasmatic process of identification, now haunts him, now touches and inhabits his life, now comes to be seen as "his": a death that is the life of his life, and in which he exists and lives, not as dead, but as dying. He exists, like the first actors who "separated themselves from the community by playing the role of the Dead," in "a body simultaneously living and dead" (*CL* 31/*CC* 56). That this experience of living at the threshold of death and life is another name for the experience of love—for what takes place in our relation to the one we love—is confirmed when, in *A Lover's Discourse,* Barthes confesses: "I have projected myself into the other with such power that when I am without the other I cannot recover myself, regain myself: I am lost, forever."[14] While he suggests that this loss of self occurs especially in relation to the absent other, he also implies that it happens even when the other is presumably "present," since the very relation between a self and an other means that, because each already inhabits the other, neither the self nor the other can return to himself (or, in the case of his mother, to "herself"): the self and the other deconstitute one another precisely in their relation.

If neither Barthes nor his mother can remain simply themselves, it is because, bearing the trace of the other, each can become identified with the other. The possibility of this transformation of the one into the other is confirmed in an extraordinary moment in which Barthes claims, in an extreme temporal reversal, to have given birth to his mother, and therefore to have become a mother himself. After recalling that the Greeks "entered into Death backward," Barthes claims, on discovering the Winter Garden Photograph of his "mother as a child," to have "worked back" in relation to this photograph "through a life, not my own, but the life of someone I love." He goes on to suggest that, while taking care of his ailing mother "at the end of her life," he is able to experience the backward "movement of the Photograph"—its capacity to take him back to the childhood of his mother—in "reality" (*CL* 71/*CC*, 111–112). "During her illness," he explains, "I nursed her, held the bowl of tea she liked because it was easier to drink from than from a cup; she had become my little girl, uniting for me with that essential child she was in her first photograph. . . . Ultimately I experienced her, strong as she had been, my inner law, as my feminine child. Which was my way of resolving Death . . . if after having been reproduced as other than himself, the individual dies, having thereby denied and transcended himself, I who had not procreated, I had, in her very illness, engendered my mother" (*CL* 72/*CC* 112–113). Acknowledging that his mother always had been his "inner law," Barthes suggests that she was already in him before he was himself; she was already stronger or more forceful than he: from the very beginning, she had left an imprint on him and therefore given birth to him, reproduced him, "as other than himself." As a mechanism for reproduction, the mother reproduces—like a camera—not the same thing, but something else: she therefore kills (Barthes says he "dies") at the same time that she engenders, produces, gives birth, brings to the light of day, and gives something to be seen. He confirms this death—this death that attends birth—when, as happens in this passage, he encounters himself in the figure of the mother. In experiencing the mother's alterity, in experiencing alterity in the mother, he experiences the alteration "in him" that infinitely displaces and delimits his singularity. This is why, from the moment of his birth, Barthes already experiences a kind of death in relation to the maternal body—a body whose material residue lives on in his body and therefore retrospectively confirms not only his body's passage through her body but also his capacity to retain a relation to the mother's body, even after her death. Embodying both the past and the present, death and life, Barthes's body bears the traces of the place where he once lived (and lived in order to begin dying): his mother's dark womb (or, as we might put it, his mother's "darkroom"). As he notes, "Freud says of the maternal body that 'there is no other place of which one can say with so much certainty that one has already been there'" (*CL* 40/*CC* 68). The condition of possibility for a process of reproduction that gives something to be seen, the mother's body is at once camera, developer, and photographic darkroom. Giving birth to an image, the mother is another name for photography. This bond between photography and the mother is legible throughout Barthes's text, and it is not restricted to those moments in which he refers to the mother explicitly: he structures his entire text around a photograph of his dead mother that he does not reproduce, but from which he wishes to derive all photography, and he conceives of photography in maternal terms, as a process of reproduction that, like the mother, gives birth to a series of images—through chemical means—which create, preserve, and destroy their subjects, and which are joined to the observing subject by a kind of umbilical cord. Within the world of *Camera Lucida,* the mother is an incunabulum of images.

If Barthes's mother remains "in him," even after her death, even after she has disappeared and passed away, this is because, beyond the material traces, the material imprint her body has left on his, she remains in him in a series of memories and scenes that are nothing else than images: she leaves "in him" only images.[15] Recalling his mother (but what else, other than the mother, can we remember?), Barthes associates her with a series of different, but related images—first the image of her during her illness, then the image she becomes when she is his "feminine child" or "little girl," and then the image of the one whom he "engenders." It is not an accident, however, that he identifies with the mother, with the maternal function, at the very moment when his "mother," not yet a mother, is the "essential child" in her "first photograph." Like the mother who reproduces the self as an other, Barthes reproduces his mother as an other (as a series of others). Incorporating his dead mother into his own spectral identity, he enables a kind of "resurrection" (*CL* 82/*CC* 129), another "birth," and thereby counters her death with an element of life (perhaps his "own"), but a life that already was there in the mother's living death. If the photograph bespeaks a certain horror, Barthes notes, it is because "it certifies that the corpse is alive, *as corpse:* it is the living image of a dead thing" (*CL* 78–79/*CC* 123); it is because, in other words, within the photograph, the dead and the living become undead.[16]

The general relay between photography and the mother suggests that the photograph— and, in this instance, the photograph we know as the son who becomes the mother— is endowed with a magical and uncanny power to procreate, and this is confirmed in one of the most remarkable passages in *Camera Lucida,* a passage that brings together light, the body, the gaze, the self, the referent, and the maternal body. Barthes writes: "The photograph is literally an emanation of the referent. From a real body, which was there, proceed radiations which ultimately touch me, who am here; the duration of the transmission is insignificant; the photograph of the missing being touches me like the delayed rays of a star. A sort of umbilical cord links the body of the photographed thing to my gaze: light, though impalpable, is here a carnal medium, a skin I share with anyone who has been photographed" (*CL* 80–81/*CC* 126–127).[17] Evoking Democritus and his theory of *eidolas*—in which bodies give off emanations, material vestiges of the subject, that travel through the medium of light to the eyes of a spectator[18]—Barthes suggests that the photograph brings together a distant past and a present moment in the same way that the "delayed rays of a star" join what is most distant to what is closest at hand, and that it is also bound to the spectator's gaze by a kind of umbilical cord composed of light. As Elissa Marder suggests in her reading of this passage,

If the photograph transforms the living and the dead into the living dead—if it binds the living to the dead in a kind of "amorous or funereal immobility, at the very heart of the moving world"; if life and death are "glued together, limb by limb, like the condemned man and the corpse in certain tortures" (*CL* 6/*CC* 17)—it is also because, like the mother, the photograph kills at the same time that it gives birth. As Barthes puts it, "once I feel myself observed by the lens, everything changes. . . . I feel that the Photograph creates my body or mortifies it, according to its caprice" (*CL* 10–11/*CC* 25). Like the mother, the photograph exists between life and death, the past and the present, interiority and exteriority, body and image, and subject and image. It opens onto a future whose lineaments are not yet known, even if what can be known enables us to delineate the contours of the horizon and limit of death. This is why the mother—Barthes's mother, but also all mothers—is nothing more nor less than a figure for the birth and death of photography.

VI

If the Winter Garden Photograph is indeed the "invisible *punctum*" of Barthes's elegiac book[20]—even though it does not belong to the series of photographs he exhibits and analyzes, it nevertheless haunts the entire book; we could even say that, as the wound that "signs" the book, there is no sentence in the book that is not touched by it—he soon suggests that, in thinking of the photograph, we must think of something other than simply light or photography: we must think of what he calls the "last music," the song of his mother and of his grief at her death, and, in general, a kind of accord or correspondence. As he notes: "The Winter Garden Photograph was for me like the last music Schumann wrote before collapsing, that first *Gesang der Frühe* that accords with both my mother's being and my grief at her death: I could not express this accord except by an infinite series of adjectives" (*CL* 70/*CC* 110).[21] While he already had stressed the relation between photography and music in his discussion of the *studium* and *punctum*—"Having thus distinguished two themes in Photography," he writes, "(for in general the photographs I liked were constructed in the manner of a classical sonata), I could occupy myself with one after the other" (*CL 27/ CC* 49)—his reference to Schumann's last music is particularly resonant here, since, among other things, it evokes his 1979 essay "Loving Schumann" and an earlier essay from 1976 on Schumann and Schubert entitled "The Romantic Song." In the latter text, he explains that, while listening to the Schumannian lied, he addresses himself to "an Image: the image of the beloved in which I lose myself and from which my own image, abandoned, comes back to me." "I struggle with an image," he goes on to say, anticipating his later understanding of his relation to the Winter Garden Photograph, "which is both the image of the desired, lost other, and my own image, desiring and abandoned."[22] After his mother's death, however, the figure of the "desired, lost other" evoked by Schumann's music becomes associated specifically with his mother and her death, and with the loss of self to which this relation and death give birth. He makes this point explicit in "Loving Schumann," when he claims that Schumann is the musician of "solitary intimacy, of the amorous and imprisoned soul that *speaks to itself . . .* in short, of the child who has no other link than to the Mother," and when he states that Schumann's music is "at once dispersed and unary, continually taking refuge in the luminous shadow of the Mother (the lied, copious in Schumann's work, is . . . the expression of this maternal unity)."[23] Suggesting that we have a relation to the Mother even when we are alone and speaking only to ourselves (and this because we internalize her trace just as we internalize the trace of the music we hear), Schumann's music, like photography, joins love to a force of arrest, and the "Mother" to photography. Associated with the light and darkness within which photography emerges, the Mother also turns out to be linked to the rhythms and scansions of music "itself."

What is perhaps most remarkable about this series of associations—among music, love, death, mourning, and the mother—is that it transcribes music onto a shadowy representation of mortality and finitude. This relation between music and death is evoked in André Malraux's 1933 account of the early days of the Chinese Revolution, *The Human Condition.* Malraux notes that "music only can speak of death."[24] If, on the one hand, he suggests that of all the arts only music can speak of death, on the other hand, he tells us that music can only speak of death, can speak of nothing but death. What makes music music, in other words, is that, in our experience of it, we encounter what is always about to vanish. This is why, for Barthes, music is linked to mourning, and, in particular, within *Camera Lucida,* to the relation between love and mourning. Indeed, it is precisely this latter relation that is evoked by the Winter Garden Photograph and that draws him toward Photography, since it is in relation to this particular photograph that he claims to understand that he must "interrogate the evidence of Photography . . . in relation to what we romantically call love and death" (*CL 73/CC* 115). Like love and death, music begins in its fugitive, transitory character, in the impossibility of our ever comprehending it. This is why music often has been understood as "an art beyond signification."[25] In the experience of music, we always encounter an aleatory (but sonorous, audible, evocative) oversignification. We might even say that music is, as it were, the least incorporated matter. Like the other who always remains beyond our comprehension—as we know, this incomprehension is, for Barthes, a condition of love and its many enigmas—music remains, even after we hear it, even after we incorporate its trace, somewhere beyond us, resonating at a distance, in an exteriority that extends in every direction and that we experience as the opening of the world. Music has no hidden surface, even when it remains unseen; like Barthes's mother, it appears "without either showing or hiding" itself (*CL* 69/*CC* 107). It is fugitive and evanescent. Like love and death, it has the capacity to dispossess its subjects, and, since it determines us by displacing us, by disappropriating us, by making us inaccessible to ourselves, we could even say that it means *the vanishing of the subject.*

To say that music "only speaks of death," then, is to say that, like photography and love, music always signals our departure from ourselves, our imminent death. It is also to say that music has always been a means of experiencing traces, a form of inscription or writing. Like photography, it has the power to leave an imprint or trace—and it has this power because, among other things, it is rhythm itself. When Mallarmé says in *Music and Letters* that "every soul is a rhythmic knot,"[26] he recalls the archaic sense of the word "music": *rhythm,* which meant "type," "letter," "character," and even "scheme." This is why music always implies the violent imposition of a certain form; it is the impression that, in some malleable material (wax or vinyl, for example)—and, again, not unlike photography—produces an effigy. To designate an operation of this kind, the Greeks used the verb *tupein,* from *tupos*: the mark, the imprint, engraved characters. Emile Benveniste (for whom Barthes often confessed his admiration and love)[27] confirms this point in his 1966 essay "The Notion of 'Rhythm' in Its Linguistic Expression," noting that *rhuthmos* means originally *skhema* (form, figure, schema) and that it also characterizes (and belongs to) a generalized process of differentiation and distinction often exemplified by the letters of the alphabet.[28]

This relation between rhythm and inscription, between rhythm and letters, evokes the question of writing in general, a question on the basis of which it seems possible, passing through the works of Barthes, to think about the subject's preinscription within writing. But, as Philippe Lacoue-Labarthe notes in his analysis of Benveniste's essay, we should not move too quickly through the steps of Benveniste's argument.[29] Benveniste in fact insists that *skhema* is only an approximation of *rhuthmos*. If *skhema* designates "a fixed, realized form posited as an object," *rhuthmos* is "the form at the moment it is taken by what is in movement, mobile, fluid, the form that has no organic consistency." It is, he adds, "improvised, momentaneous, modifiable" form.[30] This means, among other things, that the form of rhythm is traversed by time, or, to put it differently, time is its condition of possibility. Following Lacoue-Labarthe, we can say that the word "rhythm" already implies—at the very edge of the subject's capacity to figure or represent itself—the mark, the stamp, the imprint that, inscribing us within its movement, prevents us from ever returning to ourselves, sends us back to the night and chaos that, never ordered by us, enables us to appear as what we are, as what we are not—ourselves.[31] This process of inscription and impression also characterizes the photographic space, a space in which, as Barthes suggests, we always experience the "advent" of ourselves as an other. In this sense, perhaps, "every soul is a rhythmic knot," a bringing together of stasis and movement, of stability and instability, of singularity and repetition. We are *rhythmed,* therefore[32]—which is to say that we become an impression, in particular, a photographic impression. Barthes confirms this transformation (and in the context of his relation to the beloved's voice and body) in *The Lover's Discourse* when he writes that, "in the fascinating image, *what impresses me (like a sensitized paper)* is not the accumulation of its details but this or that inflection. What suddenly manages to touch me (ravish me) in the other is the voice, the line of the shoulders, the slenderness of the silhouette, the warmth of the hand, the curve of a smile, and so forth."[33] Like the detail or *punctum* that pierces him, that wounds him, the details of his beloved's body enter him and transform him into the register, the imprint, of a series of impressions that, like the "sensitized paper" that records the other's trace, confirm his photographic character, his inscription within a photographic process. The body he loves is not unlike the music he loves, since both enter his own body and, in entering it, prevent it from remaining just "his," even if, as he suggests, "he" and his body become a kind of musical organ that "plays" this music from somewhere else as if it were emerging from "him" (like the *punctum,* the music is added to his body, even as it is already there). "Schumann's music goes much farther than the ear," Barthes explains, "it goes into the body, into the muscles by the beats of its rhythm, and somehow into the viscera by the voluptuous pleasure of its melos; as if on each occasion the piece was written only for one person, the one who plays it." "The true Schumannian pianist," he adds, is him: "*c'est moi.*"[34] Entering him and piercing him like the *punctum* of a photograph, music transforms and animates him and, in the rhythm of this process, he becomes the only one who can experience and interpret the music in a particular way, in a way that remains faithful to the madness of its movement. "Rhythmed" in this way, he is jostled back and forth until he appears to become a kind of light that, rebounding off the several surfaces it encounters, ensures that his "identity" remains nothing more than what he elsewhere calls a "fleeting index."[35] As he puts it in his analysis of the lover's discourse, displacing his interest from a musical interest to a photographic one, "in the amorous encounter, I keep rebounding—I am *light.*"[36]

In an unpublished lecture from 1977 entitled "Music, Voice, and Language," Barthes reinforces this relay between music and love by suggesting that music—in the composer's imaginary, more often associated with night than with light—in fact "derives" from the discourse of love. "Every 'successful' relation," he writes, "successful in that it manages to say the implicit without articulating it, to pass over articulation without falling into the censorship of desire or the sublimation of the unspeakable—such a relation can rightly be called musical."[37] The music of love therefore belongs to a space of relation and silence—a space without articulation—but one whose silence is linked to the "affect of the lost, abandoned subject." Barthes reinforces this claim in *Camera Lucida* in an exquisite passage on the relations among music, silence, blindness, the night, and, again, a certain accord. Immediately after noting that the *punctum* can "accommodate a certain latency," that it can appear when he is not looking at a photograph, he writes: "Ultimately—or at the limit—in order to see a photograph well, it is best to look away or close your eyes. 'The necessary condition for an image is sight,' Janouch told Kafka; and Kafka smiled and replied: 'We photograph things in order to drive them out of our minds. My stories are a way of shutting my eyes.' The photograph must be silent . . . this is not a question of discretion, but of music. Absolute subjectivity is achieved in a state, an effort, of silence (shutting your eyes is to make the image speak in silence). The photograph touches me if I withdraw it from its usual blah-blah: 'Technique,' 'Reality,' 'Reportage,' 'Art,' etc.: to say nothing, to shut my eyes, to allow the detail to rise of its own accord into affective consciousness" (*CL* 53, 55/*CC* 88–89). Encountering a photograph—like encountering music, Barthes suggests—requires a certain silence and blindness, and, together, this silence and blindness suggest a kind of withdrawal from more conventional (or less surprising) understandings of photography. If he likens the silence of the photograph to the experience of shutting his eyes to what we do not wish to see or wish to name, and to music itself (we should remember that silence, as he says, nonetheless still speaks), it is because music never gives anything to sight: it says nothing, it cannot be immobilized, it is, in Marie-Louise Mallet's words, a "'rebel' object," and this because, before everything else, it can never become an object.[38] Like love, death, and photography, it escapes the theoretical regard; it remains in the dark. This is why Nietzsche calls music the "art of the night," and why he associates it with the "night" of philosophy itself.[39] In Barthes's terms, while music may be of the order of an "event," like the photographic subject or object it appears only to disappear, and this is why it requires, at every moment, a work of mourning. This is simply to say that music names, if it names anything at all, a loss without return; it recalls death to us, and, since the night always suggests death, we could even say that, in Barthesian terms, there is no music without the night or death. As he states in relation to his love of Schumann, "Loving Schumann . . . is in a way . . . to adopt a Nietzschean word, Untimeliness, or again, to risk this time the most Schumannian word there is: Night."[40] This means, among other things, that to focus on the relation between music and the night, between music and death, is already to suggest something "untimely," since this focus menaces the projects of philosophy, knowledge, and truth. Like the Barthes who claims that he can respond to photographs only by dismissing "all knowledge, all culture," and by refusing "to inherit anything from another eye than [his] own" (*CL* 51/*CC* 82), the Barthes who loves Schumann does so *against* the age," which, as he suggests, is the only responsible way of loving. Love means: *going against the age,* since "it inevitably leads the subject who does so and says so to posit himself in his time according to the injunctions of his desire and not according to those of his sociality,"[41] and this is, he suggests, the only way to have even the slightest chance of addressing the beloved's singularity, the beloved's cherished body.

What happens, however, when, as Barthes asks, our eyes meet what they cannot see, or when they encounter what cannot be encountered—whether it be music, love, death, photography, or even the beloved's singularity? What might this experience of blindness and shadows have to do with what makes photography photography? In what way is sight essentially linked to an experience of mourning, an experience of mourning that mourns not only experience but sight itself? Why is it that only the most profound mourning can become music? Why is it that music is most expressive only in the silence of the night? As Barthes would have it: as soon as a technology of the image exists, sight is already touched by the night. It is inscribed in a body whose secrets belong to the night. It radiates a light of the night. It tells us that the night falls on us. "But even if it were not to fall on us, we already are in the night," Derrida explains,

as soon as we are captured by optical instruments that have no need for the light of day. We are already ghosts. . . . In the nocturnal space in which this image of us, this picture we are in the process of having "taken," is described, it is already night. Moreover, because we know that, once taken, once captured, such an image can be reproduced in our absence, because we know this already, we already know that we are haunted by a future that bears our death. Our disappearance is already there.[42]

Camera Lucida begins in the shadowy night of this relation to death, in this rhythmic play between life and death, presence and absence, and light and darkness. As Barthes works to demonstrate—but in accordance with the madness of what he calls a "stupid" metaphysics (*CL* 85/*CC* 133)—the entire logic of our relation to the world can be read here, and it can be read as the logic of the photograph. Like the world, the photograph allows itself to be experienced only as a fragment, only as a remnant, of what withdraws from experience. This experience—and if it were different it would not be an experience at all—is an experience of the impossibility of experience. This is why, after the death of his mother, after the death of himself in relation to his mother (a death that, as he tells us, did not have to wait until his mother's death, or even his), Barthes suggests that we remain entirely unprovided for in a world in which we must survive the impossibility of experience, in which the photograph— the photograph as we generally understand it, but also the photograph that we now can call "Barthes"—tells us, if it tells us anything at all, that it is with loss and death that we have to live, love, and experience what cannot be experienced. This music of love and death (and there can be no other) can be called, for lack of a better name, "photography."

Notes

We would like to thank Hal Foster and Benjamin Buchloh for their encouragement and support, and Roger Bellin for his diligent research assistance.

1. *Camera Lucida: Reflections on Photography,* trans. Richard Howard (New York: Farrar, Straus, and Giroux, Inc., 1981), 116–112. All references to the English translation of this text are to this edition and will be cited parenthetically as *CL.* Since, on occasion, we have modified this translation, we also include references to the original French edition; in this instance, then, the second citation can be found in *La chambre claire: Note sur la photographie* (Paris: Éditions du Seuil, 1980), 179, 28. All references to the French edition are given following the English citation and will be cited as *CC.*

2. Barthes not only invents a set of Latinate neologisms but he also ceaselessly marks and remarks even familiar terms in such a way that, in each instance, they break away from what generally has been conceived or meant by them. He chooses Latin as the "mother tongue" of photography—an archaic language to describe a modern technology, a dead language to evoke a technology organized around death—because modernity can only be understood in relation to the past from which it emerges. For an excellent discussion of this point, see Elissa Marder, "Nothing to Say: Fragments on the Mother in the Age of Mechanical Reproduction," *L'Esprit Créateur* 40, no. 1 (Spring 2000), esp. 28–30.

3. Barthes's stylistic strategies—his use of capitalization, in particular—have been commented on extensively. Perhaps the most elaborate account is provided by Andrew Brown, *Roland Barthes: The Figures of Writing* (Oxford: Clarendon Press, 1992), esp. chaps. 1 and 2.

4. Jacques Lacan, "Agency of the Letter in the Unconscious," in *Écrits: A Selection,* trans. Alan Sheridan (New York: W. W. Norton and Co., 1977), p. 166.

5. Within this amorous relation, what evokes and attracts the gaze is called "adventure" (*CL* 19/*CC* 38). Like any adventure, the photographic adventure is linked to particularity—"contingency, singularity, adventure" (*CL* 20/*CC* 40) form a series in *Camera Lucida*—and to the adventurer's confrontation with the other. Like all adventure, the photographic adventure implies the risk of an "internal agitation, an excitement, a certain labor, too, the pressure of the unspeakable which wants to

be spoken" (*CL* 19/*CC* 37). Like music, the photograph breaks into the subject and produces a kind of agitation and interruption that—and here is the effect of the risk (and of all risk)—transforms the subject and thereby prevents him from remaining "himself." This is why, when Barthes suggests that, "In this glum desert, suddenly a specific photograph reaches me; it animates me, and I animate it" (*CL* 20/*CC* 39), he implies that the adventurer's risk is never that of losing his life, but of passing through an experience that, at the edge of death, "animates" him, gives him the life he did not have, an other life. But this risk is also, at the same time, and like the adventure of love, very trivial. This is why what makes a photographic experience an adventure is precisely the enactment of an incredible feat that works to transform this triviality into a field in which the power of adventure can unfold in unexpected and transformative ways. To say that there can be no photography without adventure means, among other things, that there can be no adventure without a force of animation and trans-formation. This is why, we might say, love (as another name for the photographic adventure) means: adventure, animation, a transformation that displaces the lover onto a new terrain, one in which neither he nor his beloved (neither the observed subject nor the subject observing) can remain who they were "before" their encounter.

6. This is why the very possibility of love depends on our being able to love a photograph. For Barthes, to love a photograph is to experience "an internal agitation, an excitement" (*CL* 19/*CC* 37), to experience the adventure of what cannot be spoken or known, and to take "into my arms what is dead, what is going to die" (*CL* 117/*CC* 179). To love a photograph is to embrace the mortality of the other, to experience a kind of madness, and to find and lose oneself in relation to the beloved, and inside the beloved, since, as we know, the beloved has, like the viewer of a photograph, internalized a trace of the lover, the lover's "prick." the lover's *punctum*. To love an other, then, to love another living person, means to love a photograph—to love what, wounding us, piercing us, and entering us, can no longer be thought or experienced as entirely other than us.

7. See Jacques Derrida, "The Deaths of Roland Barthes," trans. Pascale-Anne Brault and Michael Naas, in *The Work of Mourning,* ed. Pascale-Anne Brault and Michael Naas (Chicago: University of Chicago Press, 2001), 41.

8. As a means of visualizing this paradox, the front cover of the Spanish edition of *Camera Lucida* presents an image of an antique camera—a machine that reminds us of the daguerrotype or of a certain auratic moment—in the process of copying or taking a photograph. The camera is there, in the center of the cover, between two large quotation marks that, like citation, love, mourning, or photography, infinitely reproduce its originality.

9. For early discussions of the concept of indexicality, see Rosalind Krauss, "Notes on the Index," in *The Originality of the Avant-Garde and Other Modernist Myths* (Cambridge, Mass.: MIT Press, 1985), 196–219; and Jean-Marie Schaeffer, *L'image précaire. Du dispositif photographique* (Paris, Éditions du Seuil, 1987). While we have evoked many aspects of these discussions, we also have sought, following Barthes, to indicate our distance from them.

10. See Roland Barthes, "The Third Meaning," in *The Responsibility of Forms: Critical Essays on Music, Art, and Representation,* trans. Richard Howard (Berkeley: University of California Press, 1991), 56; *Empire of Signs,* trans. Richard Howard (New York: Hill and Wang, 1982), 83; and *Roland Barthes by Roland Barthes,* trans. Richard Howard (Berkeley: University of California Press, 1977), 54–55.

11. In this sentence (and not including the citation from *Camera Lucida*), the first cited phrase is from "The Third Meaning," 56; and the last two cited phrases are from *Empire of Signs,* 83 and 84, respectively.

12. For a discussion of the fetishistic character of the photograph, see Christian Metz's "Disavowal, Fetishism," in *The Imaginary Signifier: Psychoanalysis and the Cinema,* trans. Ben Brewster et al. (Indiana: Indiana University Press, 1986), 69–80, and his "Photography and Fetish," in *October* 34 (Fall 1985), 81–91.

13. The mother's death is also legible, proleptically, and as a kind of analog, in the mortality of the Winter Garden Photograph's material support. "The photograph was very old," Barthes writes, "[t] he corners were blunted from having been pasted into an album, the sepia print had faded" (*CL, 67/ CC* 106). Like all photographs, it shares the common "fate of paper (perishable)" and, "even if it is attached to more lasting supports, it is still mortal: like a living organism, it is born on the level of the sprouting silver grains, it flourishes a moment, then ages. . . . Attacked by light, by humidity, it fades, weakens, vanishes" (*CL* 93/*CC,* 145–146).

14. Roland Barthes, *A Lover's Discourse: Fragments,* trans. Richard Howard (New York: Farrar, Straus, and Giroux, 1978), 49.

15. On this point, see Jacques Derrida, "By Force of Mourning," trans. Pascale-Anne Brault and Michael Naas, in *The Work of Mourning,* 159.

16. If Barthes desires to resurrect his mother, if he wishes to recover and revivify her body, we should not be surprised by his effort to reverse the trajectory of her life, to bring her back to life, and perhaps beginning from her death. This effort is legible, in its most secret and hidden form, in the very structure of *Camera Lucida,* at least insofar as we can claim—and we believe we can—that the structure and writing of the text embodies his desire. We can begin to read this effort by first noting that the text is composed of two parts, with each part consisting of twenty-four chapters, for a total of forty-eight chapters. It was written between April 15 and June 3, 1979, which means that it was written in forty-eight days. There are twenty-five photographs reproduced within the book, but, since the first one, Daniel Boudinet's 1979 color photograph *Polaroid,* is, strictly speaking, outside of the text, there are twenty-four photographs within the text proper. The number twenty-four seems particularly significant within the context of the book, since it evokes the number of still frames—the number of photograms—that pass through a film projector every second as well as the number of hours in a day, that is, the number of hours that constitute the cycle between day and night and light and darkness. The number forty-eight perhaps becomes more significant, however, if we recall that Barthes's mother died at the age of eighty-four, which, read backward, is forty-eight. This reversed identification would seem to be only coincidental, and perhaps only a game of numbers and chance, but it becomes less so when we remember that Barthes claims to have discovered the Winter Garden Photograph, the photograph he associates most closely with the "essence" of his mother, "by moving back through Time." Moreover, he seems to reinforce this gesture of reversal by noting that "[t]he Greeks entered into Death backward: what they had before them was their past. In the same way I worked back through a life, not my own, but the life of someone I love" (*CL*71/ *CC* 111). While there would be much to say about these correspondences, the least we can say is that, in a very real sense, what Barthes seems to want—because of his love for his mother, because of his desire to have her alive and beside him—is to have his text embody the trajectory of his mother's

lifespan, but in reverse, as if, in doing so, it might, by reversing the movement of her life from life to death and thereby transforming it from death to life, magically restore her to him. In the same way that he claims to have started with his mother's "latest image, taken the summer before her death" and then to have "arrived, traversing three-quarters of a century, at the image of a child" (*CL* 71/*CC* 111), he states that, in taking care of his mother when she was ill, in taking care of her as if she had become his child, he experienced this backward movement in reality. It is this experience of the displacement and reversal of time that encourages him to seek to conjure his mother through an act of writing that is as much an act of desire and love as it is an act of counting.

17. This play between light and skin, between the photograph and emanations, can be registered in the French word for "film": *pellicule.* From *pellis,* the skin, *pellicule* and "film" originally have the same meaning: a small or thin skin, a kind of membrane. Although, in this passage, Barthes uses the word *peau* and not *pellicule,* he demonstrates his awareness of this etymological connection between film and skin—a connection that suggests the relation between this "carnal medium" and the photograph—in *Roland Barthes by Roland Barthes.* See *Roland Barthes by Roland Barthes,* 54.

18. For a discussion of Democritus's theory of *eidolas* in relation to photography in general, see Branka Arsic, "The Home of Shame," in *Cities Without Citizens,* ed. Eduardo Cadava and Aaron Levy (Philadelphia: Slought Books; Rosenbach Museum and Library, 2003), 36.

19. Marder, "Nothing to Say: Fragments on the Mother in the Age of Mechanical Reproduction," 32.

20. The phrase is from Derrida, "The Deaths of Roland Barthes," 43.

21. That Barthes can only "express" this accord by "an infinite series of adjectives" is critical here, and especially in relation to what he understands as the photographic character of the adjective in general. He draws this "correspondence" between adjectives and photography in the series of lectures he delivered in 1978 at the Collège de France on "The Neutral," not long after the death of his mother (a death that leaves its traces throughout the lectures) and just two years before his death. As a counter to the petrifying, death-bringing effects of the adjective, Barthes explains that, in the discourse of the lover, the lover's tendency to cover his beloved with adjectives eventually leads the lover to experience the wounding lack "from which predication suffers" and he comes "to seek a linguistic way of addressing this: that the totality of imaginable predicates will never reach or exhaust the absolute specificity of the object of his desire." When he claims that he cannot express the accord among Schumann's "last music," his mother's being, and his grief at her death "except by an infinite series of adjectives," he implies that all efforts to fix or arrest this accord inevitably will fail, which is why this effort has to begin again an infinite number of times. That his discussion of the adjective is particularly resonant with his concerns in *Camera Lucida* is reinforced when he claims, in a way that evokes his mother and her death, that "in linguistic culture" the "two objects" that are understood to be "beyond predication either in horror or in desire" are "the corpse and the desired body." See Roland Barthes, *The Neutral: Lecture Course at the Collège de France (1977–1978),* trans. Rosalind E. Krauss and Denis Hollier (New York: Columbia University Press, 2005), 52, 58.

22. Roland Barthes, "The Romantic Song," in *The Responsibility of Forms,* 290.

23. Roland Barthes, "Loving Schumann," in *The Responsibility of Forms,* 293–294.

24. Malraux, *La condition humaine* (Paris: Éditions Gallimard, 1946), 334. Although Barthes rarely evokes China and its revolutionary history, he addresses both in a brief but rich text from 1975 entitled *Alors la Chine?* In a two-page coda—written in response to the negative reactions his text

elicited—he suggests that, "hallucinating" China as an object, he would like to read it as the "feminine (maternal?) infinite of the object itself." This hallucination is not "gratuitous," he explains, and it is meant to go against the popular Western hallucination of China's "directly political" and dogmatic discourse. At this moment, he makes a remarkable statement that, like Malraux, links the thought of China to music. Claiming that the intellectual or writer always moves by indirection, he notes that the aim of his little text was to offer a discourse that would be *just* (and "musically" so) in relation to the indirectness of Chinese politics. Claiming that only a certain musicality can be "just" to the indecipherability of Chinese politics, he concludes that "it is necessary to love music," and "the Chinese also." In this instance, then—and in keeping with what he suggests in *Camera Lucida*—music and love are on the side of indirection, on the side of what escapes our comprehension, and perhaps even on the side of what he dares to evoke, even if in the mode of a question, as the "maternal." See Roland Barthes. *Alors la Chine?* (Paris: Christian Bourgois Éditeur, 1975), 8, 13–14.

25. Philippe Lacoue-Labarthe makes this point in his reading of Adorno's writings on music. See Philippe Lacoue-Labarthe, *Musica Ficta (Figures of Wagner)*, trans. Felicia McCarren (Stanford: Stanford University Press, 1994), 144.

26. Stéphane Mallarmé, *La musique et les lettres*, in *Oeuvres complètes* (Paris: Gallimard, 1945), 644.

27. See, for example, Barthes's 1974 essay, "Why I Love Benveniste" (in which he explicitly situates Benveniste within the context of a discussion of the relation between love and music), in *The Rustle of Language*, trans. Richard Howard (Berkeley: University of California Press, 1989), 167.

28. See Benveniste, "La notion de 'rhythme' dans son expression linguistique," in *Problèmes de linguistiques generale*, vol. 1 (Paris: Gallimard, 1966), 330.

29. See Lacoue-Labarthe's "The Echo of the Subject," trans. Barbara Harlow, in *Typography: Mimesis, Philosophy, Politics*, ed. Christopher Fynsk (Cambridge, MA.: Harvard University Press, 1989), 196–203. In many respects, our reading of Benveniste's essay—and of the notion of "rhythm" in general—is a miniaturized photograph of Lacoue-Labarthe's argument, an argument he repeats somewhat telegraphically in *Musica Ficta*, especially on 77–83. We would suggest here that, although Barthes refers to Lacoue-Labarthe's essay, "Caesura of the Speculative," in *Camera Lucida* (see *CC* 141), it is perhaps this essay, "The Echo of the Subject," that has the most resonance with his book. A reading of Theodor Reik's *The Haunting Melody*, the latter essay is, among other things, a meditation on the relations among music, mourning, and autobiography.

30. Benveniste, "La notion de 'rhythme' dans son expression linguistique," 333.

31. See Lacoue-Labarthe, "Echo of the Subject," 202.

32. Lacoue-Labarthe makes this identical point in ibid., 202.

33. Barthes, *A Lover's Discourse*, 191.

34. Barthes, "Loving Schumann," 295.

35. Barthes, "Listening," in *Responsibility of Forms*, 248.

36. Barthes, *A Lover's Discourse*, 199.

37. Barthes, "Music, Voice, and Language," in *The Responsibility of Forms*, 284.

38. Mallet, *La musique en respect* (Paris: Éditions Galiléc, 2002), 11.

39. Nietzsche, *Daybreak: Thoughts on the Prejudices of Morality*, trans. R. J. Hollingdale (Cambridge: Cambridge University Press, 1982), 143.

40. Barthes, "Loving Schumann," 298.
41. Ibid.
42. Jacques Derrida, *Échographies de la television. Entretiens filmés* (Paris: Éditions Galilée, 1996), 131.

MICHAEL FRIED

At the crossroads of the entire oeuvre, perhaps the Theater.
—Roland Barthes, *Roland Barthes*

Roland Barthes's final book, *La Chambre claire: Note sur la photographie,* was originally published in France in 1980, the year of his tragic death, and was translated into English in 1981.[1] From the moment it appeared it has been a dominant reference for writers on photography, at least in this country and Great Britain. Above all Barthes's central distinction between what he calls the *studium* and the *punctum* has been enthusiastically taken up by countless critics and theorists, who almost without exception have found in it principally a contrast between the ostensible subject of a given photograph, or rather the general basis of that subject's presumed interest for an average viewer (the *studium*), and whatever that photograph may contain that engages and—Barthes's verbs—"pricks" or "wounds" or "bruises" a particular viewer's subjectivity in a way that makes the photograph in question singularly arresting to him or her (from here on out I shall stay with *him*). This isn't wrong—it is pretty much what Barthes explicitly states—but I want to suggest that placing all the emphasis, as is usually done, on the viewer's purely subjective response to the *punctum* ends up missing Barthes's central thought or, at any rate, failing to grasp what ultimately is at stake in his central distinction. A further question, which will arise more than once in what follows, is to what extent Barthes himself was aware of the ultimate implications of his own argument.

Barthes's announced approach in *Camera Lucida* is nothing if not personal. "I decided to take myself as mediator for all Photography," he writes early on (*CL* 8; *CC* 21–22). And: "I have determined to be guided by the consciousness of my feelings" (*CL* 10; *CC* 24). And at greater length:

I decided then to take as a guide for my new analysis the attraction I felt for certain photographs. For of this attraction, at least, I was certain. What to call it? Fascination? No, this photograph which I pick out and which I love has nothing in common with the shiny point which sways before your eyes and makes your head swim [Barthes is evidently referring to hypnotic suggestion—M. F.]; what it produces in me is the very opposite of hebetude; something more like an internal agitation, an excitement, a certain labor too, the pressure of the unspeakable which wants to be spoken. [CL 18–19; CC 37]

Further on in the same paragraph Barthes says that the best word for the attraction he felt for certain photographs was "*advenience* or even *adventure.* This picture *advenes,* that one doesn't" (*CL* 19; *CC* 38), but typically Barthes makes very little use of these words in the rest of his book (the sometimes spendthrift nature of Barthes's terminological inventions only adds to their charm). Finally, Barthes comes right out and says that in his present investigation he "borrowed something from phenomenology's project and something from its language" (*CL* 20; *CC* 40). But Barthes's heuristic or (his words) "vague, casual, even cynical" (*CL* 20; *CC* 40) phenomenology is one that, unlike classical phenomenology, attaches primary importance to desire and mourning. "The anticipated essence of the Photograph," he writes, "could not, in my mind, be separated from the 'pathos' of which, from the first glance, it consists" (*CL* 21; *CC* 42). And in the next section of the book (9 of 48), he at last moves toward introducing his central distinction by way of analyzing an exemplary photo, Koen Wessing's *Nicaragua* (1979).

"I was glancing through an illustrated magazine," Barthes begins.

A photograph made me pause. Nothing very extraordinary: the (photographic) banality of a rebellion in Nicaragua: a ruined street, two helmeted soldiers on patrol; behind them, two nuns. Did this photograph please me? Interest me? Intrigue me? Not even. Simply, it existed (for me). I understood at once that its existence (its "adventure") derived from the co-presence of two discontinuous elements, heterogeneous in that they did not belong to the same world (no need to proceed to the point of contrast): the soldiers and the nuns. I foresaw a structural rule (conforming to my own observation), and I immediately tried to verify it by inspecting other photographs by the same reporter (the Dutchman Koen Wessing): many of them attracted me because they included this kind of duality which I had just become aware of. [CL23; CC 42–44]

By the beginning of the next section Barthes attempts to characterize and name "the two elements whose co-presence established, it seemed, the particular interest I took in these photographs":

The first, obviously, is an extent, it has the extension of a field, which I perceive quite familiarly as a consequence of my knowledge, my culture; this field can be more or less stylized, more or less successful, depending on the photographer's skill or luck, but it always refers to a classical body of information: rebellion, Nicaragua, and all the signs of both. . . . Thousands of photographs consist of this field, and in these photographs I can, of course, take a kind of general interest. . . . What I feel about these photographs derives from an average effect, almost from a certain training. I did not know a French word which might account for this kind of human interest, but I believe this word exists in Latin: it is studium, *which doesn't mean, at least not immediately, "study," but application to a thing, taste for someone, a kind of general, enthusiastic commitment, of course, but without special acuity. It is by* studium *that I am interested in so many photographs, whether I receive them as political testimony or enjoy them as good historical scenes: for it is culturally . . . that I participate in the figures, the faces, the gestures, the settings, the actions. [CL 25–26; CC 47–48]*

And then (introducing the second term, one that has proven almost as popular as Benjamin's *aura*):

The second element will break (or punctuate) the studium. *This time it is not I who seek it out (as I invest the field of the* studium *with my sovereign consciousness), it is this element which rises from the scene, shoots out of it like an arrow, and pierces me. A Latin word exists to designate this wound, this prick, this mark made by a pointed instrument: the word suits me all the better in that it also refers to the notion of punctuation, and because the photographs I am speaking of are in effect punctuated, sometimes even speckled with these sensitive points; precisely, these marks, these wounds, are so many* points. *This second element which will disturb the* studium *I shall therefore call* punctum; *for* punctum *is also: sting, speck, cut, little hole—and also a cast of dice. A photograph's* punctum *is that accident which pricks me (but also bruises me, is poignant to me). [CL 26–27; CC 48–49]*

Barthes glosses this basic distinction by noting that "the *studium* is of the order of *liking,* not of loving," and further, crucially, that "to recognize the *studium* is inevitably to encounter the photographer's intentions, to enter into harmony with them, to approve or disapprove them, but always to understand them" (*CL* 27–28; *CC* 50–51). Or, as he also says, the *studium* endows the photograph "with *functions,* which are, for the Photographer, so many alibis. These functions are: to inform, to represent, to surprise, to cause to signify, to provoke desire. And I, the *Spectator,* I recognize them with more or less pleasure: I invest them with my *studium* (which is never my delight or my pain)" (*CL* 28; *CC* 51).

Most photographs, Barthes implies, are in effect all *studium;* he thinks of them as "unary" and says of one type of such photograph, the news photo, that it can shock or "shout," but it is powerless to disturb or "wound" (*CL* 41; *CC* 70). Standard pornography is also "unary," hence banal. But a few photographs are different. "In this habitually unary space," he writes at the start of section 18, "occasionally (but alas all too rarely) a 'detail' attracts me. I feel that its mere presence changes my reading, that I am looking at a new photograph, marked in my eye with a higher value. This 'detail' is the *punctum*" (*CL* 42; *CC* 71). He goes on:

It is not possible to posit a rule of connection between the studium *and the* punctum *(when it happens to be there). It is a matter of a co-presence, that is all one can say: the nuns "happened to be there," passing in the background, when Wessing photographed the Nicaraguan soldiers; from the viewpoint of reality (which is perhaps that of the* Operator*), a whole causality explains the presence of the "detail": the Church implanted in these Latin-American countries, the nuns allowed to circulate as nurses, etc.; but from my Spectator's viewpoint, the detail is offered by chance and for nothing; the scene is in no way "composed" according to a creative logic; the photograph is doubtless dual, but this duality is the motor of no "development," as happens in classical discourse. In order to perceive the* punctum*, no analysis would be of any use to me. . . . It suffices that the image be large enough, that I do not have to study it (this would be of no help at all), that, given right there on the page, I should receive it right here in my eyes. [CL 42–43; CC 71–72]*

For the remainder of the first half of his book Barthes explores the notion of the *punctum* with characteristic panache, stressing (among other features) its "power of expansion": so for example in an André Kertész photograph of a blind gypsy violinist being led by a boy (1921) what pricks Barthes is the recognition, "with my whole body, [of] the straggling villages I passed through on my long-ago travels in Hungary and Rumania" (*CL* 45; *CC* 77). (Barthes qualifies this expansion of the *punctum* via personal memory as "Proustian," for obvious reasons. More on Proust shortly.)

It's hardly surprising, then, that commentators on *Camera Lucida,* when glossing the *punctum,* have stressed the importance of the individual viewer's sheerly personal response (Victor Burgin: "It is the *private* nature of the experience which defines the punctum").[2] And in fact almost all the first half of the book is written from that point of view, while the second half, devoted to the mystery of the so-called Winter Garden Photograph of Barthes's mother as a young girl, carries the subjective emphasis to the farthest possible extreme. But one short section of Barthes's book, comprising a single page of print, embodies a radical shift in perspective:

Certain details may "prick" me. If they do not, it is doubtless because the photographer has put them there intentionally. [Remember, for Barthes "to recognize the studium *is inevitably to encounter the photographer's intentions."] In William Klein's "Shinohiera, Fighter Painter" (1961), the character's monstrous head has nothing to say to me because I can see so clearly that it is an artifice of the camera angle. Some soldiers with nuns behind them served as an example to explain what the* punctum *was for me (here, quite elementary); but when Bruce Gilden photographs a nun and some drag queens together (New Orleans, 1973), the deliberate (not to say, rhetorical) contrast produces no effect on me, except one of irritation. Hence the detail which interests me is not, or at least is not strictly, intentional, and probably must not be so; it occurs in the field of the photographed thing like a supplement that is at once inevitable and delightful [the French reads "inévitable et gracieux," which is not exactly the same thing; see n. 35 below—M. F.]; it does not necessarily attest to the photographer's art; it says only that the photographer was there, or else, still more simply, that he could not not photograph the partial object at the same time as the total object (how could Kertész have "separated" the dirt road from the violinist walking on it?). The Photographer's "second sight" does not consist in "seeing" but in being there. And above all, imitating Orpheus, he must not turn back to look at what he is leading—what he is giving to me! [CL 47; CC 79–80]*

That's it—that's all Barthes has to say, with respect to the *punctum,* about the point of view, the activity, of the photographer (the "Operator") as distinct from the response of the viewer. But I think it's enough.

By that I mean it's enough to situate *Camera Lucida* in relation to the all-important current of *antitheatrical* critical thought and pictorial practice, which (in my trilogy *Absorption and Theatricality, Courbet's Realism,* and *Manet's Modernism*)[3] I have tried to show runs from Denis Diderot and Jean-Baptiste Greuze in the 1750s and 1760s through David, Géricault, Daumier, Courbet, Millet, Legros, and Fantin-Latour (among others, along with a matching list of art critics) until it reaches a crisis of unsustainability in the art of Edouard Manet in the 1860s and 1870s. Thereafter it undergoes a fundamental change that on the one hand indicates that the Diderotian project—of effectively denying the presence before the painting of the beholder—was no longer feasible in any of its classic forms but on the other suggests that the problem of the beholder—of acknowledging his presence while not addressing him in the wrong way—was now absolutely fundamental to advanced painting and sculpture, in the first place in France, where the antitheatrical tradition arose, and eventually in the United States. (The chief critical text in the latter regard is my essay of 1967, "Art and Objecthood,"[4] which has been a focus of controversy since the day it appeared and which I shall suggest has certain claims in common with Barthes's little book.) Understood in this context, Barthes's observation in section 20 of *Camera Lucida* that the detail that strikes him as a *punctum* could not do so had it been intended as such by the photographer is an antitheatrical claim in that it implies a fundamental distinction, which goes back to Diderot, between seeing and being shown.[5] The *punctum,* we might say, is *seen* by Barthes but not because it has been *shown* to him by the photographer, for whom it does not exist; as Barthes recognizes, "it occurs [only] in the field of the photographed thing," which is to say that it is a pure artifact of the photographic event—"the photographer could not *not* photograph the partial object at the same time as the total object" is how Barthes phrases it—or, perhaps more precisely, it is an artifact of the encounter between the product of that event and one particular spectator or beholder, in the present case, Roland Barthes.[6] This is in keeping with Diderot's repeated injunction that the beholder be treated as if he were not there, standing before a painted or seated before a staged *tableau* or, to put this slightly differently, that nothing in a painted or a staged *tableau* be felt by the beholder to be there *for him.* Works of painting or stagecraft that failed to meet this experiential criterion were pejoratively characterized as *théâtral,* theatrical, which would be one way of paraphrasing Barthes's irritation with the too deliberately contrastive photograph by Bruce Gilden of a nun and drag queens (not reproduced by him) that he compares unfavorably with Wessing's *Nicaragua,* in which, it is implied, the presence of the nuns appears fortuitous, unintended, as if they entered the photographic field without the photographer being fully aware that they were there. (I don't deny that this seems an unlikely scenario; Barthes's point appears to be that unless he, the Spectator, felt that such a scenario was in play, he would not experience the nuns as a *punctum.*) By no means coincidentally, Diderot sharply criticizes the too-obvious use of contrast on the part of the artist.[7]

There is one other moment in the first half of *Camera Lucida* (section 14) at which Barthes considers his topic from the point of view of the photographer. He writes:

I imagine (this is all I can do, since I am not a photographer) that the essential gesture of the Operator *is to surprise something or someone (through the little hole of the camera), and that this gesture is therefore perfect when it is performed unbeknownst to the subject being photographed. From this gesture derive all photographs whose principle (or better, whose alibi) is "shock"; for the photographic "shock" (quite different from the* punctum*) consists less in traumatizing than in revealing what was so well hidden that the actor himself was unaware or unconscious of it. Hence a whole gamut of "surprises" (as they are for me, the* Spectator; *but for the Photographer, these are so many "performances"). [CL 32; CC 57]*

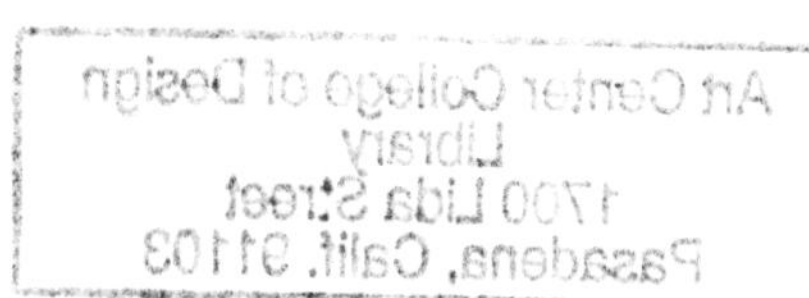

Barthes goes on to discuss several different kinds of "surprises," none of which he likes, but unfortunately he says nothing more about the large class of photographs taken of persons who are unaware of being photographed. The latter is a major element in twentieth-century (and for that matter twenty-first-century) street photography,[8] as for example in Walker Evans's "subway portraits," made with a hidden camera on the New York subway in 1938–41,[9] or as in the contemporary Swiss artist Beat Streuli's telephoto videos of moving crowds on thoroughfares or street corners in different cities of the world, the filming taking place without the knowledge of those being recorded. (Streuli also makes photographs of individual pedestrians on the same basis.)[10] Evans's and Streuli's projects may be understood as attempts to realize an ideal of naturalness that goes back to Leonardo da Vinci's notebooks and was restated in no uncertain terms just a few years before the publication of *Camera Lucida.* "There is something on people's faces when they don't know they are being observed that never appears when they do," Susan Sontag writes in *On Photography* (1977). "If we did not know how Walker Evans took his subway photographs (riding the New York subways for hundreds of hours, standing, with the lens of his camera peering between two buttons of his topcoat), it would be obvious from the pictures themselves that the seated passengers, although photographed close and frontally, didn't know they were being photographed; their expressions are private ones, not those they would offer to the camera."[11]

This is, of course, an antitheatrical ideal, and both Evans's subway photos and Streuli's videos and photos are also updated versions of the Diderotian project of depicting figures who appear deeply absorbed in what they are doing, thinking, and feeling and who therefore also appear wholly oblivious to being beheld (that's the crucial point). In Evans's and Streuli's work (as in that of other street photographers like Robert Frank, Garry Winogrand, Lee Friedlander, and Philip-Lorca diCorcia) absorption shades into distraction, a less "deep" condition, but the same fundamental problematic is in force. And in fact manifestly absorptive motifs continue to work their magic down to the present day. To demonstrate this as succinctly as possible, see Chardin's superb *The Card Castle* (ca. 1737) in the National Gallery of Art in Washington, D.C., a quintessentially absorptive picture.[12] Or two representative works by leading contemporary artists: first, Jeff Wall's light-box Cibachrome transparency, *Adrian Walker, Artist, Drawing from a Specimen in a Laboratory in the Dept. of Anatomy at the University of British Columbia, Vancouver* (1992); and, second, Gerhard Richter's photograph-based painting *Reading* (1994). Both are indisputably absorptive images (Wall explicitly describes *Adrian Walker* in those terms),[13] and both owe a large measure of their appeal, I would like to say of their persuasiveness as images of reality, to that basic fact.[14] Now one of the most original features of *Camera Lucida* is that Barthes has no interest whatever in scenes of absorption or distraction—and more broadly in the capturing of personages unaware of being photographed—as a representational strategy for the simple reason that not only does such a strategy not seem to him on the side of antitheatricality, it strikes him, on the contrary, as quintessentially theatrical in that although the "actor," that is, the subject being photographed, appears unaware of what the photograph reveals about his state of mind and/or body, for the photographer the images that result "are so many 'performances'"—obviously a pejorative notion in this context (as is "actor," I suppose).[15] In short for a photograph to be truly antitheatrical for Barthes it must somehow carry within it a kind of ontological guarantee that it was not intended to be so *by the photographer*—a requirement that goes well beyond anything to be found in Diderot or for that matter any eighteenth- or nineteenth-century critic or theorist. The *punctum,* I am suggesting, functions as that guarantee.[16]

Or consider Barthes's contention (in section 22) that "sometimes . . . the *punctum* [is] revealed only after the fact, when the photograph is no longer in front of me and I think back on it. I may know better a photograph I remember than a photograph I am looking at, as if direct vision oriented its language wrongly, engaging it in an effort of description which will always miss its point of effect, the *punctum*" (*CL* 53; *CC* 87). This is a surprising claim, but it leads to a still more remarkable one: "Ultimately—or at the limit—in order to see a photograph well, it is best to look away or close your eyes. 'The necessary condition for an image is sight,' Janouch told Kafka; and Kafka smiled and replied: 'We photograph things in order to drive them out of our minds. My stories are a way of shutting my eyes'" (*CL* 53; *CC* 88). "The photograph touches me," section 22 concludes, "if I withdraw it from its usual blah-blah: 'Technique,' 'Reality,' 'Reportage,' 'Art,' etc.: to say nothing, to shut my eyes, to allow the detail to rise as if of its own accord into affective consciousness" (*CL* 55; *CC* 89). Nothing could better illustrate the extremity of Barthes's antitheatricalism in his final book—or at least in the first half of that book—than the hyperbolic removal from the scene of response of the actual photograph, the visible material artifact, itself.

I have just acknowledged that there is a second half to *Camera Lucida,* which begins immediately following a short section (24) in which Barthes abruptly and without warning gives up the project he has been pursuing until then on the grounds that "I had not discovered the nature (the *eidos*) of Photography. I had to grant that my pleasure was an imperfect mediator, and that a subjectivity reduced to its hedonist project could not recognize the universal. I would have to descend deeper into myself to find the evidence of Photography, that thing which is seen by anyone looking at a photograph and which distinguishes it in his eyes from any other image. I would have to make my recantation, my palinode" (*CL* 60; *CC* 95–96). That recantation or palinode takes place under the sign of Barthes's love for his deceased mother, with whom he had lived for much of his adult life, and finally focuses on a single image—a faded sepia print of his mother at the age of five and her seven-year-old brother "standing together at the end of a little wooden bridge in a glassed-in conservatory, what was called a Winter Garden in those days" (the year was 1898) (*CL* 67; *CC* 106). This is the so-called Winter Garden Photograph, a photograph, he tells us, that for once "gave me a sentiment as certain as remembrance, just as Proust experienced it one day when, leaning over to take off his boots, there suddenly came to him his grandmother's true face, 'whose living reality I was experiencing for the first time, in an involuntary and complete memory'" (*CL* 70; *CC* 109).[17] And yet Barthes will shortly remark, "The Photograph does not call up the past (nothing Proustian in a photograph). The effect it produces upon me is not to restore what has been abolished (by time, by distance) but to attest that what I see has indeed existed" (*CL* 82; *CC* 129). As he says later on: "Not only is the Photograph never, in essence, a memory . . . but it actually blocks memory, quickly becomes a countermemory" (*CL* 91; *CC* 142). Barthes's willingness to let these passages chafe against one another is puzzling (how could he have failed to note their irreconcilability?),[18] but I take that chafing as an indication that the logic or analogy that binds *Camera Lucida* to Proust's immortal masterpiece and even more pointedly to the preface of *Contre Sainte-Beuve* was in the end beyond his grasp.[19] Let me spell this out: in the preface Proust discovers and then explains the mode of action of what he calls involuntary memory, the almost magical operation of which is dramatized in the famous madeleine-dipped-in-tea episode in *Du côté de chez Swann,* volume one of *À la recherche du temps perdu.* But the preface insists on an insight that to the best of my knowledge is never made explicit in the novel: that any deliberate attempt on the part of a subject to imprint a contemporary scene on his memory will not only fail to capture its reality, it will actually render the latter irrecuperable in the future by the action of involuntary recall.[20] Put more strongly, only scenes and events that escape the subject's conscious attention in the present are eligible to be recovered in the future and thus, according to Proust, to be truly experienced for the first time. The analogy between this claim and Barthes's notion that the effect of a *punctum* on a viewer depends on its nonexistence for the photographer should be obvious; conversely it is as though Proust's deliberately imprinted image—the product of voluntary memory—were itself "unary," hence powerless to resurrect the past.

Now as no reader of *Camera Lucida* needs to be told, Barthes never reproduces the Winter Garden Photograph.[21] He explains in a parenthesis: "I cannot reproduce the Winter Garden Photograph. It exists only for me. For you, it would be nothing but an indifferent picture, one of the thousand manifestations of the 'ordinary.'. . . At most it would interest your *studium:* period, clothes, photogeny; but in it, for you, no wound" (*CL* 73; *CC* 115). This makes perfect sense as far as it goes, but I want to go a step further and suggest that Barthes's declaration of the Winter Garden Photograph's structural unreproducibility should be understood as still another measure of the not quite explicit antitheatrical animus of his overall argument: as though for Barthes that unreproducibility epitomized his utter rejection of the "exhibition-value" that Walter Benjamin famously associated with the photographic in "The Work of Art in the Age of Its Technological Reproducibility."[22] Not that Barthes mentions Benjamin, who was doubtless a less imposing figure in 1980 than he is today; nor does he mention a famous text by a great French writer that climaxes with the revelation of a painting of a beloved woman that could be seen as such only by its creator, Balzac's *Le Chef-d'oeuvre inconnu.* It's hard to believe that the author of *S/Z* was unaware of the latter connection.[23]

With the Winter Garden Photograph at the center of his reflections, Barthes proceeds to zero in on the association, as he sees it, between the photograph and the past and beyond that between the photograph and death—in the first instance, the future death of the photograph's human subject (that is, future relative to the "time" of the photograph): at the epoch of the writing of *Camera Lucida* Barthes's mother was dead, as was Lewis Payne, photographed in prison by Alexander Gardner in 1865, soon thereafter to be hanged for his role in Lincoln's assassination ("The photograph is handsome, as is the boy: that is the *studium.* But the *punctum* is: *he is going to die*" [*CL* 96; *CC* 148–150]); and in the second instance, or ultimately, the future death of one particular viewer, Barthes himself.[24] "I am the reference of every photograph," he writes, "and this is what generates my astonishment in addressing myself to the fundamental question: why is it I am alive *here and now?*" (*CL* 84; *CC* 131). Of course, being alive here and now inescapably implies that a day will come when he will no longer be alive, which is why, in Barthes's words, "each photograph always contains this imperious sign of my future death" (*CL* 97; *CC* 151). All this is to say that in addition to the *punctum* of the detail, the main concern of the first half of his book, there is another *punctum,* "no longer of form but of intensity," namely, "Time, the lacerating emphasis of the *noeme* ('*that has been*'), its pure representation" (*CL* 96; *CC* 148). An obvious conclusion follows, one that Barthes himself does not draw, either because he prefers his readers to do so for themselves or, as I suspect, because his thought here too stops just short of its furthest implications. Time, in Barthes's sense of the term, functions as a *punctum* for him precisely because the sense of something being past, being historical, cannot be perceived by the photographer or indeed by anyone else *in the present.* It is a guarantor of antitheatricality that comes to a photograph, that becomes visible in it, only after the fact, *après-coup,* in order to deliver the hurt, the prick, the wound, to future viewers that Barthes evidently craves.

This has the somewhat unexpected consequence that *any* photograph of a present scene will undergo that development—hence Barthes's claims that he is the reference of "every" photograph and that "each" photograph contains an imperious sign, the *punctum* of intensity, of his future death—though his discussions of particular images, such as Gardner's prison portrait of Lewis Payne and a fortiori the Winter Garden Photograph, indicate that some photographs are far more wounding than others in this regard. One such class of photographs, Barthes recognizes, are those taken in and therefore of earlier epochs. "This *punctum*," Barthes writes,

more or less blurred beneath the abundance and the disparity of contemporary photographs, is vividly legible in historical photographs: there is always a defeat of Time in them: that is dead and that is going to die. These two little girls looking at a primitive airplane above their village (they are dressed like my mother as a child, they are playing with hoops)—how alive they are! They have their whole lives before them; but also they are dead (today), they are then already dead (yesterday). [CL 96; CC 150–151][25]

Actually, the word "blurred" isn't quite faithful to the French here; the original word is "gommé," which might better be translated as "erased" or "rubbed out." In either case, however, the thought itself seems slightly errant; it would be truer to Barthes's less than fully articulated argument to think of the *punctum* of death as *latent* in contemporary photographs, to be brought out, developed (as in the photographic sense of the term), by the inexorable passage of time.[26] More broadly, there is at least the hint of a contradiction, if not in logic at any rate in the realm of feeling, between the absolute uniqueness of the Winter Garden Photograph ("Something like an essence of the Photograph floated in this particular picture" [*CL* 73; *CC* 114]) and the claim that all photographs, virtually regardless of subject matter, are potentially carriers of the *punctum* of time and death. Which may have something to do with Barthes's hyperbolic (or Heideggerean?) pronouncement, a page or so earlier, that modern society has made of the photograph precisely a means of "flattening" death:

so that everything, today, prepares our race for this impotence: to be no longer able to conceive duration, *affectively or symbolically: the age of the Photograph is also the age of revolutions, contestations, assassinations, explosions, in short, of impatiences, of everything which denies ripening.—And no doubt, the astonishment of* "that-has-been" *will also disappear. It has already disappeared: I am, I don't know why, one of its last witnesses . . . and this book is its archaic trace.* [*CL 93–94; CC 146–147*][27]

Barthes thus comes to understand himself as commenting on an image-making or perhaps more accurately an image-consuming regime that is all but defunct, not because of any material alteration in the photographic artifact but because of what he takes to be a profound transformation of society—the world—at large.

In fact two such material alterations were either on the way or currently taking place: digitalization, which by the 1990s would thoroughly transform the ontology of the photograph, and a considerable increase in the size of art photographs, which already in 1980 was enabling works such as Jeff Wall's light-box transparencies or Thomas Ruff's blown-up portrait photographs of art students to address more than a single beholder at the same time. Intimately related to the increase of size was the display of those photographs on gallery and museum walls or, rather, the fact that photographs like Wall's and Ruff's were made in order to be so displayed.[28] It should be evident that both developments are at odds with the vision of photography in *Camera Lucida*. In the first place, the advent of digitalization, with its implication that the contents of the photograph have been put there by its maker, threatens to dissolve the "adherence" of the referent to the photograph[29] that undergirds the claim, basic to the *punctum* of the detail, that "the photographer could not *not* photograph the partial object at the same time as the total object." (A partial object in the photograph that might otherwise prick or wound me may never have been part of a total object, which itself may be a digital construction.)[30] And, in the second place, as Barthes specifies in connection with the *punctum* of time and death: "Photographs . . . are looked at when one is alone. I am uncomfortable during the private projection of a film . . . , but I need to be alone with the photographs I am looking at" (*CL* 97; *CC* 152).[31] In both respects *Camera Lucida* is indeed a swan song for an artifact on the brink of fundamental change. (Perhaps the frontispiece illustration, a color Polaroid photograph by Daniel Boudinet of drawn turquoise linen curtains with a pillow and presumably a bed in the foreground—an image unmentioned in the body of the text—may be read allegorically in terms of the first of these changes. That is, the curtain is only barely transparent to the daylit scene beyond it, as if screening the viewer from whatever referent might lie out there.)

A further dimension of Barthes's antitheatricalism emerges when we consider his engagement with the *pose,* the theatrical element in photography par excellence. Early on in *Camera Lucida,* in section 5, he speaks of his considerable experience of being photographed while aware that that is taking place. Specifically, he describes the alteration that comes over him when this happens: "Now, once I feel myself observed by the lens, everything changes: I instantly constitute myself in the process of 'posing,' I instantaneously make another body for myself, I transform myself in advance into an image. This transformation is an active one: I feel that the Photograph creates my body or mortifies it, according to its caprice" (*CL* 10–11; *CC* 25). And further on: "In front of the lens, I am at the same time: the one I think I am, the one I want others to think I am, the one the photographer thinks I am, and the one he makes use of to exhibit his art. In other words, a strange action: I do not stop imitating myself, and because of this, each time I am (or let myself be) photographed,

I invariably suffer from a sensation of inauthenticity, sometimes of imposture (comparable to certain nightmares)" (*CL* 13; *CC* 29–30). This sense of theatricalization, for that is what it amounts to, would seem to be an inevitable consequence of posing, not just for Barthes but for anyone, but consider:

1) Not just the Winter Garden Photograph but every photograph of his mother "manifested the very feeling she must have experienced each time she 'let' herself be photographed: my mother 'lent' herself to the photograph, fearing that refusal would turn to 'attitude'; she triumphed over this ordeal of placing herself in front of the lens (an inevitable action) *with discretion* (but without a touch of the tense theatricalism of humility or sulkiness); for she was always able to replace a moral value with a higher one—a civil value. She did not struggle with her image, as I do with mine: she did not *suppose* herself" (*CL* 67; *CC* 105). The quotation marks, like the italics, show how difficult Barthes found it to characterize his mother's relation to the camera; in the end there were no words for what he wished to say. As for the Winter Garden Photograph, "The distinctness of her face, the naïve attitude of her hands, the place she had docilely taken *without either showing or hiding herself* [emphasis added—M. F.], and finally her expression, which distinguished her, like Good from Evil, from the hysterical little girl, from the simpering doll who plays at being a grownup—all this constituted the figure of a sovereign *innocence* . . . , all this had transformed the photographic pose into that untenable paradox which she had nonetheless maintained all her life: the assertion of a gentleness" (*CL* 69; *CC* 107).[32] In the rarest of instances, then, it is possible to neutralize the theatricalizing effects of the pose by a kind of gift of nature on the part of the sitter, which is also to say without any intention to do so on her part.

2) Toward the end of *Camera Lucida* Barthes returns to the topic of his mother's characteristic expression and generalizes it in the concept of "the *air* (the expression, the look)" (*CL* 107; *CC* 167).[33] "The *air* of a face is unanalyzable," he goes on to say. "The air is not a schematic, intellectual datum, the way a silhouette is. Nor is the air a simple analogy—however extended—as is 'likeness.' No, the air is that exorbitant thing which induces from body to soul—*animula,* little individual soul, good in one person, bad in another" (*CL* 107–109; *CC* 167). And after a short digression on photographs of his mother: "The air (I use this word, lacking anything better, for the expression of truth) is a kind of intractable supplement of identity, *what is given as an act of grace* [emphasis added—M. F.], stripped of any 'importance': the air expresses the subject, insofar as that subject assigns itself no importance" (*CL* 109; *CC* 168). (In Richard Avedon's photograph of the late leader of the American Labor Party, A. Philip Randolph [1976, fig. 9], Barthes reads "an air of goodness [no impulse of power: *that is certain*]" [*CL* 110; *CC* 169].)[34] What especially intrigues me in these formulations is the phrase I have italicized: the air as "given as an act of grace." (The

French reads: "cela qui est donné gracieusement.") "Art and Objecthood," notoriously, ends with the sentence: "Presentness is grace." Is it possible that the essential, all but ineffable qualities that Barthes and I believed we found respectively in certain photographs and certain abstract paintings and sculptures are at bottom the same?[35]

3) Also in the second half of the book Barthes goes so far as to propose that "what founds the nature of Photography is the pose" (*CL* 78; *CC* 122), a claim that on the one hand is consistent with his previously expressed distaste for the "performance" of photographing "actors" unaware of the presence of the photographer but on the other would appear to install an essentially theatrical relationship at the very heart of the photographic project. He goes on to explain (brilliantly, to my mind):

The physical duration of this pose is of little consequence; even in the interval of a millionth of a second (Edgerton's drop of milk) there has still been a pose, for the pose is not, here, the attitude of the target or even a technique of the Operator, *but the term of an "intention" of reading: looking at a photograph, I inevitably include in my scrutiny the thought of that instant, however brief, in which a real thing happened to be motionless in front of the eye. I project the present photograph's immobility upon the past shot, and it is this arrest which constitutes the pose. [CL 78; CC 122]*

The pose, in instantaneous photographs, is thus an artifact of the encounter of the product of the photographic event and the viewer—just like the *punctum.* Barthes continues (equally brilliantly): "This explains why the Photograph's *noeme* deteriorates when this Photograph is animated and becomes cinema: in the Photograph, something *has posed* in front of the tiny hole and has remained there forever (that is my feeling); but in cinema, something *has passed* in front of this same tiny hole: the pose is swept away and denied by the continuous series of images: it is a different phenomenology, and therefore a different art which begins here, though derived from the first one" (*CL* 78; *CC* 122–123). One might expect Barthes to prefer cinema precisely on the grounds that it thereby escapes or avoids theatricality—mechanically, automatically—but that may well be the deep if unacknowledged reason why he attaches a greater value to photography: because the latter is faced with the task of *defeating* theater in and through the *punctum* or, in the case of the Winter Garden Photograph, through his mother's sheer innocence of nature. (Mechanically escaping or avoiding theater isn't so much antitheatrical as, merely, nontheatrical.) This chimes with a similar claim about the movies in "Art and Objecthood," where I further contend that the fact that cinema escapes, and therefore doesn't face the task of seeking to defeat, theater makes cinema something other than a modernist art.[36] Once again the closeness of the two texts, obviously not the result of any influence of the American on the French, is suggestive.[37]

4) A final reach of Barthes's thematics of the pose concerns his liking—far too mild a word—for photographs that look him, as he puts it, *"straight in the eye"* (*CL* 111; *CC* 172). (Avedon's portrait photographs are exemplary for him in that regard. The great missed encounter among the photographers of the 1960s and 1970s, however, is with the work of Diane Arbus; one would like to know what he would have made of her often disturbing images of frontally posed subjects.)[38] This corresponds to a major strain, which I call "facingness," in modernist painting since Manet[39] and is said in connection with a further avowal of his lack of interest in photographs that seem to ignore him, in particular news photographs of scenes of "death, suicide, wounds, accidents" (*CL* 111; *CC* 171). "No, nothing to say about these photographs in which I see surgeons' gowns, bodies lying on the ground, broken glass, etc. Oh, if there were only a look, a subject's look, if only someone in the photographs were looking at me! [But what of Kertész's *The Violinist's Tune, Abony, Hungary* or Alfred Stieglitz's classic *The Horse-Car Terminal,* another image Barthes admires, neither of which contains such a look? On the other hand, there *are* facing figures in Wessing's Nicaragua photographs, William Klein's *Mayday, Moscow,* and indeed in most of the other images Barthes illustrates.—M. F.] For the Photograph has this power—which it is increasingly losing, the frontal pose being most often considered archaic nowadays—of looking me *straight in the eye* (here, moreover, is another difference: in film, no one ever looks at me: it is forbidden—by the Fiction)" (*CL* 111; *CC* 171–172). Barthes is right about the diegetic structure of film, or at any rate of traditional narrative film with its implicit injunction against all direct solicitation of the viewer,[40] but turns out to have been wrong about photography's abandonment of the frontal pose. Apart from Avedon and Arbus (and Robert Mapplethorpe, two of whose portrait photos he reproduces), reliance on such a pose was already implicit in Bernd and Hilla Becher's documentary photographs of industrial buildings and constructions, which they had begun to make in 1959 and which starting around 1980 would emerge as central to the practice of younger photographers such as Thomas Ruff, Thomas Struth (both students of Bernd Becher in Düsseldorf), and Rineke Dijkstra. More broadly, the frontal pose has come to play a crucial role as ambitious photography increasingly has claimed for itself the scale and so to speak the address of abstract painting. So perhaps we should say that Barthes was forward-looking in his attachment to the frontal pose, even if his taste for Avedon in particular is at odds with recent developments.

The question, of course, is how, within the logic of the arguments we have been tracking, photographs based on the frontal pose, and thereby foregrounding the subject's awareness of the fact of being photographed, can succeed in defeating theatricality in the case of subjects who are not, like Barthes's mother at age five or A. Philip Randolph, humanly exceptional. Barthes's attempt at a solution (in section 46) takes off from a real-life situation in which a young boy entered a café and looked at him without his being sure that the boy was seeing him. This leads to the proposal that "the Photograph separates attention from perception, and yields up only the former, even if it is impossible without the latter. . . . It is this scandalous movement which produces the rarest quality of an air. That is the paradox: how can one have an *intelligent air* without thinking about anything intelligent, just by looking into this piece of black plastic? It is because the look, eliding the vision, seems held back by something interior" (*CL* 113; *CC* 172–174).[41] This too is brilliant in an ad hoc sort of way, but appealing as it does to the photograph as such it fails to explain why only *some* frontal portraits are felt by Barthes to succeed in this respect (is that really what is at stake in Kertész's great portrait of the fiercely intellectual Mondrian [1926; fig. 10], which Barthes illustrates in this connection?), and it appears to have nothing to do with the ontological and affective themes of what has gone before. At this juncture the impetus of his discourse gives out and the book is near its end. But we can at least say that Barthes's avowed taste for photographs of the frontal type, precisely because of the difficulties they would seem inevitably to present for an antitheatrical esthetic, further suggests that for him overcoming, not avoiding, theatricality is what has to be accomplished and perhaps also that success in that endeavor can be imagined to take place only against the grain of the photographer's intentions.[42]

Two points by way of conclusion. In "Art and Objecthood" and related essays, I drew a sharp distinction between modernist painting and sculpture and the work and writings of the minimalists or, as I mainly called them, literalists—Donald Judd, Robert Morris, Carl Andre, and Tony Smith (among others). To the literalists, what mattered or ought to matter were not the relationships within a work of art, as in modernist painting and sculpture, but the relationship between the literalist work and the beholder, as the beholder was invited to activate (and in effect to produce) that relationship over time by entering the space of exhibition, approaching or moving away from the work (or, in the case of Carl Andre's floor pieces, literally walking on them), comparing changing views of the work with an intellectual comprehension of its basic form, and so on. What mattered, in other words, was the beholder's *experience* of the work or rather of the total situation in which the work was encountered, a situation that, as I put it in "Art and Objecthood," "virtually by definition, *includes the beholder*"[43]—which is also to say that to refer to the relationship in question as lying "between" the work and the beholder doesn't quite capture the literalist idea (nor does the term *beholder* wholly fit the case). The literalist work, in other words, was incomplete without the experiencing subject, which is what I meant by characterizing such work as theatrical in the pejorative sense of the term. Modernist paintings and sculptures, in contrast, I claimed were fundamentally antitheatrical in that (to speak only somewhat metaphorically) they took no notice of the beholder, who was left to come to terms with them—to make sense of the relationships they comprised—as best he could. (That modernist paintings like Morris Louis's *Unfurleds* may be said to face the beholder with extraordinary directness only makes their structural indifference to his actual presence before them all the more perspicuous.) A further contrast, which in "Art and Objecthood" remains largely implicit, concerns the fact that whereas in modernist paintings and sculptures the constitutive relationships were intended to be what they are by the artist,[44] the relationship between the literalist work and the beholder, although conditioned in a general way by the circumstances of exhibition, was understood by the literalists themselves as emphatically not determined by the work itself and therefore as not intended as such by its maker. On the contrary, the primacy of experience in the sense stated above meant that meaning in literalism was essentially indeterminate, with every subject's necessarily unique response to a given work-in-a-situation standing on an equal footing with every other's.[45] And this brings us back to Barthes, for whom in *Camera Lucida* nothing is more imperative than somehow to evade, elide, or otherwise get round the photographer's intentions and for whom the crucial element in the photographs that move or wound him, the *punctum,* is known only in and through a particular viewer's subjective experience (the *punctum* has no existence apart from that experience). These are literalist notions,[46] but I think it would be hasty to identify Barthes's position in that book as literalist *tout court.* For one thing, that would be to overlook the oddness of some of his claims (for example, that the best way to experience the *punctum* of a given photograph may be to shut one's eyes and let the crucial detail rise into one's consciousness) and, for another, much more seriously, it would be to fail to do justice to the depth and pervasiveness of his antitheatrical commitments. What we find revealed in *Camera Lucida* is the impossibility of constructing a radically antitheatrical photographic "esthetic" (another less than ideal term but let it stand), while at the same time acknowledging more fully than any previous thinker the inherently theatrical nature of the photographic artifact, without that "esthetic" giving rise to the sorts of literalist consequences that have just been cited.[47]

Finally, the present essay as a whole raises a different sort of question, namely, the status of antitheatricalism elsewhere in Barthes's oeuvre. A thoroughgoing attempt to answer that question would have to consider at least his early writings on the theater both before and after his epochal 1954 encounter with the Berliner Ensemble and the plays and theories of Brecht (a highly ambiguous figure with respect to the issue of theatricality); the articles "Baudelaire's Theater," "Rhetoric of the Image," and "Diderot, Brecht, Eisenstein"; his more covert involvement with Artaud; the essay "The Third Meaning: Research Notes on Several Eisenstein Stills" (points in which anticipate ones in *Camera Lucida*); and the exhilarated pages on the *bunraku* puppet theater in *Empire of Signs.*[48] It is not to be expected, given the several intellectual peripeteias in Barthes's career, and also in view of the fact that even in *Camera Lucida* he remains incompletely aware of the ultimate import of key distinctions and arguments, that the story would be simple.

NOTES

1. See Roland Barthes, *La Chambre claire: Note sur la photographie* (Paris, 1980), hereafter abbreviated *CC;* trans. by Richard Howard under the title *Camera Lucida: Reflections on Photography* (New York, 1981), hereafter abbreviated *CL.*
2. Victor Burgin, "Re-reading *Camera Lucida,*" *The End of Art Theory: Criticism and Postmodernity* (Atlantic Highlands, N.J., 1986), 78.
3. See Michael Fried, *Absorption and Theatricality: Painting and Beholder in the Age of Diderot* (1980; Chicago, 1988), *Courbet's Realism* (Chicago, 1990), and *Manet's Modernism, or, The Face of Painting in the 1860s* (Chicago, 1996). See also Fried, "Caillebotte's Impressionism," *Representations,* no. 66 (Spring 1999): 1–51; rpt. in *Gustave Caillebotte and the Fashioning of Identity in Impressionist Paris,* ed. Norma Broude (New Brunswick, N.J., 2002), 66–116; and "Roger Fry's Formalism," in *The Tanner Lectures on Human Values,* ed. Grethe B. Peterson (Salt Lake City, 2004), 3–40.
4. See Fried, "Art and Objecthood," *Art and Objecthood: Essays and Reviews* (Chicago, 1998), 148–172.
5. On the distinction between seeing and being shown, see Stephen Bann, *The True Vine: On Visual Representation and the Western Tradition* (Cambridge, 1989), 43–45, 89, where he makes clear the relation of that distinction to the reading of Diderot put forward in *Absorption and Theatricality.* In fact Barthes, as we have seen, inserts the qualifiers "not strictly" and "probably" in his initial formulation of this law, but the passage as a whole expresses no uncertainty.
6. A few commentators have noted this simple but decisive point; see, for example, Gregor Stemmrich, "Between Exaltation and Musing Contemplation: Jeff Wall's Restitution of the Program of *Peinture de la Vie Moderne,*" in *Jeff Wall: Photographs,* ed. Edelbert Köb (exhibition catalog, Cologne, Museum Moderner Kunst Stiftung Ludwig Wien, 22 Mar.–25 May 2003), 154: "The *punctum* is what a photograph can show without being intended by the photographer, or even being capable of being intended." Stemmrich's further claim is that "there is no *punctum* in the Barthesian sense in Wall's images [because of the degree of artistic control Wall exercises over their contents—M. F.], but indeed something that we might call the artistic use of the *idea of the punctum.*" Stemmrich goes on to relate Wall's work to my "Art and Objecthood" and *Absorption and Theatricality* (155–156). See also Naomi Schor, "Desublimation: Roland Barthes's Aesthetics," in *Critical Essays on Roland Barthes,* ed. Diana Knight (New York, 2000), 228, where she writes: "Like Proust's *madeleine*—and *Camera Lucida* is Barthes's *Recherche*—the *punctum* does not come under the sway of the will. It escapes the intentionality of both the photographer and the spectator." For more on Proust and the *punctum,* see below. Miriam Bratu Hansen, in a superb recent essay, remarks that for Walter Benjamin in his brilliant "Little History of Photography" (1931), the "mechanically mediated moment [of split-second photographic exposure] may preserve 'a tiny spark of contingency,' an element of alterity that speaks to another—and 'other'—in the future beholder" (Miriam Bratu Hansen, "Room-for-Play: Benjamin's Gamble with Cinema," *October,* no. 109 [Summer 2004]: 39). She adds in a note:

The technologically-based disjunction between storage and release allows for an unconscious element to enter at two levels, the moment of inscription and the time of reading. In the case of the photograph, this distinction may involve an uncanny sense of futurity (as in Benjamin's example of the wedding picture of the photographer Dauthendey and his wife who was to commit suicide after the birth of their sixth child)—something that was not visible or knowable at the time speaks to the later beholder of his form of death. . . . It is no coincidence that this particular staging of the optical unconscious has invited comparison with Roland Barthes's notion of the "punctum," the accidental mark or detail of the photograph which "pricks," stings, wounds the beholder. [Ibid., n. 97]

(More on the *punctum* and death below. See Walter Benjamin, "Little History of Photography," trans. Edmund Jephcott and Kingsley Shorter, *Selected Writings,* trans. Rodney Livingstone et al., ed. Michael W. Jennings, Howard Eiland, and Gary Smith, 4 vols. [Cambridge, Mass., 1999], 2: 507–530.) But in the bulk of the secondary literature on *Camera Lucida* (or at least in the bulk of the literature that I have read—the total mass is enormous) the structural invisibility of the *punctum* to the photographer has gone unrecognized, and in the few instances where that is not the case the antitheatrical implications of that invisibility have not been pursued.

7. For example: "Le contraste mal entendu est une des plus funestes causes du maniéré. Il n'y a de véritable contraste que celui qui nait du fond de l'action, ou de la diversité, soit des organes, soit de l'intérêt." ("Contrast wrongly understood is one of the most disastrous sources of mannerism. The only true contrast is that which arises from the depths of the action, or from the diversity of organs or of interests.") (Denis Diderot, *Essais sur la peinture,* in *Oeuvres esthétiques,* ed. Paul Vernière [Paris, 1959], 672; my trans.).

8. On the past fifty years of that tradition, see, for example, Kerry Brougher and Russell Ferguson, *Open City: Street Photographs since 1950* (exhibition catalog, Oxford, Museum of Modern Art, 6 May–15 July 2001).

9. See Walker Evans, *Many Are Called* (1966; New Haven, Conn., 2004). See also Mia Fineman, "Notes from Underground: The Subway Portraits," in *Walker Evans* (exhibition catalog, New York, The Metropolitan Museum of Art, 1 Feb.–14 May 2000), 108, and Judith Keller, "Walker Evans and *Many Are Called:* Shooting Blind," *History of Photography* 17 (Summer 1993): 152–165.

10. See the photographs reproduced in *Beat Streuli: New York City, 2000–2002* (Ostfildern-Ruit, 2003).

11. Susan Sontag, *On Photography* (New York, 1977), 37; hereafter *OP.* Before Evans, Paul Strand used hidden cameras to record anonymous figures in the street. Evans too used such a camera; specifically, he used "a 'decoy' false lens screwed onto his camera at a right angle, hoping, by catching his subjects off guard, to capture on film a certain elusive 'quality of being'" (Fineman, "Notes from Underground," 111).

Strand had to be "invisible" so as not to disturb his subjects in their unselfconscious expressions, for he wished to capture whatever mood or mind was most symptomatic of their nature off-guard. To fix this essence involved his projection of empathic interest to establish—for a suspended moment—a connection with a stranger wholly unaware that he had become a partner in a tightrope act performed on a busy street by a spellbound photographer juggling a cumbersome machine. The process was, Strand said repeatedly, "nerve-racking," for the rapt quality of his intensity naturally attracted the attention of his subjects, yet if they gave it, the photograph was ruined. [Maria Morris Hambourg, Paul Strand: Circa 1916 *(New York, 1998), 37]*

In his essay in the Beat Streuli volume cited above, Vincent Katz writes that Streuli

engages in empathetic response to his subjects . . . paradoxically, as a voyeur, using a telephoto lens, some-times ensconced inside a cafe, while photographing people passing outside. By not entering into a personal relationship with his subjects, he captures them in their natural, unguarded state. . . . Because Streuli sees without being seen, it is almost as if we are given access to the interior mental workings of his walkers. They inhabit the moment in which awareness and absorption are seamlessly blended. [Vincent Katz, "The New York Photographs of Beat Streuli," in Beat Streuli, *205]*

12. See the discussion of that painting in Fried, *Absorption and Theatricality,* 46–49.

13. See Jeff Wall, "Restoration: Interview with Martin Schwander" (1994), in Thierry de Duve et al., *Jeff Wall,* 2d ed. (London, 2002), 126–127. The crucial exchange reads:

Schwander: With Adrian Walker *you made a portrait of a young man who is concentrating so intensely on his work that he seems to be removed to another sphere of life.*
Wall: But I don't think it is necessarily clear that Adrian Walker *is a portrait. I think there is a fusion of a couple of possible ways of looking at the picture generically. One is that it is a picture of someone engaged in his occupation and not paying any attention to, or responding to the fact that he is being observed by, the spectator. In Michael Fried's interesting book about absorption and theatricality in late eighteenth century painting, he talks about the different relationships between figures and their spectators. He identified an "absorptive mode," exemplified by painters like Chardin, in which figures are immersed in their own world and display no awareness of the construct of the picture and the necessary presence of the viewer. Obviously, the "theatrical mode" was just the opposite. In absorptive pictures, we are looking at figures who appear not to be "acting out" their world, only "being in" it. Both, of course, are modes of performance. I think* Adrian Walker *is absorptive.*

14. In several writings I have suggested that historically there exists a close link between pictorial realism and a thematics of absorption. See in particular Fried, *Realism, Writing, Disfiguration: On Thomas Eakins and Stephen Crane* (Chicago, 1987), 42–45. The point is further developed in *The Moment of Caravaggio,* a book-in-progress based on the A. W. Mellon Lectures in the Fine Arts that I gave at the National Gallery of Art in the spring of 2002, as well as in a chapter on the art of Jeff Wall in another book-in-progress, the one on recent photography, of which the present essay will be a part.

15. Among the sources of Barthes's resistance to absorption is undoubtedly his previous engagement with Brecht. That is, there is an important sense in which the "realistic" theater that was the heritage of the Diderotian *tableau,* with its inbuilt injunction to treat the audience as if it did not exist (thereby transfixing it before the stage), was exactly what Brecht felt it imperative to overthrow. In Barthes's words: "Now comes a man . . . who tells us, despite all tradition, that the public must be only half-committed to the spectacle so as to 'know' what is shown, instead of submitting to it; that the actor must create this consciousness by exposing not by incarnating his role; that the spectator must never identify completely with the hero but must remain free to judge the causes and then the remedies of his suffering; that the action must not be imitated but narrated; that the theater must cease to be magical in order to become critical, which will still be its best way of being passionate"

(Barthes, "The Brechtian Revolution," *Critical Essays,* trans. Howard [Evanston, Ill., 1972], 37–38). In the later article "Diderot, Brecht, Eisenstein," Barthes compares and contrasts the thought of all three theorists with respect to the *tableau,* but owing to his unhistorical allegiance to Brecht's theories he completely misses the antitheatrical import of Diderot's views. See Barthes, "Diderot, Brecht, Eisenstein," *The Responsibility of Forms: Critical Essays on Music, Art, and Representation,* trans. Howard (New York, 1985), 89–97. A further, almost shocking instance of Barthes's misreading of Diderot is found in the late *A Lover's Discourse: Fragments,* trans. Howard (New York, 1978), where he associates Diderot's notion of the *coup de théâtre* with "the 'favorable moment' of a painting" (200), an association that runs exactly counter to Diderot's ideas.

16. And yet there is a sense in which the formal structure Barthes attributes to the copresence of *studium* and *punctum*—a "field" or "extent" punctured (also punctuated) by a detail that "shoots out" from the former "like an arrow" to "pierce" the viewer—is analogous to the structure of the Diderotian *tableau,* with its axes of absorption and address orthogonal to each other (as in Chardin's *The Card Castle* for example). Indeed the details in Chardin's genre pictures that underscore the subject's utter absorption, hence *oubli de soi,* often have the character of "wounds" or "tears" in his or her garments, as in the various versions of *Young Student Drawing* in Stockholm, Fort Worth, and elsewhere, in which there is a hole in the back of the young man's coat (a red undergarment shows through it), or as in *Soap Bubbles* in the National Gallery of Art, in which we cannot fail to notice an even larger tear near the armpit of the young man's jacket. In *The Card Castle* the boy's clothing is intact but the drawer opened toward the viewer in the bottom foreground plays a comparable role (we intuitively sense that the drawer lies outside the boy's range of awareness).

    On a thematic rather than a structural level, blindness—as in Kertész's *The Violinist's Tune, Abony, Hungary*—is claimed by me to be akin to absorption, in that it implies the depicted figure's unawareness of being beheld; see Fried, *Absorption and Theatricality,* 69–70, 145–160, 175–178.

    Finally, the necessarily unintended nature of the *punctum* amounts to a radicalization of the gap between intention and action that Walter Benn Michaels brilliantly discusses in relation to the automatic nature of photography in "Action and Accident: Photography and Writing," *The Gold Standard and the Logic of Naturalism: American Literature at the Turn of the Century* (Berkeley, 1987), 215–244. See also the penultimate paragraph of the present essay.

17. Fascinatingly, Barthes neglects to mention that photography is implicated in Proust's epiphany. In Brassaï's marvelously original study, Brassaï's [Gyula Halász], *Proust in the Power of Photography,* trans. Howard (Chicago, 2001), the same episode is rehearsed in greater detail:

The narrator stays with his grandmother at the Grand Hôtel de Balbec. One day, he surprises her dressed up in her finest clothes. She explains with some satisfaction that Saint-Loup wants to photograph her. The narrator feels "slightly irritated by this childishness" and by discovering in the old lady a coquetry he had never suspected.

Upon Françoise's insistence, however, he decides to let Saint-Loup go ahead with his project, while expressing some reservations, "a few ironic and cutting remarks intended to neutralize the pleasure my grandmother seemed to take in being photographed" (Within a Budding Grove*). He succeeds so well that the grandmother poses for her picture quite uncomfortably. Some years pass, and the narrator is once again at Balbec. As he bends over to remove his boots, suddenly the memory of his grandmother occurs* *to him, and for the first time since her death a year before, he rediscovers her in her "living reality," even as he realizes at last that he has lost her forever. And he is immediately overcome with remorse for all the pain he had caused her, "like that day when Saint-Loup had taken grandmother's photograph and when, having made no secret of the almost ridiculous coquetry she revealed in posing for him, . . . I had allowed myself to be heard murmuring several impatient and hurtful remarks, which she had indeed heard and been wounded by. . . . Never again could I erase that painful uneasiness I had been responsible for in her expression"* (Sodom and Gomorrah*).*

Françoise surprises him in his grieving contemplation of his grandmother's photograph, but what she then tells him redoubles his remorse: The day Saint-Loup took that photograph, the old lady was very ill, but she had forbidden her grandson to be told. She had merely made this recommendation to Françoise: "If something happens to me, I want him to have a photograph of me." [65–66]

Obviously the circumstances of the taking of the Winter Garden Photograph have nothing in common with those discovered by Proust's narrator. But might there nevertheless be in this intertextual connection the merest hint of a fantasy: that Barthes's mother *wanted* him to have that particular photograph of her?

Proust's grandmother is also the focus of a scene that exposes the potential cruelty of the absorptive *dispositif*. In Brassaï's retelling:

The Guermantes Way *doubtless affords the most magnificent example of this a-human vision, in which the [Proustian] narrator's eye functions like a camera. Back from Doncières, the narrator, eager to see his grandmother, surreptitiously enters the salon where she is reading, unaware of her grandson's arrival. "I was there, or rather I was not there since she didn't know it. . . . But of me—by that fugitive privilege when we have, during the brief moment of a return the faculty of suddenly attending our own absence— there was only the witness, the observer still wearing a hat and overcoat, the stranger who is not of the house, the photographer who comes to 'shoot' places that will not be seen again. What, quite mechanically, occurred in my eyes when I caught sight of my grandmother at that moment was indeed a photograph."*

And the narrator concludes, his heart aching: "I for whom my grandmother was still myself, I who had never seen her except within my own soul, always in the same place in the past, through the transparency of continuous and superimposed memories, suddenly, in our salon . . . for the first time and only for a moment, for she disappeared very quickly, I glimpsed on the couch, under the lamp, red, heavy, and coarse, ill and half asleep, her eyes wandering wildly over her book, a feeble old woman I did not know." [Pp. 121–122]

The thought of this episode could only have confirmed Barthes in his distaste for the idea of taking the photographic subject by surprise.

18. As he also writes (a few pages before the discovery of the Winter Garden Photograph):

As a living soul, I am the very contrary of History, I am what belies it, destroys it for the sake of my own history (impossible for me to believe in "witnesses"; impossible, at least, to be one; Michelet was able to write virtually nothing about his own time). That is what the time when my mother was alive before me is—History (moreover, it is the period which interests me most, historically). No anamnesis could ever make me glimpse this time starting from myself (this is the definition of anamnesis)—whereas, contemplating a photograph in which she is hugging me, a child, against her, I can waken in myself the rumpled softness of her crêpe de Chine and the perfume of her rice powder. [CL 65; CC 102]

19. Two more references to Proust in *Camera Lucida* should perhaps be cited. Barthes writes about his mother: "To the Mother-as-Good she had added that grace of being an individual soul. I might say, like the Proustian Narrator at his grandmother's death: 'I did not insist only upon suffering, but upon respecting the originality of my suffering'; for this originality was the reflection of what was absolutely irreducible in her, and thereby lost forever" (*CL* 75; *CC* 117–18). (The notion of grace will be touched on below.) And on the capacity of photography to reveal what Barthes calls "a certain persistence of the species": "Proust (again) said of Charles Haas (the model for Swann), according to George Painter, that he had a short, straight nose, but that old age had turned his skin to parchment, revealing the Jewish nose beneath" (*CL* 105; *CC* 162).

20. Marcel Proust, *Contre Sainte-Beuve* (Paris, 1954), 58–59:

> *Non seulement l'intelligence ne peut rien pour nous pour ces résurrections, mais encore ces heures du passé ne vont se blottir que dans des objets où l'intelligence n'a pas cherché à les incarner. Les objets en qui vous avez cherché à établir consciemment des rapports avec les heures que vous viviez, dans ceux-là elle ne pourra pas trouver asile. Et bien plus, si une autre chose peut les ressusciter, eux, quand ils renaîtront avec elle, seront dépouillés de poésie.*
>
> *Je me souviens qu'un jour de voyage, de la fenêtre du wagon, je m'efforçais d'extraire des impressions du paysage qui passait devant moi. J'écrivais tout en voyant passer le petit cimetière de campagne, je notais des barres lumineuses de soleil sur les arbres, les fleurs du chemin pareilles à celles du* Lys dans la Vallée. *Depuis, souvent j'essayais, en repensant à ces arbres rayés de lumière, à ce petit cimetière de campagne, d'évoquer cette journée, j'entends cette journée* elle-même, *et non son froid fantôme. Jamais je n'y parvenais et je désespérais d'y réussir, quand l'autre jour, en déjeunant, je laissai tomber ma cuiller sur mon assiette. Et il se produisit alors le même son que celui du marteau des aiguilleurs qui frappaient ce jour-là les roues du train, dans les arrêts. A la même minute, l'heure brûlante et aveuglée où ce bruit tintait revécut pour moi, et toute cette journée dans sa poésie, d'où s'exceptaient seulement, acquis pour l'observation voulue et perdue pour la résurrection poétique, le cimetière de village, les arbres rayés de lumière et les fleurs balzaciennes du chemin.*

   Contre Sainte-Beuve is not cited in the bibliography to *La Chambre claire* (the English translation carries no bibliography).

21. This has led to speculation that no such photograph ever existed. See, for example, Margaret Olin, "Touching Photographs: Roland Barthes's 'Mistaken' Identification," *Representations,* no. 80 (Fall 2002): 99–118.

22. See Benjamin, "The Work of Art in the Age of Its Technological Reproducibility: Third Version," *Selected Writings,* 4: 257–258.

23. See Barthes, *S/Z,* trans. Richard Miller (New York, 1974). In this connection it should be noted that Sontag discusses Benjamin, whom she calls "photography's most important and original critic" (*OP,* 76) and that Barthes lists Sontag's book in his bibliography.

24. Compare *OP,* 15: "All photographs are *memento mori.* To take a photograph is to participate in another person's (or thing's) mortality, vulnerability, mutability. Precisely by slicing out this moment and freezing it, all photographs testify to time's relentless melt." And 69: "Photographs state the innocence, the vulnerability of lives heading toward their own destruction, and this link between photography and death haunts all photographs of people." Sontag's book was translated into French in 1979.

25. The passage continues: "At the limit, there is no need to represent a body in order for me to experience this vertigo of time defeated. In 1850, August Salzmann photographed, near Jerusalem, the road to Beith-Lehem (as it was spelled at the time): nothing but stony ground, olive trees; but three tenses dizzy my consciousness: my present, the time of Jesus, and that of the photographer, all this under the instance of 'reality'—and no longer through the elaborations of the text, whether fictional or poetic, which itself is never credible *down to the root* [as a photograph is or can be, presumably— M. F.]" (*CL* 96–97; *CC* 151). The fact remains that Barthes's selection of exemplary photographs is almost exclusively devoted to images of persons (no views of Paris by Atget, for example).

26. To Proust's question: "But what is a memory we no longer recall?" which evokes that realm of the existence or nonexistence of memory-phantoms, this other question corresponds: "But what is a photograph that has never been developed?" No memory, and no latent image, can be delivered from this purgatory without the intervention of that deus ex machina which is the "developer," as the word itself indicates. For Proust, this will habitually be a present resemblance which will resuscitate a memory, as a chemical substance brings to life a latent image. The role of the developer is identical in both cases: to bring an impression from a virtual to a real state. [Brassaï, *Proust in the Power of Photography*, 139]

27. Section 38 begins:

All those young photographers who are at work in the world, determined upon the capture of actuality, do not know that they are agents of Death. This is the way in which our time assumes Death: with the denying alibi of the distractedly "alive," of which the Photographer is in a sense the professional. For Photography must have some historical relation with what Edgar Morin calls the "crisis of death" beginning in the second half of the nineteenth century. . . . For Death must be somewhere in a society; if it is no longer (or less intensely) in religion, it must be elsewhere; perhaps in this image which produces Death while trying to preserve life. Contemporary with the withdrawal of rites, Photography may correspond to the intrusion, in our modern society, of an asymbolic Death, outside of religion, outside of ritual, a kind of abrupt dive into literal Death. Life/Death: the paradigm is reduced to a simple click, the one separating the initial pose from the final print. [CL 92; CC 143–144]

The reference is to Edgar Morin's *L'Homme et la mort* (Paris, 1970), cited in the original bibliography.

Earlier in *Camera Lucida*, in a passage that seems strangely out of place where it occurs, Barthes writes:

Yet is not (it seems to me) by Painting that Photography touches art, but by Theater. Niepce and Daguerre are always put at the origin of Photography (even if the latter has somewhat usurped the former's place); now Daguerre, when he took over Niepce's invention, was running a panorama theater animated by light shows and movements in the Place du Château. The camera obscura, in short, has generated at one and the same time perspective painting, photography, and the diorama, which are all three arts of the stage; but if Photography seems to me closer to the Theater, it is by way of a singular intermediary (and perhaps I am the only one who sees it): by way of Death. We know the original relation of the theater and the cult of the Dead: the first actors separated themselves from the community by playing the role of the Dead: to make oneself up was to designate oneself as a body simultaneously living and dead: the whitened bust of the totemic theater, the man with the painted face in the Chinese theater, the rice-paste makeup of the Indian Katha-Kali, the Japanese No mask. . . . Now it is this same relation which I find in the Photograph;

however "lifelike" we strive to make it (and this frenzy to be lifelike can only be our mythic denial of an apprehension of death), Photography is a kind of primitive theater, a kind of Tableau Vivant, *a figuration of the motionless and made-up face beneath which we see the dead. [CL 31–32; CC 55–56]*

28. In this connection, see the important essay by Jean-François Chevrier, "Les Aventures de la forme tableau dans l'histoire de la photographie," in *Photo-Kunst: Arbeiten aus 150 Jahren: Du XXème au XIXème siècle, aller et retour* (exhibition catalog, Stuttgart, Staatsgalerie, 1989), 47–81.

29. Barthes in section 2:

A specific photograph, in effect, is never distinguished from its referent (from what it represents), or at least it is not immediately *or generally distinguished from its referent (as is the case for every other image, encumbered—from the start and because of its status—by the way in which the object is simulated): it is not impossible to perceive the photographic signifier (certain professionals do so), but it requires a secondary action of knowledge or of reflection. . . . It is as if the Photograph always carries its referent with itself. . . . The photograph belongs to that class of laminated objects whose two leaves cannot be separated without destroying them both. . . . In short the referent adheres. [CL 5–6; CC 16–18]*

30. On digitalization, see, for example, Philip Rosen, *Change Mummified: Cinema, Historicity, Theory* (Minneapolis, 2001).

31. For Barthes, being alone with a photograph seems above all to have meant being alone with the reproduction of a photograph in a book or magazine; hence his remark, quoted above, that in order "to perceive the *punctum . . .* it suffices that the image be large enough, that I do not have to study it (this would be no help at all), that, *given right there on the page,* I should receive it right here in my eyes" (*CL* 42–43; *CC* 71–72; emphasis added). Compare Proust's fundamental disagreement with John Ruskin's account of reading as a conversation with men wiser and more interesting than those one normally has occasion to meet. Against Ruskin, Proust maintains

that reading cannot be assimilated in this way to a conversation, even with the wisest of men; that the essential difference between a book and a friend is not their greater or lesser wisdom, but the manner in which we communicate with them, reading being the exact opposite of conversation in consisting for each one of us in having another's thought communicated to us while remaining on our own, that is while continuing to enjoy the intellectual authority we have in solitude and which conversation dispels instantly, while continuing to be open to inspiration, with our mind yet working hard and fruitfully on itself. [Proust, On Reading, *trans. John Sturrock (Harmondsworth, 1994), 26]*

Further on in that essay Proust speaks of reading as "an intervention which, though coming from another, is produced deep inside ourselves, the impulsion of another mind certainly, but received in the midst of our solitude" (35). Does it go too far to suggest that such a conception of the act of reading is essentially antitheatrical? The French original of *On Reading,* "La Lecture," appeared first as an article in *La Renaissance latine* in 1905 and a year later as the introduction to Proust's translation of Ruskin's *Sesame and Lilies;* see John Ruskin, *Sésame et les lys: Traduction et notes de Marcel Proust,* ed. Antoine Compagnon (Paris, 1987), 62, 72.

32. Jacques Derrida too is struck by the phrase I have italicized. "Without either showing or hiding herself," he writes,

This is what took place. She had already taken her place "docilely," without initiating the slightest activity, according to the most gentle passivity, and she neither shows nor hides herself. The possibility of this impossibility derails and shatters all unity, and this is love; it disorganizes all studied discourses, all theoretical systems and philosophies. They must decide between presence and absence, here and there, what reveals and what conceals itself. Here, there, the unique other, his mother, appears, that is to say, without appearing, for the other can appear only by disappearing. And his mother "knew" how to do this so innocently, because it is the "quality" of a child's "soul" that he deciphers in the pose of his mother who is not posing. Psyche without mirror. He says nothing more and underscores nothing. [Jacques Derrida, "The Deaths of Roland Barthes," trans. Pascale-Anne Brault and Michael Naas, The Work of Mourning, *ed. Brault and Nass (Chicago, 2001), 48]*

From the perspective of the present essay, of course, the "possibility of [an] impossibility" that Derrida elaborates on here is that of a quintessentially antitheatrical artifact (photograph, painting, sculpture, and so on), if not of antitheatricality as such.

33. The French text says only "*c'est l'air*"—nothing about the expression or the look, which the translator has added by way of clarification.

34. The whole of the brief passage containing this phrase reads: "Perhaps the air is ultimately something moral, mysteriously contributing to the face the reflection of a life value? Avedon has photographed the leader of the American Labor Party, Philip Randolph (who has just died, as I write these lines); in the photograph, I read an air of goodness (no impulse of power: *that is certain*)" (*CL* 110; *CC* 168–169).

35. In a brief discussion of a Kertész portrait of the young Tristan Tzara, Barthes refers to "the gift, the grace of the punctum" (*CL* 45; *CC* 74). Compare also the characterization of the *punctum* of the detail as occurring "dans le champ de la chose photographiée comme un supplément à la fois inévitable et gracieux" (*CC* 80). The translation in *Camera Lucida* renders "gracieux" as "delightful" (47), but here too "given as an act of grace" (or, more simply, "freely given") seems nearer Barthes's meaning.

36. See Fried, "Art and Objecthood," 164. Compare Stanley Cavell, *The World Viewed: Reflections on the Ontology of Film,* rev. ed. (Cambridge, Mass., 1979), 90:

One impulse of photography, as immediate as its impulse to extend the visible, is to theatricalize its subjects. One may object that the command is given not to achieve the unnaturalness of theater but precisely to give the impression of the natural, that is to say, the candid; *and that the point of the direction is nothing more than to distract the subject's eyes from fronting on the camera lens. But this misses the point, for the question is exactly why the impression of naturalness is conveyed by an essentially theatrical technique. And why, or when, the candid is missed if the subject turns his eye into the eye of the camera.*

And 118–119: "Setting pictures to motion mechanically overcame what I earlier called the inherent theatricality of the (still) photograph. The development of fast film allowed the subjects of photographs to be caught unawares, beyond our or their control. But they are nevertheless *caught;* the camera holds the last lanyard of control we would forgo."

37. The cinema comes up earlier in *Camera Lucida* (section 23), where Barthes begins by saying that the *punctum* is an addition, something he adds to the photograph "and *what is nonetheless already there*" (*CL* 55; *CC* 89), and goes on to ask: "Do I add to the images in movies? I don't think so; I don't

have time: in front of the screen, I am not free to shut my eyes; otherwise, opening them again, I would not discover the same image; I am constrained to a continuous voracity; a host of other qualities, but not *pensiveness;* whence the interest, for me, of the photogram" (*CL* 55; *CC* 89–90). And toward the end of the book he cites "the fictional [that is, narrative—M. F.] cinema" as one of several forces contributing to the "taming" or "domestication" of the photograph (*CL* 117; *CC* 180–181). See Steven Ungar, "Persistence of the Image: Barthes, Photography, and the Resistance to Film," in *Critical Essays on Roland Barthes,* 236–249. On Barthes's "resistance to cinema," see also Barthes, *Roland Barthes,* trans. Howard (New York, 1977), 54–55.

38. It seems unlikely that Barthes would not have been familiar with at least some of Arbus's photographs by the time he came to write *Camera Lucida.* Might he have been influenced against her by Sontag's criticism of what she regarded as Arbus's exploitation of her human subjects? See Sontag, *On Photography,* pp. 32–48.

39. See Fried, *Manet's Modernism,* pp. 405–406. A thematics of facing is also at work in my earlier writing on abstract art, as for example in "Morris Louis" (1966–1967), *Art and Objecthood,* pp. 100–131.

40. See, for example, Edward Branigan, *Narrative Comprehension and Film* (London, 1992), 53: "A glance [in a narrative film] impies an interaction with an object. In fact, glances are so important to narrating a story world that the only glance that is generally avoided is a glance into the lens of the camera. A look into the camera breaks the diegesis because it makes the conventional reverse shot or eyeline match impossible. (Such a match would reveal the camera itself; its absence would be just as revealing.)" For a fuller treatment of the transgression constituted by "a look and a voice addressed to the camera," also characterized as "an infraction of canonical proportions, an affront to the 'proper' functioning of representation and filmic narrative," see Francesco Casetti, *Inside the Gaze: The Fiction Film and Its Spectator,* trans. Nell Andrew and Charles O'Brien (Bloomington, Ind., 1998), esp. chap. 2, "The Figure of the Spectator," 16, 17. My thanks to Dudley Andrew for both references.

41. The phrase "intelligent air" ("air intelligent") is not italicized in the French.

42. See also Barthes's late, possibly unfinished essay, "Right in the Eyes," *The Responsibility of Forms,* 237–242. "As we have seen apropos of Avedon," the essay closes,

it is not excluded that a photographed subject should gaze at you—i.e. gaze at the lens: the direction of the gaze (one might say: its address*) is not pertinent in photography. [One sees what Barthes means, but that isn't exactly his view in* Camera Lucida, *where at least toward the end figures gazing out of the photograph are privileged.—M. F.] But it is so in the cinema, where it is forbidden for an actor to look at the camera, i.e., at the spectator. I am not far from considering this ban as the cinema's distinctive feature. This art severs the gaze: one of us gazes at the other, does only that: it is my right and my duty to gaze; the other never gazes; he gazes at everything, except me. If a single gaze from the screen came to rest on me, the whole film would be lost. [If true this would make the movies a radicalization of the Diderotian* tableau.—M. F.] *But this is only the literal truth. For it can happen that, on another, invisible level, the screen . . . does not cease gazing at me. [242]*

43. Fried, "Art and Objecthood," 153. Michaels comments on this statement as follows:

The "virtually" here is a little misleading because, as Fried goes on to say, although the "object, not the beholder, must remain the center or focus of the situation," "the situation itself belongs to the beholder—it is his situation." The presence of the beholder is structural rather than empirical, since without him there is no situation and therefore no literalist art. The point here is not a kind of general idealism, not the idea that the object comes into existence only when the beholder encounters it and therefore that there is some sense in which he creates it. Although this position will quickly emerge as central to certain forms of literary theory, in Fried's account of Minimalism, the object exists on its own all right; what depends on the beholder is only the experience. But, of course, the experience is everything—it is the experience instead of the object *that Minimalism values. [Michaels,* The Shape of the Signifier: 1967 to the End of History *(Princeton, N.J., 2004), 89]*

Michaels's book is a wide-ranging critique of recent theoretical and fictional texts all of which make the analogous error of "think[ing] of literature in terms of the experience of the reader rather than the intention of the author, and [of substituting] the question of who people are for the question of what they believe" (from the book jacket).

44. Probably this is made most nearly explicit in certain remarks about the work of the British sculptor Anthony Caro. For example: "It is as though Caro's sculptures essentialize meaningfulness *as such*—as though the possibility of meaning what we say and do *alone* makes his sculpture possible. All this, it is hardly necessary to add, makes Caro's art a fountainhead of antiliteralist and antitheatrical sensibility" (Fried, "Art and Objecthood," 162).

45. On the logical connection between literalism and indeterminacy, see Jennifer Ashton, "'Rose Is a Rose': Gertrude Stein and the Critique of Indeterminacy," *Modernism/Modernity* 9, no. 4 (2002): 581–604 and "Modernism's 'New' Literalism," *Modernism/Modernity* 10, no. 2 (2003): 381–390.

46. My thanks to Walter Benn Michaels, who read the present essay in manuscript, for insisting on this point.

47. All this will eventually have to be understood in the context of the book on recent photography I am currently writing (see n. 14 above). Without wishing to anticipate my argument in that book, I will simply say that Barthes's hyperbolic desire to sever the (ideal) photograph from the intentions of its maker subsequently found its mirror image in the increasing use of digital techniques by ambitious photographers in order to make photographic artifacts every bit of which may be seen as potentially the manifestation of an artistic intention (or as I say earlier in this essay, as having been put there by their maker). Even more striking in this connection is Thomas Demand's signature project of making photographs in which the photographer's intentions are everywhere foregrounded by the practice of replacing his ostensible subjects (typically scenes devoid of persons where something criminal or otherwise noteworthy has taken place) with brilliantly, but not perfectly, verisimilar constructions and then photographing them.

48. It scarcely seems necessary to give detailed references to all the texts mentioned or implied here. See, however, Timothy Scheie, "Performing Degree Zero: Barthes, Body, Theatre," *Theatre Journal* 52, no. 2 (2000): 161–81, which brings out the significance of Artaud; Jean-Pierre Sarrazac, "Le Retour au théâtre," *Parcours de Barthes, Communications,* no. 63 (1996): 11–23, a brilliant analysis of the vicissitudes of a different sort of "theatricality" in Barthes's oeuvre; and Sarrazac, "The Invention of 'Theatricality': Rereading Bernard Dort and Roland Barthes," *Substance* 31, nos. 2–3 (2002):

52–72. There is much that might be said about the relationship between "The Third Meaning" and *Camera Lucida,* but probably the most important point is that the elements in a film still Barthes associates with the "third" or "obtuse" meaning cannot have been intended as such by the filmmaker; see Barthes, "The Third Meaning," 41–62. A very useful compilation of pertinent texts is Barthes, *Écrits sur le théâtre,* ed. Jean-Loup Rivière (Paris, 2001), with a brief but excellent preface. Two items in that volume are particularly interesting in connection with the present essay: "Sept photo modèles de *Mère Courage*" and "Commentaire: Préface à Brecht, *Mère Courage et ses enfants*" (also based on photos of an actual production). For example, in "Commentaire" Barthes distinguishes between Brechtian "realism" (which he deeply admires) and ordinary "verism" (which he pretty much despises), characterizing the latter as "un art synchronique, sommatif, il veut représenter une accumulation de choses dans leur état, il veut donner l'illusion qu'elles sont incréés *et comme simplement surprises*" (275; emphasis added)—as if "verism" as Barthes understands it aspires to the effect of the surprise-based photographs that get short shrift in *Camera Lucida. Écrits sur le théâtre* opens with Barthes's brief text of 1965 for *Esprit,* the first sentence of which reads, "J'ai toujours beacoup aimé le théâtre et pourtant je n'y vais presque plus" (19), a remark cited and discussed in Sarrazac, "Le Retour au théâtre."

What Do We Want Photography to Be?

A Response to Michael Fried

James Elkins

Although Michael Fried is easy on previous readings of the *punctum,* it has arguably been one of the two most often misused terms in recent photography theory (the other candidate would be Charles Peirce's idea of indexicality).[1] The *punctum* is used to speak about viewers' responses that are taken to be idiosyncratic, unpredictable, or essentially incommunicable; yet, by citing the *punctum* to theorize such responses, historians and critics make it public and accessible to other readers, which is, I take it, the exact opposite of what Barthes intended. In effect the *punctum* becomes an unusual example of the *studium,* which Barthes disparagingly calls "a kind of education."[2]

This problem of the *punctum* is nestled within the problem of what can best be made of *Camera Lucida.* It is strange that after all the critical writing of the last twenty-five years Barthes's "little book"—so he called it, reminding us how much is really in it—remains a central text, cited almost by default as a source of insights about photography's "essential features" (*CL,* p. 3). This is despite the fact that readings by Derrida and others have shown how the text fails to provide the theory it initially promises and how it enacts that failure by contradicting both its claims to universality ("I wanted to learn at all costs what Photography was 'in itself'") and to privacy ("what I can name cannot really prick me" [*CL* 3, 51]).[3] For Patrick Maynard, *Camera Lucida* has no purchase on photography at all and is instead a meditation on mourning and representation that happens to use images as catalysts.[4] Nancy Shawcross has argued that *Camera Lucida* is an experiment in what Barthes called the "third form" between essay and novel, making it unavailable, except by wilful misreadings, as a source of theory.[5] Either way, it seems that *Camera Lucida* is of limited value in the history or criticism of photography. These criticisms, I take it, comprise a general consensus; yet, at the same time, writers continue to pluck the *punctum* out of the text in order to speak about private experience. There is perhaps no better evidence of the disarray of contemporary theorizing on photography than the fact that a book as problematic as *Camera Lucida* is still read and cited as a source of insights about photography.

Michael Fried's "Barthes's *Punctum*" is the kind of strong reading that *Camera Lucida* requires if it is going to be used as a source for theorizing about photography rather than an occasion for reflecting on the impossibility of building theories around personal experiences of certain photographs or as an opportunity to poach a poetic concept. I expect Fried's reading will put a stop to some of the looser uses of the *punctum,* not by demonstrating how strange *Camera Lucida* is (that doesn't seem to have helped), but by making explicit what is entailed in subscribing to the *punctum.* For theory-building purposes Fried is right to stress that "the detail that strikes . . . as a *punctum* could not do so had it been intended as such by the photographer" (Michael Fried, "Barthes's *Punctum,*" *Critical Inquiry* 31 [Spring 2005]: 546), precisely because the point is arguable and pulls the *punctum* out of its solipsistic private-language doldrums. Fried links the claim about the absence of intentionality to what he calls the antitheatrical tradition and, via a reading by Stephen Bann, to a distinction made by Diderot between "seeing" and "being shown." "The *punctum,*" Fried glosses, "is *seen* by Barthes but not because it has been *shown* to him by the photographer, for whom, literally, it does not exist." Regarding the second half of *Camera Lucida,* in which the passage of time is proposed as a *punctum,* Fried points out that "the sense of something being past, being historical, cannot be perceived by the photographer or indeed by anyone else *in the present*"; hence the *punctum* understood as a sign of the passage of time is another "guarantor of antitheatricality" and a parallel instance of seeing without being shown (560).

"Barthes's *Punctum*" is not an easy text to critique. It would be unhelpful, I think, to criticize the reading of Barthes for being narrow and selective; Fried knows it is both and has good reasons. Nor would it be fruitful to characterize the essay as a rescue mission directed at just a brief passage ("one short section . . . comprising a single page of print" [543]) in a text that is otherwise irrecoverable for theory. (How else could it be rescued?) "Barthes's *Punctum*" is a *necessary* reading in the specific sense that it is impelled by the thematic of antitheatricality that Fried has explored over the last twenty-five years, and it is supported by examples that have much richer contexts elsewhere.[6] I take it that his work on the antitheatrical tradition is both fundamental and indispensable for the interpretation of modernism, so it wouldn't be sensible to approach "Barthes's *Punctum*" as if it could open the question of antitheatricality or its potential applications in the present; those themes are in the books, not in this essay.[7]

"Barthes's *Punctum*" is a part of a work in progress on photography, and I imagine that when the book appears much of the reaction will center on the jump in Fried's interests from painting to photography. It's not just that Fried hasn't written much on photography (mainly a page-long footnote that hangs, anomalously, from a meditation on realism in *Courbet's Realism*); it's that modernist criticism has long been identified with claims about the specificity of media that would apparently prohibit the move in "Barthes's *Punctum*."[8] I do not think either of these points should be worrisome. The footnote in *Courbet's Realism* contains several of the arguments in "Barthes's *Punctum*," including the parallel with Chardin and the crucial stress on Barthes's idea that the photographer can "not *not* photograph the partial object at the same time as the total object." The note is appended to a consideration of the properties of realism in Courbet's painting, and the passage leading up to the note concludes: "the starkness of the opposition between Realism and photography points to their rootedness in the same historical conjuncture." Thus the genealogical tree that could present photography as a modernist art form "entangled with a problem of theatricality" was already in place in *Courbet's Realism*. The second point, concerning the specificity of media, may seem troublesome because in "Barthes's *Punctum*" Fried applies several of the same criteria to photography as he has applied to painting, apparently breaching the medium-specificity that has been central to modernist criticism since Greenberg. But it is one thing to claim that some recent "ambitious photography increasingly has claimed for itself the scale and so to speak the address of abstract painting" (570–571)—a claim I'll consider at the end of this response—and another to try "to learn at all costs what Photography [is] 'in itself,'" as Barthes says (*CL* 3). Fried doesn't write about photography because it is "faced with the task of *defeating* theater in and through the *punctum*" (568) but, I take it, in order to justify the importance of some contemporary photographic practices by demonstrating their connections with themes that, as he says in the footnote in *Courbet's Realism*, were first articulated "around the middle of the eighteenth century." If this appears as a betrayal of modernist faith in media-specificity, I wonder if that isn't because modernist criticism has a structural inability to determine what constitutes the specificity of a medium. Medium-specificity is either presented as a given—an inherent set of properties comprising "all that [is] unique in the nature"[9] of each medium—or else as an historical fable, now jettisoned in the "age of the post-medium condition."[10] "Barthes's *Punctum*" steps around that inbuilt and unproductive choice by paying attention to the pressure exerted on the present by the historically specific forms media have taken, while at the same time acknowledging the possibility that media co-opt properties from one another, thereby rearranging, blurring, or simply switching their historical roles.

Given all that, it seems to me that the most interesting questions to be asked about "Barthes's *Punctum*" only appear when its reading of the *punctum* is accepted. What I want to know then is: What kind of photography does the newly theorized *punctum* give us?

And—a separate question—what kind of photography does "Barthes's *Punctum*" give us? Here I'll propose features and kinds of photographs that are compatible with the *punctum* as it is read in "Barthes's *Punctum*," but are not countenanced in the essay. These new features and examples bring Fried's reading into areas that are, I take it, not of interest to him—areas that, as we know from *Camera Lucida,* were also of no interest to Barthes. The point here is to ask how strictly the reading in "Barthes's *Punctum*" constrains the *punctum* and where antitheatricality and the *punctum* can go when it comes to current photography. The answer to the latter question is: much further than either Fried or Barthes wants them to go.

For both *Camera Lucida* and "Barthes's *Punctum*," much depends on what is made of phenomenology. Toward the end of a series of acknowledgements that Barthes's approach "is nothing if not personal," Fried remarks that Barthes's sense of phenomenology "is one that, unlike classical phenomenology, attaches primary importance to desire and mourning" (539, 540). Barthes only mentions phenomenology twice in *Camera Lucida:* once in a passage Fried quotes, in which Barthes acknowledges that his phenomenology is "vague, casual, even cynical," and again in section 14, in the course of expositing photographic "'shock.'"

"'Shock'" (always, in section 14, in quotation marks), Barthes says, is "quite different from the *punctum*" in that "'shock'" is less about "traumatizing" than revealing what had been hidden. "'Shock'" comes in five flavors, which Barthes calls "'surprises,'" also in quotation marks.[11] The third "'surprise'" is "prowess": "For fifty years, Harold D. Edgerton has photographed the explosion of a drop of milk, to the millionth of a second."[12] The only other comment Barthes has about prowess is in a parenthesis appended to this sentence: "(little need to admit that this kind of photography neither touches nor even interests me: I am too much of a phenomenologist to like anything but appearances to my own measure)" (*CL* 33). In that one remark Barthes compresses a massive rejection—so much of photography has to do with appearances incommensurate with human measure—with a significant distortion of the concept of phenomenology. This is not "vague" or "casual" phenomenology, if only because it could be defended by appealing to Merleau-Ponty's own rejection of scientific epistemology and his interest in embodied knowledge of the world. I assume Barthes would not want to follow that line of argument because it is also the case that a photograph of milk droplets can, in a reading wholly dependent on Merleau-Ponty, elicit a strongly embodied reaction. How, in a phenomenological account, could a milk drop fail to be seen *as if* it were human-scaled? Indeed, what can be apprehended—in Kant's sense of that term, in which it is opposed to what can be comprehended—without being taken as an image made to our own measure?

I am not fond of this parenthesis of Barthes's because the lack of argument on a point so crucial to the book's axial theme of embodied experience can only function, it seems to me, as a sign that a region of photography is being hastily and arbitrarily closed off. Photography is domestic and domesticated in *Camera Lucida* because it is identified with what is called vernacular photography: *Little Italy, Idiot Children in an Institution, Savorgnan de Brazza* (*CL* 46, 50, 52). Barthes is attracted to pictures of race, of mental debilitation, of romantically lost places and people, and above all to pictures of what he thinks are unusual costumes, demeanors, and faces.[13] But what if even vernacular photography included something less human, less immediately freighted with national, social, ethnic, and familial significance, less perfectly suited to Barthes's own family history? What if the concerted search for personal engagement that impels Barthes in *Camera Lucida* is better described as an elaborate way of failing to find a more difficult sense of photography?

Consider this thought experiment: imagine the Winter Garden Photograph—as good an exemplar of vernacular photography as any, especially since it exists only in the collective imagination of Barthes's readers—and take your eyes off the central figures. Look instead, in your mind's eye, at the things that surround the children. You will see almost nothing. A bit of railing on a "little wooden bridge" and a "glassed-in conservatory" is all the picture contains, provided your imagination does not add anything Barthes doesn't mention (*CL* 67). (When I tried this, I found my memory added some details of their clothing and drooping plants on either side.) The absence of visual incident makes sense because for Barthes the photograph exists only as a way to think about his mother; and, by extension, in Barthes's account photographs are opportunities to meditate on such things as the passage of time and the modulations of memory, loss, and pain.

If I perform this same exercise with any actual family snapshot, something quite different happens: I become aware of half-occluded pieces of furniture, I notice a mess of foliage outside a window, I see the overexposed glare of a white wall—all the particular matter of the world that was not the point of the photograph. Such details can be hard to look at because they will not adhere to my thoughts, which remain bent on the photograph's subject, the one the photograph was meant to pluck out of the matrix in which it is, in fact, embedded. Those nearly unseeable pieces and forms, shapes and parts are the *on-and-on* of the world, its apparently unending supply of usually dull and sometimes uninterpretable *stuff,* and for me they are proof of a difference between whatever photography is and the agendas of vernacular photography in particular.

Or take an example reproduced in *Camera Lucida,* Alexander Gardner's *Portrait of Lewis Payne,* the one of whom Barthes says "the *punctum* is: *he is going to die*" (*CL* 96). All Barthes says of the background is that Gardner photographed Lewis "in his cell." The wall is apparently two iron sheets, welded together with enormous rivets. The photograph was taken not in Lewis's cell but in the Navy Yard in Washington, so it is possible Payne was posed in front of a ship. But it goes without saying that even discovering the exact location would not remove the mass of apparently unimportant detail that *is* the photograph, apart from the small portion that depicts the "handsome" boy (*CL* 96).[14] This is—just to be literal about it—an image of scratches and scrapes on iron sheets, with a figure interposed.

These ordinarily unnoticed forms can prick me, as the *punctum* is supposed to do. But more often they thrive in my peripheral vision like an infestation. They resist interpretation not so much because they are irrelevant to the production and dissemination of photographs, and certainly not because they are likely to be fragmentary and therefore illegible, but mainly because they tend to be *boring;* they are only available to be seen because the photograph has placed them there. In Gardner's photograph I find the scratches—including those on the print itself—more absorbing than the "handsome" boy, more "wounding" and "bruising" (to use two of Barthes's words) than his shiny manacles or his prison-issue woollen shirt and pants, and certainly more "poignant" than his fixed, off-center stare (*CL* 27). What is this stuff if not the texture of antitheatrical meaning in vernacular photography, seldom "intended as such by the photographer" and rarely even noticed by viewers?[15]

Peripheral stuff is a problem for the *punctum* as it is presented in "Barthes's *Punctum*"— not because it disturbs the argument but because it implies that the *punctum* is wider, and wilder, than accounts of vernacular photography can admit. This is where my interests diverge from Fried's reading and from *Camera Lucida*. I prefer another photography, one that is not vernacular, does not rely on figures or recognizable scenes, that is less clearly a mirror of any viewer's memories.[16] Vernacular photography is a particular moment within photography and no longer, I think, its most characteristic one.

Fried mentions the subject I have in mind when he says digital photographs undermine the conditions of the *punctum* by making it possible that "a partial object in the photograph that might otherwise prick or wound me may never have been part of a total object, which itself may be a digital construction" (563). In the sentence just preceding that, Fried notes that digitalization "threatens to dissolve the 'adherence' of the referent to the photograph," thus eroding the fundamental claim that "the photographer could not *not* photograph the partial object at the same time as the total object." There are two claims here: first, that digitalization makes it possible (or easier, since darkroom manipulations can generate the same result) to detach the referent from the photograph; second, that this detachment can also work *within* the object, detaching the part object from the full object. I am not convinced that the *punctum,* or the image's antitheatricality, are necessarily threatened by either possibility. The presence and efficaciousness of the part object are independent of digitalization because the concept of the part object arises from a certain understanding of the internal structure of pictures and objects. Part objects can be found as readily in photographs of galaxies, which are assembled from layers of cleaned and enhanced digital images, as in the background of Wessing's *Nicaragua*. Nor does the detachment of the photograph from its referent threaten the operation of the *punctum* because photographs with subjects that are wholly digitally constructed can be understood as having overlooked elements waiting to be discovered by each viewer. I take it the perception of the presence of overlooked forms, like the discovery of the part object, are effects of habits of viewing we have inherited from figural photography and painting; digitization is epiphenomenal to those habits and does not affect them. On the other hand particular nonfigural digital images can be understood as extensions, into unfamiliar territory, of the *punctum* and of problems attending antitheatricality. I will give one example.

A number of electron microscope technologies, all of them digital, involve image-making procedures that are unknown in previous photography.[17] Scanning probe microscopes are an interesting development in this regard because they do away with lenses altogether, substituting a tiny pencil-shaped tip that hovers just over the atoms in the sample. By various means, the tip registers the atoms' presence, typically by waving back and forth in response to the surface, and that vibration generates the picture.

A kind of scanning probe microscope called a scanning tunnelling microscope (STM) produces pictures that can be manipulated to look like ordinary surfaces.[18] Each lump in the "topography" is said to represent an atom, but, more precisely, STM images do not resolve atoms at all; they measure a probability function, which depends on the likelihood of electrons tunnelling between the atoms of the sample and a tiny probe that hovers overhead.[19] What seem to be atoms as solid as little hills are really mathematical functions of properties of the atoms.[20]

One step further away from familiar vision is the atomic-resolution scanning acoustic tunnelling microscope (SATM). The idea is to make the sample vibrate, using ordinary sound waves of very high frequencies and to watch how individual atoms move. Much of the work on SATMs has been done in a laboratory headed by Eduard Chilla at the Paul-Drude-Institute for Solid State Physics in Berlin.[21] Initially, the problem was that the materials tended to vibrate far more quickly than the scanning probe tip could manage, so that images of atoms were blurred. The key was to add an alternating current to the circuit with a slightly different frequency: then the two frequencies (the material's own "surface acoustic wave" [SAW] and the added AC frequency) mix, producing a frequency that is much slower and can be detected.

The result, in this experiment, is pictures of individual gold atoms vibrating. Such pictures show the phase and amplitude of the atoms' vibrations. In such a close view, all the atoms are in phase with one another so ideally the two pictures are uniform when the sample is perfect and flat. When the phase and amplitude pictures are enlarged, they show some fine structure, which can be modelled by computer.[22]

Consider what is being made visible in these images. These are not images of a surface (even a surface of atoms) because they record tunnelling current and not the view from one place. Nor are they images of static objects, but rather the mathematical difference of two frequencies; the object and the scanning probe tip were both vibrating in the range of 50,000 times a second. They are not pictures of heights and depths but of the orientation of vectors. We are very far from light here, and yet, strangely, we seem to be looking at what appear to be solid objects.

Now, I do not think these are particularly interesting as photographs; they are coarse and muddy, and their hidden geometry is not that surprising. They lack the density of meaning and the affective power that viewers (not including me) might want to associate with art.[23] But they are full of things the operators could not *not* capture, rich in "accidents," and "speckled with . . . sensitive points" (*CL* 27); they conform to the *punctum*. They are also, I find, deeply absorptive and at the same time reflective of their own medium and that medium's limitations, and for those reasons they cannot be excluded from a modernist discourse intent on capturing the historically significant moments of realism.

What bothers me about attempts to revise or adapt *Camera Lucida* is that they follow Barthes in shrinking photography to the dimensions of vernacular image-making, even when (as is the case with Fried's emphasis on the unintentional nature of the *punctum*) they provide theories of the structure of photographic images that are not at odds even with such arcane images as the ones produced by atomic-resolution scanning acoustic tunnelling microscopes. If I am right that the *punctum* as it appears in "Barthes's *Punctum*" goes further than Fried or Barthes want it to, then these photographs are troublesome. Or to put it differently: if at least some of contemporary photography is taken to be adequately captured by Fried's revision of the *punctum* so that it is open for consideration as a modernist art linked to the antitheatrical tradition, then it is necessary to ask what other criteria and interests work to exclude images outside vernacular photography. It is a genuine problem that images like the ones I discuss here can be used to raise questions about photography, seeing and being seen, images and image making, the *punctum,* absorption, and realism, that are more radical and less tied to the exigencies of human scale than questions raised by photographs of "desire and mourning." Vernacular photography is only a tiny portion of photography and probably its most intellectually unadventurous part. Vernacular photography is also, I think, contemporary photography's most nostalgic moment, and I'll argue that briefly by way of a conclusion.

At one point in *Camera Lucida* Barthes expresses his dislike for photographs that have no figures: "Oh, if there were only a look, a subject's look, if only someone in the photographs were looking at me!" (*CL* 111). Fried points out that several photographs reproduced in *Camera Lucida* lack figures, but he concludes that "the fact remains that Barthes's selection of exemplary photographs is almost exclusively devoted to images of persons" (561 n. 25). Aside from a few choices such as Niépce and Daniel Boudinet (whose photograph is the only color image in *Camera Lucida*), *Camera Lucida* proposes a fairly coherent canon of "images of persons" that spans several generations from Stieglitz to Sander, Kertész, Klein, Wessing, Avedon, and Mapplethorpe. Fried's choices are also "images of persons" by Thomas Struth, Jeff Wall, Walker Evans, Rineke Dijkstra, Thomas Ruff, and Beat Streuli. That is an interestingly different list from Barthes's, not least because the more recent photographers prefer "ambitious," large—sometimes enormous—formats (569).

It is true that Streuli, Ruff, Dijkstra, and Wall in particular fit well with elements of the tradition Fried has explored. Although he does not mention it in the essay, the blank looked-at-ness of some of Streuli's and Ruff's figures is provocatively similar to the animalistic presence of figures in Millet's paintings, which Fried has explored in *Manet's Modernism*.[24] It is certainly true that Streuli's and Ruff's images have their places in a longer history of frontal poses, stares, and what Fried brilliantly articulates under the term *facingness,* a problematic that began in the 1860s and continues to this day. Yet as art the new photography is often anodyne and unchallenging. Fried remarks of street photographs made by Evans, Streuli, and others that "absorption shades into distraction, a less 'deep' condition" (549). Barthes worries the same point: "how can one have an *intelligent air* without thinking anything intelligent, just by looking into this piece of black plastic?" (*CL* 30). What happens in some work by Struth, Wall, Dijkstra, and Streuli is more like a vegetative state than distraction or even the pure unreadable blankness that might, in theory, attend the act of being seen. I think Fried is right to link photographers like Ruff and Streuli to the thematic of facingness and address, but I am not convinced that the new work carries on key elements of that thematic in anything other than an enervated and grossly simplified fashion.

In Chicago's Millennium Park, for example, the Spanish artist Jaume Plensa has installed two fifty-foot high glass-brick towers.[25] The inward-facing sides of each tower have video projections of faces, tightly cropped to the corners of the eyes and the chin. They run twenty-four hours a day on four-minute loops. (The loops have one-minute extensions, which appear randomly, during which the models pout and, in summer, water pours from hidden openings in the walls behind the images of the mouths.) The project was incomplete when it was installed in July 2004; Plensa left instructions for the filming of a total of one thousand faces. The faces change expressions in slow motion, and when the models blink each closing and opening of the eye lasts around half a second, giving the faces a cowlike look.[26] At twilight, the faces glow with a uniform color-corrected orange and are visible over ten blocks away. *Crown Fountain,* as it is called, seems to work well as a public water sculpture, but the succession of blank stares and meaningless smiles is more enervating than absorptive—less perception without seeing, in Barthes's sense, than a kind of plantlike stupor.[27] I wonder if this kind of amiable emptiness, which is also typical of Streuli's work, is an interesting future for photography.

The draining-away of the sheer force of being looked at *"straight in the eye"* (CL 111), and of the strategies for avoiding sheer theatricality in doing so, is one issue; another is the tempting art historical parallels such work offers. For a decade now, Wall's work has exerted a strange fascination on art historians. Thomas Crow, Thierry De Duve, and now Fried are among the historians who have written about his work. I regard Wall's work as a trap laid for art historians, especially those familiar with the key moments in the history of art that Wall likes to take as points of departure (even, one might say, those who helped frame those very moments). A number of Wall's photographs are almost predigested for art historical consumption: they are obviously modelled on famous precedents; their treatment of those precedents is often responsive to the existing art historical literature (written, in some cases, by the same historians who now find themselves attracted to Wall's work); and they propose variations on those precedents that are themselves within the boundaries of nineteenth-century narrative and realist practice.[28] I wonder if Wall might not be a "false friend" as language teachers like to say, an artist whose interest depends on his allusions to key monuments and texts of art history. To my eye, the double affinity with nineteenth-century traditions and late twentieth-century art historical scholarship is a bad sign. It is necessary to distinguish between practices that grow out of historical traditions, taking their strength and meaning from those traditions, and practices that play off superficial links to tradition, wearing their affinities on their sleeves.[29] I think Wall's work is significant for different reasons, in particular for the "flaws" and overlooked details that persist in his tableaux despite his most meticulous efforts—effects that cannot be eradicated because the work is photography and not painting and which are at once antitheatrical and well suited to Fried's reading of the *punctum.*

For me large-scale, ambitious narrative and realist photography including Wall's, Struth's, Ruff's, Plensa's, and Streuli's does not compel conviction. I agree that "ambitious photography increasingly has claimed for itself the scale and so to speak the address of abstract painting" (570–571), but I am not taken by the results. I think it is necessary to locate contemporary art photography in Gerhard Richter and Ed Ruscha and in artists like Marco Breuer who experiment with photography's basic materials—and to locate contemporary photography as a whole not only by reference to art but to the many kinds of scientific, technological, and utilitarian images and their digital and philosophic possibilities.[30] Photography such as Wall's relies suspiciously heavily on nineteenth-century academic painting. A parallel might be made here between Wall and Robert Mapplethorpe: both have been interested in compositional strategies that can be found in nineteenth-century painting from Hippolyte Flandrin onwards. It may be that contemporary large-scale figural photography is less an interesting way forward than a last, nostalgic, academic echo of a premodernist past.

NOTES

1. I would argue two things about uses of the index and indexicality in photography theory. First, such readings have made use of a very selective reading of Peirce's semiotic, ignoring for example the interdependence of all three kinds of signs; their division into trichotomies according to function (what Peirce calls firsts, seconds, and thirds); the fact that icon, index, and symbol are taken in relation to objects and that two other divisions name signs in relations to themselves and to what Peirce calls interpretants; and their ramification into divisions and even 59,049 cases. (In short: such readings are so abbreviated that it becomes unclear in what sense they are citations of Peirce's semiotic at all.) Second, uses of the index in photography theory have tended to identify the indexicality with cause and effect, so that the work indexicality has been made to do could often have been done without any reference to Peirce. These points are discussed in my "What Does Peirce's Sign System Have to Say to Art History?" *Culture, Theory, and Critique* 44, no. 1 (2003): 5–22.

2. Roland Barthes, *Camera Lucida,* trans. Richard Howard (New York, 1981), 28; hereafter abbreviated *CL.*

3. See Jacques Derrida, "The Deaths of Roland Barthes," *The Work of Mourning,* ed. Pascale-Anne Brault and Michael Naas (Chicago, 2001), 31–67; Margaret Olin, "Touching Photographs: Roland Barthes's 'Mistaken' Identification," *Representations,* no. 80 (Fall 2002): 99–118; and Graham Allen, *Roland Barthes* (London, 2003), chap. 9, "*Camera Lucida:* The Impossible Text," pp. 125–132. Allen argues very directly that *Camera Lucida* "blends the discourse or language of method (theory) with a wholly personal discourse (of mourning) and thus unsettles and disturbs the very results it seems to present" (Allen, *Roland Barthes,* 125–126). Fried cites Olin's essay, noting that she doubts the existence of the Winter Garden Photograph, but does not comment on her argument that Barthes's desire overwhelmed his theory, compelling him to construct the photograph out of parts of existing photographs. I take it the essential point is not that the photograph must decisively never have existed but that "Barthes," the author of *Camera Lucida,* needs to "use photography to satisfy his desire to possess or commune with his mother" and that the desire displaces the *punctum,* "like an alibi" (Olin, "Touching Photographs," 115, 112). It seems to me that in Olin's essay the *punctum* in *Camera Lucida* is too unreliable to contribute to a theory of photography. Another text that reads Barthes's book as an exercise in self-subversion is Stamos Metzidakis, "Barthesian Discourse: Having Your Cake and Eating It Too," *Romanic Review* 91, no. 3 (2000): 335–347.

4. Maynard says *Camera Lucida* is not "a sustained account of photographs" but is "actually reductive to the subjects photographed, taken substantively: usually people or details of them and their attire" (Patrick Maynard, *The Engine of Visualization: Thinking through Photography* [Ithaca, N.Y., 1997],

13). A similar argument regarding Barthes's *use* of photography to make unrelated points is made in Jean-Michel Rabaté, introduction to *Writing the Image after Roland Barthes,* ed. Rabaté (Philadelphia, Pa., 1997), 1–16.

5. Nancy Shawcross, *Roland Barthes on Photography: The Critical Tradition in Perspective* (Gainesville, Fla., 1997), 67–85. Barthes introduces the "third form" in *The Rustle of Language,* trans. Richard Howard (New York, 1986), 281.

6. Let me mention and dispense with what I think may be an objection to this equation of the claim that the *punctum* is unnoticed at the time of the making of the photograph and the function of "being shown" in the antitheatrical tradition. The case of photography, so it might be said, is different from painting, where the signs of the antitheatrical thematic—such as, in Fried's examples, the open drawer in Chardin's *The Card Castle* or the torn jacket in *Soap Bubbles* (553 n. 16)—are placed in the paintings by the painters. When a photographer inadvertently includes a feature that will figure, for some future viewer, as a *punctum,* it is merely because the photographer "cannot *not*" photograph that feature. But Fried intends only a parallel of the *appearance* of not having been shown, and he emphasizes that Barthes "goes well beyond anything to be found in Diderot or for that matter any eighteenth- or nineteenth-century critic or theorist" by insisting that the photograph "carry within it a kind of ontological guarantee that it was not intended to be [antitheatrical] *by the photographer*" (553).

7. Fried's work, I think, is exemplary of modernism and *for* modernism, which is what I mean when I say that the reading in "Barthes's *Punctum*" is necessary. I discuss Fried's modernism at length in *The Master Narratives and Their Discontents* (forthcoming); I have also discussed his art criticism (especially in regard to the crucial difference between having a claim, a position, and a stance) in *What Happened to Art Criticism?* (Chicago, 2003), 65–77; and I have explored the close relation between his forms of narrative address and the claims he makes in my book *Our Beautiful, Dry, and Distant Texts: Art History as Writing* (New York, 2000), 246–252.

8. See Fried, *Courbet's Realism* (Chicago, 1990), 282–283. The footnote is anomalous in that the book is formatted with endnotes rather than footnotes, with only three exceptions, of which this is the longest. It is an asterisked footnote, a full page long, less than seven pages before the end of the book—a genuine compositional anomaly. I take that as an indication that even though the logic is consistent between the footnote and the context in *Courbet's Realism,* the historical continuity between realism (in painting) and photography remains troublesome. I thank Joel Snyder for alerting me to this note, which I'd forgotten.

9. Clement Greenberg, "Modernist Painting," *Clement Greenberg: The Collected Essays and Criticism,* ed. John O'Brian, 4 vols. (Chicago, 1993), 4:86.

10. See Rosalind Krauss, *"A Voyage on the North Sea": Art in the Age of the Post-Medium Condition* (London, 1999).

11. First surprise: the "rare"—a man "with two heads, woman with three breasts, child with a tail, etc.: all smiling." Second surprise: the "*numen* of historical painting," where we are shown the moment that "the normal eye cannot arrest": Baron Gros's *Plague-House at Jaffa,* where "Bonaparte has just touched the plague victims" and his hand withdraws. This second surprise is "habitual to Painting," but a "surprise" when it appears in photography. Fourth surprise: the "contortions of technique: superimpressions, anamorphoses." Fifth surprise: "the *trouvaille* or lucky find": "an emir in native

costume on skis." Barthes does not approve of these "surprises" because they are orchestrated and therefore, as Fried emphasizes, *shown* to the viewer instead of lying unseen in the images, waiting to be discovered. Barthes says that relying on "surprise" makes it necessary, "by a familiar reversal," to find the "surprise" in all photography, in photography itself. Instead of searching out "surprises," amateur photographers say that whatever odds and ends they photograph are automatically "notable" (*CL* 32–33).

12. Barthes copied this from a popular magazine, which reported the facts inaccurately: Edgerton's milk-drop photos were made between 1932 and 1957. See Harold Edgerton, *Stopping Time: The Photographs of Harold Edgerton,* ed. Gus Kayafas (New York, 1987), 126. Kayafas tells me that Edgerton produced about 20,000 negatives of milk drops and destroyed all but two dozen or so; see Kayafas, letter to the author, 1999.

13. I use *vernacular photography* here to denote a set of practices that include portraiture, journalism, street photography, and the snapshot. See Douglas Nickel, "Roland Barthes and the Snapshot," *History of Photography* 24, no. 3 (2000): 236–39. On Barthes's choice of images, see also Olin, "Touching Photographs."

14. The argument I am making here is parallel to one made by Maynard, *Engine of Visualization,* 29–33, in reference to scratches and doodles in a Walker Evans photograph, except that Maynard is not valorizing photography's incidental marks, but considering it as a "surface-marking" technology (34).

15. This is also where Barthes's equation of photographs with reproductions of photographs becomes especially significant. Fried puts this quite accurately: "for Barthes, being alone with a photograph seems above all to have meant being alone with the reproduction of a photograph in a book or magazine" (p. 563 n. 31). Fried goes on to talk about Ruskin and reading, and his observation about Barthes's reliance on magazines is nearly an argument that, for Barthes, looking at photographs is *reading.* Nothing is lost in reproduction as far as Barthes's theory is concerned. In "Barthes's *Punctum*" the physical presence of photographs is important, but not such things as the inevitable gloss of a photograph's water-resistant surface, the slight depth of its layers of grain, and the heft of its paper backing (or the translucency and thickness of the plastic support, in the case of a light box). The stuff that comprises photographs gets a bit lost, even though it is not necessarily a sign of theatrical address and even though it is not irrelevant in large-scale installations like Struth's or Wall's.

16. This is addressed in a work in progress, written against *Camera Lucida,* tentatively titled *Camera Dolorosa: On Visual Desperation.* An excerpt has appeared as "Harold Edgerton's Rapatronic Photographs of Atomic Tests," *History of Photography* 28, no. 1 (2004): 74–81.

17. After transmission electron microscopes (TEMs) the next to be developed were the scanning electron microscopes (SEMs). In the last fifteen years of the twentieth century there were also SPMs (scanning probe microscopes), including STMs (scanning tunnelling microscopes), AC-STMs, AFMs (atomic force microscopes), CFMs (chemical force microscopes), and—at the very end of the century—NSOMs (nearfield scanning optical microscopes). See Newbury and Williams, "The Electron Microscope"; for CFMs, see Aleksandr Noy, Dmitri Vezenov, and Charles Lieber, "Chemical Force Microscopy," *Annual Review of Materials Science* 27, no. 1 (1997): 381–421. Those basic kinds subdivide into an astonishing number of evanescent technologies: inelastic tunnelling spectroscopy, ballistic electron emission microscopy, scanning spin-precession microscopes, scanning

thermal microscopes, and a dozen others just between 1981 and 1995. These and others are cited in H. Kumar Wickramasinghe, "Progress in Scanning Probe Microscopy," *Acta Materialia* 48 (Jan. 2000): 347–358. The last few years have seen the development of scanning capacitance microscopes, magnetic resonance force microscopes, and atomic-resolution acoustic microscopes. See for example J. Schmidt et al., "Microwave-Mixing Scanning Capacitance Microscopy of *pn* Junctions," *Journal of Applied Physics,* 15 Dec. 1999, 7094–7099.

18. A good introductory text is *Scanning Tunneling Microscopy I: General Principles and Applications to Clean and Adsorbate-Covered Surfaces,* ed. Hans-Joachim Güntherodt and Roland Wiesendanger (New York, 1994). I thank Jie Liu for this reference.

19. See J. Tersoff and D. Hamann, "Theory and Application for the Scanning Tunnelling Microscope," *Physical Review Letters,* 20 June 1983, 1998–2001.

20. Nor are they electron orbitals, as is sometimes implied. See the incisive essay by Eric Scerri, "Have Orbitals Really Been Observed?" *Journal of Chemical Education* 77, no. 11 (2000): 1492–1494. I thank Davis Baird for drawing this to my attention. It is possible to locate individual chemical bonds within single molecules; see Barry Stipe, "Tuning in to a Single Molecule: Vibrational Spectroscopy with Atomic Resolution," *Current Opinion in Solid State and Materials Science* 4 (Oct. 1999): 421–428, and B. C. Stipe, M. A. Rezaei, and W. Ho, "Single-Molecule Vibrational Spectroscopy and Microscopy," *Science,* 12 June 1998, 1732–1735.

21. A more extended study of this and other imaging technologies is forthcoming as *Six Stories from the End of Representation.* An early paper is Eduard Chilla, W. Rohrbeck, and H.-J. Fröhlich, "Probing of Surface Acoustic Wave Fields by a Novel Scanning Tunnelling Microscopy Technique: Effects of Topography," *Applied Physics Letters,* 28 Dec. 1992, 3107–3109. I thank Eduard Chilla for a tour of his lab.

22. As the probe tip scans over the surface of the gold crystal, a tunnelling current passes between the gold atoms and the tip. That current always goes straight from the tip to the "topography"; sometimes the current is vertical, and other times it is slanted. The little ellipses stand up vertically in the surface, and each atom is at a particular place in its elliptical path when the probe approaches. (All the atoms in the sample are in virtually identical places because the image is "stroboscopically" rapid in relation to the size of the SAW.) When the tunnelling current is colinear with the atom's position—its displacement vector—then the phase image registers a maximum. When it is noncolinear, some intensity is subtracted. Hence the phase image is a picture of added and subtracted *vectors,* not topography in the ordinary sense. In addition the bright spots—they should not be called atoms—are elliptical because the atoms are like little spheres half-sunk in water: as they vibrate elliptically, they trace out an ellipsoidal surface, which is what the probe tip encounters. See T. Hesjedal, Chilla, and Fröhlich, "Direct Visualization of the Oscillation of Au (111) Surface Atoms," *Applied Physics Letters,* 15 July 1996, 354–357 and "Scanning Acoustic Tunnelling Microscopy and Spectroscopy: A Probing Tool for Acoustic Surface Oscillations," *Journal of Vacuum Science and Technology B* 15 (July 1997): 1569–1572.

23. They do not lack density of scientific meaning; much more can be said about the hexagons and ellipsoids that the computer simulation reveals, and that is what is of interest to Chilla's team.

24. See Fried, *Manet's Modernism; or, The Face of Painting in the 1860s* (Chicago, 1996).

25. See millenniumpark.org/crown.htm.

26. Because the loops have to be exactly four minutes long, because the artist preferred slow motion to fast motion, and because they have to blend seamlessly with the one-minute loops, each four-minute loop runs at a slightly different rate. The effect is that some appear nearly motionless, and others move at an almost natural speed. I thank John Manning for this information; Manning is a professor of film, video, and new media at the School of the Art Institute and is in charge of technical support and of producing the remainder of the tapes (Plensa produced very few).

27. It is fitting that there are also videos of water and plants that run, in random sequences, with the videos of faces.

28. *Diatribe* (1985), for example, struck Thomas Crow as similar to Van Gogh's *Outskirts of Paris* (1886–1888), partly on the basis of T. J. Clark's reading of the significance of the Parisian *banlieu* in impressionism and postimpressionism; Clark, in turn, is one of Wall's sources. See Thomas Crow, *Modern Art in the Common Culture* (New Haven, Conn., 1996), 160–161.

29. Here I seem to agree with Rosalind Krauss, "Reinventing the Medium," *Critical Inquiry* 25 (Winter 1999): 297 n. 14, in which she characterizes Wall's nineteenth-century references as "pastiche." But the reference is too brief to know exactly what she means by "pastiche," and it is made in the context of a review of "'postmedium' production" (296) that I find limits the possibilities of contemporary criticism, including the possibilities Fried explores in "Barthes's *Punctum.*"

30. For Breuer, see for example my "Renouncing Representation," in Marco Breuer and Elkins, *Tremors, Ephemera* (exhibition catalog, Roth Horowitz Gallery, New York, 22 Apr.–26 May 2000), and Breuer, *SMTWTFS* (New York, 2002).

ROSALIND E. KRAUSS

A BEGINNING IN "*MIS*-MAJOR"[1]

In his brilliant analysis of Roland Barthes's *Punctum,* Michael Fried recoils at a *mis*translation of the word *gomme* (or *gommé*) as "blurred," instead of "erased" or "rubbed out."[2]

There is an even more injurious *lapse* by the translator, however, who renders Barthes's use of *objet partiel* as "partial object" rather than, correctly, "part object," a *mis*take the effect of which is to *gomme* the importance of this concept for *Camera Lucida's* argument, a *mis*take that Fried lets pass. Barthes's references to the part object are in order here:

"Very often the *Punctum* is a 'detail,' i.e., a part object."[3]

". . . it says only that the photographer was there, or else, still more simply, that he could not *not* photograph the part object at the same time as the total object."[4]

THE *TUCHÉ*—AS IF BY CHANCE[5]

That the part object transports us into the domain of psychoanalysis, or more precisely, Jacques Lacan, is made specific from the outset of *Camera Lucida:*

. . . The This *(this photograph, and not Photography), in short what Lacan calls the* Tuché, *the Occasion, the Encounter, the Real, in its indefatigable expression. In order to designate reality, Buddhism says* sunya, *"the void"; but better still:* tathata, *as Alan Watts has it, the fact of being this, of being thus, of being so;* tat *means "that" in Sanskrit and suggests the gesture of the child pointing his finger at something and saying:* that, there it is, lo! *but says nothing else; a photograph cannot be transformed (spoken) philosophically, it is wholly ballasted by the contingency of which*

it is the weightless, transparent envelope. . . . The photograph is never anything but an antiphon of "Look," "See, "Here it is"; it points a finger at certain vis-à-vis, *and cannot escape this pure deictic language.*[6]

The translator's *absurd* rendering of Barthes's homophonic transformation of *tathata* into *Ta! da! ça!* by "that, there it is, lo!" *overlooks* the fact that in French ça is Id; so a more accurate reading would be "Look! There Id is!" Designating the part object as *objet [petit] a*, Lacan describes it as formative of the subject's ego, as he encounters it pointing at him either from the loving gaze of his mother, or from her withheld breast which he wants to interject, a fantasy that, in Melanie Klein's terms, transforms the good object into the bad, depressive object. In the form of his own body seen in a mirror and possessing the organization (gestalt) that surpasses his own experience of his disorganized, inchoate body, the *objet a* conspires paradoxically in an alienation of the subject from himself.[7]

TRIUMPH OF THE WILL

Michael Fried wants us to believe that Roland Barthes shares his own adversary within modernist aesthetic production, namely, theatricality. His reading of *Camera Lucida*, therefore, focuses on what Barthes singles out as those features of the photograph that destroy or prevent the experience of the punctum. The central one of these, he asserts, is a sense of the photographer's intention, which will prevent the detail from wounding or "pricking" Barthes as observer. This leads to the "subjectivism" often ascribed to *Camera Lucida*: That the detail must not be present as intended, shifts the entire act of experiencing its meaning over to the viewer of the image. Drawing back from this shift, Fried points out that it tips *Camera Lucida* dangerously over into "literalist" sensibility in which, as in Minimalist sculpture, the work cannot exist without the viewer to complete it, but, dangerously, every viewer's interpretation of its meaning is equivalent to every other, since the "constitutive relationships" of the work were not built into it by its maker.[8]

We have the right, however, to wonder whether Barthes identifies his foe as theatricality or instead, as he himself declares it very often: "fascism." In his Inaugural Lecture for his chair at the Collège de France, Barthes spoke of "the fascism of language," by which he meant the coercive powers of speech which force the speaker always to choose one side of the binaries that constitute him: gender, number, degree of intimacy (as in *vous* or *tu*). Because of this, Barthes longed for a "third language" the task of which would be "to release the prisoners: to scatter the signifieds, the catechisms."[9]

As many commentators have pointed out, Barthes's longing for the "third language" prepares the long gestation in his work for the idea of *punctum,* itself anticipated in his essay "The Third Meaning" by the Obtuse Meaning, which, in its own opposition to the Obvious Meaning, forecasts *Camera Lucida's* contrast of *studium* and *punctum.* In preparing for the *punctum's* escape from language through the "nothing-to-say,"[10] the Obtuse resists signification by opening onto what Barthes refers to as Julia Kristeva's concept of *signifiance.* "The Third Meaning" is, itself, a preparation for *Camera Lucida's* search for the *noeme* of a particular medium (here, cinema), which, perversely, Barthes finds in the film still or that which stops the temporal unfolding of the narrative, becoming—in its vertical piling up of substitutions for the image's meaning—what Barthes calls a "counter-narrative"—an anticipation of *Camera Lucida's* "counter-memory."

Notes on the Index

The speechlessness Barthes craves in *Camera Lucida* twice takes the form of being stunned into silence—an escape from the "fascism of language" through "amazement" or "astonishment." The first occurs in the opening of the book as Barthes tells us of the time when "I happened on a photograph of Napoleon's youngest brother, Jerome, taken in 1852. And I realized then, with an amazement I have not been able to lessen since: 'I am looking at eyes that looked at the Emperor.' Sometimes I would mention this amazement, but since no one seemed to share it, nor even to understand it . . . I forgot about it."[11] The second arrives somewhat later as Barthes identifies the *noeme* of photography as the "emanation of the referent": "Always the Photograph *astonishes* me, with an astonishment which endures and renews itself, inexhaustibly."[12]

These two aspects—the "nothing-to-say" of the Obtuse, and the "emanation of the referent"—are obviously properties of that sign C. S. Peirce designates as "index," distinguishing it from "symbol" on the one hand and "icon" on the other.[13] Barthes had long before acknowledged the mixed sign of the photograph as index plus icon when, in "The Photographic Message," he defined the photograph as an instance of a "message without a code."[14]

The penultimate course Barthes gave at the Collège de France was titled *Le neutre,* a consideration of the possible escape from the coercion of language through the avoidance of language's forced "affirmation," its dependence on "conflict"—each of these rubrics of one of his lectures. [15] The neutral is also a topic-heading of *Roland Barthes by Roland Barthes,* anticipating this important cancellation of structuralist operations.[16]

Several sections of the autobiographical book are worth quoting here, providing as they do, a sense of the constancy of Barthes's commitment to the third meaning (and thus the Neutral), as to its affective resonance:

Quand je jouais aux barres

When I used to play prisoner's base in the Luxembourg, what I liked best was not provoking the other team and boldly exposing myself to their right to take me prisoner; what I liked best was to free the prisoners—the effect of which was to put both teams back into circulation: the game started over again at zero. In the great game of the powers of speech, we also play prisoner's base: one language has only temporary rights over another; all it takes is for a third language to appear from the ranks for the assailant to be forced to retreat: in the conflict of rhetorics, the victory never goes to any but the third language. *The task of this language is to release the prisoners: to scatter the signified, the catechisms.*[17]

L'amour d'une idée

For a certain time, he went into raptures over binarism; binarism became for him a kind of erotic object. This idea seemed to him inexhaustible, he could never exploit it enough. That one might say everything with only one difference produced a kind of joy in him, a continuous astonishment. Since intellectual things resemble erotic ones, in binarism what delighted him was a figure. Later on he would find this (identical) figure again, in the opposition of values. What (in him) would deflect semiology was from the first the pleasure principle: a semiology which has renounced binarism no longer concerns him at all.[18]

Exemption of meaning

Evidently he dreams of a world which would be exempt from meaning *(as one is from military service). This began with* Writing Degree Zero, *in which is imagined "the absence of every sign"; subsequently, a thousand affirmations incidental to this dream (apropos of the avant-garde text, of Japan, of music, of the alexandrine, etc.).*

Curious that in public opinion, precisely, there should be a version of this dream; Doxa, too, has no love for meaning, which in its eyes makes the mistake of conferring upon life a kind of infinite intelligibility (which cannot be determined, arrested): it counters the invasion of meaning by the concrete; the concrete is what is supposed to resist meaning.[19]

Yet for him, it is not a question of recovering a pre-meaning, an origin of the world, of life, of facts, anterior to meaning, but rather to imagine a post-meaning: one must traverse, as though the length of an initiatic way, the whole meaning, in order to be able to extenuate it, to exempt it.

Whence a double tactic: against Doxa, *one must come out in favor of meaning, for meaning is the product of History, not of Nature; but against Science (paranoiac discourse) one must maintain the utopia of suppressed meaning.*[20]

Charlot

As a child, he was not so fond of Chaplin's films; it was later that he found a kind of delight in this art at once so popular and so intricate; it was a composite *art, looping together several tastes, several languages. Such artists provoke a complete kind of joy, for they afford the image of a culture that is at once differential and collective: plural. This image then functions* as the third term, *the subversive term of the opposition in which we are imprisoned: mass culture* or *high culture.*[21] *[emphasis added RK]*

The Neutral, the *punctum,* were already in gestation within Barthes's concerns beginning with his idea of the zero degree, and continuing throughout his curious identification of the structuralist project with fascism. We hear this in the topics of his course's lectures: as the escape from choice takes the form of "Silence"; "Tact"; and "Sleep"; while the coercion of language is registered through the figures of "Affirmation"; "Arrogance"; and "The Adjective."

NOTES

1. See Jacques Derrida, "Limited Inc," *Glyph 2* (1977): 176. Derrida cites all the uses of mis-take and mis-understanding, in John Searle's attack on his essay "Signature, Event, Context," calling this a "percussion in *mis-major.*"

2. Michael Fried, "Barthes's *Punctum,*" *Critical Inquiry,* 31 (Spring 2005): 550. In the disputed passage Barthes writes: "Ce *punctum,* plus ou moins gommé sous l'abondance et la disparité des photos d'actualité, se lit vif dans la photographie historique: il y a toujours en elle un écrasement du temps: cela est mort et cela va mourir." This passage demands not only a knowledge of French but also of the history of photography in which gum bichromate was the chemical of choice among "pictorialist" photographers, who manipulated their prints by erasing or blurring the engrafted photographic information in order to produce the "aesthetic" effects of Impressionist painting. Barthes's target here may not be so much theatricality as "artiness."

3. Roland Barthes, *Camera Lucida: Reflections on Photography* (1980), trans. Richard Howard (New York: Hill and Wang, 1981), 43.

4. Ibid., 47.

5. Jacques Lacan, "Tuché and Automatom," in *The Four Fundamental Concepts of Psycho-Analysis,* trans. Alan Sheridan (New York: Norton, 1978).

6. Barthes, *Camera Lucida,* 4–5.

7. This aspect of Barthes's meditation is addressed by Margaret Iverson in her important "What Is a Photograph?," *Art History* 17 no. 3 (September 1994): 450–464.

8.   This results in Fried's implicit dismissal of the index as an analytic tool to understand photography, since his idea of the need for artistic control over every aspect of the work leads to his support for digital imaging, as in the photography of Thomas Demand, Thomas Struth, Andreas Gursky, and others. Barthes's own commitment to the index as explained above with regard to the "pure deictic language" of *tathata*, would open a gulf separating his analysis from Fried's.

9.   Roland Barthes, "Lecture," trans. Richard Howard, *October* 8 (Spring 1979): 5; and Roland Barthes, *Roland Barthes by Roland Barthes* (1975), trans. Richard Howard (New York: Hill and Wang, 1977), 50.

10.   The pointing finger of the *tathata*, according to *Camera Lucida*, "says nothing else; a photograph cannot be transformed (spoken) philosophically, it is wholly ballasted by the contingency of which it is the weightless, transparent envelope. . . . the photograph is never anything but an antiphon of 'Look'" (5).

11.   Barthes, *Camera Lucida*, 3.

12.   Ibid., 82.

13.   Much as I abominate self-citation, my "Notes on the Index" is relevant here (*October* 4 (Fall 1977): 58–67).

14.   Roland Barthes, "The Photographic Message," *Image/Music/Text,* trans. Stephen Heath (New York: Noonday Press, 1988), 17.

15.   Roland Barthes, *Le neutre: cours au Collège de France (1977–1978),* (Paris: Seuil, 2002); in English as *The Neutral,* trans. Rosalind Krauss and Denis Hollier (New York: Columbia University Press, 2005).

16.   Barthes, *Roland Barthes by Roland Barthes*, 132.

17.   Ibid., 50.

18.   Ibid., 51.

19.   Ibid., 87.

20.   Ibid., 87.

21.   Ibid., 54.

Gordon Hughes

Near the end of *Camera Lucida,* Roland Barthes makes a veiled but unmistakable reference to E.T.A. Hoffmann's 1816 story "The Sandman." Barthes has been trying to describe the "madness" and "hallucinatory" effect of photography ("Here is where the madness is. . . . The photograph becomes a bizarre medium, a new form of hallucination . . . a sort of tempered hallucination"),[1] when we find this:

The same evening of a day I had again been looking at photographs of my mother, I went to see Fellini's Casanova *with some friends. I was sad, the film exasperated me; but when Casanova began dancing with the young automaton, my eyes were touched with a kind of acute and delicious pain, as if I were suddenly experiencing the effects of a strange drug; each detail, which I was seeing so exactly, savoring, so to speak, every last part of it. . . . At which moment I could not help thinking about Photography. . . . Was I not, in fact, in love with the Fellini automaton? Is one not in love with certain photographs?"*[2]

The reference is clear. In Hoffmann's story, young Nathaniel's nurse tells him that if he doesn't sleep, the sandman will come and steal his eyes (Barthes: "my eyes were touched with a kind of acute and delicious pain"). One evening, this frightening figure comes to Nathaniel's house, discovers the boy spying, and is about to drop hot coals into the boy's eyes when his father intervenes. Later in the tale, Nathaniel falls in love with a neighbor's oddly inanimate daughter, who turns out to be the automaton Olympia ("Was I not, in fact, in love with the Fellini automaton?"). This misdirected love, along with the reappearance of the sandman, eventually leads Nathaniel into madness ("Here is where the madness is").

Barthes's allusion to "The Sandman" is a reference within a reference—not so much to Hoffman's story as to Freud's famous reading of it in his 1919 essay "The Uncanny" (*"Das Unheimliche"*). Indeed, Barthes's interest in tying photography's madness to "The Sandman" is not to forge a simple equation with Nathaniel's mental illness. He is not saying that photography is madness, pure and simple. Rather, Barthes is pointing toward the radical indeterminacy that Freud sees at the heart of Hoffmann's story. This indeterminacy is epitomized for Freud in the bizarre episode where Nathaniel is discovered and almost blinded by the sandman. As Freud writes: "Hoffmann already leaves us in doubt whether what we are witnessing is the first delirium of the panic stricken boy, or a real succession of events which are to be regarded in the story as being real."[3] For Freud (and this is crucial to Barthes's understanding of photography), both alternatives involve a mixing of realism and madness, such that, like "the effects of a strange drug" (as Barthes writes above), one is indistinguishable from the other. Photography, for Barthes, manifests *la vérité folle* (the crazy truth);[4] it is an "insane image, rubbed with the real."[5]

Real *and* mad: this paradoxical cohabitation of opposites is one of many such noncontradictory contradictions that generate the effect Freud describes. This "intellectual uncertainty," as Freud calls it, is perhaps most famously performed in the German word *unheimlich* (homely) itself. As analyzed at length in the beginning of Freud's essay, *heimlich* (homely) folds into its opposite, *unheimlich* (unhomely). Significantly, the former term appears in *Camera Lucida* in relation to Barthes's description of an 1854 photograph by Charles Clifford: "such then would be the essence of the landscape (chosen by desire): *heimlich*, awaking in me the Mother (not in the least disturbing)."[6] In evoking the homeliness of the landscape, however, Barthes recognizes that the *heimlich* is always imprinted over its opposite, for this passage is prefaced with Freud's description of the uncanny maternal body: "There is no other place of which I can say with so much certainty that one has already been there."[7] The quote, lifted straight from Freud's essay, shifts Clifford's homely landscape into the unhome—*unheimlich* in its sense of *heimlich*. But in addition to collapsing the *unheimlich* mother into the *heimlich* landscape, Freud's description of the uncanny maternal body that Barthes quotes—"I can say with so much certainty that one has already been there"—resonates conspicuously with Barthes's description of the photographic *noeme*: "in photography I can never deny that *the thing has been there*." Photography, in all of its hallucinatory detail—as the *has been there* of the *noeme*—manifests the *home* and *not home* of the mother. All of which circles back to Barthes's own mother, whose absent photograph represents, "something like an essence of the Photograph."[8]

A strikingly similar image of photography as simultaneously intimate and foreign appears in *The Guermantes Way* (1920),[9] the third volume of Marcel Proust's *In Search of Lost*

Time. A book well known to Barthes (and no doubt fresh in his mind following his lectures on it at the Collège de France in 1978 shortly before writing *Camera Lucida*), it seems safe to assume that he would have been struck by Proust's scattered allusions to photography. Indeed, Barthes references Proust throughout *Camera Lucida*, twice relating the narrator's grandmother to the Winter Garden Photograph of his own mother.[10] The ties between mother and grandmother are reinforced in one particular passage in *The Guermantes Way*. In it, the narrator walks into a drawing room and, seeing his grandmother absorbed in her reading, realizes that she is oblivious to his presence. Unobserved, he scrutinizes her appearance, seeing her for a fleeting second not through the distorting eyes of affection but in a cold objective light that reduces her to an image—a "ghostly image," as Proust puts it, that is simultaneously beloved, trapped in "the perpetual motion" of his "incessant love," and unfamiliar, "a crushed old woman whom I did not know."[11] As Proust states, this doubling of beloved and stranger takes place as though through the alienating lens of someone else's eyes—as though through the lens, in fact, of a photographer: "The only part of myself that was present . . . was the witness, the observer, in travelling coat and hat, the stranger to the house, the photographer who has called to take a photograph of places that will never be seen again."[12] This fixing of a living person into a ghostly image is for Proust the condition of photography: "What my eyes did, automatically, in the moment I caught sight of my grandmother, was to take a photograph."[13]

The photography, for Proust, places us at a remove from the living vortex of our affections and memories. As Barthes states referencing Proust, "The photograph does not call up the past (nothing Proustian in a photograph)."[14] Or again, "Not only is the photograph never, in essence, a memory . . . but it actually blocks memory, quickly becoming a counter-memory."[15] This view of photography is deeply sympathetic with Proust's own, right down to their shared sense of death. "With the photograph we enter into *flat death*,"[16] Barthes writes. Proust puts it this way:

But if, instead of our eyes, it should happen to be a purely material lens, a photographic plate, that has been watching things, then what we see . . . may prevent the intelligent devotion of our affection from rushing forward in time to hide from our eyes what they ought never linger upon, and outstripped by chance, they get there first, with the field to themselves, and start to function mechanically like photographic film, showing us, not the beloved figure who has ceased to exist, and whose death our affection has never wanted to reveal, but the new person it has clothed, hundreds of times each day, in a lovingly deceptive likeness.[17]

To view the world photographically, for Proust, is to posit a new kind of world—a world where we are estranged from our intimates and where we are confronted with a new sense of time: "suddenly, in our drawing room, which had now become part of a new world, the world of Time, inhabited by the strangers we describe as 'aging well,' for the first time, and for a mere second, since she vanished almost immediately, I saw her sitting there on the sofa, beneath the lamp, red-faced, heavy, and vulgar, ill, her mind in a daze, the slightly crazed eyes wandering over a book, a crushed woman I did not know."[18] This world of time—the world viewed photographically as "pure representation"—is also central to Barthes's view of photography. "I know that there exists another *punctum*," Barthes writes. "This new *punctum*, which is no longer of form but of intensity, is Time, the lacerating emphasis of the *noeme* ('*that has been*'), its pure representation."[19]

If the Winter Garden Photograph of Barthes's mother as a child guides Barthes through the labyrinth of "all the world's photographs," the Ariadnian thread that he both follows and seeks is the *punctum*. Quoting Nietzsche's prophecy that "a labyrinthine man never seeks the truth, but only his Ariadne,"[20] this quest through the labyrinth ends, in the conclusion of *Camera Lucida*, with madness: "Nietzsche . . . threw himself in tears on the neck of a beaten horse: gone mad for pity's sake."[21] The image of labyrinthine man who is lost to madness in a world stripped of truth is found in the same paragraph where Barthes equates the uncanny paradigm of falling in love with an automaton to falling in love with certain photographs ("Was I not, in fact, in love with the Fellini automaton? Is one not in love with certain photographs?"). But crucially, this knotting of photography with uncanny madness is also tied to the wounding of the *punctum*—a wounding that Barthes has carefully followed throughout the maze of his book:

In the love stirred by Photography (by certain photographs), another music is heard, its name oddly old-fashioned: pity. I collected in a last thought the images which had "pricked" me (since this is the action of the punctum*), like that of the black woman with the gold necklace and the strapped pumps. In each of them, inescapably, I passed into the unreality of the thing represented, I entered crazily into the spectacle, into the image, taking into my arms what is dead, what is going to die, as Nietzsche did when, as Podach tells us, on January 3, 1889, he threw himself in tears on the neck of a beaten horse: gone mad for pity's sake.*[22]

The *punctum* gathers "what is dead, what is going to die"—oddly suspended, like a ghost, between life and death. "This *punctum*," Barthes writes earlier, ". . . *that* is dead and *that* is going to die. These two little girls . . . how alive they are! They have their whole lives before them; but they are also dead (today), they are then *already* dead (yesterday)."[23] Like the uncanny figure of the automaton, the *punctum* moves the inanimate photograph into animation, fusing death with life, and life with death. The *punctum* preserves the living person whose death is captured in the future anterior, the will-have-been of the photograph. If photographs entomb the living, then, by the reverse token, they also bring the dead to life. Describing photographs of certain dead bodies, Barthes writes, "if the photograph then becomes horrible, it is because it certifies, so to speak, that the corpse is alive, as *corpse:* it is the living image of a dead thing."[24]

Many if not most photographs are *not* this uncanny mix of living and dead for Barthes. Quite the contrary, they are lifeless objects, pure and simple, that do not move him. On the whole, photographs and the people who populate them are dead to Barthes. And yet, "In this glum desert, suddenly a specific photograph reaches me; it animates me, and I animate it. So that is how I must name the attraction which makes it exist: an *animation.*"[25] In this lifeless landscape of photographs—"in this glum desert"—a kind of mirage appears, hovering like a madness or hallucination between there and not there, animate and inanimate. And the term that Barthes gives to the special, ineffable quality that separates inanimate photographs from those that come to life is the *punctum*: "Many photographs are, alas, inert under my gaze. . . . they have no *punctum* in them."[26] The *punctum* animates the inanimate. It is what captures our desire and propels our love, like Nathaniel's gaze onto Olympia.[27]

If most photographs are dead to Barthes, the opposite is true of cinema. Too alive, film functions as too much a continuation of life: "Yet the cinema has a power which at first glance the photograph does not have . . . the man or woman who emerges from it continues living: a 'blind field' constantly doubles our partial vision."[28] The "blind field" names the capacity of cinema to animate, to extend the life of its actors. It is this blind field—this spark of life, this *punctum*—that most photographs lack:

Now, confronting millions of photographs, including those that have a good studium, *I sense no blind field: everything which happens within the frame dies absolutely once this frame is passed beyond. When we define the Photograph as a motionless image, this does not mean only that the figures it represents do not move; it means that they do not* emerge, *do not* leave: *they are anesthetized and fastened down, like butterflies.*[29]

Most photographs, as Barthes states, have no blind field: they are dead "absolutely." "Yet once there is a *punctum*," Barthes continues, "a blind field is created (is divined)."[30] The *punctum* breathes life into the dead photograph creating an uncanny object, spectral in its absence/presence, life/death. Such is the case, for Barthes, of an 1863 photograph of Queen Victoria: "The *punctum* fantastically 'brings out' the Victorian nature (what else can one call it?) of the photograph; it endows this photograph with a blind field."[31] Not fully animate, as with cinema, the *punctum* stirs the immobile photograph, bringing it halfway back from the dead.

For Barthes, photography "touches art" not through cinema but through theater: "if Photography seems to me closer to the Theater," Barthes writes, "it is by way of a single intermediary (and perhaps I am the only one who sees it): by way of Death."[32] Film is too alive, too animate, but in the oddly false live action of theater Barthes sees an uncanny mix of life and death: "The first actors separated themselves from the community by playing the role of the Dead: to make oneself up was to designate oneself as a body simultaneously living and dead."[33] Crossing life with death, theater, for Barthes, overlaps photography.

In addition to photographs of others, Barthes sees uncanny doubling in his own photographic image. Posing in front of the camera, Bathes feels himself divided—split between the "(mobile) image" of the photograph and the "(profound) 'self'" that is "the precious essence of my individuality."[34] "The photograph," Barthes writes, "is the advent of myself as other: a cunning dissociation of consciousness from identity."[35] This doubling of the self transforms Barthes into a kind of ghost: "I am neither subject nor object, but a subject who feels he is becoming object: I then experience a micro-version of my own death (of parenthesis): I am truly becoming a specter."[36] Barthes watches as photography ungrounds him, turning him into a kind of automaton—thing and person, subject and object. In his photograph, Barthes sees the ghost of his dead body. And indeed, ghosts and dead bodies represent, for Freud, "the acme of the uncanny"—an uncanniness that has "anything to do with death, dead bodies, revenants, spirits, and ghosts."[37]

What, then, are we to make of Barthes's privileging of the uncanny in photography? And how is this emphasis on the photographic uncanny situated in relation to the state of photography circa 1980, when *La chambre claire* was first published? Answers to these questions must begin, I believe, with the recognition that Barthes's view of photography is at root conservative. Quite literally so for *Camera Lucida* is motivated by an effort to conserve a particular kind of photographic experience along with a particular kind of photograph that is capable of carrying that experience. And this experience—described throughout *Camera Lucida* in terms of the uncanny—was, as Barthes correctly surmised, under threat in 1980. This threat is registered, for example, when he writes, "And no doubt, the astonishment of *'that-has-been'* will disappear. It has already disappeared: I am, I don't know why, one of its last witnesses . . . and this book is its archaic trace."[38] As Michael Fried describes this passage, Barthes voices an almost Heideggerean sense of loss as "modern society has made of the photograph precisely a means of 'flattening' death."[39] This sense of a flat, simply inanimate photographic death (flat because it has no *punctum*, no pulse of desire) is evident for Barthes in disaster or shock photographs. What these photographs lack, Barthes claims, is "a look, a subject's look"—a look that is increasingly lost to contemporary photography. Again, Barthes registers a sense of loss in his belief that the look has become imperiled: "For the photograph has this power—which it is increasingly losing, the frontal pose being most often considered archaic nowadays—of *looking me straight in the eye.*"[40] In the conclusion of the book (in section forty-eight, directly following the penultimate section containing the passage on Fellini's *Casanova*), Barthes most strongly voices his opposition to contemporary photography. "Society is concerned to tame the photograph," Barthes writes, "to temper the madness which keeps threatening to explode in the face of whoever looks at it."[41]

Barthes ends *Camera Lucida* by extending the sense of loss and mourning that pervades the book to the *punctum* itself. By taming the photograph—by "tempering its madness"— contemporary photography circa 1980 exorcizes the spectral force of the *punctum*, driving it out into the flat death of mere interest. Photography in our current era becomes, like film, "the opposite of an hallucination, it is simply an illusion." Worse still, contemporary photography is agent and symptom, cause and effect, of a fundamental reversal—a reversal in which photography's uncanny capacity to animate the dead is flipped, tragically, into photography's capacity to deaden the living. Rather than photography moving the dead into the world of the living, the opposite occurs: the living move into an ever-mortified world of photography:

Looking at the customers in a café, someone remarked to me (rightly): "Look at how gloomy they are! Nowadays the images are livelier than the people." One of the marks of our world is perhaps this reversal: we live according to a generalized imaginary. Consider the United States, where everything is transformed into images: only images exist and are produced and are consumed. . . . Such a reversal necessarily raises the ethical question: not that the image is immoral, irreligious, or diabolic . . . but because, when generalized, it completely derealizes the human world of conflicts and desires, under cover of illustrating it.[42]

Photography, Barthes states on the second page of *Camera Lucida,* is distinct in its capacity to touch the real, to capture "what Lacan calls the tuché, the Occasion, the Encounter, the Real."[43] On the second-from-last page, this is reversed: the "archaic trace" of photography's ability to capture "the human world of conflicts and desires" has been lost, as the real is derealized into a world that is supersaturated with vacant images. No longer cut by photographs barbed with the immediacy of desire, contemporary photography, for Barthes, instead functions to mediate and distance desire. This photographic derealization of the world is ethical for Barthes, not because it is "immoral, irreligious, or diabolic" but because it deindividuates and dehumanizes. For Barthes ethics resides in the face of the other—in the look that exposes individuality ("For the photograph has this power—which it is increasingly losing, the frontal pose being most often considered archaic nowadays—of looking me straight in the eye"). The straight-in-the-eye look catches us in its individuality, pierces us in its unmediated sense of person, captures our love and desire. This punctum is lost or is being lost. In its place, Barthes sees its opposite: he sees what drains photography of its uncanny not-quite life, as the sharp edges of animate photography are blunted by a contemporary world of image-mediated desire.

In its concern "to tame the photograph," society, Barthes claims, "has two means at its disposal": the first is art, and the second is flat, systematic, and banal generalization. Generalization kills what Barthes calls the "air" of the person photographed. In excess of resemblance and illusion, the air "is not schematic, intellectual datum, the way a silhouette is."[44] On the contrary, the air is what overflows photographic verisimilitude: "No, the air is that exorbitant thing which induces from body to soul—animula, little individual soul, good in one person, bad in other."[45] Photographs devoid of air have no soul for Barthes—no sense of person, no grace: "The air . . . is a kind of intractable supplement of identity, what is given in an act of grace."[46]

Generalizing the irreducible air of the person is closely related to art, the other threat that Barthes identifies in contemporary photography. Art threatens the hallucinatory madness of the photograph because "no art is mad." Indeed, for Barthes, art is present in photography when "there is no longer any madness in it, when its noeme is forgotten and consequently its essence no longer acts on me."[47] Art voids photography of its essential madness, emptying the photographic uncanny into the simply familiar or strange but never both. But how are we to understand Barthes's disparagement of "art" given that so many of the examples he discusses, reproduces, and clearly admires are works by "art photographers"—André Kertész, Robert Mapplethorpe, Alfred Stieglitz, William Klein, Nadar, Richard Avedon, August Sander, Lewis H. Hine. Barthes also speaks with evident respect of the "great" photographer: "Polaroid? Fun, except when a great photographer is involved,"[48] and "one day an excellent photographer took my picture." For Barthes, excellence and greatness are clearly distinct from a more pedestrian or merely professional command of photography. But above all, excellence is distinct from art. So what makes for a great photograph? And what distinguishes photographic excellence from entering into the negative condition of art? Greatness, for Barthes, is in the details:

Hence the detail which interests me is not, or at least not strictly, intentional, and probably must not be so; it occurs in the field of the photographed thing like a supplement that is at once inevitable and graceful; it does not necessarily attest to the photographer's art; it says only that the photographer was there, or else, still more simply, that he could not not *photograph the partial object at the same time as the total object. . . . The photographer's "second sight" does not consist in "seeing" but in being there. And above all, imitating Orpheus, he must not turn back to look at what he is leading—what he is giving to me!*[49]

The detail Barthes describes here—the mark of photographic excellence—is the *punctum.*[50] As Barthes states, this detail cannot be intentional. As first described in *Camera Lucida,* the detail of the *punctum* is "a role of the dice. A photograph's *punctum* is that accident which pricks me."[51] As Fried has argued, the experience of the *punctum* lives or dies for Barthes according to the absence or presence of intentionality on the part of the photographer; if there is visible intention, there is no *punctum.* That the *punctum* can exist only in the absence of intention is consistent, Fried claims, with his distinction between "seeing" (understood positively as antitheatrical) and "being shown" (understood negatively as theatrical).[52] The possibility of the *punctum* is cancelled if bound to the photographer's intention—if we are *shown* what can only be seen. As Fried states: "The *punctum,* we might say, is *seen* by Barthes but not because it has been *shown* to him by the photographer, for whom it does not exist; as Barthes recognizes, 'it occurs [only] in the photographic field of the photographed thing,' which is to say that it is not a pure artifact of the photographic event."[53] The *punctum,* Fried writes, serves as, "a kind of ontological guarantee that it was not intended to be so *by the photographer.*"[54] To be shown the photographer's intention, in other words, is to be shown the photographer's art. And in these two words, art and intention, Barthes names the same thing—the demise of the *punctum.*

Barthes chose to bring *Camera Lucida* to a close in two particular ways—first, by equating his misplaced love for Fellini's automaton to his love for certain photographs (most notably the Winter Garden Photograph of his mother) to emphasize the uncanny nature of the *punctum,* and second, by arguing against contemporary photography. This decision speaks to the contested state of the photographic uncanny in the decades leading up to 1980. Indeed, Barthes's championing of the photographic uncanny and his polemic against contemporary photography appear to place *Camera Lucida* squarely on the side of the presence of the uncanny in postwar photography and against its avant-garde counterparts. This simple for-and-against, however, is not as simple as it might appear.

Although the photographic uncanny is present in photography in varying degrees from its inception, it erupts with particular force in the 1920s and 1930s *Neue Sachlichkeit* ("new objectivity") photographs of August Sander, a photographer who is discussed by Barthes early in *Camera Lucida.* Best known for his massive archival project, *Citizens of the Twentieth Century* (1910–1934), Sander attempted to photograph a comprehensive physiognomic typography of Weimar society. Yet as critics have argued, the systemic rationalism that grounds Sander's photographic archive unwittingly flips into its mirror opposite because it is ungrounded by the very irrationalism that it sought to expel.[55] The reason-based impetus of Sander's archival system is thus twinned, against its will, with its opposed double, the unreason of the uncanny. This is most evident in the double images that appear as uncanny faultlines in Sander's archive. Giving form to one of Freud's most famous examples of the *Unheimlich*, these images of uncanny doubling (most notably in photographs such as *Farm Girls*, *Usherettes*, and *Midgets*) are presented in the service of the rational and yet resonate uncannily with the viewer's own internal doubling (ego and superego, conscious and unconscious).

The internal tension within Sander's work—between the rational effort to conceive of a systematically determined archive and the irrational, uncanny fissures in this system—is intimately bound to another tension within Sander's project. For while Sander's project attempts to push the individual photographic portrait into the larger social system of Weimar society, it does so by supporting individual, physiognomic-based portraiture.[56]

The internal tensions within Sander's photographs become sites of contestation in the 1960s and 1970s, as his reception is divided into two primary and opposing branches. Representing the first branch of this divide are photographers such as Diane Arbus and Richard Avedon who align themselves or are aligned by critics with the uncanny effects of Sander's portraiture.[57] Sander's double portrait *Farm Girls,* for example, is frequently cited as the historical antecedent to Diane Arbus's famous photograph of uncannily identical twins. On the opposite and opposing branch are avant-grade photographers such as Bernd and Hilla Becher, Andy Warhol, Edward Ruscha, and Thomas Struth who flatten the discrete photograph through the use of serial structures, systems, or archives. These photographers drain the individualized photograph of physiognomic or subjective content, shifting the single image into a systematic and generalized collection of typographies. As Benjamin Buchloh states of Bernd and Hilla Becher, for instance, their photographs collect apparently authorless architectural forms (we have no idea who designed these water towers, gasometers, lime kilns, etc.) in such a way that this already anonymous image is gridded into a larger system of typological difference. This double gesture, Buchloh claims, asserts the general social system over the individual (and individualizing) photograph: "[the Bechers'] insistence on the anonymity of the architectural authors and on the absence of the producers from the sites of production has clearly allied itself as an artistic gesture with a concept of collective subjectivity rather than with one of Bourgeois individuality." Indeed, as Buchloh states, the deindividuation of the Bechers—both in subject and in format—is directly at odds with the opposing, uncanny branch of Sander's reception: "This principle of excluding the social subject, embodied in photographic figuration, was also precisely what had distinguished the Bechers' work most notably from the spectacular and grotesque distortions of subjectivity in New York school photography."[58] It is precisely this avant-garde effort to push individuality into a systematic concept of "collective subjectivity" that Barthes sees as part of a larger social tendency towards "generalization." As Barthes states in no uncertain terms:

The other means of taming photography is to generalize, to gregarize, banalize it until it is no longer confronted by any image in relation to which it can mark itself, assert its special character, its scandal, its madness. This is what is happening in our society. . . . when generalized, it completely de-realizes the human world of conflicts and desires, under cover of illustrating it . . . . [It is] as if the universal image were producing a world that is without difference (indifferent), from which can rise, here and there, only the cry of anarchisms, marginalisms, and individualisms: let us abolish the images, let us save immediate Desire (desire without mediation).[59]

So if Barthes appears to enter the fray of contemporary photographic polemics on the side of uncanny photography against the avant-garde, why are Arbus's photographs—those paradigmatic exemplars of uncanny photography—so conspicuously absent from *Camera Lucida*? The answer, I believe, returns to the question of art and intention. For although systemic reason and uncanny unreason could cohabit, however discordantly, in Sander's early twentieth-century archive, by the 1960s and 1970s it was evident that these two tendencies stood in stark and irreconcilable opposition. For this reason, I believe that Arbus, faced with the systematic leveling of subjectivity by the avant-garde, self-consciously employed a hyperbolic use of the uncanny as a means to combat the flattening of subjectivity within photography. Responding to the hollowing of photographic interiority described by Barthes—a hollowing actively promoted by the avant-garde—Arbus programmatically ratcheted-up uncanny effects in her photographs in defense of an increasingly imperiled sense of what Barthes calls the "soul," "grace," or "air" of the subject.

Arbus's best defense against the flattening of photographic portraiture thus appears as a strong offense, but this double defense/assertion comes at some cost. In certain key respects, Arbus's portraiture cuts its historical losses. First, it recognizes that an adamantly subjective form of late-modern portraiture must abandon a discredited, more-or-less physiognomically based attempt to reveal the subjective ground of the photographic subject. In its stead, Arbus attempts to activate not the subjective core of the person who was photographed but the subjectivity of the person who is viewing the photograph. The vehicle for this shift in accent, from subject to viewer, is uncanny affect. Unable to sustain portraiture's historical claim to capture interior essence, Arbus attempts to salvage subjective effect through an altogether different mode of interiority—through uncanny resonance within the viewer. Second, as famously indicted by Susan Sontag in *On Photography* (1977, listed in the bibliography of *La chambre claire*), to achieve this subjective reversal—from those photographed to those viewing photographs— Arbus's camera is notoriously unkind to its subjects. And third, Arbus fully intends to show the uncanny. As Sontag states, Arbus aspires to twist normality into abnormality—to make the familiar strange as a conscious act of will: "[Arbus's] camera has the power to catch so-called normal people in such a way as to make them look abnormal. The photographer chooses oddity, chases it, frames it, develops it, titles it."[60] This intention to capture the uncanny—to choose, chase, frame, develop, and title it—is, from Barthes's point of view, to lapse into the negative condition of "art." For in *showing* us the uncanny with "insistent sameness" (as Sontag puts it)—rather than simply allowing us to *see* it—Arbus separates the uncanny from the *punctum*. There is thus a fundamental difference between Arbus's vision of the photographic uncanny and Barthes's. Arbus attempts to pinpoint the uncomfortable strangeness in which we all reside, to draw it out of the everyday, to show it again and again with exacting deliberation. This is diametrically opposed to Barthes's view of the uncanny, in which the dead photograph has the capacity to take on life through the accidental animation of the *punctum*—a blind field that must remain blind, always, to the photographer.

The absence of Arbus from *Camera Lucida* is all the more conspicuous in that several of the photographs reproduced or discussed by Barthes are so evidently Arbus-like, most notably Lewis H. Hine's *Idiot Children in an Institution, New Jersey, 1924* and, pages earlier, William Klein's *Little Italy, New York, 1954*. As Sontag states, Hine's photograph "could be a late Arbus (except that the pair of mongoloid children posing on the lawn are photographed in profile rather than frontally)."[61] The profile noted by Sontag is important as it marks the essentially documentary nature of Hine's photographic practice. Much like Sander's images, the uncanny nature of Hine's photograph exists within a larger project of documenting American life in the 1920s. In a crucial way, Hine's aim is not to track down and foreground the *unheimlich* as it is with Arbus. Even still, Barthes distances his notion of the photographic uncanny as belonging to the *punctum* from the strangeness of this photograph in two ways—first, by emphasizing that its "monstrous" aspect (its uncanniness) belongs to the *studium*—to interest, to facts, to the documentary nature of Hine's practice; and second, by insisting that he sees only "the off-center details":

I too, in the photograph of two retarded children at an institution in New Jersey (taken in 1924 by Lewis H. Hine), hardly see the monstrous and pathetic profiles (which belong to the studium*); what I see . . . is the off-center detail, the little boy's huge Danton collar, the girl's bandaged finger.*

. . . I dismiss all knowledge, all culture. I refuse to inherit anything from another eye other than my own.[62]

In his refusal "to inherit anything from another eye other than my own," Barthes insists that uncanny effect—or at least his version of it—is carried in the subtlety of details that are blind to intention. The elements of the photography that lend it a superficial resemblance to Arbus are therefore precisely *not* where the uncanny resides for Barthes. Likewise, in Klein's *Little Italy* photograph (a photograph reminiscent of Arbus's later *Boy Holding a Toy Hand-Grenade, Central Park, New York*), the incidental detail of the child's bad teeth—not the overtly uncanny effect of the toy gun pressed against the grinning child's head—captures Barthes's gaze. By the same token, Barthes is resolutely not interested in another example of the "monstrous"—the head in Klein's *Shinohiera, Fighter Painter*: "[it] has nothing to say to me because I can see so clearly that it is an artifice of the camera angle."[63] To use the example discussed by Fried, Barthes distains Bruce Gilden's uncanny coupling à la Arbus of a nun and a drag queen (taken in 1973, the year after Arbus's retrospective at the Museum of Modern Art) because the "deliberate (not to say, rhetorical) contrast produces no effect on me, except perhaps one of irritation."[64]

The concluding paragraph of *Camera Lucida* presents two alternatives for photography: "Such are the two ways of the photograph. It's up to me to choose: to submit its spectacle to a civilized code of perfect illusions or to confront in it the awakening of an intractable reality."[65] To civilize photography—to codify or systematize it, to reduce it to a record of the facts, to transform it into art—is, for Barthes, to cure its madness. This first, negative possibility for photography includes both avant-garde efforts to void photographic affect *and* forms of photography, epitomized by Arbus, that overtly demonstrate, in no uncertain terms, the photographic uncanny. This is what Barthes resists. His choice is the alternative— "to confront in it the awakening of an intractable reality," to confront the dormant details of the photograph that capture his desire. Barthes's choice is squarely conservative: it is to awaken the "soul," the "pity," the "intractable reality" from the dead material of the inanimate photograph. In so choosing, Barthes positions himself against two dominant strains of contemporary photography circa 1980: the desubjectivizing efforts of the avant-garde and the emotional extremism of Arbus and her cohorts. Looking at the childhood photograph of his now dead mother, Barthes mourns, grieving not only the loss of the person but the loss of a form of photography that was able to touch him.

Notes

Many thanks to Jennie King, Charles Palermo, Geoffrey Batchen, and Diarmuid Costello for their generous feedback.

1. Roland Barthes, *Camera Lucida: Reflections on Photography*, trans. Richard Howard (New York: Hill and Wang, 1981), 115. In the English translation of this passage from the original French, *La chambre claire: note sur la photographie* (Paris: Gallimard Seuil, 1980), 177, Richard Howard mistranslates the verb *tempérée* as "temporal" ("a temporal hallucination") rather than "tempered." I have used Howard's translation except in instances where I felt modification was necessary, in which case page references are given to both *Camera Lucida* (henceforth *CL*) and *La chambre claire* (henceforth *CC*).

2. Ibid., *CL*, 115–116.

3. Sigmund Freud, "The Uncanny" (1919), *Writings on Art and Literature* (Stanford: Stanford University Press, 1997), 203.

4. Barthes, *CL*, 113. The phrase is Julia Kristeva's.

5. Ibid., *CL*, 115; translation modified, *CC*, 177.

6. Ibid., *CL*, 40; translation modified, *CC*, 68.

7. Ibid., *CL*, 40.

8. Ibid., 73.

9. Marcel Proust, *The Guermantes Way* (1920), trans. Mark Treharne (New York: Viking Penguin, 2005).

10. In the first, Barthes writes of the Winter Garden Photograph: "For once, photography gave me a sentiment as certain as remembrance, just as Proust had experienced it one day when leaning over to take off his boots, there suddenly came to him his grandmother's true face, 'whose living reality I was experiencing for the first time, in an involuntary and complete memory.'" Barthes, *CL*, 70. And again, five pages later, Barthes describes his suffering at the loss of his mother: "I might say, like the Proustian Narrator at his grandmother's death: 'I did not insist only upon suffering, but upon respecting the originality of my suffering.'" Ibid., 75.

11. Proust, *The Guermantes Way*, 134–135.

12. Ibid., 134.

13. Ibid., 134.

14. Barthes, 82.

15. Ibid., 91.

16. Ibid., 92.

17. Proust, 135.

18. Ibid.

19. Barthes, *CL*, 96.

20. Ibid.

21. Ibid., 117.

22. Ibid., 116–117.

23. Ibid., 96.

24. Ibid., 78–79.

25. Ibid., 20.

26. Ibid., 27.

27. As Carol Armstrong writes, "the '*punctum*' that Barthes theorizes as being essential to the disquiet resident in photography, is nothing else but the photographic uncanny, buried in the homely, everyday, banal details of every-photograph." Carol Armstrong, "From Clementina to Käsebier: The Photographic Attainment of the 'Lady Amateur,'" *October* 91 (Winter 2000): 102.

28. Barthes, *CL,* 55–57.

29. Ibid.

30. Ibid.

31. Ibid.

32. Ibid., 31.

33. Ibid.

34. Ibid., 11–12.

35. Ibid., 12.

36. Ibid., 14.

37. Freud, "The Uncanny," 148. According to Freud, the fear associated with ghosts is fundamental to the effect of the uncanny. Unconscious repression, Freud claims, resonates with external forms that are felt to be uncanny so that consciousness feels itself to be haunted from within, doubled by an unknowable force that eludes reason and yet somehow shapes and determines us: "If psychoanalytic theory is right in asserting that every affect arising from an emotional impulse—of whatever kind— is converted into fear by being repressed, it follows that among those things that are felt to be frightening there must be one group in which it can be shown that the frightening element is something that has been repressed and now returns. This species of the frightening would then constitute the uncanny." Ibid., 147.

38. Barthes, *CL,* 93–94.

39. Michael Fried, "Barthes's *Punctum,*" *Critical Inquiry* 31 (Spring 2005): 561.

40. Barthes, *CL,* 111. Carol Armstrong emphasizes the uncanny nature of the frontal poses that pervade *Camera Lucida*: "the photograph, as the trace of the beloved face, looking at us, from beyond the grave, 'directly in the eyes,' which is enhanced by the frontal pose (*Camera Lucida* is full of faces and frontal poses) . . . speak of the uncanny." Armstrong, "From Clementina to Käsebier," 106–107.

41. Barthes, *CL,* 117.

42. Barthes, *CL,* 118; translation modified, *CC,* 181–182.

43. Barthes, *CL,* 4.

44. Ibid., 109.

45. Ibid.

46. Ibid.

47. Ibid, 117.

48. Ibid., 9. The reference here is probably to Daniel Boudinet's 1979 color Polaroid, reproduced as the book's frontispiece.

49. Barthes, *CL,* 47; translation modified, *CC,* 79–80.

50. As Barthes writes, "In this habitually unary space, occasionally (but alas all too rarely), a 'detail' attracts me. I feel that its mere presence changes my reading, that I am looking at a new photograph, marked in my eyes with a higher value. This 'detail' is the *punctum* (that which pierces me)." Barthes, *CL*, 42; translation modified, *CC*, 71.

51. Barthes, *CL*, 27.

52. Fried develops the terms "theatrical" and "antitheatrical" in a trilogy of books: Michael Fried, *Absorption and Theatricality: Painting and Beholder in the Age of Diderot* (Chicago: University of Chicago, 1980), *Courbet's Realism* (Chicago: University of Chicago, 1990), and *Manet's Modernism, or, The Face of Painting in the 1860s* (Chicago: University of Chicago, 1996).

53. Fried, "Barthes's *Punctum*," 546. I am much indebted to Fried's essay in what follows.

54. Ibid., 553.

55. See, for example, George Baker, "Photography between Narrativity and Stasis: August Sander, Degeneration, and the Decay of the Portrait," *October* 76 (Spring, 1996): 72–113.

56. As Benjamin Buchloh notes, Walter Benjamin championed Sander's structural archive only through turning a blind eye to the singular, physiognomy of his portraits: "Sander's serial approach to the traditionally unique, single-frame portrait must have engendered Benjamin's enthusiastic response to the first publication of a small selection of Sander's work [published as *Antlitz der Zeit*—"The Features of Time"—in 1929]. . . . Shifting the individual, depicted in the artificiality of the photographer's studio, to the representation of subjects constituted within social relations as much as by their professional identity, Sander's emphasis on a serial and contextual conception of identity was systematically embodied in the structuring of *Antlitz der Zeit* . . . as a larger project in forty-five portfolios, each containing twelve photographs." Benjamin Buchloh, "Residual Resemblance: Three Notes on the End of Portraiture," in Melissa E. Feldman, ed., *Face-Off: The Portrait in Recent Art* (Philadelphia: Institute of Contemporary Art, 1994), 57.

57. As Baker remarks on Sander's divided legacy: "As far as photographic history is concerned . . . [Sander's] legacy has been taken up in at least two directions. Inasmuch as photographers have realized the unconscious and social crisis posed by Sander's portraiture and typological practice, they manage to achieve a truly political function for photography—to an extent, this legacy has been realized by Bernd and Hilla Becher and Thomas Struth, among others. However, to the extent that photographers remain blind to the obsolete historical aspects of Sander's project, they end up repeating and replaying the historical crisis embodied there—not as tragedy, to quote from Marx, but as farce. This, if anything, has been the photographic contribution of such esteemed portrait photographers as Arbus (at her worst) and Richard Avedon (at his best)." Baker, "Photography between Narrativity and Stasis," 72.

58. Benjamin H. D Buchloh, "Portraits/Genre: Thomas Struth," in *Thomas Struth: Portraits* (Munich: Schirmer-Mosel, 2001), 159 n. 17. Buchloh also notes how the exclusion of the photographic portrait in the work of Ruscha is part of a larger critique of photographic portraiture among postwar photographers. Buchloh writes: "The *exclusion* of figures and faces has now become a strategy as significant as their traditional *inclusion* had been, and that it is precisely this decision to eliminate the representable subject altogether that will make a reading of the resulting iconography all the more complex. What is at stake in the exclusion of the figure seems to be precisely the fundamental and irresolvable dialectic: A subject is only to be recognized, in fact will be most visible, in the socially

mediated forms of object production and service exchange." Buchloh, "Residual Resemblance," 62. As Buchloh notes, the very *exclusion* of the individual photographic subject in favor of the infrastructural conditions that contribute to its formation (Becher's industrial conditions of production) foregrounds the concern with photographic portraiture in the work of Ruscha and the Bechers.

59. Barthes, *CL,* 118.

60. Susan Sontag, *On Photography* (New York: Anchor Books, 1977), 34.

61. Ibid., 46.

62. Barthes, *CL,* 51.

63. Ibid., 47.

64. Ibid. Barthes's irritation in the face of contrived contrast supports Fried's view of him as a "Diderotian" critic. Thus, in Denis Diderot's *Notes on Painting To Serve as an Appendix to the Salon of 1765* [1765], we find a condemnation of forced contrast similar to that of Barthes's: "Contrast that's poorly understood is one of the most deadly causes of mannerism. Genuine contrast derives from an action's essence, or from a diversity of agents or interests. . . . No contrast should be sought out other than what's needed to individuate them; so much is genuine, any more would be shabby and false." Denis Diderot, *Notes on Painting To Serve as an Appendix to the Salon of 1765,* in *Diderot on Art I,* trans. John Goodman (New Haven: Yale University Press, 1995), 195.

65. Barthes, *CL,* 119; translation modified, *CC,* 183–184.

BLACK AND BLUE

THE SHADOWS OF *CAMERA LUCIDA*

CAROL MAVOR

Le punctum *d'une photo, c'est ce hazard qui, en elle, me point (mis aussi me meutrit . . .).*
[A photograph's punctum *is that accident which pricks me (but also bruises me . . .).]*
—Roland Barthes, *La chambre claire [Camera Lucida]*[1]

The quality we call beauty, however, must always grow from the realities of life, and our ancestors forced to live in dark rooms, presently came to discover beauty in shadows, ultimately to guide shadows towards beauty's end.
—Jun'ichiro Tanizaki, *In Praise of Shadows*[2]

AT THE BEGINNING

For a long time, I dwelt on the *studium* of Barthes's reading of the Van der Zee portrait—his seemingly obvious, erroneous readings of race. As he writes about the Van der Zee image:

Voici une famille noire américaine, photographiée en 1926 par James Van de Zee. Le studium est clair: je m'intéresse avec sympathie, en bon sujet culturel, à ce que dit la photo, car elle parle (c'est une «bonne» photo): elle dit la respectabilité, le familialisme, le conformisme, l'endimanchement, un effort de promotion sociale pour se parer des attributs du Blanc (effort touchant, tant il est naïf). Le spectacle m'intéresse, mais il ne me « point » pas. Ce qui me point. Chose curieuse à dire, c'est la large ceinture de la soeur (ou de la fille)—ô négresse nourricière—ses bras croises derrière les dos, à la façon d'une écolière, et surtout ses souliers à brides . . . Ce punctum-là remue en moi une grande bienveillance, presque un attendrisssement. (74)

[Here is a family of American blacks, photographed in 1926 by James Van der Zee. The studium *is clear: I am sympathetically interested, as a docile cultural subject, in what the photograph has to say, for it speaks (it is a "good" photograph): it utters respectability, family life, conformism, Sunday best, an effort of social advancement in order to assume the White Man's attributes (an effort touching by reason of its naïveté). The spectacle interests me but does not prick me. What does, strange to say, is the belt worn low by the sister (or daughter)—the "solacing Mammy"— whose arms are crossed behind her back like a schoolgirl, and above all her strapped pumps. . . . This particular* punctum *arouses great sympathy in me, almost a kind of tenderness. (43)]*

It was not hard to "out" Barthes's racist tendencies when it came to his reading of the Van der Zee picture with the talk of "Sunday best," "conformism," and other such "White Man's attributes," "touching by reason of its naïveté."[3] (If it is ironical, it is not ironical enough.) My mouth always falls open when I confront this passage by Barthes, not only in French but particularly in the English translation. I especially cannot get past that "solacing Mammy."[4] Richard Howard has translated *ô négresse nourricière* as "the 'solacing Mammy,'" with the addition of quotes around his all-out bang of "Mammy," suggesting his own bafflement of how to name the darkness of race as inflected by *ô négresse nourricière.* I have no answer on how to accurately translate this French phrase for an English-speaking audience. The quotation marks and the qualifying adjective of "solacing" hardly soften the blow. But perhaps that was the intention of Barthes's most brilliant translator and cherished friend. (There is an essay in that translation alone.[5]) And because Betye Saar's own "Mammy," her 1972 *Liberation of Aunt Jemima* (figure 12.1), is in my "image repertoire" (if not Barthes's) and both nourishes me with my own childhood memories of pancakes with Aunt Jemima's syrup and also carries a gun, I am taken aback. I am fed and shot. I stumble here on Barthes, on Van der Zee, on the maternal, on race, on myself. I am finding something that verges on my own *punctum,* which pricks me—if on a mixed-up and delayed route through Barthes, through Van der Zee, through Saar, through my own mother pouring syrup onto my Saturday morning pancakes.

Reading this passage of Barthes's and looking at the Van der Zee photograph, I feel bruised. The *punctum* can "accommodate a certain latency (but never any scrutiny)" (53), claims Barthes. Nevertheless, he does scrutinize it, and so will I, as it accommodates a "certain latency" of this essay.[6]

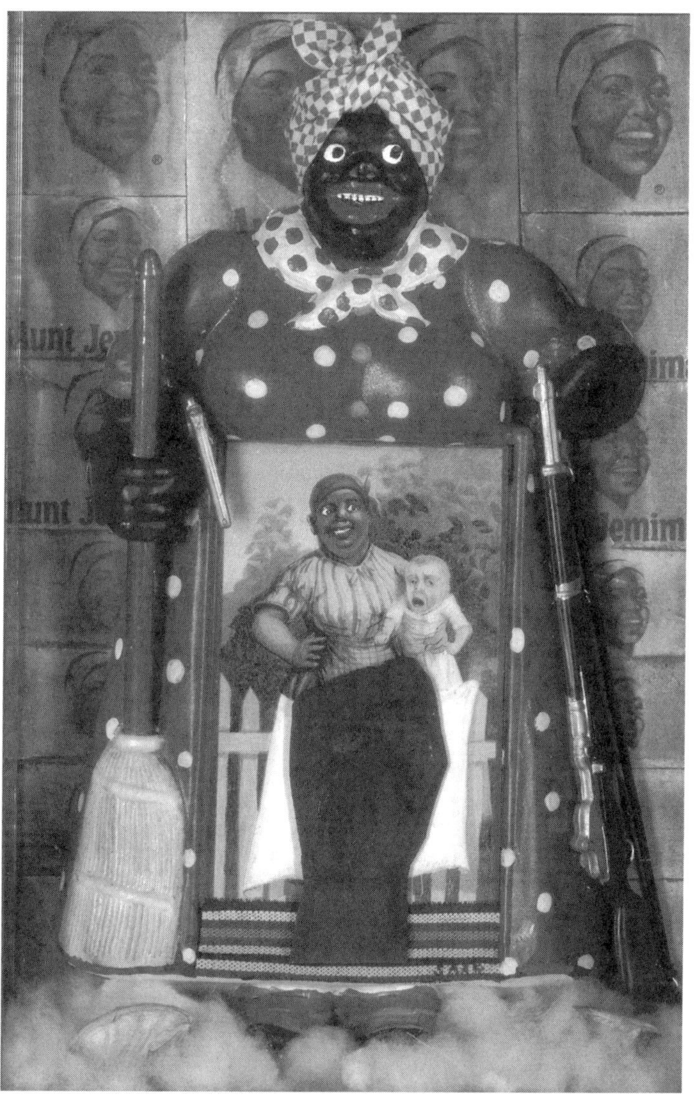

Figure 12.1   *Betye Saar,* The Liberation of Aunt Jemima, *1972. University of California Berkeley Art Museum.*

Camera Lucida is Barthes's book (part novel, part philosophy) on desire (*punctum*) and "the art of fixing a shadow" (photography). When race meets the photograph, desire (*punctum*) resides in the shadows: "The *punctum* shows no preference for morality or good taste" (43). Even Barthes knows that.

I have never *not* noticed the four photographs of blacks in *Camera Lucida*—three of African Americans (two portraits by Richard Avedon and a family photograph by Van der Zee) and one by Nadar of the African men who bookend the Italian-turned-French Savorgnan de Brazza, the so-called "peaceful conquerer" who opened up entry to France along the right bank of the Congo. How could I not notice? Although Barthes notes the matter-of-factness of the photograph as equivalent to "the child pointing his finger at something and saying 'that, there it is, lo!' but says nothing else" (5), Frantz Fanon starts "The Fact of Blackness" with "'Dirty nigger!' or simply 'Look, a Negro!'"[7] The fact of blackness is as stubborn as the photograph's link to the referent.

Blackness has shadowed my own hunger for *Camera Lucida*. It has touched me, even bruised me, but it has not, until now, touched my writing.

Elsewhere, I have written about how Barthes's story of childish wonder is fed by a deep desire to find his mother (his beloved Henriette) in boxes of old photographs, as if he were a child lost in a crowd looking for his mother,[8] and how, as a result of her death, Barthes's hunger is nourished by the texture of what might hold her—the photograph. Barthes's Maman fed his writing, just as Maman fed his beloved Proust. This *maman* sustenance is the stuff of both *Camera Lucida* and also *A Lover's Discourse* (where the ultimate lover-couple is a reflection of D. W. Winnicott's notion of the mother and child as "the nursing couple") and even in *Empire of Signs* (where much of the touch of Japan is maternalized). It is along these *maman* lines that this standing woman in the 1926 Van der Zee photograph (whom Barthes hails as "*ô négresse nourricière*") finds herself bumping up against the famed 1898 Winter Garden Photograph (the image of Barthes's mother Henriette at age five, a picture we hear much about but never see). Both the Winter Garden Photograph and the Van der Zee *Family Portrait* are the most significant keepers and feeders of *punctum* in the book. Both mother and blackness nourish *Camera Lucida*.

What is the shutter cord, the umbilicus, the ribbon of gold that links the Winter Garden Photograph together with Van der Zee's *Family Portrait*? How does this "queer" couple "shimmer" in a kind of Derridean nondialectical middle? *Shimmer* is one of Barthes's terms, under his rubric of the neutral (*le neutre*), that sets into play those oppositions, which subtly and boldly enlighten dominant cultural ideologies.[9] In Barthes's words: "The Neutral is the shimmer: that whose aspect, perhaps whose meaning, is subtly modified according to the angle of the subject's gaze."[10]

Barthes's novel(esque) *Camera Lucida* is a story of a desire for the maternal that is nurtured by photography, whose very texture tells the story of the nourishment of race. (Carrie Mae Weems has both swallowed it up and chewed it into a thousand little pieces in her 1988 photograph entitled *Chocolate Colored Man* (figure 12.2) from her series *Colored People.*)[11] The skin of the photograph hails what Fanon has termed a "racial epidermal schema."[12] If (as Balzac metaphorically proposed) a thin layer of skin is taken with each photograph, then what is the racial epidermal of the photograph's ghostlike membrane?

Photography, at least at its conception and for many years after, is a story of dark and light. In the early days, photography was called "the black art": the collodion would stain your fingers with evidence of what you had been up to (perhaps a key to Charles Dodgson's obsession with white gloves). Even after photography grew out of its sepia days of "the black art" and the slickness of black and white, photography would become "colored." Photography (light writing) has always been struck by racial adjectives and metaphors. "Black art" was "colored" long before the first color photograph of a tartan ribbon was presented by James Clerk Maxwell in 1861. Again, I am touched by Weems's *Colored People,* from *Chocolate Covered Man,* to *High Yella Girl,* and for the purposes of this essay, I especially feel the punch of *Blue Black Boy* (figure 12.3).

Both Richard Dyer and Kobena Mercer have remarked that the very texture of photography is raced. In the words of Dyer, "I suspect that there is some very interesting work to be done on the invention of photography and the development of lighting codes in relation to the white face, which results in the technicist ideology that one sometimes hears of it being 'more difficult' to photograph black people. Be that as it may, it is the case that the codes of glamour lighting in Hollywood were developed in relation to white women, to endow them with a glow of radiance that has correspondences with the transcendental rhetoric of popular Christianity."[13] Without a blush, Dyer gives a reasonably straight trajectory from the invention of photography to Hollywood film (with its degradation of the black body) to the radiant glow of white women, which is both sexualized and purified by Christian white "light."

Attending to "the prints of darkness,"[14] Kobena Mercer has located in Robert Mapplethorpe's photographs a fetishization of dark skin that speaks directly to the more generalized notion of the photograph as fetish (as so poignantly coined by Christian Metz).[15] In Mercer's words: "The glossy, shining, fetishized sheen of black skin thus serves and services the white man's desire to look and enjoy the fantasy of mastery precisely through the scopic intensity that the pictures solicit."[16] Or like "a blank page, the very blackness of

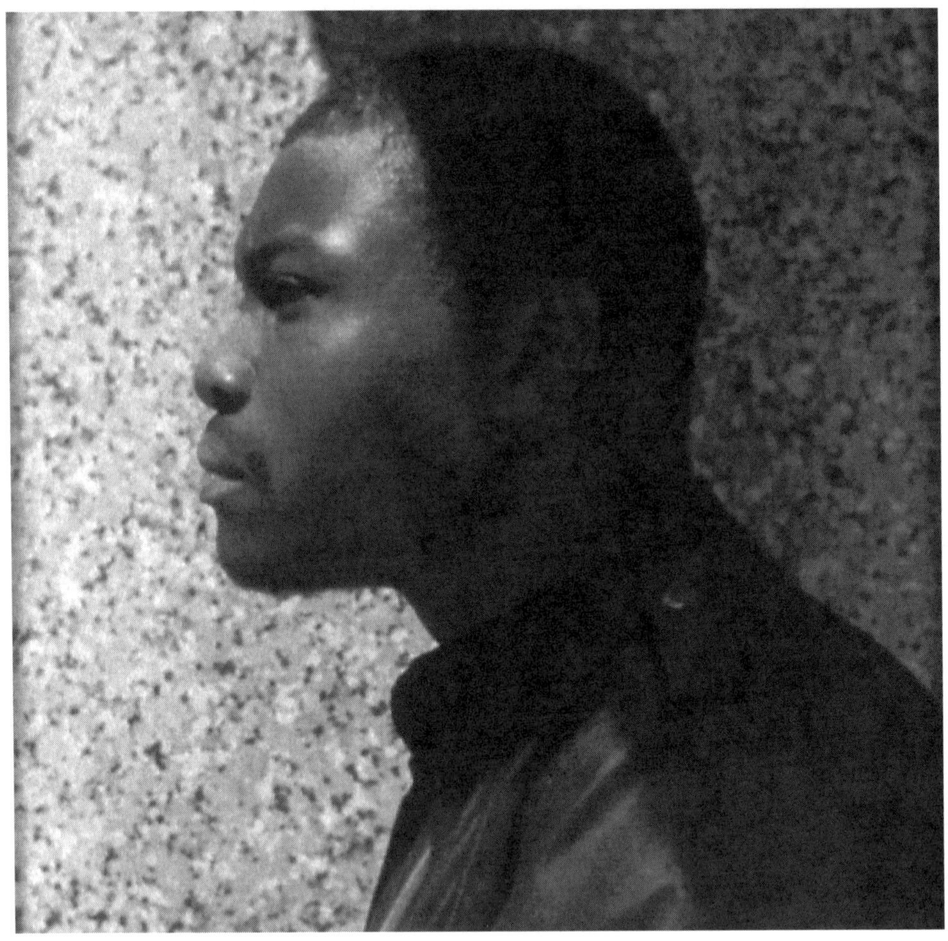

FIGURE 12.2 *Carrie Mae Weems,* Chocolate Colored Man *(from the series* Colored People*), 1988. Courtesy of Jack Shainman Gallery, New York.*

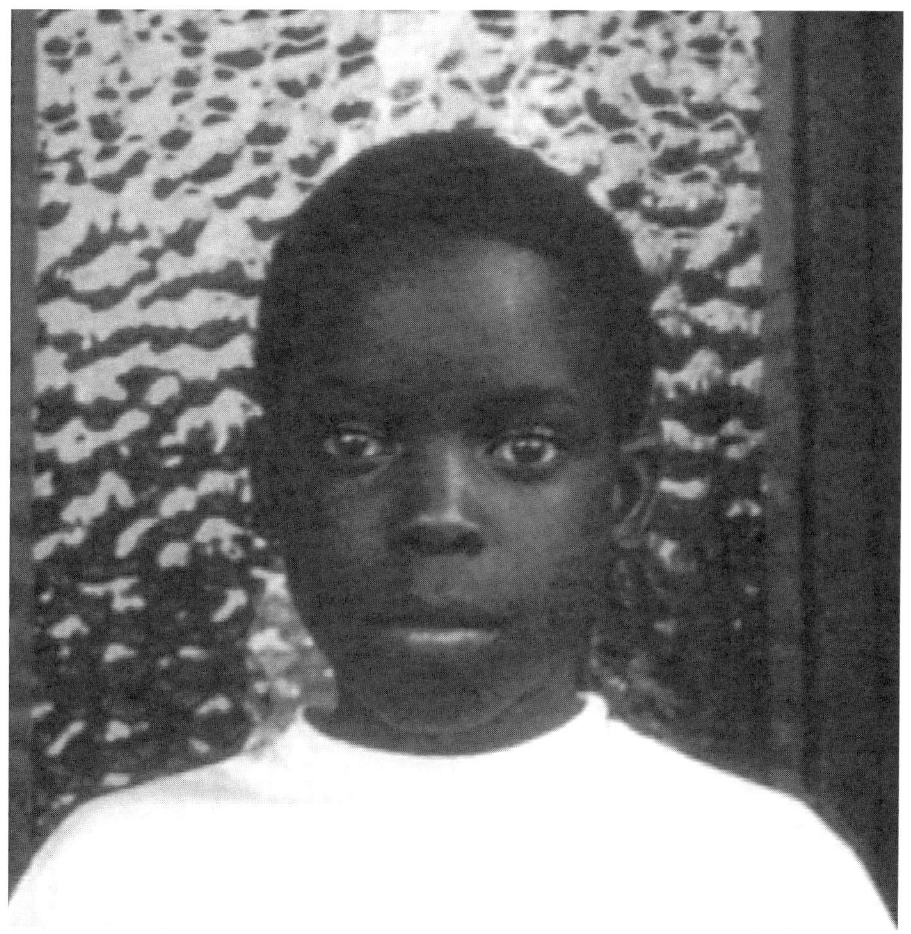

FIGURE 12.3 *Carrie Mae Weems,* Blue Black Boy *(from the series* Colored People*), 1988. Courtesy of Jack Shainman Gallery, New York.*

black skin acts as a tabula rasa for the inscription of a look that speaks primarily of a white European sexuality."[17] (More recently, Mercer has rethought Mapplethorpe's photographs as analogously supplying a powerful and pleasurable site of fetishization not just for white men but precisely for black gay men. Without naming it as so, Mercer's newfound negative and positive ambivalence enacts *le neutre* on Mapplethorpe's photographs, giving them a Barthesian "shimmer" by modifying them according to the angle of his own subjectivity—a desiring, black, gay man.[18])

Given the texture of photography as essentially raced, it is little wonder then, as Zeynep Çelik has noted in her essay on photography and the colonizing of Algeria, that "the history of photography is intertwined with the history of colonialism and both are connected with the project of modernity."[19] More germane to Çelik's own project is the fact that "photographs of Algeria relied upon and contributed to knowledge of the colony as well as its definition . . . thereby enabling a shorthand identification of France's most significant possession of *outre-mer*."[20]

In *outre-mer,* I hear *autre mère* because words are not just read; they are also heard, especially if one is schooled in Barthes's neither-nor school of "writing aloud."[21] And I hear more. I hear in the distance the approaching footsteps of Freud, with his mumblings on the female body as a "dark continent," her mystical Otherness afloat with "oceanic feelings."[22] I hear and feel the blue ocean as an overseas mother (*outre-mer*). I hear and feel the black continent as mother (*autre mère*). Blue-black.

Punctum at times may be just a little sting, but when it is coupled with some hard-hitting *studium* (like the fact of blackness, like the racing of photography, like color and women as nourishing), it is affectively bruising. It makes you black and blue.

Blue, so claims Brian Masumi, is the color of affect.[23]

In French, *bleu* can mean both blue and bruise.

For now, let it suffice to say that the Van der Zee *Family Portrait* is a black picture, and the Winter Garden Photograph is a blue picture.[24] I am developing them together, turning them into a composite print. The resulting photograph speaks of desire: it reveals a shimmer, a nondialectical convergence of "*ô négresse nourricière*" and Barthes's Winter Garden Photograph.

My story of Barthes's photograph is not black and white. It is a Barthesian *third language* of black and blue.

Like the camera lucida itself, the simple photographic, light-writing instrument consisting of drawing (imagination) and mirroring (exactitude) is a tool of dark and light contradictions.[25] Neither an instrument of just science nor an instrument of just art, the camera lucida, which always hails the camera obscura, is a neither-nor thing that Barthes names, possibly a little too adorably, as la *critique ni-n*i or *ninisme* (neither-norism). (In French, *neither-nor* is constructed as *ni-ni*.) As Barthes writes about himself (in the third-person) in *Roland Barthes by Roland Barthes*, the novel/nonfiction, biography/autobiography with "Barthes" as both object and subject: "For a certain time, he went into raptures over binarism: binarism became for him a kind of erotic object. This idea seemed to him inexhaustible, he could never exploit it enough. That one might say everything *with only one difference* produced a kind of joy in him, a continuous astonishment . . . intellectual things resemble erotic ones."[26]

Likewise in *Camera Lucida*, Barthes flutters his way through the photograph's pleasures of neither here nor gone, neither negative nor positive, neither dead nor alive, neither melancholic nor utopic, neither black nor white, neither the work of the amateur nor the artist, neither the real nor the image, and on and on. Nurtured by the photograph's vast oppositional consciousness, Barthes confesses: "Always the Photograph *astonishes* me, with an astonishment which endures and renews itself, inexhaustibly" (82).

In sum, *Camera Lucida* is a physical embracement and a philosophical study of Barthes's cherished concept of *le neutre,* the term itself shadowed by a range of *ni-ni* ninnies—from neither male nor female (*le neutre*) to the domain of international law (Switzerland as neutral) to the neutrality that journalists supposedly embody while telling both sides of the story. Indeed, as Rosalind Krauss has thoughtfully pointed out, Barthes's penultimate course, "Le Neutre,"[27] is evidence of a steady conjecture, an obedience to this "third language" (as played out by the neutral) from his early book *Writing Degree Zero* to his final teachings at the Collège de France. [28]

Always tearing himself apart Rumpelstilzchen style over the opposites that fascinated him as a structuralist and then as its very opposite as the poststructuralist that he was: as soon as readers hold him between their fingers, we find that he becomes shadow, memory, light-writing without weight. We touch the case of the daguerreotype, but the image slips and fades away. Words from Barthes's seminar on *le neutre* float from his mouth as if carried by ribbons of banderol in a painting by Van der Weyden, spoken but not written, slow, smooth, gentle and unforced, without (it seems) direction or purpose, they drift: "The present-day world is full of it (statements, manifestos, petitions, etc.), and it's why it is so wearisome: hard to float, to shift places. (However, to float, i.e., to live in a space without tying oneself to a place = the most relaxing position of the body: bath, boat.)" [29]

A shadow floats: "And yet there are situations when the appearance of a shadow testifies to the solidity of an object, for what casts a shadow must be real."[30]

Talbot took the camera obscura elsewhere,[31] inventing the negative-positive process, sending photography forever adrift under the spell of its binaries—not only the profundity of the play between negative and positive but also what Barthes calls the "stubbornness of the Referent" (6): "The Photograph belongs to that class of laminated objects whose two leaves cannot be separated without destroying them both: the windowpane and the landscape, and why not: Good and Evil, desire and its object: dualities we can conceive but not perceive" (6). The phrase "dualities that we can conceive but not perceive" creates such a shimmering, allowing the light of the past to touch us "like the delayed rays of a star" (81). Such a glimmer, a flash, draws the "artist-professor" (Thomas Clerc's name for Barthes[32]) to Talbot, who called his invention "the art of fixing a shadow."[33]

Barthes suffered and took pleasure in a game of two languages—the ascetic and the hedonist, the supposed real and its fantastic shadows. Barthes was the poet of the fragment, the professor of gluttonous desire *and* the famed structuralist, the professor of withholding anorexia: "In this plenitude you leave me nothing else than nothing to desire."[34] Always the man and his shadow *and* the boy without his shadow. His irrevocable choice of neither-nor criticism, the shadow as appealingly empty (Japan) and the shadow as full (the West), Barthes was as fickle as J. M. Barrie's Peter Pan. Like Peter, he envisaged leaving off his shadow all together (remaining sprite, eternal boy, child without death) or sticking it back on with soap (becoming earthly, real boy, man with death). For both Roland the real and Peter the fantasy, a little mother (Wendy/Henriette) sewed a shadow on her ancient boy.

Barthes's mother Henriette sewed a luminous shadow onto her son: he recognized it in the mourning-glory blue light after her death. It became a "twinkling"—what Barthes called *punctum* in *Camera Lucida*, *jouissance* in *The Pleasure of the Text*, and chocolate eggs in *Sollers écrivain*: "I seek what will touch me (as children we hunted in the countryside for chocolate eggs that had been hidden there). . . . I await the fragment that will concern me and establish meaning for me."[35] Finding what Joseph Cornell called the "zest." What Baudelaire called "*correspondances*." What Freud called "fetish" and Lacan *objet petit a*. What Barthes called in *Empire of Signs* "*satori*." What Barthes's beloved Proust called *mémoire involontaire*.

Punctum is always personal (not universal like the *studium* of a photograph, which speaks clearly to a docile subject with intended meanings that are unproblematically discerned). *Punctum* comes unexpectedly, just as pleasure (*jouissance*) does in *The Pleasure of the Text*: "The *studium* is ultimately always coded, the *punctum* is not" (51). As one of my students once wrote referring to Barthes's excessive use of parentheses: "For me, the text outside of the secretive punctuation is my *studium*, and what lay within, my *punctum*. While *Camera*

Lucida can only be described as a personal journey, it is within the parentheses that I find the author. They are the gaps in the text, where contradiction finds a home."[36] *Punctum* is intimate. It keeps you coming back, like it kept Barthes coming back to the Van der Zee photograph. At first, it was "the belt worn low" and then the "strapped pumps" that touched him, and finally, he landed on the "necklace" (like a child who plays beyond but keeps returning to the circle of the mother). *Punctum* works. We saw the trace of this play in his famed inaugural lecture, not long before he wrote *Camera Lucida*: "I should therefore like the speaking and the listening that will be interwoven here to resemble the comings and goings of a child playing beside his mother, leaving her, returning to bring her a pebble, a piece of string, and thereby tracing around a calm center a whole locus of play."[37]

But Barthes is not just playing around a calm center. And neither am I. He is, to hail Toni Morrison's brilliant book, "playing in the dark."[38] *Punctum* forecloses closure because desire itself can never be fully attained. *Punctum*, unlike *studium*, cannot be shellacked and immobilized. Whether intentional or not, Barthes's impolite parts demand a criticism that is not "too polite or too fearful to notice a disrupting darkness" before our "eyes"—no matter what color the eyes of the object or its reader.[39] When looking at the fateful page of Barthes's riddled with "White Man's attributes" and "*ô négresse nourricière*," I had acknowledged only what I had understood as "the politically correct"—what was easy, straightforward to read. You could say that I saw only the *studium* of Barthes's work on *punctum*.

Beyond *studium* (but not excluding it), *punctum* is difficult, conflicted and riddled with desire. *Punctum* is bodily: it is as if one were being punctured and stitched, umbilically resewn to the mother's body. Perhaps it is not surprising that the umbilical cord becomes a shimmering real/reel, a "carnal medium" twice in *Camera Lucida*:

The photograph is literally an emanation of the referent. From a real body, which was there, proceed radiations which ultimately touch me, who am here; the duration of the transmission is insignificant; the photograph of the missing being, as Sontag says, will touch me like the delayed rays of a star. A sort of umbilical cord links the body of the photographed thing to my gaze: light, though impalpable, is here a carnal medium, a skin I share. (80–81)[40]

and

Thus the air is the luminous shadow which accompanies the body; and if the photograph fails to show this air, then the body moves without a shadow, and once this shadow is severed, as in the myth of the Woman without a Shadow, there remains no more than a sterile body. It is by this tenuous umbilical cord that the photographer gives life; if he cannot, either by lack of talent or bad luck, supply the transparent soul its bright shadow, the subject dies forever. (110)[41]

In his course on "The Neutral," Barthes admits to a dark cloud of mourning for his mother, yet the course also sprouted twenty-three dandelion seeds of what Barthes called "twinklings"—figures that embody the neutral (sleep, for example) as well as in the antineutral (arrogance, for example): "The task of this language is to release the prisoners: to scatter the signified, the catechisms."[42] "My mother, she too sewed an umbilical shadow on me that has its own twinkling." And now it is time "to release the prisoners: to scatter the signifiers, the catechisms."

It all must be considered as if spoken by a character in a novel.
—*Roland Barthes by Roland Barthes*[43]

The Tarzan stories, the sagas of twelve-year-old explorers, the adventures of Mickey Mouse, and all those "comic books" serve actually as a release for collective aggression. The magazines are all put together by white men for little white men. This is the heart of the problem.
—Frantz Fanon, *Black Skin, White Masks* [44]

I grew up as an only child, with no shadow of a brother or sister to stick to or to stick to me. Although I had more than enough toys, mostly dolls, I grew up in a sterile house (white, white, white and clean, clean, clean) that was rather empty of books, song, and poetry. At first glance, the *mise-en-scène* of my childhood bedroom/my kiddish mind might seem to be akin to the stilled, cold, always-frozen-tundra mausoleum nursery of Rachel Whiteread's 1990 *Ghost,* with hardly a shadow to be found—no dust, no thought, no dirt, no dark, save for the smudge of ash in the fireless hearth.[45] But my childhood house—without traces of words and song, dirt and smudge—provided an adequate setting for shadow (play) that came to be about a *writerly,* not a *readerly,* childhood.[46]

I invisibly decorated my empty white house with the theater of my mind. Talking to my toys, I dreamed of childish exiles caused by divorce, abandonment, or a move to far away places that I knew nothing about. Joyfully imagining a glorious split between my parents (who are still to this day married), their permanent departure from home, our move to Bangkok, or my imprisonment in my bedroom and never being allowed to come out, or my self-imprisonment in the bathroom and choosing to never come out, I was practicing the *third language.*

My childhood fantasy life was fueled by what I already was—alone. As Charles Baudelaire writes in his "Philosophy of Toys": "All children talk to their toys: the toys become actors in the great drama of life, reduced by the camera obscura of their brains."[47] I made stories

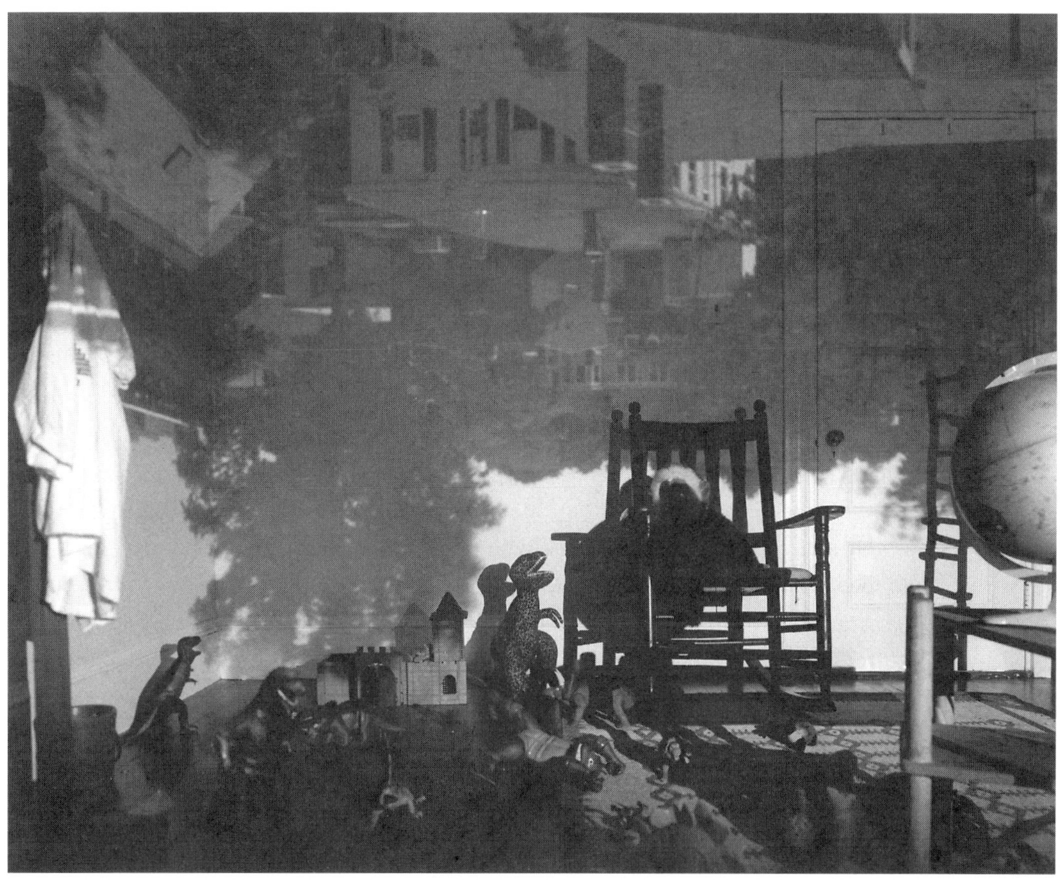

FIGURE 12.4 *Abelardo Morell,* Brookline View in Brady's Room, *1992.*
© *Abelardo Morell / Courtesy Bonni Benrubi Gallery, NYC.*

without books and documented them in the camera obscura of my girl brain. Abelardo Morell (figure 12.4) has brought to life a magical image of his son's bedroom turned into a camera obscura—an enchanting elevated view of the trees and rooftops of Brookline, Massachusetts, clapboard homes (all upside down, as if one were looking through a large-format camera). In *Brookline View in Brady's Room* (1992), the shadowy, transparent image of his wrong-way-up neighborhood, like a ghost-thing that flatly grazes the walls, moves up and over the plastic Tyrannosaurus rex, Triceratops, Brachiosaurus, Playmobil castle, wooden rocking chair, globe and abandoned teddy bear. I see it and think, as if I were a child again: "I want to live there." "I want to live there," writes Barthes below the the Alhambra, the famed Moorish palace (enclosed city and fortress) pictured by Charles Clifford.

When I played in my bedroom—like little Brady Morell in his Brookline bedroom and like children a hundred years before—I made my own fairy cottages and filled them with bugs, made up words to my own songs, wrote an awkward poem or two, and told tales that were more Disney than Grimm, more plastic than wooden. (Late twentieth-century toys were a disappointment to Barthes, who pined for the metal and wood toys of his own childhood: "The bourgeois status of toys can be recognized not only in their forms, which are functional, but also in their substances. Current toys are made of a graceless material, the producer of chemistry, not of nature. Many are now moulded from complicated mixtures; the plastic material of which they are made has an appearance at once gross and hygienic, it destroys all the pleasure, the sweetness, the humanity of touch."[48])

I remember that my mother would recite Robert Louis Stevenson's 1885 poem "My Shadow" to me. [49] She had memorized it in school (poems that she had learned by rote were some of the gifts that she retained from her depression-era Arkansas education). And Stevenson's poem was at the center of the only book that I remember from my childhood, a volume that, tattered and worn, still sticks with me—*The Gateway to Storyland*, first published in 1956, edited by Watty Piper. The poem, nearly my only literary memory, is where it all began—my *Mnemosyne*.

Like "a little shadow that goes in and out with me," with its hereness and goneness marking absence and presence, it plays the game of the photograph that marks the split nature of Barthes himself or of little Brady Morell looking at his own shadow on his bedroom wall (figure 12.5).

Like *Camera Lucida*, my beloved storybook had its own stories of desire spelled out through other "shadows" of blackness that I tucked into bed with me, into the corners of my sheets, into the wrinkles of my memory. (As Peter Stallybrass has taught me, in the technical jargon of sewing, wrinkles are called *memory*.[50]) As my father read, I made rabbit shadows on my white, white wall: my index and middle fingers were ears, my ring finger made a wiggly

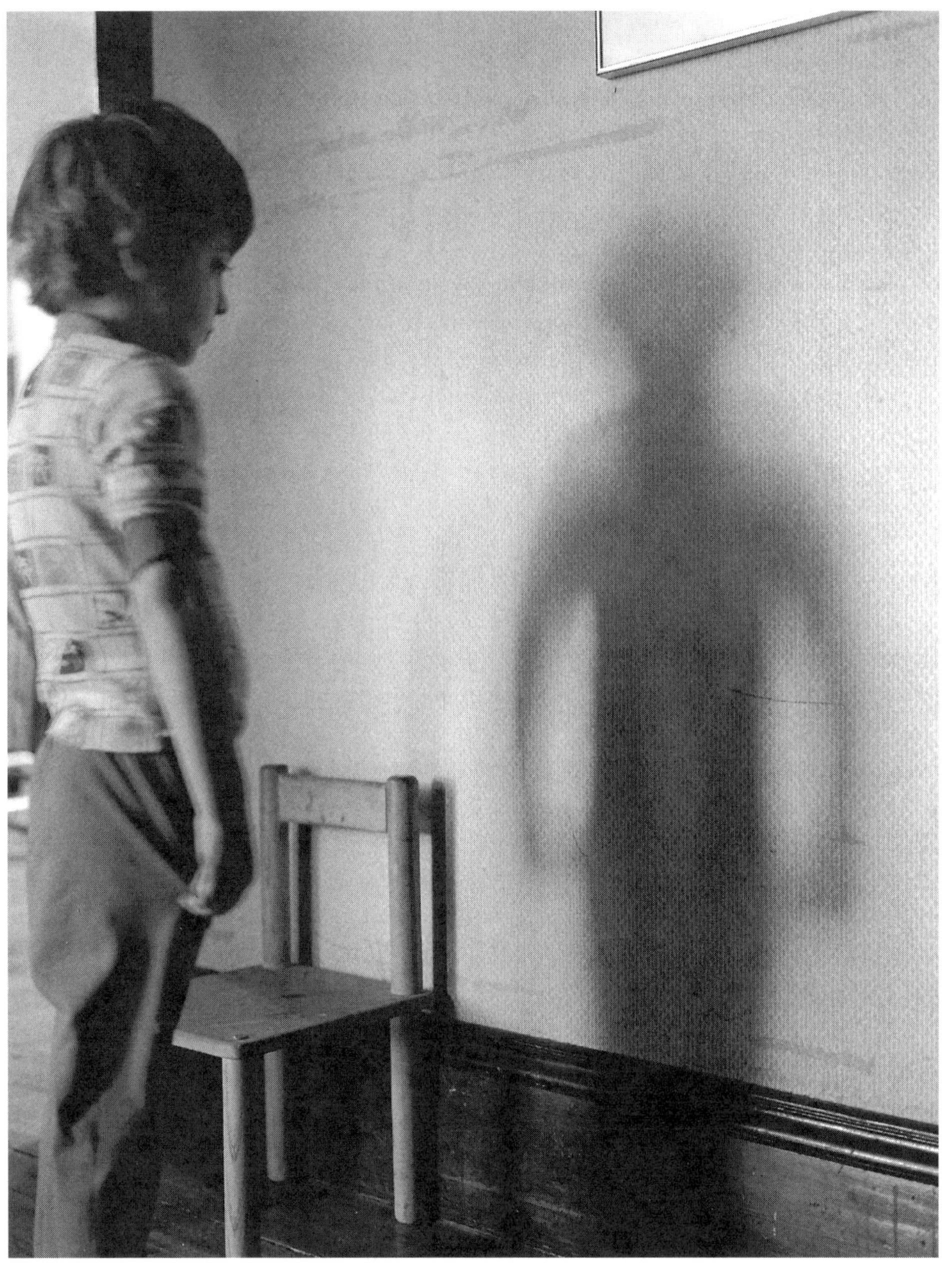

Figure 12.5 *Abelardo Morell,* Brady Looking at His Shadow, *1990.*
© *Abelardo Morell / Courtesy Bonni Benrubi Gallery, NYC.*

nose, my thumb and my pinky touched to make an eye. And I heard not only "My Shadow" but also "Little Black Sambo" and "The Little Tar Man" (the latter without the black dialect of Joel Chandler Harris's Br'er Rabbit stories). Living in my white house with my white liberal family, hearing stories of blackness in my white little-girl's room, I was confused by these stories of black children, and I was confused by my mother's stories of her girlhood in Arkansas: an uncle of hers said that a dark-skinned child was a result of a "n_ _ _ _ _ in the wood pile," and a grandmother called Brazil nuts "n_ _ _ _ _ toes."

When I looked at Richard Avedon's 1963 portrait of William Casby, *Born a Slave,* tucked in between the sheets of *Camera Lucida,* I remembered myself as a little girl in bed listening to racist stories. While a real man who had been born a slave walked around, I was read stories that confirmed his past. The past slapped me in the face with its presentness: slavery existed.

In bed, I began my long apprenticeship on the intricacies of desire and its claims on race (and on gender and class). It all happens long before we lose our milk teeth and make shadows on the wall.

BLACK VEIL

As Margaret Olin has demonstrated, one needs to ask a whole series of questions that turn on Barthes's use of the word *naïve* when describing the Van der Zee photograph:

Why are the sitters naïve? To think that the acquisition of "Sunday best" and jewelry (or to have themselves photographed in such costumes), will make them like whites? Or are they naïve to think that whites will treat them better if they see them in such garb? Which attributes does Barthes mean: Why does Barthes take the "American Way of Life" to mean "attributes du Blanc," rather than attributes of the middle class, surely an aspiration of many of Van Der Zee's sitters, and entry into which a portrait by Van Der Zee may already have certified?[51]

Yet as Olin points out, Barthes elsewhere has more "clearly" taken to task the myths that white people held of black people, as in "Bichon and the Blacks," which appeared in the original French edition of *Mythologies.*[52] Or what about Barthes's careful and powerful analysis of the photo of a young black soldier wearing a French uniform on the cover of *Paris-Match,* in which he shows how the myth of France as a great empire without discrimination works through the signifiers of this picture?

Rather than simply labeling Barthes as naïve to the contradictions that he is setting at play, he instead seems to be casting the Van der Zee picture into a shadow among shadows (in his own magic lantern show), where as "a phosphorescent jewel gives off its glow and color in the dark and loses its beauty in the light of day."[53] After all, the Van der Zee picture is where we first learn to see *punctum*, which is a pierce, a wound, a puncture, a hole. *Punctum* is a shadow of sorts. It is a dark place.

As Barthes tells his readers: "In order to see a photograph well, it is best to . . . close your eyes. . . . My stories are a way of shutting my eyes" (66). This is a real necessity here, given that *"ô négresse nourricière"* has no "slender ribbon of braided gold," as Barthes claims. She seems to be wearing, as Olin suggests in her brilliant essay, pearls. But in Barthes's mind, the African American woman is wearing the "same necklace (a slender ribbon of braided gold)" that had been worn by his Aunt Alice. Like Barthes, she had "never married, lived with her mother" (53) for her entire life. You can find her in *Roland Barthes by Roland Barthes*: she stands, again as Olin points out, in a family portrait in the same position as "*ô négresse nourricière*." In the photograph, she is wearing a necklace (perhaps gold but certainly not a "slender ribbon"). Barthes "adheres" to this aunt, like the photograph and its referent, like Stevenson's boy and his shadow ("I'd think shame to stick to nursie as that shadow sticks to me!"). This shame is known to Barthes's beloved Proust, who stuck to his own Maman, a shame that was familiar to some unmarried "boyish men" who remained in the households of their mothers in a culture of what Sedgwick calls "effiminiphobia."[54]

Barthes was nursed and nourished by the blackness of the Van Der Zee woman—the black twin (at least in his mind) of his Aunt Alice. Barthes hails the black *punctum*-feeding woman of the Van Der Zee photograph as "*ô négresse nouriciere*." Depite his claims otherwise, Barthes does not always "behave as a well-weaned subject," feeding himself "on other things besides the maternal breast."[55] "The neutral," Barthes notes, can be seen "as scandal."[56] Like an adolescent, he perhaps recklessly unveils desire as raced, queered. Yet he sticks to this black woman—like Maman, like Aunt Alice—as if he was her. An auntie is a pansy is a nancy boy.

Barthes was at times mockingly referred to by the students of the Collège de France as being a *tante* (not only "aunt" but slang for "queer"). Barthes identifies himself with both Aunt Alice and the Auntie of the Van Der Zee photograph.

Barthes sees in a pearl necklace "a slender of braided gold" that threads him to his aunt who lived with her mother and never married. She probably was queer in Sedgwick's expansion of the term, a kind of *neutre* like himself—the old maid and "the old queen" (the latter anxiety of identity grows in Barthes's posthumously published *Incidents*). If Sedgwick can declare herself to be a gay man trapped in a woman's body, perhaps Barthes can be understood as a lesbian trapped in a man's body. One of the subheadings for his book on Michelet, in fact, is "Michelet's Lesbianism."[57] As Barthes writes on this beloved writer, a figure he beatifies as much as his Proust: "For Michelet, relations between man and woman are therefore not at all based on the difference between the sexes. . . . Michelet turns himself into a woman, mother, *nurse*."[58]

Barthes himself writes that the light of every photograph becomes "a carnal medium, as skin that I share with him or her who was photographed" (81). He portrays himself, if subtly so, via the body of his own nourishing mother, as sharing a skin with the black woman with the "belt worn low" and the "strapped pumps": "[For Michelet, there is] no more difference between algae and fish than between skin and the silk which covers it. When Michelet amorously describes the tunic coiled around woman, there is no doubt that he longs to be that garment."[59] Through the "carnal medium" of photography, the effect is both touching and erotic. It pricks him.

Barthes couples himself and his aunt under the shade of the woman he salutes as "*ô négresse nourricière*," who is the most shadowed figure both allegorically and formally in Van der Zee's family portrait. And Barthes becomes the solacing nurse to his own mother in her illness: "During her illness, I nursed her, held the bowl of tea she liked because it was easier to drink from than from a cup: she had become my little girl, uniting for me with that essential child she was in her first photograph" (72).

This is not the only time that Barthes will see *punctum* through a black veil. It happens two more times. The second time occurs in a study (which as often happens with Barthes, becomes a personal confession) of Lewis H. Hine's *Idiot Children in an Institution* (New Jersey, 1924). A few pages past the cords that draw him to the absent/present slender gold necklace, Barthes claims to "hardly see the monstrous heads and pathetic profiles" (which belong to the *studium*). No he gets a *punctum*—a cut from "the girl's finger bandage" and the little boy's huge Danton collar" (51). Barthes compares his skewed vision to "Ombredane's blacks." (51). Here, Barthes is referring to the 1949 experiment done by André Ombredane, in which people in the Belgian Congo were shown a film about daily hygiene. The Congolese were fascinated by what the film's makers would consider an unimportant detail—"the tiny hen which crosses the village in a corner of the film."[60] The Congolese see the chicken as primary and will not retain the lesson of the film. Like Barthes, they scatter "the signified, the catechisms" by making the chicken into a gastronomically inflected *punctum*.

Barthes plays this game of neither black nor white (his *ni-ni* criticism) for the third time when he compares the Winter Garden photograph to Avedon's picture of one of the leaders of the American civil rights and labor movements—Phillip Randolph.

BLUE AND BLACK VEILS

His writing is sweeping, blue, aerated.
—Philippe Sollers, *R.B.*[61]

The first page of *Camera Lucida* is an image. *Polaroid,* as it is called, is a nearly monochrome blue photograph of a bed taken in 1979 by Daniel Boudinet. We are born from mothers in bed. We die in bed. We have sex in bed. We write in bed. We eat in bed. And, it seems, we begin to learn the intricacies of desire as raced. It is the only photograph in the book about which Barthes says nothing. For me, *Polaroid* is the companion of the Winter Garden Photograph—the photograph that Barthes talks most about but never reproduces.[62]

Searching through old photographs of Henriette, Barthes reminisces on the luminosity of his mother's eyes: "For the moment it was a quite physical luminosity, the photographic trace of a color, the blue-green of her pupils" (66). As Diana Knight points out: "This . . . is the mediating light that will lead him at last to the essence of her face, a blue-green luminosity which is also that of the Boudinet polaroid."[63] *Polaroid* has no text; the Winter Garden Photograph has no image. They are a queer couple, not unlike Barthes and his mother.

Womblike, the light from *Polaroid*'s window is diffused by gauzy curtains. Bits of light creep in through the loose weave of the fabric. Light leaks (where the curtains barely part, near the pillow) and drifts (through a small number of thin, select tears in the fabric). By invoking at once a watery membrane and aging sagging skin at once, the curtains pull at the delicate and somber texture of *Camera Lucida,* suggesting seeing through his mother's blue eyes, seeing through a blue veil. As Stacy Waddell has suggested, Barthes seems to be living in his own double-consciousness, akin to Du Bois's black double-consciousness. In Barthes's case, it was of the gay man in a straight world. When Du Bois speaks of a life lived in "twoness" (as an "American" and as a "Negro," with "two unreconciled strivings," with "two warring ideals in one dark body"), he invokes the folk notion of being born with the veil or the caul, the inner fetal membrane that occasionally envelops the newborn's head. In African American culture, this is understood as a "gift" that can "foretell luck or precognitive powers."[64] But Du Bois inverts this "good" notion of the veil to explain the double consciousness of black existence. For Du Bois, to be born with the veil is more curse than gift. It is to be born under the rule of a white consciousness that has predetermined who that black baby is, even before he has left the embryonic sac, even before the caul has been pulled away from his eyes.

Barthes, the invert, is both blessed and cursed by his mother's blue veil: it invokes protectiveness, love, tenderness, awkwardness, "Mama's boy," eternally adolescent. As Tzvetan Todorov has remarked: "There was always something adolescent, even childish, in him. He had no truth to impose upon others, nor even upon himself. . . . He always seemed to be the age of the students in his latest seminar. . . . *A Lover's Discourse* is also rooted in adolescent language . . . the book concerns love, not desire."[65] And that love was ultimately a love for his mother.

A gay man, Barthes fulfilled the stereotype of being too passionately close to the mother. Barthes played best (perhaps even solely/wholely) with his mother. As queer (left-handed, child of a single mother, a Protestant in a Catholic country, brother of a child born out of wedlock, poor as a child, unmarried, lover of men), he was metaphorically stuck in the hole:

When I was a child, we lived in a neighborhood called Marac; this neighborhood was full of houses being built, and the children played in the building sites; huge holes had been dug in the loamy soil for the foundations of the houses, and one day when we had been playing in one of these, all the children climbed out except me—I couldn't make it. From the brink above, they teased me: lost! alone! spied on! excluded! (to be excluded is not to be outside, it is to be alone in the hole, *imprisoned under the open sky:* precluded*); then I saw my mother running up; she pulled me out of there and took me far away from the children—against them.*[66]

Soaked in precious robin's-egg blue, *Polaroïd* is the only color photograph among a total of twenty-five. Its color hails invert. The lovely color—a range of creamy green blues, gray green blues, and charcoal blues, infused with flickers of white light—is a surprise. Barthes does not like color photographs. I get stuck on this photograph like I get stuck on Van der Zee's woman with the low belt. Barthes writes in *Camera Lucida*: "I always feel . . . that . . . color is a coating applied *later on* to the original truth of the black-and-white photograph." Here color invokes a putting on (a veiling over) that is at play in the "double consciousness" that arises from the more minor and the extremely severe "minority situation"[67]—from Boudinet to Van der Zee.

In our seminar devoted to Barthes, Thu-Mai told us this story:

My high school French teacher told us this story about a trip she took to Japan. She was on a train traveling through the Japanese countryside. Across from her, a little boy and an elderly woman were obviously looking at her as they spoke to one another in their native Japanese. For a blonde-haired American woman, a rare sight in this part of Japan, the attention was not unusual. After more discussion with the old woman, the little boy finally approached my teacher and said, "My grandmother wants to know if you see blue through your blue eyes."

Blue is not as innocent or as true-blue as it professes to be, whether it is a woollen hat covering the heads of little blue boys or the dress of the Virgin Mary or the sky of the heavens. One cannot see through blue eyes without its prerequisite white skin, with or without a calling card from the world that controls the veil. In *The Bluest Eye*,[68] Tony Morrison devastates us with Pecola, the black girl who dreams of having "Morning-glory-blue eyes. Alice-and-Jerry-blue-storybook-eyes."[69] In *A Patch of Blue,* the 1965 Guy Green movie, a girl's blindness to Sydney Poitier's "color" is highlighted by her memory of a "patch of blue." In *The Souls of Black Folk,* Du Bois notes that, as a child, the sky was the bluest when he beat his fellow white students at exams and foot races. Nevertheless, Du Bois recalls the moment when he first realized the vastness of the white world that shut him out. He had no desire to tear it. He lived above it:

It is in the early days of rollicking boyhood that the revelation first bursts upon one, all in a day, as it were. I remember well when the shadow swept across me. I was a little thing, away up in the hills of New England, where the dark Housatonic winds between Hoosac and Taghkanic to the sea. In a wee wooden schoolhouse, something put it into the boys' and girls' heads to buy gorgeous visiting-cards—ten cents a package—and exchange. The exchange was merry, till one girl, a tall newcomer, refused my card,—refused it peremptorily, with a glance. Then it dawned upon me with a certain suddenness that I was different from the others; or, like mayhap, in heart and life and longing, but shut out from their world by a vast veil. I had thereafter no desire to tear down that veil, to creep through it; I held all beyond it in common contempt, and lived above it in a region of blue sky and great wandering shadows. That sky was bluest when I could beat my mates at examination-time, or beat them at a foot-race, or even beat their stringy heads.[70]

Du Bois: black and blue.

SHADOWS "COLORED" BLACK AND BLUE

During the summer of the year 1743 I observed in the case of more than thirty dawns and as many sunsets that shadows falling on a white surface, such as a white wall, were sometimes green most often blue, and a blue as vivid as the finest azure. I pointed this phenomenon out to several persons, who were as surprised as myself. It being summer-time was not a factor, for only eight days ago I saw blue shadows, in November.[71]

To speak of the truth of the photograph as in truly seeing his mother in the Winter Garden Photograph, Barthes uses the word "air" (*gaz*):

The air is not a schematic, intellectual datum, the way a silhouette is. Nor is the air a simple analogy . . . as is "likeness." No, the air is that exorbitant thing which induces from body to soul—animula, little individual soul, good in one person, bad in another. Hence I was leafing through the photographs of my mother according to an initiatic path which led me to . . . finally,

*the Winter Garden Photograph . . . in which I discover her: a saddening awakening. . . . The air
(I use this word), lacking anything better, for the expression of truth). (109)*

Not only does Barthes find this special "air" in the Winter Garden Photograph, captured
quite by accident by an amateur photographer, but he finds it in a photograph by Richard
Avedon of Phillip Randolph, a black man. This odd ("tenuous umbilical") tie between
Randolph and Henriette becomes another "touching" connection that hails the coupling
of the woman with the low belt in the Van der Zee family portrait and Barthes's aunt.
Randolph, one of the giants of the American labor movement, organized the first union of
predominantly black workers (the Brotherhood of Sleeping Car Porters) and led 250,000
people in the historic 1963 March on Washington, a display of the solidarity of black and
white workers. (Randolph hoped for a dynamic integration of race and labor, another loop
of black and blue.)[72]

What could the Winter Garden Photograph, a family picture of a white French woman
taken by an amateur, share with its structural opposite, an art photograph of a famous black
American man taken by one of the most famous portraitists of all time? Both share, via
Henriette's "assertion of gentleness" and Randolph's "No impulse of power" (108), an "air of
goodness" through a seemingly profound embodiment of *le neutre*.

As Barthes writes (here I repeat one of his umbilical passages):

*I read an air of goodness (no impulse of power: that is certain). Thus the air is the luminous
shadow, which accompanies the body; and if the photograph fails to show this air, then the body
moves without a shadow, and once this shadow is severed, as in the myth of the Woman without
a Shadow, there remains no more than a sterile body. It is by this tenuous umbilical cord that the
photographer gives life; if he cannot, either by lack of talent or bad luck, supply the transparent soul
its bright shadow, the subject dies forever. . . . Since neither Nadar nor Avedon has photographed
my mother, the survival of this image has depended on the luck of a picture made by a provincial
photographer who, an indifferent mediator, himself long since dead, did not know that what he
was making permanent was the truth—the truth for me. (110)*

I am reminded of not only Barthes's concept of *le neutre* but also an embodiment of
that term (Barthes before Barthes) when Tanizaki describes the darkness of a study bay in a
traditional Japanese house within the faint white glow of the shoji: "The light from the pale
white paper, powerless to dispel the heavy darkness of the alcove, is instead repelled by the
darkness, creating a world of confusion where dark and light are indistinguishable."[73]

Fairy-Tale Ending

And this led me to reflect on the inimitable beauty of the picture of nature's paintings which the glass lens of the Camera throws upon the paper in its focus—fairy pictures, creations of a moment, and destined as rapidly to fade away.
—Talbot, "A Brief Historical Note on the Invention of the Art"[74]

In the Photograph, Time's immobilization assumes only an excessive, monstrous mode: Time is engorged (whence the relation with the Tableau Vivant, *whose mythic prototype is the princess falling asleep in* Sleeping Beauty*).*
—Barthes, *Camera Lucida* (91)

Camera Lucida begins as if it all were a fairy tale: "One day, quite some time ago, I happened on a photograph of Napoleon's youngest brother, Jerome, taken in 1852. And I realized then, with an amazement I have not been able to lessen since: "I am looking at eyes that looked at the Emperor" (3). I like to think that Barthes does not reproduce this first image of the book to hold onto its fairyish magic, in much the same, if very different, spirit of the *animula* of the Winter Garden Photograph. Fairies bring back the magic of childhood, like a photograph. In fact, for Barthes, the magic of photography—which is its peculiar, inexplicable connection to the real, its stubbornness when it comes to its (umbilical) tie to the referent, what he calls elsewhere its "message without a code" (*Image, Music Text*). The magic of photography is likened throughout the book to a child's experience of the world—one of profound immediacy: "In order to designate reality, Buddhism says *sunya*, the voice; but better still: *tathata*, as Alan Watts has it, the fact of being this, of being thus, of being so; *tat* means *that* in Sanskrit and suggests the gesture of the child pointing his finger at something and saying: *that, there it is, lo!* but says nothing else; a photograph cannot be transformed (spoken) philosophically, it is wholly ballasted by the contingency of which it is the weightless, transparent envelope" (5). Like a shadow, a photograph carries its referent with itself. It just is. Barthes chooses to dismiss culture, science, and, it seems, even language, in his fairy-tale "Once upon a time" story—experienced with his eyes closed.

One might even say that photographs themselves are fairyish,[75] specifically in the fairy-tale notion of the suspension of time, of nodding off as if stuck in wet collodion. Close your eyes and think of "Sleeping Beauty," as told by Perrault. In this magical tale, the good fairy acts like a camera to protect Beauty. For the good fairy knows that if Beauty is asleep for some hundred years, she is going to be shocked to find the world around her radically transformed. So the good fairy puts to sleep the entire castle, even the whole process of cooking is suspended (as if in emulsion). To photograph is in a sense to act as Perrault's good fairy—to make the world "doze off" into "the permanence of a single, monotonous, and interminable moment."[76] The photograph nourishes many desires (racial, sexual), but here it feeds the desire to hold time, to keep death abate, as if it could be fed like hunger ("Time is engorged") (91).

The fairy-tale suspension of Barthes's *Camera Lucida* twinkles throughout. There are the fairy-tale beginning and the child-like wonder in understanding a photograph, which is pushed to its limits when Barthes chooses to see the photograph with his hedonistic self-serving eyes closed: "I am a . . . child . . . I dismiss all knowledge, all culture, I refuse to inherit anything from another eye than my own" (51). Even his own "wakening" comes *Sleeping Beauty*–style on the final page of the book ("the wakening of intractable reality").

Barthes eventually turns to Strauss's opera, *The Woman without a Shadow*. The story of *The Woman without a Shadow* is a fairy tale. The emperor catches a gazelle who turns into a woman that he marries. As daughter of Keikobad, king of the spirits, she is a woman without a shadow. Part spirit, she is as shadowless as a ghost, and this means that she cannot bear children. But she gains her shadow by the end of the twelfth moon, which allows her to become fertile and full of shadows and to escape being turned into stone. For Barthes, the photograph that he ties to mother and the womb is "sterile" when it does not reproduce the "air" of its sitter (whether that person is the amateur photographer's Henriette, Nadar's Ernestine, or Avedon's Philip Randolph): "and if the photograph fails to show this air, then the body moves without a shadow, and once this shadow is severed, as in the myth of the Woman without a Shadow, there remains no more than a sterile body" (110).

After his mother's death, Barthes found himself to be "without his shadow"—with no desire to write, no fecundity left, no life. He was sterile. He had found himself to be perhaps the most fecund at the time right before her death when he became mother with Henriette as his child: "Ultimately I experienced her, strong as she had been, my inner law, as my feminine child. . . . I who had not procreated, I had in her very illness engendered my mother" (72). Such fantasies are hailed by Barthes's own queerness, for a gay man can be seen as a sterile, feminized being—a woman without a shadow. Without his mother, without his "transparent soul," without his "bright shadow," he was an allegory of death.

Barthes had to fly back to a time without time, to a Neverland island, to a time before Barthes. He flew through photograph after photograph, from box to box, until he landed on his mother's childish head when Henriette was five.

Five is an especially magical time when it comes to children and their shadows. As Robert Casati Writes in *The Shadow Club:* "The child is bewitched by the shadow. . . . Children really seem to think so. Even if they won't admit it when pressed, they still may think that shadows are like real people—for example, that shadows exist even in the dark."[77] According to Jean Piaget, little children who do not know how shadows are produced are imaginative about how they are conceived. Piaget's five-year-old child imagines that shadows are conceived as a collaboration between two sources, two opposites, the external and the internal world. For five-year-old children, shadows are not cast. They emanate in a play between two worlds, not unlike Strauss's gazelle-empress who is half spirit and half earthly, not unlike Barthes and his mother.

Barthes had to go back to the time before their division, before the inevitable cut of the cord, before the drama of his first breath and the exhaustion of her last breath to a utopian time when Barthes was nothing more, nothing less than a sweet in his five-year-old mother's clenched hand.

As a result, the Winter Garden Photograph is filled with luminous shadows. There you can make your own shadows, like a child on his bedroom wall making his hand into rabbits and ducks. There you can write and erase. There you can be with your mother, your mother the child. But there you also learn about desire and race, about Br'er Rabbit and Little Black Sambo, about shadows that will go in and out with you, about gorgeous visiting cards refused with a glance of blue eyes, about "Morning-glory-blue eyes. Alice-and-Jerry-blue-storybook-eyes," about a lingering "patch of blue."

While *Gateway to Storyland* is the first book that I remember reading, *Camera Lucida* was the last book that Barthes wrote. *Camera Lucida* is always under the shadow of Barthes's death but not the bright shadow of its luminous title. *Camera Lucida* has become far more tragic than the sorrowful book was perhaps meant to be. The first reviews of *Camera Lucida* were published before his death, and they were at times snide, humorous, critical—one might even say afloat—but after his death they took on a dark, beatifying mournful tone.

Let us hold Barthes in the true spirit of the book, as camera lucida *and* camera obscura, as immortalized by silver (photography), as enchanted by a metal of alchemy. Given such an elixir, Barthes is dead but also alive. Barthes becomes "the loved body . . . immortalized by the mediation of a precious metal, silver (monument and luxury): to which we might add the notion that this metal, like all the metals of Alchemy, is alive" (81). Let's read Barthes with and without shadows, as light and dark, black and white, as good and bad. Let us not wait a hundred years to break the good fairy's spell; let us wake Barthes, even if it has been only twenty-five years. (A twenty-fifth wedding anniversary is celebrated with a gift of silver.) This means reading Barthes's last book as we would read his first, without much solacing.

In my earlier work on Barthes, I suggested that Boudinet's *Polaroid* and the Winter Garden photograph were a couple. That was a nice, blue (queer) story of desire. Not as nice but perhaps more helpful is this more ambivalent story of black and blue. Although still imbued with my love for Barthes, I now believe that the truest story comes from pairing the "blue" Boudinet with the "black" Van der Zee. (As I learned from my beloved teacher James Clifford: "If we are condemned to tell stories we cannot control, may we not, at least, tell stories we believe to be true."[78])

I believe true is black *and* blue.

NOTES

1. Roland Barthes, *La chambre claire: note sur la photographie* (Paris: Gallimard, 1980), 49, in English *Camera Lucida: Reflections on Photography*, trans. Richard Howard (New York: Hill and Wang, 1981), 27 (hereafter, all references to these two books appear in the body of the text within parentheses).

2. Jun'ichiro Tanizaki, *In Praise of Shadows* (1933–1934), trans. Thomas J. Harper and Edward G. Seidensticker (New Haven, CT: Leete's Island Books, 1977), 18, originally published as *In'ei raisan* in *Keizai orai* (December 1933 and January 1934).

3. The complications of reading Van der Zee's documentation of the African American middle and upper classes is best attended to by the leading critic on the photographer—Deborah Willis. In her groundbreaking *VanDerZee* (New York: Abrams, 1993), she writes: "Since the rediscovery of James VanDerZee's photographic archive in 1969, when his photographs were included in the Metropolitan Museum of Art's controversial exhibition, Harlem on My Mind, VanDerZee's images of the people of Harlem have been celebrated as an important and beautiful historical document. If in the years since, critics and historians have come to value them primarily as a visual record of the emergence in America of the African middle and upper classes, we should not be surprised, but we should not let this judgement limit our responses to the photographs themselves" (8). Willis published this early book under the name Deborah Willis-Braithwaite. There are several variations on the spelling of VanDerZee. Willis's "VanDerZee" is the most accurate, but in this essay I use the spelling that appears in Barthes's text.

4. I began thinking more seriously about Barthes's handling of the Van der Zee picture through discussions with José Estaban Muñoz. I shared José's reading with my students, particularly David C. Hart, who developed some of this material into his intriguing master of arts thesis, *Differing Views: Roland Barthes, Race and James Vanderzee's Family Portrait* (Chapel Hill: University of North Carolina, 1996).

5. *Négresse nourricière* is used here by Barthes to describe the person who nursed and raised the child. The word *nègre* or *négresse* has been used in French to describe someone who works hard and does all the work (the person being of color or not). Like the American *mammy*, the words *nègre* and *négresse* come from the time of slavery, and the words have kept their pejorative connotation. Yet the word *négresse* as a pejorative term is then troubled by Barthes's expression of "*ô négresse nourricière*," suggesting that the author is paying homage to what Howard names for us as the "solacing Mammy." I thank Anne Calvignac for helping me with the difficulties and subtleties of this translation.

6. Barthes loves to contradict himself because contradictions fuel him. Consider how he posits Japan as fictive in *Empire of Signs* but nonetheless fills it with history, with facts, with concrete observations. His use of parentheses is another case in point, taken up briefly in the body of this essay.

7. Frantz Fanon, *Black Skin, White Masks: The Experiences of a Black Man in a White World,* trans. Charles Lam Markman (New York: Grove Press, 1967), 109, first published in French as *Peau Noire, Masques Blancs* (Paris: Editions du Seuil, 1952).

8. Carol Mavor, "Roland Barthes's Umbilical Referent," in Richard Meyer, ed., *Representing the Passions: Histories, Bodies, Visions* (Santa Monica, CA: Getty Research Institute, 2003); Carol Mavor, *Reading Boyishly: J. M. Barrie, Roland Barthes, Jacques Henri Lartigue, Marcel Proust and D. W. Winnicott* (Durham, NC: Duke University Press, 2006).

9. Barthes's *le neutre* is akin to Louis Marin's use of the term in his *Utopics: The Semiological Play of Textual Space,* trans. Robert A. Volrath (Atlantic Highlands, NJ: Humanities Press, 1990), first published as *Utopiques: jeux d'espaces* (Paris: Editions de Minuit, 1973). See my explanation of the relationship between Barthes and Marin on the topic of *le neutre* in my *Pleasures Taken: Performances of Sexuality and Loss in Victorian Photographs* (Durham, NC: Duke University Press, 1995), 20–22.

10. Roland Barthes, *The Neutral: Lecture Course at the Collège de France (1977–1978),* trans. Rosalind E. Krauss and Denis Hollier, text established, annotated, and presented by Thomas Clerc under the direction of Eric Marty (New York: Columbia University Press, 2005), 51.

11. This series of images speaks at once to darkness and desire and its variations in the fantasies of both white and black culture. These "imaginaries" necessarily include the appetite for lighter skin as it is produced within the black community, as well as the feeding on darkness by whites.

12. Fanon, *Black Skin, White Masks,* 112.

13. Richard Dyer, "White," *The Matter of Images: Essays on Representations* (New York: Routledge, 1993), 160.

14. Kobena Mercer, "Reading Racial Fetishism: The Photographs of Robert Mapplethorpe," in Emily Apter and William Pietz, eds., *Fetishism as Cultural Discourse* (Ithaca, NY: Cornell University Press, 1993), 308.

15. Christian Metz, "Photography and Fetish," *October* 34 (Fall 1985): 81–85.

16. Mercer, "Reading Racial Fetishism," 311.

17. Ibid., 317–318.

18. This more positive read, a rereading of Mapplethorpe's photographs, takes up the second half of "Reading Racial Fetishism," resulting in a hate-turned-love "ambivalence" for these troubling images.

19. Zeynep Çelik, "Framing the Colony: Houses of Algeria Photographed," *Art History* 27. no. 4 (September 2004), 616–626.

20. Ibid., 617.

21. Roland Barthes, *Pleasure of the Text,* trans. Richard Howard with a note on the text by Richard Miller (New York: Farrar, Straus and Giroux, 1975), 66. Originally published as *Le plaisir du texte* (Paris: Éditions du Seuil, 1973).

22. For an excellent discussion of Freud's notion of the dark continent and its relation to oceanic feelings, see Ranjana Khanna, *Dark Continents: Psychoanalysis and Colonialism* (Durham, NC: Duke University Press, 2003).

23. Brian Masumi, "Too Blue," *Parables for the Virtual: Movement, Affect, Sensation* (Durham, NC: Duke University Press, 2002).

24. Some have argued that the Winter Garden Photograph never existed. But in our imaginations, it is a black-and-white picture.

25. Philip Steadman, *Vermeer's Camera: Uncovering the Truth behind the Masterpiece* (Oxford: Oxford University Press, 2002), provides a useful and simple description of the camera lucida: "The camera lucida is a four-sided glass prism and lens combined supported on a stand. The artist looks through with one eye through the prism at his piece of paper, and simultaneously with the other eye at the object or scene to be drawn, and sees an image of the second superimposed on the first. He can thus trace the image. The camera lucida is generally taken to be an early 19th-century invention with the credit shared between the Englishman Wollaston and the Italian Amici" (24).

26. Roland Barthes, *Roland Barthes by Roland Barthes* (1975), trans. Richard Howard (New York: Hill and Wang, 1977), 50, first published as *Roland Barthes par Roland Barthes* (Paris: Editions du Seuil, 1975).

27. This was the last course that he taught, but he did not finish it because of the accident that led to his death—"The Preparation of the Novel."

28. Rosalind Krauss, Introduction, in Barthes, *The Neutral.*

29. Barthes, *The Neutral,* 19.

30. E. H. Gombrich, *The Depiction of Cast Shadows in Western Art* (London: National Gallery Publications, 1995), 17.

31. See Geoffrey Batchen's excellent history and theoretical understanding of Talbot's contributions in *Burning with Desire: The Conception of Photography* (Cambridge, MA: MIT Press, 1997).

32. Thomas Clerc, Introduction, in Barthes, *The Neutral,* xxv.

33. Henry Fox Talbot, "Some Account of the Art of Photogenic Drawing" (1839), in *Photography: Essays and Images, Illustrated Readings in the History of Photography* (New York: Museum of Modern Art, Boston: New York Graphic Society, 1980), 25, as discussed in Batchen, *Burning with Desire,* 91.

34. Barthes, *The Neutral,* 153.

35. Roland Barthes, *Sollers écrivain* (Paris: Seuil, 1979), 58.

36. Meg Sheehan, "Inside the 'Winter Garden Photograph,'" essay written for the course Photographies and Sexualities, University of North Carolina, Fall 1989.

37. On January 7, 1977, Barthes gave his inaugural lecture as the chair of literary semiology, Collège de France. See "Inaugural Lecture, Collège de France," trans. Richard Howard, in Susan Sontag, ed., *A Barthes Reader* (New York: Hill and Wang, 1982), 476–467, originally published in French as *Leçon: leçon inaugurale de la chaire de sémiologie littéraire du Collège de France, prononcée le 7 janvier 1977* (Paris: Éditions du Seuil, 1978), 42–43.

38. Toni Morrison, *Playing in the Dark: Whiteness and the Literary Imagination* (New York: Vintage Books, 1992).

39. I am using the final lines of Morrison's *Playing in the Dark,* in which she concludes (in response to the perhaps "easier" personification of racism in some of our greatest literature): "But it would be a pity if the criticism of that literature continued to shellac those texts, immobilizing their complexities and power and luminations just below its tight, reflecting surface. All of us, readers and writers, are bereft when criticism remains too polite or too fearful to notice a disrupting darkness before its eyes" (91).

40. In French, *La chambre claire,* 126–127.

41. Ibid., 169.

42. Barthes, *The Neutral,* xiii.

43. Barthes, *Roland Barthes by Roland Barthes,* unpaginated opening page that begins the book's discussion of select (mostly personal and family) photographs.

44. Fanon, *Black Skin, White Masks,* 146.

45. Whiteread's *Ghost* shares with photography the notion of the double, of freezing an image, a moment, forever. But her "capture" of the past is not small like "flies in amber" (the phrase comes from Peter Wollen, "Fire and Ice," in Liz Wells, ed. *The Photography Reader* (2003), 76. Originally published in *Photographies* 4 [1984]); it is gigantic. Whiteread's *Ghost* allows no possibility of Proust's *mémoire involontaire.*

46. Our role in reading, according to Barthes, is to be writerly (*scriptible*) rather than readerly (*lisible*): we must write along with the author. Embracing what he understands as the inherent "performativity" of writing (resulting in a subject-subject status as opposed to the traditional subject-object status), Barthes turns language's natural inadequacies to our advantage. Instead of a subject-writer who subjects the object-reader to an authorial reign of writer as god, both reader and author both play as subjects. Barthes refuses to privilege writer over reader. Barthes envisions writerly readers through what he calls the *writerly text*: "The writerly text is . . . . *ourselves writing* before the infinite play of the world (the world as function) is traversed, intersected, stopped, plasticized by some singular system (Ideology, Genus, Criticism) which reduces the plurality of entrances, the opening of networks, the infinity of languages." Roland Barthes, *S/Z,* trans. Richard Miller (New York: Hill and Wang, 1975), 5.

47. Charles Baudelaire, "A Philosophy of Toys," in Jonathan Mayne, ed. and trans., *The Painter of Modern Life and Other Essays* (New York: De Capo Press, 1964), 198, originally published in French as "Morale du Joujou," *Monde littéraire,* April 17, 1853.

48. Roland Barthes, "Toys," in Annette Lavers, ed. and trans., *Mythologies* (New York: Hill and Wang, 1972), 54, first published in French as *Mythologies* (Paris: Editions du Seuil, 1957).

49. Robert Louis Stevenson's 1885 poem follows:

My Shadow

I have a little shadow that goes in and out with me,
And what can be the use of him is more than I can see.
He is very, very like me from the heels up to the head;
And I see him jump before me, when I jump into my bed.

The funniest thing about him is the way he likes to grow—
Not at all like proper children, which is always very slow;
For he sometimes shoots up taller like an India-rubber ball,
And he sometimes gets so little that there's none of him at all.
He hasn't got a notion of how children ought to play,
And can only make a fool of me in every sort of way.
He stays so close beside me, he's a coward you can see;
I'd think shame to stick to nursie as that shadow sticks to me!

One morning, very early, before the sun was up,
I rose and found the shining dew on every buttercup;
But my lazy little shadow, like an arrant sleepy-head,
Had stayed at home behind me and was fast asleep in bed.

50. Peter Stallybrass, "Worn Worlds: Clothes, Mourning and the Life of Things," *Yale Review* 81, no. 2 (1993): 36.

51. Margaret Olin, "Touching Photographs: Roland Barthes's 'Mistaken' Identification," *Representations* 80 (Fall 2002): 104. Olin's carefully nuanced essay has been instrumental in my writing and teaching.

52. Barthes begins his little essay as follows, setting up the white petit-bourgeois as a straw dog: "*Match* has printed a story which has a good deal to say about our petit-bourgeois myth of the Black: a young couple, both professors, have made an expedition into Cannibal country to do some painting; they have taken with them their months-old baby, Bichon. *Match* goes into ecstasy over the courage of all three" (35). Roland Barthes, "Bichon and the Blacks," *The Eiffel Tower and Other Mythologies* (1979), trans. Richard Howard (Berkeley: University of California Press, 1997).

53. Tanizaki, *In Praise of Shadows,* 30.

54. Eve Kosofsky Sedgwick, "How to Bring Up Your Kids Gay," *Tendencies* (Durham, NC: Duke University Press, 1993.

55. Roland Barthes, *A Lover's Discourse,* trans. Richard Howard (New York: Hill and Wang, 1978), 14.

56. Barthes, *The Neutral,* 72.

57. Roland Barthes, *Michelet,* trans. Richard Howard (Berkeley: University of California, Press), 152, originally published in French as *Michelet* (Paris: Editions du Seuil, 1954).

58. Barthes, *Michelet,* 152–153.

59. Ibid., 153.

60. Antoine Compagnon, "La poule d'Ombredane, le soldat de Baltimore et la baromètre de Mme Aubain," in *R/B: Roland Barthes* (Paris: Editions du Seuil, 2002), 75 (translation is mine), published in conjunction with the exhibition R/B: Roland Barthes, under the direction of Marianne Alphant and Nathalie Léger, November 27, 2002–March 10, 2003, at the Centre Pompidou.

61. Phillipe Sollers, "R.B," in Diana Knight, ed., *Critical Essays on Roland Barthes* (New York: Hall, 2000), 98.

62. See my essay "Becoming: The Photographs of Clementina Hawarden, 1859–1864," *Genre* 29, nos. 1–2 (1996): 93–134; and my book *Reading Boyishly,* especially 398–432.

63. Diana Knight, "The Woman without a Shadow," in Jean-Michel Rabaté, *Writing the Image after Roland Barthes* (Philadelphia: University of Pennsylvania Press, 1997), 138.

64. Donald B. Gibson, Introduction, in W. E. B. Du Bois, *The Souls of Black Folk* (1903) (New York: Penguin, 1996), xv (originally published by A. C. McClurg).

65. Tzvetan Todorov, "The Last Barthes," *Critical Inquiry* 7, no. 3 (Spring 1981): 452.

66. Barthes, *Roland Barthes by Roland Barthes,* 121–122, in French *Roland Barthes par Roland Barthes,* 125.

67. Barthes is sympathetic to what he terms the "minority situation" because of his own queer tendencies, yet he acknowledges that his situation is minor—in "no way severe." Barthes, *Roland Barthes by Roland Barthes,* 130–131.

68. Again, I thank Stacy Waddell, this time for reminding me of this book's link to my project.

69. Tony Morrison, *The Bluest Eye* (1970) (New York: Plume, 2005), 46.

70. Du Bois, *The Souls of Black Folk,* 4.

71. Georges-Louis Leclerc, comte de Buffon, from a paper on "accidental" colors, as cited in Michael Baxandall, *Shadows and Enlightenment* (New Haven, CT: Yale University Press, 1995), 112.

72. For an excellent study of Randolph, see Leon Fink, *Progressive Intellectuals and the Dilemmas of Democratic Commitment* (Cambridge, MA: Harvard University Press, 1997), 184–213.

73. Tanizaki, *In Praise of Shadows,* 22.

74. William Henry Fox Talbot, *Some Account of the Art of Photogenic Drawing* (1839), unpaginated introductory remarks on the first fascicle of *The Pencil of Nature* (London, 1844); Talbot, *On the Art of Fixing a Shadow,* in *Some Account,* 11; Batchen, *Burning with Desire,* 85–86.

75. See Carol Mavor, "Photographs Are Fairyish," *Archive* (Bradford, England: National Museum of Photography, 2004), 24–29.

76. Louis Marin, *Food for Thought,* trans. and afterword by Mette Hjort (Baltimore, MD: Johns Hopkins Press, 1989), 136, originally published in French as *La parole mangée et autres essays théologico-politiques* (Libraries des Méridiens, Klincksieck, 1986).

77. Robert Casati, *The Shadow Club: The Greatest Mystery in the Universe—Shadows—and the Thinkers Who Unlocked Their Secrets,* trans. Abigail Asher (New York: Knopf, 2003), 30–31.

78. James Clifford, "On Ethnographic Allegory," in Clifford Marcus and G. Marcus, eds., *Writing and Culture: The Poetics and Politics of Ethnography* (Berkeley: University of California Press, 1986), 121.

Race and Reproduction in *Camera Lucida*

Shawn Michelle Smith

In his influential study of photography, *Camera Lucida: Reflections on Photography,* Roland Barthes makes himself the measure of photographic meaning.[1] The book is his attempt "to formulate the fundamental feature" of photography "starting from a few personal impulses" to a few photographs (8–9). Barthes seeks to discover the essential elements of photography through his own particular responses to images. This profoundly personal treatment of photography lends *Camera Lucida* both its evocative power and its frustrating limitations.

Barthes's work has been important and generative, both theoretically and methodologically, for photography scholars, especially for those who study family photography. As this work has demonstrated, the personal can be a powerful point of departure for critical analysis, and as feminist scholars of family photography insist, "the personal is political."[2] Reconsidering Barthes's individualized path to the universal in *Camera Lucida* is an opportunity to recognize the political import of his own "personal impulses." A close reading of the text reveals that many of Barthes's most important and influential insights are informed by complicated and sometimes vexing personal-political inclinations. Indeed, Barthes's very conception of photography is laden with anxieties about race and reproduction.[3]

Focusing on Barthes's articulation of the *punctum* (the detail that draws a viewer inexplicably to an image) and the *that-has-been* (the photograph's unique testimonial), this chapter traces manifestations of sexual and racial inquietude in *Camera Lucida*. It explores the tangle of racial and sexual problematics that pervades Barthes's text with the ultimate aim of suggesting how Barthes's most compelling and significant insights might be used without reproducing the racial and sexual impulses that his text sets forth.

In *Camera Lucida*, Barthes identifies two elements that are fundamental to discerning photographic meaning—the *studium* and the *punctum*. The *studium* includes the cultural knowledge that informs one's reading of a photograph and is shaped by "a certain training" (26) that evokes a culturally prescribed reading of a given visual field. The *punctum* is a more personal response to certain details in the photograph that "wound" or pierce an individual viewer—punctuating or breaking through the trained reading of the *studium* (25–27). Barthes claims that "in order to perceive the *punctum*, no analysis would be of any use to me," thereby suggesting that the *punctum* cannot be codified or predicted for any individual viewer. As readers of Barthes's text, however, we can nonetheless assess the examples he uses to describe the *punctum* and note the subtle patterns that inform them. In short, we can analyze Barthes's *punctum* for both personal and cultural schemas.

Barthes argues that the *punctum* "is a kind of subtle *beyond*—as if the image launched desire beyond what it permits us to see" (59). It is consistently the detail—the something in a photograph—that triggers a relay of thoughts and emotions back into his personal history. The *punctum* is the trace that launches Barthes "beyond" the "that has been" of the photograph, beyond the photograph's referential denotation, and into his own experience. It unsettles the fixity of the image, making it available to Barthes's personal narrative.

Barthes explains the workings of the *punctum* through his reaction to a James Van Der Zee photograph, a group portrait made in 1926. Barthes's *studium* description of the image is notably condescending. He states that the photograph "utters respectability, family life, conformism, Sunday best, an effort of social advancement in order to assume the White Man's attributes (an effort touching by reason of its naïveté)" (43). Barthes's explanation of the *studium* is laden with a paternal racism that readers are asked to ignore in pursuit of what really interests Barthes—the *punctum*. He describes the photo's *studium* as if it is self-evident—as if this lovely formal portrait could not be read in any other way, as if all readers would share Barthes's bemused reaction to the image and its subjects. Although Barthes's reading might be attributed to a predictable set of European cultural codes, readers are not asked to "see" racism as part and parcel of the *studium* but instead to see through it to the *studium* meaning that Barthes presumes. In other words, Barthes's text asks readers to view racist paternalism as natural or beside the point rather than as a culturally codified part of the *studium* that can be put under examination.

The foundation from which Barthes moves to a discussion of the *punctum* in the Van Der Zee photograph is thus troubling. And his extended rumination on the *punctum* in relation to this photograph is also curious. Considering the image further, Barthes suggests that what truly interests him in the image—the *punctum,* the details that prick him—are the strapped pumps worn by the woman who stands in the photograph. He notes: "strange to say," "this particular *punctum* arouses great sympathy in me, almost a kind of tenderness" (43). Here the shiny shoes of an unnamed woman provide the *punctum* for Barthes, the inexplicable something that compels him and captures his imagination.

Recalling the Van Der Zee photograph in a later explanation of the *punctum* as latent— as the prick that returns to the viewer only after the image itself is no longer under view, only after it has been transformed into a visual memory—Barthes muses:

Reading Van der Zee's photograph, I thought I had discerned what moved me: the strapped pumps of the black woman in her Sunday best; but this photograph has worked *within me, and later on I realized that the real* punctum *was the necklace she was wearing; for (no doubt) it was this same necklace (a slender ribbon of braided gold) which I had seen worn by someone in my own family, and which, once she died, remained shut up in a family box of old jewelry (this sister of my father never married, lived with her mother as an old maid, and I had always been saddened whenever I thought of her dreary life). I had just realized that however immediate and incisive it was, the* punctum *could accommodate a certain latency (but never any scrutiny). (53)*

Barthes's protestations aside, I would like to place this *punctum* under a bit of scrutiny. In Barthes's memory, the *punctum* of a woman's strapped pumps transmutes into the *punctum* of her necklace—"a slender ribbon of braided gold" that resembles a necklace worn by Barthes's aunt. And yet if one refuses to rely on Barthes's recollection of the Van Der Zee photograph and instead simply looks at it, one finds that both women (not one woman) in this photograph wear necklaces and that they are pearl necklaces, not the ribbons of braided gold that prick Barthes. What, then, is the *punctum?* Barthes says that "it is what I add to the photograph," but it is also *"what is nonetheless already there."* And yet here it would seem that "what is there" in the photograph (the actual detail, which is the pearl necklace) can be obfuscated by what Barthes brings to the photograph (the ribbon of braided gold). Whatever pierces the surface of the photograph may not be visible in the photograph itself.[4] Indeed, the punctum may refer to an entirely subjective signification system.

Barthes's failure to remember the precise attributes of a piece of jewelry is only a slight offense, but it indicates a fundamental interpretive slippage whereby personal connotation can efface representational denotation through the mechanism of the *punctum.* What is disturbing is not the erasure of a pearl necklace for a gold but the effacement of an African American woman under the sign of Barthes's aunt. One is left to wonder whether this erasure, effected by the *punctum,* is in part a result of the *studium,* a racist paternalism that disregards an African American woman's self-representation as trite.

Although Barthes cannot be faulted for remembering his aunt when contemplating the Van Der Zee photograph, neither can other viewers be blamed for being less curious about Barthes's aunt than about the people actually represented in the photograph. They are, in fact—Mattie, Estelle, and David Osterhout—the maternal aunts and uncle of their photographer, James Van Der Zee.[5] Barthes's musings are compelling for those who are interested in Barthes, but they are nevertheless of little use in reading this image in its historical specificity.[6] Indeed, here Barthes sidesteps his most powerful insight into the distinguishing characteristics of photographic signification—the "that-has-been," the undeniable referentiality of the photograph. In Barthes's *punctum* response to the Van Der Zee photograph, he effaces people who have existed for a personal memory (of another person who has been), obscuring the indexicality of the photograph with a memory that might have been evoked by any other sign system. Here the *punctum* seems to evade the photograph itself, enclosing Barthes in a solipsistic reverie. In making himself (and his memories) the measure of photographic meaning, Barthes obfuscates the presence of other historical subjects and, in so doing, disregards his most compelling claims about photography as a unique sign system—the evocative, provoking presence, or present-absence, of those represented on photographic film.[7] The racism registered in his *studium* response seems to enable Barthes to devalue those who have been, subsuming them under himself, under his own personal history, under the inadequate prick of the *punctum*.

THE PHOTOGRAPH, THE MASK, THE SLAVE

Van Der Zee's portrait of his aunts and uncle is not the only image of African Americans that Barthes calls on to define the attributes of photography. His discussion of Richard Avedon's 1963 portrait of William Casby, "born a slave," is also instructive in this regard. In this portrait, Barthes proclaims to see "the essence of slavery" "laid bare" (34) and also to understand photographic meaning as a kind of mask. According to Barthes, the photograph means nothing. It communicates only "that has been" unless it becomes a mask, an abstraction greater than a particular subject, a type divorced from an individual, a culturally translated symbol. In language that he used to describe the photographic sign in his earlier studies, the "message without a code" signifies only to the degree to which it can be abstracted and, in fact, codified. It cannot enter the world of signs proper unless its specificity is transformed. In Barthes's reading, the portrait of William Casby enters the realm of meaning as it comes to signify "slave" and ceases to register a singular face. Barthes collapses William Casby under the sign of slave, seeing in this portrait not a man who must have lived most of his life as an autonomous subject but instead "the essence of slavery laid bare." In Barthes's reading, a subject is transformed into an object; in Frederick Douglass's famous words, "a man is made into a slave." Barthes then uses the objectification of Casby to comment on the nature of photographic meaning: photographs become readable through a similar process of abstraction and categorization. The photograph enters meaning as its specific subject is transformed into a cultural object.

Elsewhere in *Camera Lucida,* this process of objectification troubles Barthes. Indeed, it particularly disturbs him when he thinks about photographic portraits of himself. As Jane Gallop has recently noted, Barthes rarely considers photographs of himself in *Camera Lucida,* choosing instead the role of spectator, of viewer, of the self as a politically autonomous subject who is authorized to look.[8] Musing on the process of being photographed, Barthes suggests that the photograph "represents that very subtle moment when, to tell the truth, I am neither subject nor object but a subject who feels he is becoming an object" (14). Resisting such objectification, Barthes proclaims: "It is my *political* right to be a subject which I must protect" (15).[9] The political right of subjecthood is precisely what is denied to the enslaved individual; he or she is legally recognized not as a subject but as an object.

In Barthes's analysis, the photograph is in some ways equated with the slave; the cultural meaning of both is accorded by the extent to which they function as objects. Thus, Barthes's choice of the William Casby portrait is telling, for it amplifies the objectification that is central to Barthes's experience of the photographic process and to his description of photographic meaning. In Barthes's musings, the slave figures as the objectified individual who most explicitly emblematizes photography's transformation of private subjects into public objects. The slave is the objectified subject par excellence. Through the portrait of William Casby, Barthes transfers the position of the objectified that he resists for himself to enslaved men and women. Maintaining his own political right to be a subject, Barthes collapses William Casby into the category of the photographed that signifies slave.

That-Has-Been

Slavery surfaces again in Barthes's articulation of the photographic sign's most unique characteristic—its indexical testimonial "that-has-been." For Barthes, one of the images that registers most powerfully the very ontology of photography, this "that-has-been," is a photograph that he cut from a magazine as a child and carefully saved—a photograph that "showed a slave market: the slavemaster, in a hat, standing; the slaves, in loincloths, sitting." The image provoked the child Barthes's "horror and fascination," for as a photograph it proclaimed with "*certainty* that such a thing had existed" (80).

According to Barthes, the photographic sign, unlike the linguistic sign, first exists as both a temporal fact and a tactile fact: the photograph records light rays reflected off an object, impressing themselves onto photographic film in a fraction of a second. As Barthes puts it, "The photograph is literally an *emanation* of the referent" (80). Although the photograph may not be able to tell us much more about the subject that it makes visible without textual interpretation, it undeniably testifies "that has been." Through the magic of light and chemistry, "that" (as it existed for a fraction of a second) impressed itself on film. This incontrovertible presence is what fascinated and horrified Barthes about the slave market photograph: the photograph gave evidence of slavery, proving its existence with certainty—as Barthes says, "without mediation" (80). To the child Barthes, the photograph made slavery uniquely present and even palpable; it impressed the fact of slavery into the time and space of Barthes's consciousness.

Following his brief discussion of the slave market photograph, Barthes notes a secondary effect of the photograph's power to proclaim "that-has-been"—the sense that the viewer is literally touched by the subject photographed: "From a real body, which was there, proceed radiations which ultimately touch me, who am here. . . . A sort of umbilical cord links the body of the photographed thing to my gaze: light, though impalpable, is here a carnal medium, a skin I share with anyone who has been photographed" (80–81). The light that touches the surface of the subject photographed, captured on film, also touches the viewer, rebounding (in Barthes's imagination) from subject to photograph to viewer. Perhaps this underscores what is shocking for Barthes about the slave market photograph. The photograph testifies to the existence of slavery and also *touches* Barthes. In his imagination, Barthes shares a skin with the enslaved men and women. In this provocative shared corporeality, Barthes's own position as a free, white, self-possessed European viewer is unsettled, for his "shared skin" metonymically links him with slavery, blackness, and objectification under a white gaze. He achieves for a moment, perhaps, a recognition of what Franz Fanon has called the racial epidermal schema of colonial and postcolonial Europe, the sense of having one's subjectivity subsumed under the sign of one's skin.[10] The "shared skin" that links Barthes to enslaved people must unsettle his own sense of (political) self-possession, reminding him of what he refuses—his own potential to be objectified. But even as the slave market photograph instills anxiety, it also enables him, once again, to pass off the position of the objectified onto others.

By nature of its literal absence in the text, the slave market photograph occupies a position that is intriguingly parallel to *Camera Lucida*'s most famous image, the Winter Garden Photograph of Barthes's mother as a child. This latter photograph sets the second half of Barthes's meditations in motion (73). Mourning his mother's death, Barthes seeks and finds a photograph that captures her essential self and in so doing also captures the intrinsic nature of photography, the medium's unique capacity to make the absent present. In the Winter Garden Photograph, Barthes finds his mother's essence captured in the photograph's "that-has-been." In this image, the mask of photographic meaning suddenly vanishes, and Barthes is left in the presence of his mother's soul (109). In this photograph the "that-has-been" overwhelms the cultural meaning of the image. The portrait is not confined to or delimited by likeness; it offers truth and identity. As Barthes declares: "The Winter Garden Photograph was indeed essential, it achieved for me, utopically, the *impossible science of the unique being*" (71). If the portrait of William Casby exemplifies the mask of photographic meaning whereby a unique individual is translated into a cultural sign, the Winter Garden Photograph secures precisely the opposite; it removes the mask to reveal the unique individual. The Winter Garden Photograph becomes for Barthes a "treasury of rays" that "emanated" from his mother, "from her hair, her skin, her dress, her gaze, *on that day*" (82). An image deeply personal and important to Barthes, it is one he refuses to reproduce for later viewers. Thus, the essential images, those that make the "that-has-been" most powerfully apparent, are the images that ultimately remain absent from Barthes's text—the slave market photograph and the Winter Garden Photograph.

Barthes's refusal or inability to reproduce examples of his most powerful evidence is curious in such a heavily illustrated text. One can easily understand his reluctance to share the Winter Garden Photograph because it is profoundly important to him but might prove, for other viewers "nothing but an indifferent picture, one of the thousand manifestations of the 'ordinary'" (73).[11] And yet Barthes's decision not to reproduce this image also leaves his readers, once again, only with Barthes's rendition. The photographic evidence is obscured and indeed replaced by his reading. There is no chance for the represented to stand and meet the gaze of others, and there is no opportunity for another viewer to be authorized. Denied one's own response to the image, ultimately the reader can respond only to Barthes himself. This accords with Barthes's preferences, for one of the things he claims to have admired about his mother is that he had never known her to make "a single 'observation'" (69). In Barthes's account, she never looked and considered and critiqued.[12] She never performed the intellectual work that was Barthes's entire purpose. She was there to be observed only and, in the case of the Winter Garden Photograph, to be observed only by Barthes.

An Umbilical Cord of Light

As discussed above, Barthes explains the impact of the photograph's "that-has-been," its "intractable reality" (119), through the metaphor of a "shared skin" that links viewer and viewed (81). This "shared skin" is a provocative image, especially if one imagines Barthes gazing at the slave market photograph that so intrigued and astonished him as a child. Even more provocative, perhaps, is the kind of skin that Barthes imagines links him as viewer to the photographed subject. In Barthes's articulation, "light" becomes not simply a "carnal medium" but an "umbilical cord" (81), joining viewer and viewed in a surprisingly filial—in fact, maternal—relation.

If the photograph is the conduit for the umbilical cord of light, exactly who stands in the place of the mother in this relationship—the viewer or the viewed? Once again, Barthes's discussion of the Winter Garden Photograph is instructive here. In this image, Barthes sees his "mother-as-child" (71) and recognizes how childlike she became in her last days. Musing on the end of her life, Barthes suggests, "She had become my little girl, uniting for me with that essential child she was in her first photograph" (72). As Barthes's mother becomes his little girl, Barthes enters, briefly, the procreative model of generation, of reproduction; he becomes a kind of parent. He declares, "I who had not procreated, I had, in her very illness, engendered my mother" (72). Barthes, the gay male intellectual without children, is linked through his mother, by becoming his mother's mother, to what he deems the universal; he transcends himself, his particularity, his death, by momentarily creating a child (his ailing mother). And yet because this child, his elderly mother, will not live past his own inevitable death, Barthes's parenting provides only a taste of the "Life Force" through which—according to "so many philosophers," so many heteronormative philosophers—the individual transcends death through his or her procreative role in the reproduction of "the race, the species" (72).

Barthes proclaims that after his mother's death his vision of himself as gay male progenitor also dies. After the death of the mother-as-child, Barthes declares that he can no longer do anything but wait for his "total, undialectical death" (72).[13] And yet Barthes also supposes that his procreative capacity might be reinvisioned in a utopian sense whereby he might transcend finality through writing: he might live beyond himself through the texts that he generates. In this sense, writing provides an escape from the body that dies or fails or refuses to procreate. Writing enables the proliferation and expansion of the self beyond the awkward limitation and finality of the body.

As Barthes argues in his autobiography, *Roland Barthes by Roland Barthes,* writing also liberates the self from the limitations of its "narrative continuity," from its autobiography, from its place in the "'family romance.'"[14] For Barthes, that discreet, continuous self, the self that must be liberated from its singularity and confinement, is construed and anchored by "imagery," by an "image-repertoire"—by family photographs.[15] One's visual insertion into the family line connects and confines one to a genealogy. However, writing—marking, for Barthes, the beginning of "productive life"—can surpass the image repertoire.[16] Here, then, photographs represent the domain of the discreet, autobiographical, ultimately unproductive self, while writing represents the domain of the self that is liberated from its private definitions and made productive. The photograph adheres one to a body; the written text only to an abstract signifier. In Barthes's autobiography, as in *Camera Lucida*, the photograph, like the body it represents, ultimately signifies death. Writing, on the other hand, relying on the abstract linguistic signifier, can liberate one's meaning from the body and thereby signify beyond life and death.

Following Barthes's ruminations on photography in his autobiography, one might also associate the photograph, as Victor Burgin has, with a kind of expanded semiotic sphere (in Julia Kristeva's sense), an extended presymbolic stage in which the body, its sensations, and the mother's body dominate self-perception.[17] For Barthes, the image repertoire and the biography that it anchors ends with one's youth, ends as one enters the public social sphere through the production of writing. The semiotic, associated with the image (and the mother), ends with mastery of the symbolic.

The images that introduce Barthes's autobiography reinforce such a psychoanalytic reading. A photograph of the infant Barthes held by his mother, both of them looking out at the camera, is playfully entitled "The mirror stage: 'That's you.'"[18] Clearly referencing Lacan's mirror stage, in which the infant comes to recognize himself in and as an image, Barthes's photograph anchors early self-perception in the image and in the arms of the mother. Another, later photograph, "The demand for love," replicates "The mirror stage" image, with the child Barthes held in his mother's arms, and both again looking out at the camera.[19] The repetition of the pose is strained, however, by the size of the boy Barthes, who is no longer able to fit easily in his mother's arms. In D. A. Miller's wonderful reading of this image, the photograph announces what he calls "a certain gay male body." According to Miller, "His ungainly lower limbs betray the boy. . . . They are too long for short pants, and too long to justify what the boy nonetheless evidently persists in wanting: to be carried by his mother."[20] Refusing the mythos of the (presumably straight) male body's autonomy in his display of the "mothered body," "every image of Barthes, whether fully grown or all alone," according to Miller, "materially reinscribes his mother in the characteristically dejected posture of his body, always ducking and drooping, as though always wanting, but never any longer able, to drop into her arms."[21] In *Camera Lucida*, two things are certain—a temporal fact (the "that-has-been" of the photograph) and a spatial fact (as "Freud says of the maternal body," "that 'there is no other place of which one can say with so much certainty that one has already been there'") (40).

Those things that must be superseded by writing to liberate the productive self in Barthes's autobiography—the image repertoire and the mother's body—become the source of a procreative impulse and power in *Camera Lucida*. Indeed, in Barthes's final text, a powerfully procreative image emerges in his thoughts on photography. As light becomes an umbilical cord that links the photographed to Barthes himself, a vision of the gay male progenitor reemerges. Photography becomes a doubly reproductive medium: as light becomes a carnal medium, mechanical reproduction serves as a kind of surrogate for sexual reproduction.

In an inventive alteration of what one might traditionally think of as photography's creative function, Barthes does not place the photographer in the position of progenitor but instead evokes the viewer—the spectator, Barthes himself—as the origin point for reproduction. In a stunning statement, Barthes declares: "I am the reference of every photograph" (84). If every photograph refers to Barthes and if he becomes the subject of every photograph, then the images also reproduce him. They become his reproductions, his generative offspring. Suddenly the "that-has-been"—the intractable certainty of a temporal real, of the momentary presence-in-absence of the thing photographed—is subsumed under the sign of the viewer, referring to that viewer, representing and reproducing him. Through this articulation, Barthes becomes, in his own imagination, the mother of all photographs. What is one to make of this?

Returning, as Barthes himself often does, to the Van Der Zee portrait, it is illuminating to reconsider the *punctum* in light of these thoughts on reproduction. Revisiting Barthes's ruminations on this photograph, one finds that only one woman, Estelle Osterhout (the woman who stands), and the details of her attire trigger the *punctum* for Barthes. Her low belt, her strapped pumps, and finally her pearl necklace spark Barthes's mournful response to the photograph. He describes this woman as "the 'solacing Mammy'" (43), and once again, his *punctum* response is informed by a specific *studium* training. The African American woman becomes "Mammy" only through the lens of a racialized and gendered class system. Subsuming the woman of color under the white fantasy of the "Mammy," Barthes symbolically harnesses her procreative energies to raising a white brood, effacing her own potentially reproductive role as mother.[22]

The necklace that Osterhout wears recalls for Barthes the "slender ribbon of braided gold" that belonged to his aunt. Van Der Zee's aunt reminds Barthes of his own aunt, whom he describes, once again, as follows: "This sister of my father never married, lived with her mother as an old maid, and I had always been saddened whenever I thought of her dreary life" (53). (Estelle Osterhout never married either.[23]) Deeming his aunt an "old maid," Barthes seems to denigrate her for failing in her procreative role. And yet this aunt's "dreary life" closely mirrors Barthes's own. Barthes himself "never married" and lived his entire adult life with his mother.[24] Indeed, Barthes's pity for his aunt may mask an anxiety about his own family position. In a brief discussion of the photograph's capacity to capture a "genetic feature," Barthes declares: "In a certain photograph, I have my father's sister's 'look'" (103).[25]

Ultimately, the *punctum* in Van Der Zee's photograph is activated by Barthes's nervous identification with his own aunt. Through a signifying slippage, Van Der Zee's aunt recalls Barthes's aunt, who finally recalls Barthes himself. What Barthes sees in this image of a woman who stands behind and to the side of her relatives, slightly in the shadows, is an image of his own aunt and ultimately of himself—an image of the one who stands to the side of the family narrative. Barthes is never really the mother of all photographs but always the aunt.[26]

Barthes's anxieties about race and reproduction thus merge in his response to the Van Der Zee photograph. They also intersect elsewhere in his text, notably in his references to Francis Galton, the nineteenth-century founder of eugenics. Galton defined eugenics both as a science of race and a program of controlled breeding, and he used photographs to construct the physical signs of familial lineage and race.[27] In Barthes's discussion of family photographs, he evokes the eugenicist idea of biological inheritance in his discussion of "the stock" made manifest in the faces of family members caught on film (103–105). Here he bemoans his resemblance to his aunt (103). The family likeness that links Barthes to his aunt also evokes their similar role in refusing to reproduce. They carry but will not continue the reproduction of "the stock." Photographs of their faces may testify to eugenicist thinking, but they will not fulfill eugenicist goals.

Barthes refers to Galton in the final pages of his text, celebrating the eugenicist's attempt to read the signs of madness in photographed faces (113). Remarkably, this madness conjured by Galton, one of the thinkers most closely associated with race and reproduction, might release Barthes from the limitations of his own racial and sexual problematics. Deeming Galton's photographic experiments a failure (113), Barthes nevertheless discovers in those mugshots, those frontal stares, a different kind of madness. Barthes declares that the photograph "bears the effigy to that crazy point where affect (love, compassion, grief, enthusiasm, desire) is a guarantee of Being. It then approaches, to all intents, madness" (113).

Ultimately, then, the photograph insists on its referent. However much the *punctum* may launch one beyond the photograph's subject, that subject's temporal presence cannot be denied. Perceiving that presence engulfs the viewer in a kind of madness, for the "effigy" (the person photographed) must live, the representation must be real, the absent must be present: "The Photograph then becomes a bizarre *medium*, a new form of hallucination" (115). The photograph transports the photographed into the time and space of the viewer. To recognize this is to go mad, for ghostly traces become real and present; they touch and haunt the viewer. It is finally this disruptive madness that Barthes champions.[28] This madness releases him from the solipsism effected, in part, by the racism registered in the *studium*. Choosing to recognize the radical presence of photographed subjects, Barthes can no longer subsume them under the sign of himself.

In the end, even Estelle Osterhout, the subject elided most extensively in Barthes's meditations on photography, is asserted in her photograph. Finally, Barthes must bear witness to her. Trying to understand the link between "Photography, madness" and love (116), Barthes returns, once again, to the Van Der Zee photograph:

In the love stirred by Photography (by certain photographs), another music is heard, its name oddly old-fashioned: Pity. I collected in a last thought the images which had "pricked" me (since this is the action of the punctum*), like that of the black woman with the gold necklace and the strapped pumps. In each of them, inescapably, I passed beyond the unreality of the thing represented, I entered crazily into the spectacle, into the image, taking into my arms what is dead, what is going to die . . . gone mad for Pity's sake. (117)*

Here Barthes offers a different model of the possible relationship between viewer and viewed. Entering into a photograph, one might embrace its subject, allowing one's self to be touched without demanding reference or representation. One might identify without subsuming or consuming the other. In other words, the presence of the present-absent might be maintained in the face of one's own response. The that-has-been might be allowed to coexist with the *punctum*.

This model of photographic engagement acknowledges the that-has-been much more powerfully than mere *studium* recognition. It maintains the urgency and intensity of response accorded by the *punctum* without allowing the viewer's own stories to overwhelm the subject who is photographed. Such a method of photographic inquiry depends on the labor of the viewer.[29] Such mad recognition requires a viewer who is willing to enter the spectacle of the photograph and embrace its subject. It requires the effort of a devoted son, perhaps, or an obsessive scholar. This is the viewer that Barthes finally commits himself to being, and this is the viewer that Barthes cannot be certain his own images will secure.

In ending, I would like to look at Barthes—to look at this Barthes who has persistently placed himself in his text, representing and reproducing himself, symbolically grasping at what he calls the life force. Once again, his search for his mother's trace, recorded in a photograph, compels Barthes's thoughts on that life force. Looking through photographs to find the truth of the person he loved, Barthes must also wonder who will perform this tender act of mourning for him. Will his own photographs, like his aunt's necklace, remain "shut up in a family box" (53), neglected by more distant relations? Will they become the abandoned and discarded images that David Deitcher describes in his search for a gay archive? Reflecting on one such image, Deitcher states: "The knowledge that no children of my own will survive to remember me contributes to [my] morbid predisposition; as does the suspicion that among my eight nieces and nephews, some will forget me too."[30]

If the writing life frees one from the family narrative, so does a refusal to reproduce. But the latter "liberation" from the family romance is filled with anxiety for Barthes because it is also a return to the finitude to which that family narrative, supported by his childhood photographs, seemed to confine him. To this point, Barthes has lived on through his writings, and his present-absence remains profound. But existential mournfulness and anxiety pervade *Camera Lucida,* his last text. After the death of his mother, Barthes cannot be certain that his demands for love will be met. Standing to the side of the family narrative, Barthes finds himself faced with what he calls, once again, "total, undialectical death" (72). No heir will reproduce him; no child will mourn his death and cherish his photograph.

Barthes's personal exploration of photographs demands, in part, a personal response— one I now undertake with some trepidation. I find that I can meet Barthes part way by choosing a path of "sympathy" to his madness. Using the *punctum* as pathway to the that-has-been, I will try to meet Barthes as living effigy. As one aunt, I will consider another and agree to imagine, at least, that I see Barthes in one of the images he has left behind. I am drawn to a photograph of the adult Barthes preparing himself to tackle the blank slate of his writing tablet.[31] It is an unusual photograph, perhaps taken on vacation. The typically dark-clad Barthes, usually pictured in enclosed wooden offices, here sits perched on a plush white rug in a bright airy room, dressed entirely in summer whites. It is an image of the adult Barthes who has liberated himself from the family romance through the symbolic practice of writing. But it is also an image in which his short pants recall that earlier photograph of his "demand for love," of his demand to be central in the family narrative. I gaze at him from behind and to the side and wonder which close admirer might have taken this photograph. I marvel at my access to this intimate scene. Entering into the image of Barthes, embracing what is dead, this is the photograph I promise to keep. This is the one I will rescue from the advance of a life force that forgets and obscures those who do not biologically reproduce. This is the image I will save from Barthes's own self-referential practice. Finally, then, as one aunt reflecting on another, I find I can both be mad and also go mad, for sympathy's sake.

NOTES

1. Roland Barthes, *Camera Lucida: Reflections on Photography* (1980), trans. Richard Howard (New York: Hill and Wang, 1981), 9 (subsequent citations in parentheses in the text).

2. I am thinking especially of the following work: Jane Gallop, *Living with His Camera*, photographs by Dick Blau (Durham, NC: Duke University Press, 2003); Marianne Hirsch, *Family Frames: Photography, Narrative, and Postmemory* (Cambridge, MA: Harvard University Press, 1997), and Marianne Hirsch, ed., *The Familial Gaze* (Hanover, NH: University of New England, 1999); bell hooks, "In Our Glory: Photography and Black Life," in Deborah Willis, ed., *Picturing Us: African American Identity in Photography* (New York: New Press, 1994), 43–53; Annette Kuhn, *Family Secrets: Acts of Memory and Imagination*, 2nd ed. (New York: Verso, 1995, 2002); Sandra Matthews and Laura Wexler, *Pregnant Pictures* (New York: Routledge, 2000); Carol Mavor, *Becoming: The Photographs of Clementina, Viscountess Hawarden* (Durham, NC: Duke University Press, 1999); Jo Spence, *Putting Myself in the Picture: A Political Personal and Photographic Autobiography* (Seattle, WA: Real Comet Press, 1988); Deborah Willis, *Family, History, Memory* (Irvington, NY: Hylas, 2005).

3. I agree with Fred Moten that "blackness and maternity play huge roles in the analytic of photography Roland Barthes lays down in *Camera Lucida*," but I take a different critical path through Barthes's text. Fred Moten, *In the Break: The Aesthetics of the Black Radical Tradition* (Minneapolis: University of Minnesota Press, 2003), 202.

4. Margaret Olin makes a similar observation in her wonderful essay (reproduced as chapter 5 in this volume), "Touching Photographs: Roland Barthes's 'Mistaken' Identification," *Representations* 80 (Fall 2002): 99–118, 104–107.

5. David C. Hart provides this biographical information in his master's thesis, "Differing Views: Roland Barthes, Race and James VanDerZee's *Family Portrait*," University of North Carolina, Chapel Hill, August 1996, 1, 11. For further information about Van Der Zee, see also Deborah Willis-Braithwaite, with biographical essay by Rodger C. Birt, *VanDerZee, Photographer: 1886–1983* (New York: Harry N. Abrams, in association with The National Portrait Gallery, Smithsonian Institution, 1993).

6. I agree with Richard Powell's assessment of the limitations of Barthes's analysis of the Van Der Zee photograph. Richard J. Powell, "Linguists, Poets, and 'Others' on African American Art," *American Art* (Spring 2003): 16–19, 17.

7. As Fred Moten has argued, in *Camera Lucida* "historical particularity . . . becomes egocentric particularity." Moten, *In the Break,* 208.

8. Gallop, *Living with His Camera*, 19.

9. Maren Stange reminded me of the political nature of Barthes's resistance to objectification in a lecture she gave in the 2003–04 American Visual Culture Speaker Series at the Contemporary Art Museum in St. Louis, Missouri. Maren Stange, "Documenting the Private," American Visual Culture Speaker Series, St. Louis, Missouri, April 1, 2004.

10. Frantz Fanon, *Black Skin, White Masks: The Experiences of a Black Man in a White World* (1952), trans. Charles Lam Markmann (New York: Grove, 1967), 112.

11. I also agree with Diana Knight that the Winter Garden Photograph may actually be the image reproduced later in *Camera Lucida* as "The Stock," for in this image of the mother as child, "her pose, her expression, and the position of her hands exactly match Barthes's description of the Winter Garden Photograph." Diana Knight, "Roland Barthes, or The Woman without a Shadow," in Jean-Michel Rabaté, ed., *Writing the Image after Roland Barthes* (Philadelphia: University of Pennsylvania Press, 1997), 132–143, 138.

12. As Jane Gallop states, "The mother in that book [*Camera Lucida*] is defined precisely as never doing what the author does—observe and comment." "He observes; she does not; she is observed." Gallop, *Living with His Camera*, 26.

13. As Diana Knight has argued, "The idea that Barthes himself has reproduced neither the family line nor the human species is omnipresent in the second half of the book," and "this is obviously linked to the death of his mother and a new awareness of his own mortality." Knight, "Roland Barthes, or The Woman without a Shadow," 133.

14. Roland Barthes, *Roland Barthes by Roland Barthes* (1975), trans. Richard Howard (New York: Hill and Wang, 1977), 4, 3.

15. Ibid., 3, 4.

16. Ibid., 4.

17. Victor Burgin, "Re-reading *Camera Lucida*," *The End of Art Theory: Criticism and Postmodernity* (New York: Macmillan, 1986), 84–85.

18. Barthes, *Roland Barthes by Roland Barthes,* 21.

19. Ibid., 5.

20. D. A. Miller, *Bringing Out Roland Barthes* (Berkeley: University of California Press, 1992), 32.

21. Ibid., 33. In Miller's reading, Barthes is defined by his demand for his mother. In her own work with Barthes's, Carol Mavor takes an interesting theoretical turn, choosing for herself the position of the mother whose "desire is to be demanded." Carol Mavor, *Pleasures Taken: Performances of Sexuality and Loss in Victorian Photographs* (Durham, NC: Duke University Press, 1995), 124. Jane Gallop also writes about Barthes's *Camera Lucida* from the position of the mother, but while Mavor chooses the writing mother, Gallop chooses the photographed mother. See especially Jane Gallop, "Observations of a Photographed Mother," *Living with His Camera*, 19–54.

22. See also David C. Hart's reading of this image in "Differing Views," 31–36, 45.

23. According to Hart, none of the Osterhout sisters ever married. Hart, "Differing Views," 15.

24. Olin, "Touching Photographs," 112.

25. Barthes reproduces a photograph of his aunt in *Roland Barthes by Roland Barthes*, giving it the caption: "The father's sister: she was alone all her life" (14).

26. Diana Knight has similarly argued: "Of all Barthes's delvings into the past generations of both sides of his family, I am struck by the sympathetic identification with his aunt. If Barthes perceives his lineage as 'a disturbing entity' of which he represents the end point (*CL*, 98), his aunt, too, has contributed to the collapse of the paternal line." Knight, "Roland Barthes, or The Woman without a Shadow," 140.

27. Francis Galton, *Hereditary Genius: An Inquiry into Its Laws and Consequences* (London: Macmillan, 1892); Galton, *Inquiries into Human Faculty and Its Development*, 2nd ed. (London: Dent, 1907); Galton, *The Life History Album* (London: Macmillan, 1884).

28. John Tagg also discusses "Barthes's final ecstatic embrace of the evidential power of the photograph" (299). John Tagg, "The Pencil of History," in Patrice Petro, ed., *Fugitive Images: From Photography to Video* (Bloomington: Indiana University Press, 1995), 285–303, especially 298–299.

29. Taking a different path through Barthes's work, Victor Burgin similarly concludes that *Camera Lucida*'s "significance for theory is the emphasis thus placed on the active participation of the viewer in producing the meaning/affect of the photograph." Burgin, "Re-reading *Camera Lucida*," 88.

30. David Deitcher, "Looking at a Photograph, Looking for a History," in Deborah Bright, ed., *The Passionate Camera: Photography and Bodies of Desire* (London: Routledge, 1998), 22–36, 33. See also David Deitcher, *Dear Friends: American Photographs of Men Together, 1840–1918* (New York: Abrams, 2001), especially 13–25.

31. The photograph is reproduced in *Roland Barthes by Roland Barthes* on page 39 as the final image in a short series of photographs of Barthes at his desk on pages 37 and 39.

CAMERA LUCIDA

ANOTHER LITTLE HISTORY OF PHOTOGRAPHY

GEOFFREY BATCHEN

Those of us interested in providing an appropriate historical framework for photography are faced with a veritable mountain of methodological problems. Photography implodes reality and representation, time and space, leading Roland Barthes to describe it as "an anthropological revolution in man's history"—a "truly unprecedented" type of consciousness.[1] Writing a history for such an entity is a crucial task. But photography's peculiarities— its faithful replication of what it sees; its simultaneous articulation of past, present, and future; its capacity for endless reproduction and shifting of shape; the infinite number of its products—represent a seemingly insoluble historiographic challenge.

After all, how do you write a history of a "consciousness"? How do you write a history for something that escapes easy definition, has no discernible boundaries, and operates on the principle of reflection? (How, for example, do you separate a photograph from what it's of or from the unfolding context of its reception?) How do you invent a voice (or voices) for this history that can speak to photography's emotional effects as well as its physical and formal characteristics and economic and political ramifications? How can you speak of and from a local position and yet encompass photography's global reach? The problem is to transform the way that the history of photography is represented so that this history can, for the first time, engage with photography in all of its many aspects and manifestations. One place that we might look for a model of how to go about conceiving such a history is Barthes's own little history of photography—his last book, *Camera Lucida*.[2]

Some have said that *Camera Lucida* was the worst thing that ever happened to photographic discourse because the book appears to abandon Barthes's earlier commitment to the political analysis of images in favor of a textual hedonism. And it's certainly true that *Camera Lucida*—with its stated dissatisfaction with sociology, semiology, and psychoanalysis as systems of analysis; its epicurean, autobiographical tone; and its interest in formulating "the fundamental feature, the universal without which there would be no photography" (*CL* 9)—seems in every respect to be the antithesis of this same author's work from the 1950s and 1960s. Having seemingly abandoned both the science of semiotics and the politics of Marxism, the Barthes of *Camera Lucida* instead ruminates on the nature of the photographic medium, seeking, as he says on his first page, "to learn at all costs what Photography was 'in itself,' by what essential feature it was to be distinguished from the community of images" (*CL* 3). He pursues this "ontological desire," as he calls it, by way of his own personal responses to various photographs (perversely, the most important of these—a portrait of his recently deceased mother as a child—is never reproduced). All this seems very different from the trenchant ideological analysis that motivated the essays in Barthes's *Mythologies*.[3] Despite this apparent divergence of aims, there is a sustained politics at work in *Camera Lucida,* and this politics is found in the way that Barthes deals with history. I propose, therefore, that *Camera Lucida* is best read not as a book of critical theory but as a history of photography.

Most discussions of *Camera Lucida* tend to focus on the problem of distinguishing *studium* from *punctum,* the intricacies of Barthes's rhetorical flourishes and learned asides, and the allure of the book's subtheme—death (photography's, his mother's, and his own). *Camera Lucida* doesn't look or read like our standard histories, which has, I suspect, distracted attention from the broader structure of the book and from its carefully calibrated survey of photography's history.

Camera Lucida has two parts, each divided into twenty-four sections, so that one half of the book is a mirror image of the other. Such a structure is not unprecedented in the history of small histories of photography. As Sabine Gölz has pointed out, Walter Benjamin's 1931 essay, "Little History of Photography," employs the same kind of division. In a comparison of the final printed version with an earlier manuscript, Gölz argues that Benjamin even swapped paragraphs around to ensure that his key definition of *aura* remained at the exact halfway point in the text, becoming the fulcrum around which turns his argument about the political potential of photography. Gölz also describes how Benjamin's dense montage of references and strategic metaphors of light and shadow set out to textually "photograph," or assimilate, both reader and author, as if we are looking into the reflective surface of a daguerreotype and seeing ourselves staring back.[4]

Like Barthes, Benjamin illustrates his history with relatively banal photographs.[5] But these pictures nevertheless induce a number of poetic readings from him, as if Benjamin is seeking to explain the *punctum*-like effect of his own subjective response to certain photographs. He speaks, for example, of the "unruly desire" evoked in him by Hill and Adamson's photograph of a Newhaven fishwife and, even more powerfully, of "an irresistible urge" to search a picture of Dauthendey and his fiancée for signs of her future suicide. He looks, he says, for "the tiny spark of contingency, of the Here and Now, with which reality has so to speak seared the subject, to find the inconspicuous spot where, in the immediacy of that long-forgotten moment, the future subsists so eloquently that we, looking back, may rediscover it."[6] This dizzying temporal convolution is again reminiscent of Barthes's description of his own photographic experiences in *Camera Lucida.*

Other correspondences between these two little histories are more subtle. Carolin Duttlinger, for example, has noted that Benjamin misidentifies (she says deliberately) the woman with Dauthendey in the photograph that has inspired his temporal rhapsodies. For this woman is Dauthendey's second wife, not his first wife, the one who had six children and later went on to commit suicide. Benjamin drew the details from a biographical account written by Dauthendey's son but apparently chooses, in the interests of positing a photographically induced delirium, not to remember exactly what he read there. The photograph therefore ends up inducing an emotive response to something other than itself.[7]

Barthes too is guilty of a strategically faulty memory. As Margaret Olin and others have recognized, Barthes thinks back to a photograph reproduced earlier in his book and realizes that "the real *punctum* was the necklace she was wearing . . . a slender ribbon of braided gold" (*CL* 53). However, if we look back ourselves, we see that both women in the Van Der Zee photograph are actually wearing pearl necklaces. The gold necklace he remembers is worn instead by Barthes's aunt in a family photograph reproduced in *Roland Barthes by Roland Barthes.* Olin links this slippage from one photograph to another to a more disturbing possibility—that the famous Winter Garden Photograph of Barthes's mother never actually existed.[8] Could Barthes have intended it to function only as a fictional archetype, the *ur*-photograph? If so, it's a clever rhetorical strategy. Whether real or imaginary, its place in his book is a space into which readers project their own *punctum* and enact their own primal relationship to a lost loved one. In both cases, both Barthes and Benjamin seem to be willing to cross the line into fiction when it suits their purposes; that is, they lie when it allows them to describe a greater truth.[9] Despite these various similarities, Barthes notoriously fails to reference Benjamin's work in his bibliography or marginal notes (both of which are unfortunately deleted from the English edition).[10]

The structural duality of *Camera Lucida*, however, obediently reflects Barthes's enduring interest in the complexities of binary thinking. "For a certain time," Barthes writes in *Roland Barthes by Roland Barthes*, "he went into raptures over binarism; binarism became for him a kind of erotic object."[11] We see the evidence of this in Barthes's frequent coupling of binary terms as a means of description and especially in his descriptions of the functioning of photographs: denotation/connotation and *studium/punctum* are the most obvious examples.[12] It is not surprising, therefore, to find Barthes manifesting this same binarism as the very infrastructure of *Camera Lucida*. But what has to be decided is the function of this structure and the significance of its duality.

There are twenty-four black-and-white photographs illustrated in *Camera Lucida* and one color reproduction of a Polaroid image by French photographer Daniel Boudinet. It's interesting to consider this selection of pictures free from the framing text that informs their meanings in the book. The illustrations appear at regular, if unpredictable, intervals and come to us in no particular chronological order. Ten of them are from the nineteenth century, with the earliest (which Barthes mistakenly captions as "The first photograph") dated to 1823. The latest, including Boudinet's work, were taken in 1979, the year in which the book was written. So while claiming to make only himself "the measure of photographic 'knowledge'" (*CL* 9), Barthes nevertheless manages to offer his readers a full survey of photography, including examples from the 1820s, the 1850s, the 1860s, the 1880s, the 1890s, 1900, the 1920s, the 1930s, the 1950s, the 1960s, and the 1970s—not a bad coverage for a selection that pretends to be arbitrary and entirely personal.

Certain photographers and thus certain kinds of photography are privileged within this selection—four pictures by Kertész and two each by Nadar, Koen Wessing, Richard Avedon, Robert Mapplethorpe, and William Klein. There are also two pictures by unknown photographers. Some have complained about Barthes's bad taste and about the bourgeois mediocrity of his choices. As it happens, Barthes has a bit to say about the role of taste in his book, claiming to be able to transform his own individual preferences into a "science of the subject," into a "generality" (*CL* 18). The continued popularity of the book, despite the banality of his picture selection, lends some credence to this claim. Certainly, by making himself such a central rhetorical element of his account of photography, Barthes makes us self-consciously aware of his authorial role, both as writer and curator.

This is unusual in history books, which usually prefer to adopt a tone of distanced objectivity, as if history thereby magically gets to speak itself. This is not so in *Camera Lucida*, which opens with a first-person account of the author's "amazement" at the contiguous relationship that photography enjoys with the past and is inflected with Barthes's voice throughout. We are always aware of him as the producer of the text we read and of his historical account as an entirely subjective, and therefore biased and contestable, one.

Barthes also emphasizes his own amateurism. He speaks, he tells us, not as a photographer but from the point of view of the spectator, as an everyman. His choice of pictures seems equally amateur, very much in keeping with his own taste and interests (accordingly, his bibliography includes a 1976 issue of *Rolling Stone* as well as books by Lacan and Proust). Late in the book, however, he claims a special privilege for this taste—the taste of the amateur—at least as far as photographic practice is concerned: "it is the amateur . . . who is the assumption of the professional: for it is he who stands closer to the *noeme* of Photography" (*CL* 99). The implication of *Camera Lucida* is that the amateur historian is similarly privileged and is able to offer insights into photography beyond the capacity of the blinkered professional.[13]

Looking at the images that Barthes chooses as illustrations, there's no doubt that he prefers to talk about photojournalism and portraiture—that is, about public forms of photography—rather than about other, more visually innovative genres. These are, for the most part, familiar sorts of pictures—the kind you might see in your daily newspaper or might encounter through a casual perusal of certain popular photography books (he takes many of them from the same 1977 special issue of *Nouvel Observateur* where he would have also read a French translation of Benjamin's "Little History"). But his choices are still politically inflected in a number of interesting ways.

One portrait by Richard Avedon, for example, is, Barthes tells us, of a man who was born a slave, while another features an African American labor leader who has just died: "I read an air of goodness," Barthes says, "no impulse of power: that is certain" (*CL* 110). Another group portrait just happens to be by a relatively neglected African American photographer, James Van Der Zee, which Barthes relates to struggles for racial justice. Other pictures show a political leader (Queen Victoria) and a political assassin (Lewis Payne). We also get two scenes of the civil war in Nicaragua in 1979. None of these is an innocent choice. Nor are Barthes's occasional references to his own homoerotic desires: "the photograph is handsome, as is the boy" (*CL* 96). Once again, the presence of the personal and the narrowness of the choices signal to the reader that this selection is not—cannot be—comprehensive and makes no claims to be so. This distinguishes Barthes's approach from that taken by most other historians, who present their selection as *The*, rather than *A*, history of photography.[14]

His idiosyncratic selection of photographs suggests that the photographs are not as important as the way they are analyzed. History, for Barthes, is a mode of reading, not a procession of self-evident masterworks. The implication is that these pictorial selections could be changed over and over again and that if we could each develop the capacity for critical reading, all of us could curate our own history of photography. *Camera Lucida* demonstrates, in other words, that same shifting in power from author to reader that Barthes had advocated in 1967 in his essay "The Death of the Author."[15]

Most striking about his selection, however, is his total disinterest in avant-garde practice (note the absence, for example, of anything overtly coded as art), and this, I suspect, is taken by some critics to be his real offense. The assumption behind such a criticism is that avant-garde practice is, by definition, political practice. The function of good art history is to privilege the historical avant-garde in the medium's history and to thereby provide a model (both artistic and social/political) for similarly transgressive action in the present. Despite his own association with avant-garde literature and abstract painting, Barthes did not seem to be convinced of the efficacy of this approach to the history of photography. Perhaps he recognized that a normative history that privileges avant-garde practice—even those practices that at some point contested the establishment of their own time—is still a normative history. It merely feeds an art-world economy for which such "dead" avant-gardes are only so many commodities, intellectual and otherwise.[16] In *Camera Lucida*, Barthes seems to be exploring the possibility of inventing an avant-garde form of history, not providing yet another history of avant-garde pictures. In any case, the purpose of the book is to discover the nature of the photographic experience. Photography, he argues, is an experience offered by every photograph, no matter how humble or poorly composed. An evaluation of photographs, a privileging of good ones over bad ones, would be entirely beside the point.

The bibliography in *La chambre claire* cites Beaumont Newhall's 1964 edition of *The History of Photography*, published by the Museum of Modern Art and still the founding model for most of our prevailing survey histories of photography. Recent examples of the genre by Michel Frizot and Mary Warner Marien have added breadth to Newhall's story but have otherwise retained his chronological narrative structure (with its inevitable hints at linear progress) and his art-historical value system (with its emphasis on origins and originality).[17] These kinds of histories actually tell us relatively little about their subject, even if they tell us a lot about certain select photographers, and a bit about a few individual photographs. By this means, history is subsumed to the demands of biography and art rather than being shaped by the specific qualities of its subject. In these books, we are presented with photographers (the masters) and photographs (the masterpieces) but are told almost nothing about photography as an historical phenomenon and cultural experience.

This is precisely what, in its few short pages, *Camera Lucida* tells us quite a lot about. Barthes had an intense and sustained interest in history and in photography's place in it.[18] In *Camera Lucida*, he repeats his argument that "it is the advent of the Photograph—and not, as has been said, of the cinema—which divides the history of the world" (*CL* 88). In Barthes's historical schema, the study of photography enjoys an exhilarating urgency and importance, and his personal ruminations about various photographs take on an unexpected weight for they bear on the whole history of modern life. Moreover, by adopting the voice of the generic spectator, Barthes provides the beginnings of a history of photography's reception. He tells us what a photograph looks like but also how that look feels, at least to him. He thereby opens up the whole question of the photographic experience—of the emotions stirred by photographs—as something proper to the concerns of critical historians.

Sentiment and emotion, along with first-person pronouns and autobiography, are bound to make some academics a little nervous. Not only do they border on narcissism, but the resulting text also loses the rhetorical attachment to objective science that gives third-person histories like Newhall's their scholarly tone and ability to persuade. (*Camera Lucida*, by contrast, offers a photography one could cry over.) But Barthes's point is surely that the personal must be taken seriously as the field within which the political operates.

His turn to the personal is also in keeping with Charles Sanders Peirce's theory of the index, which is key to Barthes's ontological definition of photography. "I am looking at eyes that looked at the Emperor" (*CL* 3) is Barthes's response to his viewing of a photograph of Napoleon's brother. This amazement, he tells us, is the prompt that led to the writing of the rest of the book. An index is, Peirce says, "in dynamical (including spatial) connection both with the individual object, on the one hand, and with the senses of memory of the person for whom it serves as a sign, on the other. . . . Psychologically, the action of indices depends upon association by contiguity."[19] Peirce's notion of indexical semiosis collapses any sharp distinction between a referent and the psychological associations that a viewer brings to it. In Peirce's theory of semiotics, there is no reality outside of the activity of representation. Equally, there is no activity of representation without "the senses of memory of the person for whom it serves as a sign." An equivalent oscillation back and forth between photograph and viewer and between text and reader is a central element of Barthes's discussion throughout *Camera Lucida*.

This leads us back to the question of politics. In his 1971 essay, "Mythology Today," Barthes offers a critique of his own earlier efforts at demystification. Barthes argues there that "it is no longer the myths which need to be unmasked. . . . It is the sign itself which must be shaken; the problem is not to reveal the (latent) meaning of an utterance but to fissure the very representation of meaning."[20] As he says, "the historical field of action is thus widened: no longer the (narrow) sphere of French society but far beyond that, historically and geographically, the whole of Western civilization." The task, he argues, is "no longer simply to upend (or right) the mythical message . . . but rather to change the object itself, to produce a new object, point of departure for a new science."[21] His discussion of photography in *Camera Lucida*, which he claims to be of the order of "a new science for each object" (*CL* 8), should be regarded as a contribution to this other "new science" as well.

Consider again Barthes's decision to divide his book into two equal parts, one a "palinode" or retraction of the other. Early in the book, he tells us that "the Photograph belongs to that class of laminated objects whose two leaves cannot be separated without destroying them both: the windowpane and the landscape, and why not: Good and Evil, desire and its object: dualities we can conceive but not perceive" (*CL* 6). He goes on to conclude that "this stubbornness of the Referent in always being there," this special relationship between a thing and its indexical trace, constitutes the essence of photography—the quality that distinguishes it from all other systems of representation, the quality that makes photography such an unprecedented type of consciousness. His mode of analysis throughout *Camera Lucida* (indeed, the organization of the book itself) therefore emulates what he sees as photography's own most "fundamental feature" (*CL* 9)—the binary economy of its composition.

Note, for example, the dualism of his own quest for the essence of photography. He seeks it first in a plurality of photographs and then in its exact opposite, the qualities of just one, and this dualism is given concrete form in the book's division into two equal parts. In similar fashion, he opens his book with a color reproduction of Boudinet's untitled picture but provides neither a caption nor any textual commentary. Compare this to his extensive commentary on the picture of his mother that he never reproduces; in *Camera Lucida*, one appears as the doppelganger of the other. Indeed, the absent presence of the Winter Garden Photograph is a void into which every reader projects their own banal snapshot, such that zero and infinity are made to turn in on each other without pause.[22] In this manner, Barthes provides a textual space into which the entire history of photography can be funneled without a single picture from it having to be reproduced.

His choice of title also deserves close analysis. A camera lucida is a drawing device that was invented before photography. Its glass prism focuses light reflected into it from both a scene and from the paper placed beneath the instrument and then merges these two light sources on to the back of the retina of an individual observer.[23] It is an instrument in which one sees an image only in one's own mind's eye, making looking an entirely private and individual experience. Barthes perversely chooses the term for this inward-looking, cameraless apparatus to represent a book that is ostensibly devoted to our common experience of looking out at camera pictures. The book is fraught with binaries of this kind, with one term inevitably presented as an inverse of another.

This is the case even with Barthes's representation of photographic time, which he describes in terms of a flickering back and forth from a "that-has-been" to a "this-will-be," a temporal oscillation that he seeks to encapsulate in the anterior future tense he ascribes to every photograph.[24] Stricken with grief over the passing of his mother two years before, Barthes initially associates photography with death: "whether or not the subject is already dead, every photograph is this catastrophe" (*CL* 96). However, the whole narrative force of Barthes's book is dependent on the capacity of photographs to suspend this catastrophe. The book was initiated, he tells us in an earlier interview, by "a fascination with what has died but is represented as wanting to be alive."[25] Accordingly, on the same page in *Camera Lucida* where he comments on the "catastrophe" that is inherent to all photographs, he also concedes that there is "always a defeat of time in them." Looking at a snapshot of two little girls, he exclaims "how alive they are!" It is precisely this suspension of time's passage, this conjuring of his mother as both alive and dead and therefore as neither, that moves him. Only photographs can provide this suspension, a quality that is, Barthes says, the source both of photography's ecstasy and its madness.

The structural dynamic I've been describing also happens to emulate the binary relationship of negative and positive that is at the heart of so many photographs (inseparably so in an ambrotype or a daguerreotype). In other words, to talk in an incisive way about the experience of photography, *Camera Lucida* is itself structured like a photograph. Framed by the anterior future tense that its author identifies with photography (Barthes is dead, and he is going to die), this book has become, before all else, a photographic object.

This in itself—this strategic reiteration of binary thinking—is not particularly remarkable. The Bush and Blair administrations, for example, insisted on a clear separation of good and evil (the very terms conjured by Barthes to describe the photograph) to justify the deaths of more than 65,000 Iraqi civilians from 2003 to 2007.[26] This particular example of binary rhetoric is a sharp reminder that politics is always already in play at this microlevel too, for, as we well know by now, every binary opposition comes to us as a hierarchy ordered to suit explicit political interests. There's no point contesting the larger argument unless you also disrupt the logic that sustains it, wherever you find it in action. In this case, to undermine the political economy that would neatly separate good from evil is to also undermine the rationalization of state-sanctioned murder. And this continuous implosion of binary terms is precisely what Barthes manages to orchestrate throughout *Camera Lucida*.

If Barthes's book indeed resembles a photograph, then perhaps it is best thought of as a daguerreotype, requiring a constant mobilization of its constituent parts to become itself. "The Photograph," he tells us, "represents that very subtle moment when . . . I am neither subject nor object but a subject who feels he is becoming an object" (*CL* 14). This undecidability is maintained in his discussion of *punctum*: he begins by distinguishing it from *studium*, "that very wide field of unconcerned desire, of various interest, of inconsequential taste" (*CL* 27), usually a collection of visual features intentionally coded in the photograph by the photographer and recognized by the spectator as a consequence of a shared cultural knowledge. *Punctum*, as we all know (the term having become one of the tired clichés of photographic discourse), is an element that somehow breaks or punctuates the *studium*, "this element which rises from the scene, shoots out of it like an arrow, and pierces me." (*CL* 26). It bruises him, giving him a pleasure mixed with pain, a sort of ecstasy. *Punctum* is not an easy thing to pin down, either. Barthes describes it as both an instrument ("like an arrow") and the vestige of its impact ("this wound . . . this mark")—as both a thing and its index, both a prick and a "little hole" (*CL* 26–27). *Punctum*, it seems, has a sexual connotation, whereas *studium*, he says, is merely "of the order of liking" (*CL* 27).

This distinction between *studium* and *punctum*, between shared and private meaning, intention and chance, has preoccupied many a faithful reader.[27] But anyone who swallows the bait and maintains this distinction and separates one from the other (who speaks, for example, of "the" *punctum*) has missed the complexity of Barthes's overall argument. What matters here is not the difference between *studium* and *punctum* but the political economy of their relationship (what matters is their poststructural inseparability).

After various refinements of his definition—"very often the *punctum* is a detail" (*CL* 43), but a detail that can also "fill the whole picture" (*CL* 45), even if only "after the fact" (*CL* 53), looking back—Barthes comes to what he calls his "last thing about the *punctum*" (*CL* 55): "whether or not it is triggered, it is an addition: it is what I add to the photograph and what is nonetheless already there" (*CL* 55). In fact, in the French edition of *Camera Lucida*, Barthes calls *punctum* a "*supplément*" rather than simply an addition. This is a significant, even a loaded choice of word.[28] Consigning *punctum* to the logic of the supplement is to displace it from certainty, to put it in motion, to turn it in on itself. The most important element of the photograph is also, apparently, something supplemental, unnecessary, in addition to requirements. Like the referent, it is both there in the photograph and not there, both natural (a matter of indexical science) and cultural (brought to the image by a human observer) and therefore not quite either. And indeed it isn't long before Part Two of *Camera Lucida* has collapsed the very distinctions that Part One has labored to establish. "I now know," he says, "that there exists another *punctum*. . . . this new *punctum*, which is no longer of form but of intensity, is Time" (*CL* 96). What was once confined to only a few select photographs is, he recognizes, a constituent element of all of them.

The photograph that pierces him most powerfully, the Winter Garden Photograph of his mother, is also so banal that he cannot show it to us. For us, it is no more than *studium*. It turns out that the same photograph can be both *studium* and *punctum* (the one is always already in the other), just as every photograph, no matter what its subject matter, speaks both of "what-has-been" and also of the catastrophe of death in the future. Barthes can no more separate *studium* from *punctum* than Saussure can sustain his separation of signifier and signified. Every photograph, like every sign, is produced within the dynamic play of this impossible relationship, of this haunting of one by its other.[29]

Despite the momentary thrill of new vocabulary, this dynamic is the most difficult and productive legacy that *Camera Lucida* offers to a new generation of photography's historians. It is difficult because the logic of supplementarity—in which neither inside nor outside, essence or context, is allowed to determine the identity of photography—is so hard to grasp and sustain in one's own work. Nevertheless it is at this level that political work must now be fought, within the grain of what makes any photograph function meaningfully as a photograph.

History remains a powerful site for that work, as is evidenced in the way that Barthes represents his own little history of photography. He abandons the linear, chronological narrative, the illusory claims to comprehensiveness, and the hierarchical values of most existing studies of photography. Instead, his history is driven by a single, unanswerable question: what is photography? By inserting this ontological anxiety at the heart of his narrative, Barthes sets no direction for that narrative in advance. Readers are taken on a quest—part philosophical rumination, part social history, part visual culture, part detective novel—that is as much about themselves (about "consciousness") as photography.

Like Benjamin before him, Barthes burrows into the very flesh of photography by taking on many of its most salient attributes so that they then become the structuring principles of his text. As I've already implied, *Camera Lucida* offers a model of a history of photography rather than a depiction of that history.[30] Within the dynamics of that model, Barthes is able to directly engage photography's dissemination and reception as well as its production, encompassing all its many aspects, whether visible (images and practices) or invisible (effects and experiences). He proposes that photography is not something that is generated by a particular technological apparatus but instead functions as a particular set of photographic meanings and expectations—a "mode of apprehension"—that are brought by viewers to certain images coded as photographs, irrespective of the exact technology of their making. He looks primarily at ordinary photographs rather than masterworks, opening up the entire field of photography for examination and abandoning any reliance on art historical prejudices. Aiming only to be representative, Barthes even proffers the possibility of a history based on just one (unseen) photograph. In short, the historical approach demonstrated by *Camera Lucida* produces a history that is actually about photography and not just of photographs.

Twenty-eight years after his death, Barthes's ghost continues to haunt our understanding of photography. Using *Camera Lucida* as a possible model for another kind of historical accounting, I propose that we also adopt its analytical oscillation, a back and forth between whatever examples of photography we encounter in the world and our own prized photographic reliquaries, between cliché and sublimity, sameness and difference, truth and fiction, public and private, infinity and zero—without letting either term rest on its laurels. It is surely only here within the unstable spacing of this kind of oscillation that a truly photographic history of photography can plausibly be staged.

This is a revised version of "*Camera Lucida*: Another Little History of Photography," in Robin Kelsey and Blake Stimson, eds., *The Meaning of Photography* (Williamstown, MA: Clark Studies in the Visual Arts, 2008), 76–91.

1. Roland Barthes, "Rhetoric of the Image" (1964), *Image Music Text*, trans. Stephen Heath (London: Fontana, 1977), 44.

2. Roland Barthes, *Camera Lucida: Reflections on Photography* (1980), trans. Richard Howard (New York: Hill and Wang, 1981) (subsequent page references are provided in parentheses in the text).

3. Roland Barthes, *Mythologies* (1957), trans. Annette Lavers (New York: Hill and Wang, 1972).

4. Sabine Gölz, "Incendiary Reading: Close-ups of Walter Benjamin's 'Little History of Photography,'" a public lecture given at the City University of New York (CUNY) Graduate Center, New York, October 3, 2003. Benjamin's "Little History of Photography" was first published in *Literarische Welt* (September and October 1931). It was first published in English in a translation by Stanley Mitchell as "A Short History of Photography," *Screen* 13, no. 1 (Spring 1972): 5–26. It was subsequently translated by Phil Patton as "A Short History of Photography," *Artforum* 15, no. 6 (February 1977): 46–51, and by Edmund Jephcott and Kingsley Shorter as "A Small History of Photography," in Edmund Jephcott and Kingsley Shorter, eds., *One-Way Street and Other Writings* (London: New Left Books, 1979).

5. I have argued elsewhere that because banal photographs lack imagination, they can shift the burden of imaginative thought from the artist to the viewer. They are an open invitation to see more than meets the eye. This might lead us to the following paradoxical proposition: the more banal the photograph, the greater its capacity to induce us to exercise our imaginations. This paradox perhaps helps to explain why such creative writers as Walter Benjamin (who favored the work of commercial photographer Jean-Eugène-Auguste Atget), Jorge Luis Borges (who illustrated a book with the most banal photographs ever produced by his countryman Horacio Coppola), W. G. Sebald (who was notorious for choosing unexceptional illustrations for his books), and Roland Barthes (who illustrated *Camera Lucida* with strikingly middle-brow pictures) picked relatively unimaginative photographs to accompany their texts. See my "Dreams of Ordinary Life: Cartes-de-visite and the Bourgeois Imagination," in Martha Langford, ed., *Image and Imagination* (Montreal: McGill-Queen's University Press and Le Mois de la Photo, 2005), 268.

6. Walter Benjamin, "A Small History of Photography" (1931), *One-Way Street and Other Writings*, 43.

7. Carolin Duttlinger, "Benjamin and Barthes: Towards a Science of the Particular?," a paper delivered at the Thinking Photography—Again conference, University of Durham, UK, July 9, 2005. See also André Gunthert, "Le complexe de Gradiva: théorie de la photographie, deuil et résurrection," *Etudes Photographiques* 2 (May 1997): 115–128.

8. Margaret Olin, "Touching Photographs: Roland Barthes's 'Mistaken' Identity," *Representations* 80 (Fall 2002): 99–118. Although it reproduces a generous selection of Barthes's family snapshots, an exhibition catalogue from the Centre Pompidou does not (cannot?) show us the Winter Garden picture. See Marianne Alphant and Nathalie Léger, eds., *R/B: Roland Barthes* (exhibition catalogue, Paris: Centre Pompidou, 2002).

9. Olin suggests that perhaps the Winter Garden Photograph is a stand-in for an image of Franz Kafka at the age of six that is mentioned by Benjamin in his "Little History." Kafka is shown standing in a kind of "winter garden" landscape of the sort constructed out of props in a photographer's studio. As Duttlinger has pointed out (see note 7 above), Benjamin discusses this photograph of Kafka in two texts and in one of them actually becomes Kafka; that is, he projects himself into the picture through a first-person account of the pose and setting. Olin argues that Barthes similarly transposes a photograph of himself as a young boy over the missing photograph of his mother at age five. See Olin, "Touching Photographs," 111.

10. Benjamin's "Little History" was in fact published in a French translation in a special issue of *Nouvel Observateur* 2 (November 1977). Barthes lists this magazine in his bibliography in *La chambre claire* but never mentions the Benjamin text by name or acknowledges his debt to it.

11. Roland Barthes, *Roland Barthes by Roland Barthes* (1975), trans. Richard Howard (New York: Hill and Wang, 1977), 51. As Susan Sontag has suggested, "the uses that binary and triadic thinking had for Barthes's imagination were always provisional, available to correction, destabilization, condensation." Susan Sontag, "Writing Itself: On Roland Barthes," in Susan Sontag, ed., *A Barthes Reader* (New York: Hill and Wang, 1982), xiii.

12. For his discussion of denotation and connotation, see Barthes, "Rhetoric of the Image," 32–51. In a striking parallel to *studium* and *punctum*, Barthes posits a similarly complex binary relationship for *plaisir* and *jouissance* in his book *The Pleasure of the Text*, first published in 1973. See Roland Barthes, *The Pleasure of the Text*, trans. Richard Miller (New York: Hill and Wang, 1975).

13. Barthes's stress on the "amateur" conjures, via an etymological association, the amorous subject he addresses in *A Lover's Discourse: Fragments* (1977). He thereby casts his interest in photography in terms of love relations and not just as nonprofessional.

14. The titles of histories are often out of their author's control. For discussions of how the titles of their histories came to be chosen, see, for example, Beaumont Newhall, *Focus: Memoirs of a Life in Photography* (Boston: Bulfinch Press, 1993), 177, and Michel Frizot, "A Critical Discussion of the Historiography of Photography," *Arken Bulletin* 1 (2002): 58–65.

15. Roland Barthes, "The Death of the Author," (1967) *Image Music Text*, trans. Stephen Heath (London: Fontana, 1977): 142–148.

16. For more along these lines, see my "*Art since 1900*: Review," *Art Bulletin* 88, no. 2 (June 2006): 376–377. Barthes expressed some skepticism about the political efficacy of avant-garde modes of writing: "It is an old trick of our criticism to proclaim its breadth of views, its modernism, by baptizing *avant-garde* what it can assimilate, thereby economically combining the security of tradition with the *frisson* of novelty." Roland Barthes, *Critical Essays* trans. Richard Howard (Evanston: Northwestern University Press, 1972), 95.

17. Michel Frizot, ed., *A New History of Photography* (Cologne: Könemann, 1998); Mary Warner Marien, *Photography: A Cultural History* (New York: Prentice-Hall, 2002).

18. Among Barthes's earliest efforts was a study of the nineteenth-century French historian Jules Michelet in which he minutely analyzed the form of Michelet's writing. As Steven Ungar has pointed out, Barthes's *Michelet par lui-même* (1954) is organized around a systematic play of image and text that, Ungar says, prefigures *Camera Lucida* and "attempts to verbalize the image and visualize the word" (166). See Steven Ungar, "The Imaginary Museum of Jules Michelet," in Jean-Michel Rabaté,

ed., *Writing the Image after Roland Barthes* (Philadelphia: University of Pennsylvania Press, 1997), 163–173.

19. Charles Sanders Peirce, "Logic as Semiotic: The Theory of Signs" (c. 1897–1910), in Justus Buchler, ed., *Philosophical Writings of Peirce* (New York: Dover, 1955), 107–108.

20. Roland Barthes, "Change the Object Itself: Mythology Today" (1971), *Image Music Text*, 167.

21. Ibid., 169.

22. Compare, for example, Barthes's discussion of the snapshot with the accounts provided by a spate of recent books devoted to this genre of photography. Uncertain about how to deal with the infinite number and banal aesthetic values of snapshot photographs, almost all of these accounts choose to isolate a few, exceptional images, usually those that resemble avant-garde art. Given that this resemblance is almost invariably a matter of chance or accident, the same logic is used to organize these books. In *Camera Lucida*, Barthes does something that these other histories of the snapshot dare not do. He describes the essential snapshot but does not make it visible, demanding that we do that work for him in our mind's eye. By that means, his chosen snapshot avoids being transformed into something other than itself. For an extended commentary on this problem, see Geoffrey Batchen, "From Infinity to Zero," in Marvin Heiferman, ed., *Now Is Then: Snapshots from the Maresca Collection* (Newark: Newark Museum / Princeton Architectural Press, 2008), 120–130, and Geoffrey Batchen, "Snapshots: Art History and the Ethnographic Turn," *Photographies*, 1, no. 2 (September, 2008): 121–142.

23. See my "Detours: Photography and the Camera Lucida," *Afterimage* 18, no. 2 (September 1990): 14–15.

24. On Barthes's rendition of time in *Camera Lucida*, see Nancy Shawcross, "Time: The Photographic Punctum," *Roland Barthes and Photography: The Critical Tradition in Perspective* (Gainesville: University Press of Florida, 1997), 86–106.

25. Roland Barthes, interviewed by Bernard-Henri Lévy and Jean-Marie Benoist on December 23, 1978, as quoted in Louis-Jean Calvet, *Roland Barthes: A Biography*, trans. Sarah Wykes (Bloomington: Indiana University Press, 1995), 220.

26. See my "Requiem," *Afterimage* 29, no. 4 (January–February 2002): 5. Although estimates of the number of Iraqis killed as a consequence of the American-led invasion vary considerably, the *New York Times* quotes Iraq Body Count when claiming that at least 30,051 civilians were killed between March 2003 and October 2005. See Sabrina Tavernise, "Rising Civilian Toll Is the Iraq War's Silent, Sinister Pulse," *New York Times,* October 25, 2005, A12. In January 2007, the Associated Press reported that the United Nations had estimated that 34,452 Iraqi civilians had been killed in Iraq during 2006, with a further 36,685 wounded. See "34,452 Iraqi Civilians Killed in 2006, U.N. Says," *New York Times,* January 16, 2007.

27. Few of these readers address themselves to the strategic politics that motivates the positing of such a division. Although the logic of his own narrative collapses any distinction between these two experiences of the photograph, Barthes argues that, given the "explosion of the private into the public," there is a political purpose, a "necessary resistance," behind his efforts to "reconstitute the division of public and private." See Barthes, *Camera Lucida*, 98.

28. Barthes's choice of this particular word conjures the work of his compatriot Jacques Derrida, particularly Derrida's "supplementary reading" of Rousseau's *Confessions* in *Of Grammatology*, first

published in 1967. As Barbara Johnson puts it, Derrida shows how "the logic of the supplement wrenches apart the neatness of the metaphysical binary oppositions." See Jacques Derrida, *Of Grammatology*, trans. Gayatri Chakravorty Spivak (Baltimore: Johns Hopkins University Press, 1976), and Barbara Johnson, "Translator's Introduction," in Jacques Derrida, *Dissemination* (1972), trans. Barbara Johnson (Chicago: University of Chicago Press, 1981), xiii.

29. As Derrida puts it, "this concept of the photograph photographs all conceptual oppositions, it traces a relationship of haunting which perhaps is constitutive of all logics." Jacques Derrida, "The Deaths of Roland Barthes" (1981), in Hugh Silverman, ed., *Philosophy and Non-Philosophy since Merleau-Ponty* (New York: Routledge, 1988), 267. My own essay is inspired by this one. Barthes admits in "Rhetoric of the Image" that the distinction between his earlier terms, *denotation* and *connotation*, has only an "operational validity, analogous to that which allows the distinction in the linguistic sign of a signifier and a signified (even though in reality no one is able to separate the 'word' from its meaning except by recourse to the metalanguage of a definition)." See Barthes, "Rhetoric of the Image," *Image Music Text*, 37. For a provocative commentary on Saussure's "impossible" definition of the sign, see also Vicki Kirby, "Corporeal Complexity: The Matter of the Sign," *Telling Flesh: The Substance of the Corporeal* (New York: Routledge, 1997), 7–50, 163–169.

30. In this regard, Barthes's writing might be said to emulate the strategy of a certain kind of avant-garde photographic art, even if this art does not appear in his book. See, for example, Jeff Wall's commentary on the deployment of photography within conceptual art of the 1960s, where he speaks of artists who offer "models of the social, not depictions of it" (37) and who do so through the adoption of vernacular idioms of photography. Jeff Wall, "'Marks of Indifference': Aspects of Photography in, or as, Conceptual Art" (1995), in Douglas Fogle, ed., *The Last Picture Show: Artists Using Photography 1960–1982* (exhibition catalogue, Minneapolis: Walker Art Center, 2004), 32–44. For a similar kind of argument about the work of Bernd Becher and Hilla Becher, see Blake Stimpson, "The Photographic Comportment of Bernd and Hilla Becher," *The Pivot of the World*: *Photography and its Nation* (Cambridge, MA: MIT Press, 2006), 137–175, 214–218.

SOURCES

CHAPTER 2. VICTOR BURGIN, RE-READING *CAMERA LUCIDA*
Originally published in *Creative Camera* 215 (November 1982): 730–734. Also published in Victor Burgin, *The End of Art Theory: Criticism and Postmodernity* (London: MacMillan, 1986), 71–92.

CHAPTER 3. JANE GALLOP, THE PLEASURE OF THE PHOTOTEXT
Originally published in *Afterimage* 12, no. 9 (April 1985): 16–18. Also published in Jane Gallop, *Thinking through the Body* (New York: Columbia University Press, 1988), and Liz Heron and Val Williams, eds., *Illuminations: Women Writing on Photography from the 1850s to the Present* (Durham, NC: Duke University Press, 1996), 394–402.

CHAPTER 4. MARGARET IVERSEN, WHAT IS A PHOTOGRAPH?
Originally published in *Art History* 17, no. 3 (September 1994): 450–464. Also published in Margaret Iversen, *Beyond Pleasure: Freud, Lacan, Barthes* (University Park, PA: Pennsylvania State University Press, 2007).

CHAPTER 5. MARGARET OLIN, TOUCHING PHOTOGRAPHS: ROLAND BARTHES'S "MISTAKEN" IDENTIFICATION
Originally published in *Representations* 80 (Fall 2002): 99–118.

CHAPTER 6. JAY PROSSER, BUDDHA BARTHES: WHAT BARTHES SAW IN PHOTOGRAPHY (THAT HE DIDN'T IN LITERATURE)
Originally published in *Literature and Theology* 18, no. 2 (June 2004): 211–212.

CHAPTER 7. EDUARDO CADAVA AND PAOLA CORTÉS-ROCCA, NOTES ON LOVE AND PHOTOGRAPHY
Originally published in *October* 116 (Spring 2006): 3–34

CHAPTER 8. MICHAEL FRIED, BARTHES'S *PUNCTUM*

Originally published in *Critical Inquiry* 31, no. 3 (Spring 2005): 539–575. Also published in Michael Fried, *Why Photography Matters As Art As Never Before* (New Haven, CT: Yale University Press, 2008).

CHAPTER 9. JAMES ELKINS, WHAT DO WE WANT PHOTOGRAPHY TO BE? A RESPONSE TO MICHAEL FRIED

Originally published in *Critical Inquiry* 31, no. 4 (Summer 2005): 938–957.

CHAPTER 13. SHAWN MICHELLE SMITH, RACE AND REPRODUCTION IN *CAMERA LUCIDA*

Originally published in J.J. Long, Andrea Noble, and Edward Welch, eds., *Photography: Theoretical Snapshots* (London: Routledge, 2009), 98–111.

CHAPTER 14. GEOFFREY BATCHEN, *CAMERA LUCIDA:* ANOTHER LITTLE HISTORY OF PHOTOGRAPHY

Originally published in Robin Kelsey and Blake Stimson, eds., *The Meaning of Photography* (Williamstown, MA: Clark Studies in the Visual Arts, 2008), 76–91.

GEOFFREY BATCHEN teaches the history of photography at the Graduate Center of the City University of New York. His books include *Burning with Desire: The Conception of Photography* (MIT Press, 1997); *Each Wild Idea: Writing, Photography, History* (MIT Press, 2001); *Forget Me Not: Photography and Remembrance* (Van Gogh Museum and Princeton Architectural Press, 2004); and *William Henry Fox Talbot* (Phaidon, 2008).

VICTOR BURGIN is Professor Emeritus of History of Consciousness, University of California, Santa Cruz, and Professor Emeritus of Fine Art, Goldsmiths College, University of London. His books include the edited volume *Thinking Photography* (Macmillan, 1982); *The End of Art Theory: Criticism and Postmodernity* (Humanities Press, 1986); *In/Different Spaces: Place and Memory in Visual Culture* (University of California Press, 1996); *Some Cities* (University of California Press, 1996); *The Remembered Film* (Reaktion, 2004); *Objets Temporels* (Presses Universitaires de Rennes, 2007); and *Components of a Practice* (Skira, 2008). His forthcoming book *About Art: Interventions and Exchanges 1969–2009* will be published by Reaktion, London.

EDUARDO CADAVA teaches in the Department of English at Princeton University, where he also is an associate member of the Department of Comparative Literature and the School of Architecture. He is the author of *Emerson and the Climates of History* (Stanford University Press, 1997) and *Words of Light: Theses on the Photography of History* (Princeton University Press, 1998) and a coeditor of *Cities without Citizens* (Slought Foundation, 2004).

JAMES ELKINS teaches at the School of the Art Institute of Chicago and the University College, Cork, Ireland. His recent books include *Visual Studies: A Skeptical Introduction* (Routledge, 2003); *Photography Theory* (Routledge, 2006); and *Six Stories from the End of Representation: Images in Painting, Photography, Astronomy, Microscopy, Particle Physics, and Quantum Mechanics, 1980–2000* (Stanford University Press, 2008).

MICHAEL FRIED is J. R. Herbert Boone professor of the humanities and director of the Humanities Center at Johns Hopkins University. His books include *Absorption and Theatricality: Painting and Beholder in the Age of Diderot* (University of Chicago Press, 1988); *Courbet's Realism* (University of Chicago Press, 1992); *Art and Objecthood: Essays and Reviews* (University of Chicago Press, 1998); and *Why Photography Matters As Art As Never Before* (Yale University Press, 2009).

JANE GALLOP is Distinguished Professor of English and Comparative Literature at the University of Wisconsin–Milwaukee. Her books include *The Daughter's Seduction: Feminism and Psychoanalysis* (Macmillan Press and Cornell University Press, 1982); *Reading Lacan* (Cornell University Press, 1985); *Thinking through the Body* (Columbia University Press, 1988); and *Living with His Camera* (Duke University Press, 2003).

GORDON HUGHES teaches in the Department of Art History at Rice University in Houston, Texas. His essays have been published in *October*, *Oxford Art Journal*, *Art Bulletin*, and *Art Journal*. In 2000 he collaborated with Hal Foster to edit an anthology of texts on Richard Serra as part of the October Files series.

MARGARET IVERSEN is Professor of Art History and Theory at the University of Essex. Her books include *Alois Riegl: Art History and Theory* (MIT Press, 1993); *Mary Kelly* (Phaidon Press, 1997); and *Beyond Pleasure: Freud, Lacan, Barthes* (Pennsylvania State University Press, 2007).

ROSALIND E. KRAUSS is a University Professor at Columbia University in New York. Her books include *The Originality of the Avant-Garde and Other Modernist Myths* (MIT Press, 1986); *Le photographique: pour une théorie des écarts* (Macula, 1990); *The Optical Unconscious* (MIT Press, 1994); and *Bachelors* (MIT Press, 2000); and she is a coauthor of *L'Amour fou: Photography and Surrealism* (Abbeville Press, 1985) and *Art since 1900: Modernism, Antimodernism, Postmodernism* (Thames & Hudson, 2005).

CAROL MAVOR is Professor of Art History and Visual Studies at the University of Manchester. Her books include *Pleasures Taken: Performances of Sexuality and Loss in Victorian Photographs* (Duke University Press, 1995); *Becoming: The Photographs of Clementina, Viscountess Hawarden* (Duke University Press, 1999); and *Reading Boyishly: J. M. Barrie, Roland Barthes, Jacques Henri Lartigue, Marcel Proust, and D. W. Winnicott* (Duke University Press, 2007).

MARGARET OLIN is a professor in the departments of art history and visual and critical studies at the School of the Art Institute of Chicago. Her books include *Forms of Representation in Alois Riegl's Theory of Art* (Pennsylvania State University Press, 1992) and *The Nation without Art: Examining Modern Discourses on Jewish Art* (University of Nebraska Press, 2007), and she is also an editor of *Monuments and Memory, Made and Unmade* (University of Chicago Press, 2004).

JAY PROSSER is a reader in humanities in the School of English, University of Leeds. His books include *Second Skins: The Body Narratives of Transsexuality* (Columbia University Press, 1998) and *Light in the Dark Room: Photography and Loss* (Minnesota University Press, 2004).

PAOLA CORTÉS ROCCA is an assistant professor in the Department of Spanish at San Francisco State University and also teaches literary theory at the University of Buenos Aires. She is a coauthor of *Imágenes de vida, relatos de muerte. Eva Perón: cuerpo y política* (Beatriz Viterbo Editora, 1998).

SHAWN MICHELLE SMITH is an associate professor of visual and critical studies at the School of the Art Institute of Chicago. She is the author of *American Archives: Gender, Race, and Class in Visual Culture* (Princeton University Press 1999) and *Photography on the Color Line: W. E. B. Du Bois, Race, and Visual Culture* (Duke University Press 2004) and a coauthor of *Lynching Photographs* (University of California Press 2007).

Page numbers in italics refer to illustrations.

Bataille, Georges, 58

Baudelaire, Charles, 4, 220, 222

Bazin, André, 50

Beceyro, Raul, 10

Becher, Bernd and Hilla, 155, 202–203

Bellevance, Leslie, 53–54

Benjamin, Walter, 10, 61–63, 81–82, 100, 143,
150, 260–261, 263, 269, 271n10

Benveniste, Emile, 40, 130–131

Berger, John, 41

Bertillon, Alphonse, 119

Binaries, 17, 34, 114, 188, 190, 219–220, 261–
262, 266–267, 271n12

Blair, Anthony Charles Lynton (Tony), 267

Blossfelt, Karl, 62

Bonaparte, Charles Louis Napoléon (Napoleon
III), 3, 6, 189, 233, 265

Bonaparte, Jérôme Napoléon, 3, 189, 233, 265

Boudinet, Daniel, 8, 11, 16–17, 27n56, 74n42,
136n16, 152, 179, 229–230, 235–236, 262,
266

   Fragments of a Labyrinth, 16

   Polaroid, 11, 16–17, 27n56, 70, 74n42,
136n16, 152, 179, 229, 235–236, 262, 266

Bourdieu, Pierre, 10

Bowers, Harry

   Black and White #6, 55

Bowie, Malcolm, 66

Brassaï (Gyula Halász), 161n17

Brazza, Savorgnan de. See Nadar

Brecht, Bertolt, 6, 157, 160n15

Breton, André, 105

Breuer, Marco, 180

Brown, Andrew, 62–63

Buchloh, Benjamin, 202

Buddhism, 10, 20, 38–39, 91–101, 187, 233

Burgin, Victor, 18–19, 144, 251

Bush, George W., 267

Cadava, Eduardo, 20

Cahiers du cinema, 8–9, 14, 94

Caillois, Roger, 67–68

Calvino, Italo, 10

Camera lucida (instrument), 10–11, 58, 80, 219,
266

Camera obscura, 10, 58, 68, 80, 219

Casares, Adolfo Bioy, 105

Casati, Robert, 234

Casby, William. *See* Avedon, Richard

Çelik, Zeynep, 218

Chaplin, Charlie, 191

Chardin, Jean Baptiste, Siméon, 173

   The Card Castle, 147, 182n6

   Soap Bubbles, 161n16, 182n6

   Young Student Drawing, 161n16

Chilla, Eduard, 177

China, 137n24

Christianity, 98, 144, 215, 230

Cinema, 50, 64, 108, 152, 154–155, 191,
197–199

Clerc, Thomas, 220

Clergue, Lucien, 17

Clifford, Charles, 11, 194, 224

Clifford, James, 236

Coleman, A. D., 17

Colorless writing, 4–5

Connotation/denotation, 7–8, 36, 94, 244–245,
261

Cornell, Joseph, 220

Cortázar, Julio, 123

Cortés-Rocca, Paola, 20

Courbet, Gustave, 145, 173

Crimp, Douglas, 18

Crow, Thomas, 180

Cupid, 49

Daguerreotype, 219, 260, 267

Daumier, Honoré, 145

Dauthendey, Karl, 61, 261

David, Jacques-Louis, 145

   *Napoleon Bonaparte Crossing the Alps at Saint-
Bernard Pass,* 6

Death, 6, 8–9, 13–14, 19, 42, 58–59, 68, 77,
81, 91, 95–101, 105–108, 111–112, 114,